Matrimonial and Domestic Injunctions

Practice and Precedents

Second edition

Mark Pelling LLB (Lond) AKC

Of the Middle Temple and the South-Eastern Circuit,
Barrister

Robert Purdie LLB (Wales)

Of the Middle Temple and the South-Eastern Circuit,
Barrister

Foreword to first edition by
Dame Margaret Booth
One of the Justices of Her
Majesty's High Court of Justice

London
Butterworths
1987

United Kingdom	Butterworth & Co (Publishers) Ltd, 88 Kingsway, LONDON WC2B 6AB and 61A North Castle Street, EDINBURGH EH2 3LJ
Australia	Butterworths Pty Ltd., SYDNEY, MELBOURNE, BRISBANE, ADELAIDE, PERTH, CANBERRA and HOBART
Canada	Butterworths. A division of Reed Inc., TORONTO and VANCOUVER
New Zealand	Butterworths of New Zealand Ltd, WELLINGTON and AUKLAND
Singapore	Butterworth & Co (Asia) Pte Ltd, SINGAPORE
South Africa	Butterworth Publishers (Pty) Ltd, DURBAN and PRETORIA
USA	Butterworths Legal Publishers, ST PAUL, Minnesota, SEATTLE, Washington, BOSTON, Massachusetts, AUSTIN, Texas and D & S Publishers, CLEARWATER, Florida

British Library Cataloguing in Publication Data

Pelling, Mark
   Matrimonial and domestic injunctions:
   practice and precedents.—2nd ed.
   1. Family violence-Law and legislation
   —England 2. Injunctions—England
   I. Title   II. Purdie, Robert
   344.2061′5   KD7972

   ISBN 0 406 33441 2

Set in 10 on 11 Linotron Times
by The Word Factory Ltd, Rossendale, Lancashire
Printed and bound in Great Britain by
Biddles Ltd, Guildford, Surrey

Foreword to first edition

The equitable remedy of the injunction, originally devised by the Courts of Chancery to overcome the rigidity of the common law, has become a powerful weapon in the armoury of those courts which exercise family jurisdiction. It is a wide ranging relief. It can provide a speedy and effective means of protecting a spouse, a child, money or property. It is available now to the unmarried couple as well as to the married couple engaged in family conflict. It may take many forms and may impose upon litigants obligations and duties as well as restraints.

In recent years the use of the injunction in relation to family disputes has steadily increased bringing with it problems which sometimes have been complex and difficult to resolve. There now exists a large body of case law relating to this and in particular to the colloquially termed ouster injunctions or orders to exclude one party from his or her home for the protection of the other or of their children. Applications for such orders have been given added impetus by the provisions of the Domestic Violence and Matrimonial Proceedings Act 1976. But this statute too has introduced further problems some of which are illustrated in the leading case of *Davis v Johnson* [1979] AC 264, HL and in the growing number of authorties on the use of the power of arrest.

So widespread and varied now are applications for injunctive orders that there is a real danger that misunderstandings may arise as to the very nature of the relief they give leading in turn to their misuse. It is, therefore, wholly appropriate and desirable that a clear and comprehensive exposition of the principles and procedures relating to this relief should be available. That is now provided by this work. It is to be welcomed for the practical guidance that the authors offer, both in the text and in the precedents, and for their learned discussion of the statute and case law which has included considerable research into many otherwise unreported decisions.

Margaret Booth
ROYAL COURTS OF JUSTICE

June 1982

Preface to second edition

In the five years which have passed since September 1982, when the first edition of this work was published, there have been many changes in the relevant law and practice. These changes are to be found in the legislation, rules, practice directions and particularly in the reported (and indeed unreported) cases.

Perhaps the most important decision is that of *Richards v Richards* where it was declared that the Matrimonial Homes Act 1967 (now the Matrimonial Homes Act 1983) was the basis of the jurisdiction for the grant of exclusion injunctions. This case was of wide public interest beyond the legal profession, being the subject of a leading article in *The Times* as well as some correspondence. Subsequent decisions in the Court of Appeal have explained various sections of the Act.

There have been significant developments in the law of contempt such as *Williams v Fawcett* and *Linnett v Coles*. The recent case of *C v S*, while most unusual, emphasises that a legal right is a precondition to the grant of an injunction. The Mareva and Anton Piller orders are now recognised as being of value in family proceedings; such orders are of increased importance with the Matrimonial and Family Proceedings Act 1984, Part III providing financial relief after overseas divorce.

The procedural changes brought about by the County Court Rules 1981 and the County Court (Forms) Rules 1982 are now well established and the County Courts Act 1984 has consolidated most of the enactments relating to county courts.

The Child Abduction Act 1984 and the Child Abduction and Custody Act 1985, which ratifies international conventions relating to the international kidnapping of children and to the international recognition and enforcement of custody orders, have made major changes to the criminal and family law. Further changes will take place when the Family Law Act 1986 is fully in force.

For the future, it seems that proposals for a Family Court may not immediately be reflected in legislation.

Considerable rewriting has been necessary to take account of these and other changes. In addition, new areas of law have been included so that this work will be of even greater use to busy practitioners. The appendices have been expanded to take account of this wider coverage. At the same time it has been felt important to produce a volume of suitable size to fit easily into a briefcase, and of a reasonable price to appeal to a wide market, while giving detailed consideration to the field of law covered. We hope that these objectives have been achieved.

We would like to thank all those who have contributed to the writing and production of this book: in particular, Elisabeth Calman, solicitor and Charlotte Jones, barrister. A special mention is owing to the staff of Butterworths for their tolerance and understanding.

Mark Pelling has produced chapters 13 and 14; the remainder of the book has been the responsibility of Robert Purdie. We regret that professional commitments have prevented Augustus Ullstein from continuing to act as Consulting Editor.

We take this opportunity to acknowledge the kind permission of Her Majesty's Stationery Office to reproduce extracts from the Cause List Notices and The Housing (Homeless Persons) Act 1977 Code of Practice, in respect of which there is Crown Copyright.

We have endeavoured to state the law as at 1st October 1987.

Mark Pelling
Robert Purdie
The Temple
1 October 1987

Stop Press

Chapter 3, page 29, fn 14: A husband may be guilty of committing an indecent assault on his wife during the subsistence of the marriage. *R* v *Kowalski* (1987) Times, 9 October, CA.

Chapter 4, page 34, fn 17: See also *Wiseman* v *Simpson* (1987) Times, 8 October, CA.

Chapter 10, section 2, Mareva injunction: See also *Law Society* v *Shanks* (1987) Times, 14 October, CA.

Extract from preface to first edition

Every day applications are made for non-molestation and ouster orders in the courts exercising family jursidiction in England and Wales. The decisions of the appellate courts on such matters are many and often too briefly reported or not reported at all. We have endeavoured therefore to collect the *rationes* of these decisions into one concise volume of suitable and convenient size for practitioners working in such courts.

In addition to the applications most commonly considered during the course of a matrimonial suit or under the domestic violence legislation in both the county and magistrates' courts, we have included chapters which deal more generally with applications relating to matrimonial relationships; the care and control of children and other orders in the nature of injunctive relief in the family context.

Contents

Table of statutes

References in this Table to *Statutes* are to Halsbury's Statutes of England (Fourth Edition) showing the volume and page at which the annotated text of the Act may be found. Page references printed in **bold** type indicate where an Act is set out in part or in full.

Table of rules and regulations

Page references printed in **bold** type indicate where the rule is set out in part or in full.

Table of cases

Page numbers in **bold** type indicate where Practice Directions and Practice Notes are set out.

B

C

Chapter 1
Jurisdiction

A General

An injunction is a court order whereby someone, usually a party to the proceedings, is restrained from doing a specific act or acts[1] or is required to do a specific act or acts.[2]

The injunction has its origins in the courts of equity and until 1854 the courts of common law had no general power to grant an injunction.[3] Since 1875 all divisions of the High Court have had jurisdiction to grant injunctions.[4]

The High Court may grant an injunction, either interlocutory or final, in all cases in which, to do so, is just and convenient.[5] The jurisdiction of the county court is similar.[6] An injunction will only be granted in support of a legal right,[7] or to protect children.[8]

There must be a close nexus between the substantive proceedings and the claim to the interlocutory injunction so that the application for the injunction arises out of, or is incidental to, the action.[9]

B Domestic Violence and Matrimonial Proceedings Act 1976

1 County Courts

The Act gives jurisdiction to every county court to grant certain injunctions whether or not any other relief is sought in those proceedings upon an

---

1 A prohibitory injunction.
2 A mandatory injunction.
3 Common Law Procedure Act 1854, s 79.
4 Supreme Court of Judicature Act 1873, now replaced by Supreme Court Act 1981, s 37(1) (11 *Halsbury's Statutes* 756 (4th edn) COURTS) and see Appendix 1.
5 Supreme Court Act 1981, s 37(1).
6 County Courts Act 1984, ss 38 and 39 (11 *Halsbury's Statutes* (4th edn) COURTS) and see Appendix 1.
7 *Montgomery* v *Montgomery* [1965] P 46, [1964] 2 ALL ER 22 and *Robinson* v *Robinson* [1965] P 39, [1963] 3 ALL ER 813.
8 *Stewart* v *Stewart* [1973] Fam 21, [1973] 1 All ER 31, *Phillips* v *Phillips* [1973] 2 All ER 423, [1973] 1 WLR 615, *Quinn* v *Quinn* (1983) 4 FLR 394, CA. See also *Beard* v *Beard* [1981] 1 All ER 783, [1981] 1 WLR 369, CA, where the exceptional nature of the jurisdiction to protect children was emphasised.
9 *Des Salles d'Epinoix* v *Des Salles d'Epinoix* [1967] 2 All ER 539, [1967] 1 WLR 553, CA; *F* v *F (Exclusion Order)* (1980) 3 FLR 202 Eastham J; *McGibbon* v *McGibbon* [1973] Fam 170, [1973] 2 All ER 836; see also *Winstone* v *Winstone* [1960] P 28, [1959] 3 All ER 580. Cf *The Siskina* [1979] AC 210, [1977] 3 All ER 803, HL at 256 and 824 f–h, per Lord Diplock; see the quotation at p ii above.

application by a party to a marriage.[10] This provision ended the need for a husband or wife seeking such injunctive relief to bring proceedings for trespass or assault claiming not only an injunction but also damages.

The marriage to which the applicant must be a party would include not just a valid marriage but also any marriage celebrated outside England and Wales which the court would recognise. It is not clear whether or not the Act applies to parties to actually polygamous marriages. It would probably apply to potentially polygamous marriages.[11] The language[12] of section 1 appears to presuppose a monogamous relationship. If the Act does not apply to polygamous marriages the court would nonetheless have jurisdiction if the parties came within the meaning of the phrase 'living with each other in the same household as husband and wife'.[13]

On the granting of a decree absolute, whether of divorce or nullity, the parties cease to be husband and wife and therefore the court would not have jurisdiction to entertain an application from a former spouse because he or she would no longer be a party to a marriage. Where an injunction is sought by one former spouse against the other, it is usually more appropriate to seek the injunction in the matrimonial cause,[14] than to commence new proceedings.

A decree of judicial separation does not bring to an end the status of husband and wife although it does relieve the petitioner of the obligation to cohabit with the respondent.[15] It follows that husbands and wives who are judicially separated from each other may apply to the court under the provisions of the Domestic Violence and Matrimonial Proceedings Act 1976.

2 High Court

The question of whether the High Court has jurisdiction to entertain proceedings to grant relief under section 1(1) of the Domestic Violence and Matrimonial Proceedings Act 1976 where no other relief is sought in the proceedings is not without difficulty. Section 1(1) of the Act of 1976 is expressed to be 'without prejudice to the jurisdiction of the High Court'. It follows that the Act does not extend the jurisdiction of the High Court.[16]

In *Crutcher* v *Crutcher*[17] it was held that section 1(1) of the Act of 1976 did not enlarge the jurisdiction of the High Court to grant an injunction and if it was desired to obtain such an injunction in the High Court, proceedings for some substantive relief must have been commenced or there must be the usual undertaking to commence proceedings forthwith. It was held further that the words in the Act 'whether or not any other relief is sought in the proceedings' referred to an application in the county court.

10 S 1(1), as therein defined; see section G below.
11 *Hussain (Aliya)* v *Hussain (Shahid)* [1983] Fam 26, [1982] 3 All ER 369, CA.
12 S 1(1)(*a*) refers to 'the other party to the marriage' while s 1(1)(*b*) and (*c*) refers to 'the other party'.
13 See ch 1, section C, below.
14 As to whether or not injunctions can be granted in matrimonial causes after decree absolute see ch 1, section C, below.
15 Matrimonial Causes Act 1973, s 18(1); *Hutchinson* v *Hutchinson* [1947] 2 All ER 792, Denning J.
16 See *Davis* v *Johnson* [1979] AC 264 at 332B , [1978], 1 All ER 1132 at 1143a–b, HL per Viscount Dilhorne.
17 (1978) 128 NLJ 981, per Payne J.

Thus although it would appear that the powers of the Family Division to grant an injunction similar to those available under section 1(1) of the Act of 1976 are limited to cases where there are already proceedings in that division for divorce, judicial separation or nullity, wardship or under the Guardianship of Minors Acts 1971 to 1973, the court in *Crutcher* v *Crutcher* does not appear to have considered the effect of the Rules of the Supreme Court.[18] These Rules made with the authority of Parliament[19] prescribe the procedure to be followed on an application by a party to a marriage[20] for an injunction containing any of the relief set out in section 1(1) of the 1976 Act. It is prescribed[1] that if no other relief is sought in the proceedings, the application should be made by originating summons.[2]   It is submitted that the decision of *Crutcher* v *Crutcher* was reached without consideration of the Rules and is therefore *per incuriam*. The effect of the words 'if no other relief is sought in the proceedings' must enable the Family Division of the High Court to grant such injunctions in summary proceedings virtually in exactly the same way as the county court.

However, it remains in doubt whether the High Court has jurisdiction where the parties are not married but are living together as husband and wife in the same household.[3] Whilst it is submitted that the High Court has jurisdiction to entertain such applications, it is to be emphasised that the overwhelming majority of such applications will be made in the county court rather than the High Court. Unless there is any special reason for commencing the proceedings in the High Court applications should be made in the appropriate county court if for no other reason than that of saving costs.

C Interlocutory relief in a matrimonial cause

From the date on which the petition is presented[4] until a decree absolute of divorce or nullity or a decree of judicial separation, the court has power[5] to enjoin one spouse for the benefit of the other.

The court on an application made ex parte before the presentation of a petition, may grant a non molestation or ouster injunction on the proposed petitioner's undertaking to file a petition for divorce, nullity or judicial separation.[6]   The jurisdiction of the court is different after the suit has been determined.[7] The court will grant an order restraining molestation

---

18 RSC Ord 90, r 30; see Appendix 3, below.
19 Supreme Court Act 1981, s 84.
20 RSC Ord 90, r 30(1) uses the phrase 'a party to a marriage within the meaning of section 1(1), Domestic Violence and Matrimonial Proceedings Act 1976.' From this it is likely that the High Court may entertain applications from persons who come within the meaning of the phrase 'a man and a woman who are living with each other in the same household as husband and wife'; see further ch 1, section C, below.
1 RSC Ord 90, r 30(1).
2 For a precedent of such an originating summons see Appendix 4, below.
3 *Seray-Wurie* v *Seray-Wurie* [1987] Fam Law 124, CA, but on the question of the jurisdiction of the High Court see [1986] CA Transcript 259.
4 That is the date on which it is filed at the court office: see Matrimonial Causes Rules 1977, r 12(5); *Alston* v *Alston* [1946] P 203, [1946] 2 All ER 62.
5 County Courts Act 1984, s 38; Supreme Court Act 1981, s 37. See Appendix 1.
6 See further ch 2, section A.2, below.
7 The suit is determined on pronouncement of a decree absolute of divorce or nullity or a decree of judicial separation. A decree of judicial separation, however, does not end the status of the parties as husband and wife; the petitioner is no longer obliged to cohabit with

after a final decree[8], however; the grant of an ouster injunction after decree absolute is by no means as easy, from the point of view of the jurisdiction of the court, as is the grant of a non molestation injunction. In general, an ouster injunction will only be granted, after decree absolute, in support of either a proprietary right[9] or for the welfare of the children.[10]Where there are no children and the spouse seeking the order has no proprietary right in the matrimonial home, the court has no jurisdiction to do more than make a non molestation order.[11] The appropriate remedy to resolve disputes about property may be to apply in the suit for ancillary relief and not to apply for injunctive relief.[12]

The right of a spouse to apply for a transfer of property order by way of ancillary relief in the suit is not a proprietary right and can not be protected by a mandatory injunction ordering the other spouse to leave the matrimonial home.[13] The court has adequate power[14] to preserve matrimonial assets so that any orders of the court made in this context will not be defeated. After decree absolute the court has jurisdiction[15] to protect the interests of children and where the children required somewhere to live, the court will grant an injunction ordering a spouse to vacate the former matrimonial home, should this be necessary. It is submitted that injunctions should not be granted after decree absolute restraining the use of the former matrimonial home by reason only of the fact that there are children of the family to whom section 41 of the Matrimonial Causes Act 1973 applies who are living in that home but that injunctions should only be granted where they are required for the protection of such children.

The Court of Appeal[16] has condemned as 'extremely undesirable and a complete abuse of the process of injunctive relief in this context' the

the respondent. See Matrimonial Causes Act 1973, s 18(1) (27 *Halsbury's Statutes* (4th edn) 700 MATRIMONIAL LAW). Other rights and obligations may continue; see 22 *Halsbury's Laws* (4th edn) 901 et seq HUSBAND AND WIFE.

8 *Robinson v Robinson* [1965] P 39, [1963] 3 All ER 813; *Montgomery v Montgomery*, above; *Webb v Webb* [1986] 1 FLR 541, CA. *Ruddell v Ruddell* (1967) 111 Sol Jo 497. After decree absolute a former spouse, with no proprietory rights in the former matrimonial home cannot rely on the inherent jurisdiction of the court to exclude his or her former spouse from the home as the applicant has no more rights than an independant adult licensee. *O'Malley v O'Malley* [1982] 2 All ER 112, [1982] 1 WLR 244, CA. It is an abuse of process to use the remedy of injunction to set the scene for ancillary relief, ibid. The decision in *O'Malley v O'Malley* does not derogate from the inherent jurisdiction of the court to grant injunctions, after decree absolute, for the protection of children. *Quinn v Quinn* (1982) 4 FLR 394, CA, *Beard v Beard* [1981] 1 All ER 783, [1981] 1 WLR 369, CA, see also *Waugh v Waugh* (1982) 3 FLR 375, CA, the actual decision in *Waugh v Waugh* might be different now by reason of Housing Act 1985, s 91(3)(b).
9 *Brent v Brent* [1975] Fam 1, [1974] 2 All ER 1211, Dunn J.
10 *Stewart v Stewart* [1973] Fam 21, [1973] 1 All ER 31; *Phillips v Phillips [1973]* 2 All ER 423, [1973] 1 WLR 615. *Quinn v Quinn*, above.
11 *Webb v Webb* [1986] 1 FLR 541, CA.
12 *Grace v Grace* [1980] CA Transcript 418.
13 *Brent v Brent* [1975] Fam 1, [1974] 2 All ER 1211, per Dunn J (obiter) which was a decision immediately after the pronouncement of a decree nisi where Dunn J held that as the decree would be made absolute in six weeks time, the position after decree absolute should be considered: following *Montgomery*, above, he held the court had not jurisdiction after decree absolute to exclude a husband from premises owned wholly by him or before decree absolute to make such an order the purpose and effect of which was to produce that result.
14 Under the Matrimonial Causes Act 1973, s 37. See further ch 10, below.
15 *Stewart v Stewart*, above.
16 *Grace v Grace*, above. See also *O'Malley v O'Malley* [1982] 2 All ER 112, [1982] 1WLR 244, CA, but see *Quinn v Quinn* (1982) 4 FLR 394, CA.

practice of ousting a spouse in order to present the court with a *fait accompli* on the hearing of an application for ancillary relief.

In cases involving the protection of children, the court will act even after the passage of some time since the grant of a decree absolute. In *Beard* v *Beard*[17] the judge at first instance, a year after decree absolute as an emergency measure for the protection of children ordered the wife to leave the former matrimonial home in which she had been looking after the children and granted interim care and control to the father. On appeal this decision was upheld and the Court of Appeal emphasised that the court has jurisdiction to make such orders for the protection of children, in emergency, during the continuance of the emergency and for the period of the emergency.[18] It is to be emphasised however that this decision was wholly exceptional and in order to invoke it the circumstances must justify the application of the term 'emergency'. It was made clear that the propositions advanced were not to be interpreted as throwing any light at all upon the jurisdiction of the court in situations other than such extreme emergency.[19] The jurisdiction of the High Court and divorce county courts to grant interlocutory injunctions are identical.[20] As a matrimonial cause can only be commenced in a divorce county court[1] any application, ex parte, before the issue of proceedings must be made in a county court.[2]

D Matrimonial Homes Act 1983

The Act[3] gives jurisdiction to the High Court[4] and county courts[5] to grant injunctions[6] relating to the occupation of a dwelling house[7] which is or has been the matrimonial home.[8] The parties must be married[9] and the marriage may have been entered into under a law which permits polygamy.[10] Where both spouses have a legal[11] interest in the matrimonial home they are each entitled to occupy the same[12] but not to the exclusion of the other. Where the title to the matrimonial home is in the sole name of one spouse he or she is entitled to occupy the same[13] and the other spouse has rights of occupation[14] namely: if in occupation, a right not to be evicted or excluded by the other except with the leave of the court;[15] if not in

---

17 [1981] 1 All ER 783, [1981] 1 WLR 369, CA.
18 [1981] 1 All ER 783 at 787d–h, [1981] 1 WLR 369 at 373B–E.
19 Ibid at 787d and 373B.
20 Supreme Court Act 1981, s 37(1); County Courts Act 1984, s 38. See Appendix 1.
1 Matrimonial and Family Proceedings Act 1984, s 33(3) (27*Halsbury's Statutes* (4th edn) 853 MATRIMONIAL LAW).
2 See further ch 2.
3 Matrimonial Homes Act 1983 (27 *Halsbury's Statutes* (4th edn) 585 MATRIMONIAL LAW). See Appendix 1.
4 Ibid, s 1(9).
5 Ibid.
6 Ibid, s 1(2).
7 As defined in ibid, s 10(1); see Appendix 1.
8 Ibid, s 1(10).
9 Ibid, s 1. The Act uses the word 'spouse'.
10 Ibid, s 10(2).
11 As opposed to equitable.
12 By virtue of joint ownership, recognised by the Matrimonial Homes Act 1983, s 9.
13 By virtue of the legal interest in the property whether freehold, leasehold or rented.
14 Matrimonial Homes Act 1983, s 1(1).
15 Ibid, s 1(1)(a).

occupation, a right to enter and occupy the home with the leave of the court.[16]

Where the matrimonial home is in the joint names of the parties either spouse may apply to the court, during the subsistence of the marriage,[17] for an order prohibiting, suspending or restricting the exercise by the other's right to occupy the home.[18] Where the matrimonial home is in the sole name of one spouse either spouse may apply, during the subsistence of the marriage,[19] for an order declaring, enforcing or terminating those rights;[20] prohibiting, suspending or restricting the exercise of those rights;[1] or, requiring the other spouse to permit the applicant to exercise his or her rights[2] of occupation.

Rights of occupation end on the death[3] of one spouse or on the other termination of the marriage[4] unless in the event of a matrimonial dispute or estrangement[5] the court directs otherwise by an order[6] made during the subsistence of the marriage. Therefore unless such a direction has been made under the Matrimonial Homes Act 1983, section 1 before decree absolute, a spouse who has no proprietary interest in the matrimonial home has difficulty in obtaining an injunction in respect of the occupation of the matrimonial home against the other.[7]

Although the Act only applies to spouses[8] where, on an application under the Act, one party alleges that there never has been a marriage, the court may treat the marriage as binding[9] unless the contrary is shown when the issue is properly determined by the court.[10]

E   Wardship

The wardship jurisdiction of the High Court is inherent and derives from the protection given by the Crown to its subjects. Those who are minors[11] are more vulnerable than adults and are given the special protection of the Crown as *parens patriæ*.[12]

Any minor who is a British subject or who is present in England or

16 Ibid, s 1(1)(b).
17 Ie before it is ended by a decree absolute of divorce or nullity.
18 Matrimonial Homes Act 1983, s 9.
19 Ie before it is ended by a decree absolute of divorce or nullity.
20 Matrimonial Homes Act 1983, s 1(2)(a).
 1 Ibid, s 1(2)(b).
 2 Ibid, s 1(2)(c).
 3 Ibid, s 2(4)(a).
 4 Ibid, s 2(4)(b), ie a decree absolute of divorce or nullity.
 5 The term 'matrimonial dispute or estrangement' is not defined but by reason of the fact that the order must be made under Matrimonial Homes Act 1983, s 1, it would seem to be limited to proceedings under the Matrimonial Homes Act 1983 or interlocutory relief in a matrimonial cause. It might include proceedings under the Domestic Violence and Matrimonial Proceedings Act 1976.
 6 Under Matrimonial Homes Act 1983, s 1.
 7 See chapter 1, section C.
 8 Matrimonial Homes Act 1983, s 1.
 9 *Seray-Wurie* v *Seray-Wurie* [1987] Fam Law 124, CA
10 Where there is no marriage the court would have jurisdiction under the Domestic Violence and Matrimonial Proceedings Act 1976 if the parties came within the meaning of the phrase 'living with each other in the same household as husband and wife'. See further chapter 1, sections B and G.
11 A minor is a person under the age of 18: Family Law Reform Act 1969, s 1(1).
12 *Re P (GE) (an infant)* [1965] Ch 568, [1964] 3 All ER 977, CA.

Wales may be made a ward of court[13] although the court may refuse to exercise the jurisdiction.[14]

A judge exercising the wardship jurisdiction has limitless power to protect the ward from any interference with his or her welfare, direct or indirect.[15] It is unfruitful to seek to define any limits to the jurisdiction.[16] The exercise of the wardship powers is discretionary.[17] The interests of the ward are the first and paramount consideration.[18] In the exercise of their discretionary powers, judges should keep a proper balance between the protection of their wards and the rights of outside parties (those parties not in a family or personal relationship with the ward) whether such rights arose by common law or statute.[19]

There is jurisdiction to restrain a party from leaving the jurisdiction if such is in the interests of the ward.[20]

F Guardianship of Minors Acts 1971 and 1973

The Acts, inter alia, give the High Court and county courts power to make orders for the legal custody of and access to minors.[21] Although the court may make some orders on the application of grandparents[1] it would appear that only a parent may be the applicant and the initial respondent.[2]

The court may grant injunctions as interlocutory relief,[3] ancillary to or in support of, an order for legal custody.[4] For example: restraining the removal of a minor from care and control, or restraining molestation of the minor. There is statutory power to restrain the removal of a minor from England and Wales.[5]

An exclusion injunction may not be made in respect of a home owned jointly by the parties.[6] It is submitted that where the applicant is entitled to

---

13 A minor becomes a ward upon the issue of the originating summons. RSC Ord 90, r 3.
14 Child in the care of the local authority see: *A v Liverpool City Council* [1982] AC 363, [1981] 2 All ER 385, HL. Minor whose parent claims diplomatic immunity see *Re: C (an infant)* [1959] Ch 363, [1958] 2 All ER 656. Child refused entry by the immigration authorities see *Re Mohammed Arif (an infant)* [1968] Ch 643, [1968] 2 All ER 145, CA; see also *Re S (minors)* (1980) 11 Fam Law 55, CA. No jurisdiction to grant a bare declaration of paternity *Re JS (a minor)* [1981] Fam 22, [1980] 1 All ER 1061, CA. The above examples are not exhaustive; see *Rayden on Divorce* (14th edn), ch 27.
15 *Re X (a minor)(Wardship: Restriction on Publication)* [1975] Fam 54, [1975] 1 All ER 702, CA; *Re R (MJ) (a minor)* [1975] Fam 89, [1975] 2 All ER 749; *Re D (a minor) (Wardship: Sterilisation)* [1976] Fam 185, [1976] 1 All ER 326; *Re J (a minor)* [1984] FLR 535, [1984] Fam Law 308.
16 Ibid.
17 Ibid.
18 Ibid.
19 Ibid.
20 *Re I (a minor)* (1987) Times, 22 May.
21 Guardianship of Minors Act 1971, s 9 (6 *Halsbury's Statutes* (4th edn) 305 CHILDREN). Guardianship Act 1973, ss 2–5 (6 *Halsbury's Statutes* (4th edn) 338 CHILDREN).
1 Guardianship of Minors Act 1971, s 14A.
2 Guardianship of Minors Act 1971, s 9. In cases where it is desired to make a non-parent a party to the proceedings it is more appropriate to invoke the wardship jurisdiction.
3 Under Supreme Court Act 1981, s 37 and County Courts Act 1984, s 38.
4 *Re: W (a minor)* [1981] 3 All ER 401, 11 Fam Law 207, CA.
5 Guardianship of Minors Act 1971, s 13A.
6 *Ainsbury v Millington* [1986] 1 All ER 73, [1986] 1 FLR 331, CA. On the particular facts of the case the applicant could not rely on the Matrimonial Homes Act 1983 as the parties were not married; furthermore, the Domestic Violence and Matrimonial Proceedings Act 1976 could not be used as the parties had not cohabited for about a year prior to the application.

occupy the property and the respondent is not so entitled, an exclusion order could properly be made against the respondent provided that it was ancillary to an order for legal custody.[7]

G Unmarried couples

The Act of 1976 provides remedies for unmarried as well as married couples[8] If the language of section 1(2) of the 1976 Act were to be interpreted strictly, its meaning would be greatly restricted since the literal meaning of the words suggest that both the parties to an application must be living together with each other at the time when an application is made. Such a literal interpretation would deprive the Act of much of its effect and rationale. On the other hand, according to the wording a wider meaning might result in serious difficulties in interpreting facts.[9]

This was finally resolved in *Davis* v *Johnson*;[10] it was held that the Act gave jurisdiction to county courts to grant exclusion injunctions where the parties, whether married or living together unmarried, had shared accommodation irrespective of any right of property vested in the person excluded whether as owner, tenant or joint tenant in the same circumstances that such an injunction would be granted under the terms of the Act to a married woman. In effect, unmarried persons living together in the same household as husband and wife are treated by the Act as if they were married.[11] It is to be emphasised however that whilst the Act represents an important extension of the family protection it is not to be regarded as 'a battered mistresses' charter'.[12] The Act extends protection to households in which a man and a woman live irrespective of whether or not they bring up children at the same time. It does not extend to a woman who has been installed in a property for the intermittent sexual enjoyment of another.[13] Difficult questions of fact arise where the relationship has ended, and some time has elapsed before an application to the court is made. The question which has to be answered in such a case is when the relationship between the man and woman concerned is to be treated as having come to an end. This is a question to which courts have yet to formulate a conclusive answer. However, it has been indicated that the longer the period of time that has elapsed between the cessation of the relationship between the parties and the issue of the summons is, the more difficult it will be for an applicant to bring himself within the section.[14]The words in the Domestic

---

7 *Re: W (a minor)* above. The applicant would have a legal right to exclude the respondent and the grant of an injunction in guardianship proceedings would avoid the institution of a separate action for trespass.
8 Domestic Violence and Matrimonial Proceedings Act 1976, s 1(2)
9 *B v B (Domestic Violence: Jurisdiction)* [1978] Fam 26, [1978] 1 All ER 821. See also *McLean v Burke* (1980) 3 FLR 70, CA.
10 [1979] AC 264, [1978] 1 All ER 1132, HL answering some of the questions raised in *B v B (Domestic Violence: Jurisdiction)* above and *Cantliff v Jenkins* [1978] Fam 47, [1978] 1 All ER 836, CA.
11 Ibid at 334E and at 1145a, per Viscount Dilhorne approved and followed by the Court of Appeal in *McLean v Nugent* (1980) 1 FLR 26, CA.
12 [1979] AC 264 at 338H, [1978] 1 All ER 1132 at 114f–g, per Lord Kilbrandon.
13 Ibid.
14 *McLean v Nugent* (1980) 1 FLR 26, CA per Ormrod LJ.

Violence and Matrimonial Proceedings Act 1976, 'living with each other in the same household as husband and wife', should be interpreted as referring to the relationship existing immediately before the incident (or series of incidents) giving rise to the application.[15] This question is one of fact and it is submitted that where there has been delay for which there is a good explanation, this should not be fatal to the application.

It is a question of fact whether on the circumstances of any particular case, a man and woman are properly to be held as living in the same household as husband and wife. The court deciding the issue must look at all the facts and ask itself whether it can be said that the parties are living together in the same household as husband and wife. In answering that question there are many different factors which must be taken into account; it will depend on the domestic relationship between the parties; their ages; the accommodation that is available and in general upon their manner of life together.[16]

Decisions and interpretations of the words 'living with each other in the same household'[17] provide some assistance in the interpretation of the Act of 1976. The phrase 'household' has an abstract meaning[18] rather than referring to something physical. Mere physical absence from the matrimonial home is not fatal to the suggestion that the parties are 'living together' unless it can also be shown that one or other of the parties has made up his or her mind that he or she will not renew the relationship of living together in the same household with the other party. Even where the parties continue to share the premises in which they had lived together, it is not certain that they can be described as living together for the purposes of the Act. So for example where two parties continue to live in a house but occupy different rooms in the property; do not speak to each other and do not take their meals together it is unlikely that they will be held to be living together for the purposes of the Act.[19]

The words 'in the same household' are to be regarded as words of limitation the effect of which is to treat persons living with each other as living apart unless they are 'in the same household'.[20] Courts construing the statute should not lose sight of the practicalities of such relationships and should be reluctant to find artificial and separate households in circumstances where the practicalities of the accommodation prevent the reality of two separate households.[1] The question is one of degree and the whole of the physical circumstances have to be looked at to determine whether the degree of separation is such as to justify the finding of two separate households. Whilst cases decided under the old law may provide some guidance, it is to be borne in mind that the old decisions were the product of judicial stretching of the law designed to get over the impossible position in which a couple had ceased to communicate altogether but neither of the

---

15 *McLean v Burke* (1980) 3 FLR 70, CA.
16 *Hills v Bushby* [1977] CA Transcript 398B.
17 Divorce Reform Act 1969, ss 2(5) and 3(6), repealed and replaced by the Matrimonial Causes Act 1973, s 2(6).
18 *Santos v Santos* [1972] Fam 247,[1972] 2 All ER 246, CA.
19 *Hollens v Hollens* (1971) 115 Sol Jo 327, Wrangham J.
20 *Mouncer v Mouncer* [1972] 1 All ER 289 at 291f, per Wrangham J and see *Hills v Bushby* above.
 1 *Adeoso v Adeoso* [1981] 1 All ER 107at 110d–f, [1980] 1 WLR 1535 at 1537 F–H, CA, per Ormrod LJ.

parties was able to leave the home they had formerly shared together because of the absence of alternative accommodation.[2] Just as it was necessary to stretch the law for the purposes of practical necessity in those cases, it may be necessary to take a quite contrary approach when determining applications under the Act of 1976, regard having been had to the fact that one or other of the parties may not be able to leave because of the impracticality of obtaining alternative accommodation in circumstances where, by reason of the proximity of the parties and the disintegration of their relationship, protection may most be needed.

The phrase 'living with each other as husband and wife' also acts as a phrase of limitation by excluding from the protection of the Act any case in which a man and a woman simply share living accommodation for the purposes of reducing their individual expenses.

For the purposes of supplementary benefit, where an applicant cohabits as man and wife with another person the requirements and resources of both will be aggregated.[3] It then becomes necessary to decide in what circumstances two people are to be regarded as cohabiting as man and wife. A number of criteria have been adopted by the Supplementary Benefits Commission[4] and whilst these criteria do not have the force of law it is submitted that they are factors which any court in deciding the issue would have regard to. The Commission would not normally regard a man as living in the same household as a woman unless he has no other home where he normally lives. Equally, the commission take the view that living together as husband and wife implies more than a very occasional or brief association.[5] Equally, whilst it is to be expected that in such a relationship one party will provide at least some partial financial support for the other, or at least a sharing of expenses, the absence of such an arrangement would not be conclusive against the finding that the parties were cohabiting. Similarly, whilst a sexual relationship is a normal and important part of marriage and therefore of living together as husband and wife, its absence does not necessarily prove that a couple are not living together as husband and wife nor does its presence prove that they are.[6] There is a strong presumption that where a couple are caring for a child or children of their union, they are living together as husband and wife. Whilst the fact that a couple have represented themselves to other persons as being husband and wife is a factor which will or may be significant[7] its absence will not since many couples living together do not wish to pretend they are actually

---

2 Ibid at 109 d–f and at 1537 F–H.
3 Supplementary Benefits Act 1976, Sch 1, para 3(1).
4 *Supplementary Benefits Handbook 1977*, para 21.
5 Cf *Davis* v *Johnson* [1979] AC 264 at 338H, [1978] 1 All ER 1132 at 1148 f–g, HL, per Lord Kilbrandon.
6 See *Adeoso* v *Adeoso* [1981] 1 All ER 107, [1980] 1 WLR 1535 CA, where the parties had not had sexual intercourse for some sixteen months prior to the application to the court yet it was held that they were living together as husband and wife and *Piper* v *Piper* (1978) 8 Fam Law 243, a case under s 1(2)(e) of the Matrimonial Causes Act 1973 in which it was held that a husband and wife were not living together in the same household in circumstances where the husband maintained his own household and regularly visited his wife at her house and stayed at weekends and sometimes during the week and that sometimes sexual intercourse took place between them.
7 See *Adeoso* v *Adeoso* [1981] 1 All ER 107 at 109 d–f and at [1980] 1 WLR 1535 at 1537 F–H, per Ormrod LJ.

married and in fact retain their separate identities publicly as unmarried persons.

Whilst it is submitted that these tests will provide some degree of assistance in attempting to decide any question of whether or not the parties to an application were living together in the same household as man and wife, it is to be remembered that these factors are not to be regarded as in any way exhaustive and each case must be looked at in its own context. All that can be said on these particular matters is that they will normally provide an indication of the likely outcome of any issue between the parties on the point. Ultimately, the question is one of fact based upon common sense.[8]

Where the parties are not married and do not come within the definition of 'living with each other in the same household as husband and wife' recourse must be had to common law actions in tort for trespass or assault.[9]

8 *Hills* v *Bushby* [1977] CA Transcript 398 B.
9 See further ch 8.

Chapter 2
Procedure

A Applications for ex parte injunctions and orders

1 Applications to the county court under the Domestic Violence and Matrimonial Proceedings Act 1976

Such applications should be made to the county court for the district in which the applicant or the respondent resides or for the district in which the matrimonial home[1] is situate.[2] The application is made by affidavit.[3] In a case of great urgency, an application may be made before the issue of the originating application[4] upon an undertaking to issue such by the party making the application or if the party is represented, then by the solicitors acting for him or her.[5]

2 Applications to the county court for interlocutory relief in a matrimonial cause

Where a cause is pending an application should be made to the court in which that cause is pending. Where no matrimonial proceedings have been commenced then an application may be made to any divorce county court.[6] The application is made on affidavit.[7]

In case of great urgency, the application may be made before the cause is commenced.[8] The court will require an undertaking that a matrimonial

---

1 'Matrimonial home' means premises in which the husband and wife live; or in the case of an unmarried couple the premises in which they live together in the same household as husband and wife: Domestic Violence and Matrimonial Proceedings Act 1976, s 1(2) (27 *Halsbury's Statutes* (4th edn) 788 MATRIMONIAL LAW).
2 CCR Ord 47, r 8(2).
3 CCR Ord 13, r 6(3). For the contents of such affidavit see Appendix 4, below. Where it is not possible to swear an affidavit, a judge will in general hear oral evidence or will permit a draft affidavit to be read to him though usually the latter course will only be adopted if the party reading it will give an undertaking to file the affidavit within a fixed time, usually 24 hours or less. It should be noted that an affidavit sworn by an applicant in support of an ex parte application for an injunction must disclose all material facts to the extent that an applicant must act *uberrima fides* or he will disentitle himself to the relief sought. This requirement is imposed by the court for its own protection and to ensure so far as is possible that the ex parte application procedure is not abused; see *R v Kensington Income Tax General Comns, ex p Princess de Polignac* [1917] 1 KB 486.
4 CCR Ord 13, 6(4).
5 A time limit will be fixed for the issue of the originating application. The time allowed will, in general, not exceed 24 hours and may be shorter depending upon the prevailing circumstances.
6 Matrimonial Causes Rules 1977 (SI 1977/344), r 12(1). For divorce county court see the Divorce County Courts Order 1978 (SI 1978/1759), as amended. See 16 *Court Forms* 95 DIVORCE for a complete list of divorce county courts.
7 CCR Ord 13, r 6(3). For the content of such an affidavit see Appendix 4, below.
8 CCR Ord 13, r 6(4).

cause will be commenced.[9] Where a proposed petitioner is frightened of the other spouse and does not wish to disclose his present residence to the proposed respondent, leave may be obtained[10] for his or her address not to be included within the petition. Application for such leave should be made upon the application for an ex parte injunction the reasons for it being set out in the affidavit which is used to support the application for an ex parte relief.

3 Applications to the county court under the Matrimonial Homes Act 1983

The application, which is made by affidavit,[11] is made to the court for the district in which the matrimonial home is situate.[12] In cases of urgency, the application may be made before the issue of the originating application,[13] upon an undertaking to issue the same.[14] Where a matrimonial cause has been commenced, or is about to be commenced, an application for relief under the Matrimonial Homes Act 1983 may be made as interlocutory relief in such proceedings.[15]

4 Applications to the county court under the Guardianship of Minors Acts 1971 to 1973

The application, which is made by affidavit,[16] is made to the county court for the district in which any of the respondents, the applicant or the minor reside.[17] In cases of urgency the application may be made before the issue of the originating application[18] upon the undertaking to issue such an application[19]

5 Applications to the High Court under the Domestic Violence and Matrimonial Proceedings Act 1976

Such application may be made either at the Principal Registry in London or any district registry of the High Court.[20] The application, which is made

---

9 An undertaking must be given to present a petition for divorce, judicial separation or nullity. A time limit will be fixed for the filing of such documents which, in general will not exceed 24 hours in respect of the petition. Longer periods of time may be allowed to file the supporting documents which are:

In the case of petition for divorce, judicial separation or nullity – (a) the marriage certificate (Matrimonial Causes Rules 1977, r 12(2)); (b) statement as to the arrangements for children (Matrimonial Causes Rules 1977, r 8(2) and Form 4 in Matrimonial Causes Rules 1977, App I); (c) certificate with regard to reconciliation (Matrimonial Causes Rules 1977, r 12(3) and Form 3 in Matrimonial Causes Rules 1977, App I).

10 Matrimonial Causes Rules 1977, r 9.
11 CCR Ord 13, r 6(3).
12 CCR Ord 4, r 8(a)(ii).
13 CCR Ord 13, r 6(4).
14 A time limit will be fixed for the issue of the originating application. The time allowed will, in general, not exceed 24 hours and may be shorter depending upon the circumstances.
15 CCR Ord 47, r 4(4).
16 CCR Ord 13, r 6(3).
17 Guardianship of Minors Act 1971, s 15(1)(b), (6 *Halsbury's Statutes* (4th edn) 321 CHILDREN).
18 CCR Ord 13, r 6(4).
19 A time limit will be fixed for the issue of the originating application. The time allowed will, in general, not exceed 24 hours and may be shorter depending upon the prevailing circumstances.
20 RSC Ord 90, r 30(1).

by affidavit,[1] may be made before the issue of an originating summons[2] upon an undertaking to issue the same.[3]

6 Applications to the High Court for interlocutory relief in a matrimonial cause

As a matrimonial cause cannot be commenced in the High Court[4] there will already be proceedings pending at the time any application for interlocutory relief is made to the High Court. The application for such relief should be made either at the Royal Courts of Justice or at the appropriate divorce town depending upon whether the suit is pending in the Principal Registry or a district registry.[5] The application is made by affidavit.[6]

7 Applications to the High Court under the Matrimonial Homes Act 1983

The application is made either at the Divorce Registry[7] or at any district registry of the High Court.[8] The application which is made on affidavit[9] may, in cases of urgency, be made before the issue of the originating summons[10] upon an undertaking to issue such originating summons.[11] Where a matrimonial cause has been commenced, or is about to be commenced, an application for relief under the Matrimonial Homes Act 1983 may be made by an interlocutory application in such proceedings.[12]

8 Applications to the High Court under the Guardianship of Minors Acts 1971 to 1973

The application is made either at the Principal Registry in London or to any district registry of the High Court.[13] The application which is made by affidavit[14] may, in cases of urgency, be made before the issue of the originating summons[15] upon an undertaking to issue such originating summons.[16]

---

1 RSC Ord 29, r 1(2).
2 RSC Ord 29, r 1(3).
3 The time limit will be fixed for the issue of originating summons. The time allowed will in general not exceed 24 hours and may be shorter depending upon the prevailing circumstances.
4 Matrimonial and Family Proceedings Act 1984, s 33(3) (27 *Halsbury's Statutes* (4th edn) 853 MATRIMONIAL LAW).
5 Matrimonial Causes Rules 1977, r 122(1)(a). See 16 *Court Forms* 95 DIVORCE for a complete list of district registries and divorce towns.
6 RSC Ord 29, r 1(2). For the contents of such affidavit see Appendix 4, below.
7 Defined as the Principal Registry of the Family Division by Matrimonial Causes Rules 1977 (SI 1977 No 344) r 2(2).
8 Matrimonial Causes Rules 1977 r 104(1) as applied by r 107(1).
9 RSC Ord 29 r 1(2).
10 RSC Ord 29 r 1(3).
11 A time limit will be fixed for the issue of the originating summons. The time allowed will, in general, not exceed 24 hours and may be shorter depending upon the prevailing circumstances.
12 Matrimonial Causes Rules 1977 r 107(2).
13 RSC Ord 90, r 5.
14 RSC Ord 29, r 1(2).
15 RSC Ord 29, r 1(3).
16 A time limit will be fixed for the issue of the originating summons. The time allowed will in general not exceed 24 hours and may be shorter depending upon the prevailing circumstances.

9 Applications in wardship proceedings in the High Court

Applications for interlocutory relief in wardship proceedings may be made either at the Principal Registry in London or at any district registry of the High Court.[17] The application is made by affidavit.[18] The application may be made before the issue of the originating summons[19] upon an undertaking to issue the originating summons.[20]

10 Procedure upon the hearing of ex parte applications

Applications for injunctions restraining molestation, exclusion injunctions and injunctions requiring the respondent to permit the applicant to enter and remain in the home or to return children and thereafter not to remove children from the care and control of a particular parent must be made to a judge of either the High Court or the county court and neither High Court or county court registrars have power to make such injunctions.[1]

Most courts have at least one day in each week when urgent ex parte applications can be made.[2] Applications at the Royal Courts of Justice are heard at 10.30 am and 2 pm each week day.[3] Urgent applications at other times may be made by arrangement with the Clerk of the Rules.

Where an applicant's solicitors notify the respondent's solicitors of an intended ex parte application and fail to notify them of its withdrawal they may be personally liable for costs incurred by those parties of attendance at the abortive hearing.[4]

The application should be made on affidavit, except in a case of great urgency when the judge should be invited to hear oral evidence. The affidavit should be as full and complete as possible.[5]

Only in exceptional circumstances should an applicant for a non-molestation or ouster injunction be asked to give an undertaking in respect of damages sustained by the respondent.[6] In general such an undertaking is unnecessary and inappropriate in matrimonial and children's cases involving personal conduct. The undertaking should not be recited automatically in the order as drawn up by the court.

In general, applications will be heard in chambers[7] though a judge may direct the matter to be heard in open court at his discretion.

Where an ex parte injunction is made, a return date will be specified at which time an inter partes hearing will take place. The return date should be made as soon as possible after the ex parte hearing.[8] The reason is that on an ex parte application, the court will be unable to reach a rational and

---

17 RSC Ord 90, r 3(1).
18 RSC Ord 29, r 1(2).
19 RSC Ord 29, r 1(3).
20 A time limit will be fixed for the issue of the originating summons. The time allowed will in general not exceed 24 hours and may be shorter depending upon the prevailing circumstances.
1 RSC Ord 32, r 11(1)(d); CCR Ord 13, r 6(1); Ord 47, r 4(2).
2 This may be at 10.30 am or at 2 pm or both. Some courts hear ex parte applications at 4 o'clock pm. The practice varies from court to court and details can always be obtained by telephoning the court office.
3 See also Notice in Daily Cause List, Appendix 2, below.
4 *Re F* (1984) Times 25 August.
5 See Appendix 4.
6 *Practice Direction* [1974] 2 All ER 400, [1974] 1 WLR 567. See Appendix 2, below.
7 CCR Ord 47, rr 4(1), 8(4); *Practice Direction* [1974] 2 All ER 1119, [1974] 1 WLR 936, Appendix 2, below.
8 *Ansah* v *Ansah* [1977] Fam 138, [1977] 2 All ER 638, CA.

balanced decision[9] with the result that delay in hearing the respondent's side of the matters which are alleged to have necessitated the application may cause him or her great injustice and inconvenience.

An ex parte injunction together with any supporting affidavit should be served on the respondent as soon as possible.[10] Furthermore, where the injunction has been obtained on an undertaking to issue substantive proceedings the originating document should be served at the same time or if this is not possible, as soon as possible thereafter. Where an undertaking is given to issue substantive proceedings 'as soon as reasonably practical' this means the same as 'forthwith'.[11] It is important that there should be no default in compliance with such an undertaking.[12] It is to be emphasised that before an injunction can be enforced by committal to prison the order must have been endorsed with a penal notice and served personally upon the respondent irrespective of whether a solicitor is on the record as acting on behalf of the respondent.[13]

11   Principles applicable to the determination of ex parte applications

In general, an application for an injunction, either under the Act of 1976 or as interlocutory relief in a matrimonial suit, should only be made or granted ex parte where there is a real immediate danger of serious injury or irreparable damage.[14] The Act of 1976 was created and designed to provide an emergency procedure to cope with the crisis incidents in domestic life[15] and it follows that only exceptional cases falling within either of the two categories will justify a departure from the normal procedure particularly where orders are sought which may have the effect of depriving a respondent of a roof over his head. Almost every application for a non molestation order, an order ousting the other party from the matrimonial home or an order that the applicant be permitted to re-enter the matrimonial home inevitably will involve a degree of emergency but such 'normal emergency' does not justify an application made ex parte. It is to be emphasised that whilst the power of the court to intervene immediately and without notice to the other party in a family dispute is essential to the administration of justice, the power must be used with great caution and only in circumstances where it is really necessary to act immediately.[16] Whilst the court is generally reluctant to grant an injunction ex parte except in the clearest cases, because to do so may result in an injustice to the respondent which will have the effect of damaging the court's authority, the court is in particular reluctant to make orders which would involve the ousting of a respondent from the matrimonial home without the opportunity of his having been heard.

9 *Rennick* v *Rennick* [1978] 1 All ER 817, [1977] 1 WLR 1455, CA, per Ormrod LJ, obiter.
10 This must be done for two reasons: firstly so that he or she becomes aware of the order and is then able to comply with it and secondly so that the order may be enforced by committal. See further ch 12, below. Furthermore service must be effected so as to give the respondent at least two clear days' notice of the return date.
11 *PS Refson & Co Ltd* v *Saggers* [1984] 3 All ER 111, [1984] 1 WLR 1025.
12 Ibid.
13 See ch 12, below for committal to prison for breach of injunctions.
14 See *Practice Direction* [1978] 2 All ER 919, [1978] 1 WLR 925 reproduced in Appendix 2, below. The contents of the Practice Direction and the need for following it was emphasised by the Court of Appeal in *Smollen* v *Smollen* [1979] CA Transcript 794 (14 December).
15 *McLean* v *Nugent* (1980) 1 FLR 26, CA, per Ormrod LJ.
16 *Ansah* v *Ansah* [1977] Fam 138 at 142H, [1977] 2 All ER 638 at 642 b–c, per Ormrod LJ.

Where such a radical remedy is sought, it is important to reach a rational and balanced decision.[17] Indeed, to make an application ex parte to oust the respondent from a matrimonial home will in the normal run of cases amount to an abuse of the process of the court with the consequence that the solicitor promoting such an application could find himself or herself liable to pay all the costs thrown away.[18] It has been emphasised by the courts on numerous occasions that the most urgent of applications when onerous relief is claimed, can be dealt with on two days' notice in matrimonial proceedings pending in the Divorce Registry for hearing at the Royal Courts of Justice[19] and the corresponding procedure in divorce county courts where a suit is pending or is about to be commenced or in which an undertaking to file can be given. Urgent applications for relief under the Act of 1976 between co-habitees or between husband and wives with no present intention of divorcing or judicially separating may be treated with equal speed.[20]

Whilst it is emphasised that courts entertaining applications made ex parte will proceed with great caution, a co-habitee or spouse should in no way be deterred from seeking ex parte relief in a case of great emergency where immediate protection for the applicant or a child is vital. It is for such cases as that that the ex parte relief procedure is available. Only the abuse of such procedure has resulted in the Court of Appeal expressing its views with such emphasis. More generally, circumstances may arise when prior notice cannot be given to the respondent in particular, where the one parent has disappeared with the children or a spouse is so frightened of the other that some protection must be provided against a violent response to service of the proceedings but in all such cases, the court must be satisfied that such protection is genuinely necessary before it will be persuaded to act.[1]

12 Time limits

Once the court, in its discretion, grants an ex parte injunction, the order, when drawn up, must clearly state the terms of the injunction and must moreover, specify the return date when the matter will be considered further by the court in the presence of both parties. The return date even if that date is only for a preliminary hearing of the matter must be as soon as practicable and should normally be a matter of days rather than weeks away from the date of the ex parte order.

In order to prevent injustice to the respondent, an order obtained ex parte must state expressly the date on which it expires.[2] Where, exceptionally, it is anticipated by the party obtaining an order ex parte that there will be difficulty in serving the other side, it may be permissible for the court to fix a longer period before the return date and to protect the respondent's interest sufficiently by incorporating into the order a liberty in the respondent to apply to the court upon short (usually twenty-four hours)

---

17 *Renick* v *Renick*, above.
18 *Masich* v *Masich* (1977) 7 Fam Law 245, [1977] CA Transcript No 291, per Ormrod LJ.
19 See *Practice Direction* [1972] 2 All ER 1360, [1972] 1 WLR 1047 reproduced in Appendix 2, below. The procedure is also set out in the Daily Cause List under the heading 'Matrimonial Causes and Matters – Urgent Applications', see Appendix 2, below.
20 See further sections on procedure.
1 *Ansah* v *Ansah* [1977] Fam 138 at 143 C [1972] 2 All ER 638 at 642 e, per Ormrod LJ.
2 Ibid at 143 D–F and at 642 f–h, per Ormrod LJ.

notice to discharge any or all of the orders made by the court on the ex parte application.[3]

It is to be emphasised that in no circumstances should an order be made upon an ex parte application which is expressed to operate 'until further order'. To make such an order upon an application made ex parte is wholly unjustifiable and improper.[4]

13   Power of arrest

In order for the court to have power to impose a power of arrest upon an order made ex parte, it will be necessary for the court to be satisfied, as it is necessary to satisfy it on all such applications, that not only has the respondent caused actual bodily harm to the applicant but also that he or she is likely to do so again.[5] Whilst there may be little or no difficulty in satisfying a judge on an application properly made ex parte that an applicant has suffered actual bodily harm at the hands of the respondent, it may well be very difficult or impossible to establish ex parte that the respondent is likely to do so again.[6] It follows, that even where the court is prepared to make an order upon an application made ex parte, it may well not be prepared to make an order endorsed with a power of arrest unless it is possible to establish on affidavit any reason for supposing that a respondent is likely to commit further actual bodily harm upon the applicant.[7] Evidence which might support such an application and which should be included in any affidavit in support of an application made ex parte where it is intended to apply to the court for a power of arrest to be attached to any order made on the application would include the allegations that previous orders of the court that had been made were flouted; that criminal convictions of violence had been recorded against the respondent prior to the incidents complained of; that by committing the offences in question, the respondent will be in breach of probation orders, suspended sentences, conditional discharges or other orders of the court should process for enforcement be taken or that the history of the particular relationship is one of persistent and protracted violence.

B   Procedure upon inter partes applications

1   Applications to the county court under the Domestic Violence and Matrimonial Proceedings Act 1976

Such applications are made by originating application[8] to the county court for the district in which the applicant or the respondent resides or in which the matrimonial home[9] is situate.[10]

3   Ibid.
4   *Morgan* v *Morgan* [1978] 9 Fam Law 87, [1978] CA Transcript 423, per Bridge LJ; a case concerning an appeal from a non molestation order made on the ex parte application of a husband against his wife.
5   *Lewis* v *Lewis* [1978] Fam 60, [1978] 1 All ER 729, CA.
6   *Morgan* v *Morgan*, above.
7   See further ch 6 below.
8   CCR Ord 47, r 8(1). For a precedent see Appendix 4, below.
9   'Matrimonial home' means the premises in which a husband and wife live; in the case of an unmarried couple the expression means premises in which they live together in the same household as the husband and wife. See Domestic Violence and Matrimonial Proceedings Act 1976, s 1(2). (27 *Halsbury's Statutes* (4th edn) 788 MATRIMONIAL LAW).
10   CCR Ord 47, r 8(2).

The applicant should swear an affidavit[11] setting out the grounds upon which he or she seeks the relief claimed.[12] The originating application together with the supporting affidavit should be served personally[13] on the respondent at least four clear days before the hearing[14] An affidavit of service of these documents should be sworn by the person serving them.[15]

Having been served with the originating application and affidavit in support, the respondent should prepare and file an affidavit in answer. The affidavit should admit or deny, as appropriate, the allegations in the affidavit of the applicant and should set out any other relevant matters upon which the respondent relies such as the availability of alternative accommodation for either himself or the applicant.

In general, applications will be heard in chambers[16] although a judge may in his discretion direct that the matter be heard in open court.

Except in a case of urgency the applicant, before the hearing, should prepare a draft of the injunction sought.[17] If the application is granted the draft should be submitted to the judge who will settle the terms of the injunction.[18] When settled the injunction will be forwarded to the proper officer[19] for filing[20] who will issue a copy to the applicant's solicitor for service. The order thus issued should be endorsed with a penal notice[1] and should be served personally[2] so that the same may be enforced by committal[3] for breach. It is good practice for the person serving the order endorsed with the penal notice upon the respondent personally to swear an affidavit of service immediately after which exhibits the order served sets out the circumstances of service so that it can be retained on file by the applicant's solicitors for use in the event of breach in an application to commit.

2 Applications to the county court for interlocutory relief

An application for an injunction in a matrimonial cause is made by notice of application[4] and should be supported by an affidavit sworn by the applicant. The application together with the affidavit in support should be served at least two clear days before the date of hearing[5] The applica-

---

11 It should include the information set out in Appendix 4, below.
12 CCR Ord 13, r 6(3).
13 Personal service is desirable in case the respondent does not attend the hearing; see CCR Ord 13, rr 1(2), (3). However it should be borne in mind that where a solicitor is on the record of the court as acting for the respondent, service upon that solicitor will be good service.
14 CCR Ord 7, r 10(5) as applied by Ord 3, r 4(6) and Ord 47, r 8(3).
15 This is to prove personal service in case the respondent does not attend the hearing. The requirement in CCR Ord 7, r 6(1)(b) that an affidavit of service should be sworn is directory and not mandatory see *Savage* v *Savage* [1979] CA Transcript 537. It follows that where service has been effected oral evidence of good service is admissible.
16 CCR Ord 47, r 8(4).
17 CCR Ord 13, r 6(6).
18 CCR Ord 13, r 6(6).
19 For the meaning of 'proper officer' see CCR Ord 1, r 3.
20 CCR Ord 13, r 6(7).
 1 CCR Ord 29, rr 1(2),(3).
 2 CCR Ord 29 rr 1(2),(3).
 3 See further ch 12, below: enforcement of injunctions.
 4 CCR Ord 13, rr 1(2),(3), as applied by Matrimonial Causes Rules 1977, r 122(1)(b). For a precedent see Appendix 4, below.
 5 CCR Ord 13, rr 1(2),(3), as applied by Matrimonial Cause Rules 1977, r 122(2).

tion and supporting affidavit should be served personally[6] and the process server should swear an affidavit of service exhibiting the documents served and setting out the circumstances in which they were served.[7]

The application is made to a judge[8] and the application will be heard at the appropriate court of trial.[9] The application like applications made ex parte and inter partes for relief under the Act of 1976 may be heard by the judge in chambers.[10]

Upon being served with the applicant's affidavit and application, the respondent should then file an affidavit in answer. The affidavit should admit or deny as appropriate the allegations contained in the affidavit in support of the application and should set out any other relevant matters which will be relied upon by the respondent at the hearing of the application.

Except in a case of urgency the applicant, before the hearing, should prepare a draft of the injunction sought.[11] If the application is granted the draft should be submitted to the judge who will settle the terms of the injunction.[12] When settled the injunction will be forwarded to the proper officer[13] for filing[14] who will issue a copy to the applicant's solicitor for service. The order should be endorsed with a penal notice[15] and the copy issued by the court to the applicant's solicitors should be served personally[16] on the respondent in order that, in the event of breach, it may be enforced by committal.[17] It is good practice for the person serving the order personally upon the respondent to prepare and swear an affidavit of service setting out the circumstances in which it was served and exhibiting the documents served which should then be retained on file by the solicitors acting for the applicant so that in the event of a committal hearing, the contemporaneous affidavit is available.

3 Applications to the county court under the Matrimonial Homes Act 1983

The application is made by originating application[18] to the county court for the district in which the matrimonial home is situate.[19] The applicant

6 Personal service is desirable in case the respondent does not attend the hearing. However, service may be effected by post to a solicitor on the record or to a party in person; see Matrimonial Causes Rules 1977, r 119. It is to be emphasised that where a solicitor is on the record as acting for a respondent, service upon that solicitor is good and effective service until such time as that solicitor is removed from the record as acting in accordance with the Rules of Court.

7 This is to prove personal service in case the respondent does not attend the hearing. The requirement in CCR Ord 7, r 6(1)(b) that an affidavit of service should be sworn is directory and not mandatory see *Savage* v *Savage*, above. The effect is that where an affidavit of service is not available at the hearing, oral evidence to prove service is admissible.

8 CCR Ord 13, r 6(1).

9 Matrimonial Causes Rules 1977, r 123(1)(b). For courts of trial see Divorce County Courts Order 1978 (SI 1978/1759) as amended. See 16 *Court Forms* 95 DIVORCE for a complete list of courts of trial.

10 *Practice Direction* [1974] 2 All ER 1119, [1974] 1 WLR 936; see Appendix 2, below.

11 CCR Ord 13, r 6(6).

12 CCR Ord 13, r 6(6).

13 For the meaning of 'proper officer' see CCR Ord 1, r 3.

14 CCR Ord 13, r 6(7).

15 CCR Ord 29, rr 1(2)(3)

16 CCR Ord 29, rr 1(2)(3).

17 See further ch 12, below, for enforcement of injunctions by committal.

18 CCR Ord 3, r 4.

19 CCR Ord 4, r 8(a)(ii)

should swear an affidavit[20] setting out the grounds of the application.[1] The originating application and supporting affidavit should be served personally[2] on the respondent at least two clear days before the return date.[3] On issue of the originating application the proper officer will have fixed the return date.[4]

Having been served with the originating application and affidavit in support the respondent should swear and file an affidavit in answer, admitting or denying the allegations, as appropriate, and setting out all relevant matters that will be relied upon at the hearing.

Where the application is for an ouster injunction it will be heard by a judge.[5] However, where it is sought to terminate the respondent's rights of occupation[6] and it appears to the registrar, on an ex parte application, that the respondent is not in occupation and his whereabouts cannot, after reasonable inquiries, be ascertained, the registrar may dispense with service and hear and determine the application.[7]

The application will be heard in chambers unless otherwise directed.[8]

Except in a case of urgency, the applicant, before the hearing, should prepare a draft of the injunction sought.[9] If the injunction is granted the draft should be submitted to the judge, who will settle the terms of the injunction.[10] When settled, the injunction will be forwarded to the proper officer for filing,[11] who will issue a copy to the applicant's solicitors for service.

The order, thus issued, should be endorsed with a penal notice[12] and served personally[13] on the respondent so that the same may be enforced by committal[14] if it is breached. It is good practice for an affidavit of service[15] to be made by the person serving the order, and filed with the court, so that it is ready in the event of an application to commit.

Where matrimonial proceedings[16] are pending between the parties in a county court an application under the Matrimonial Homes Act 1983 may be made by an interlocutory application[17] in such proceedings.[18]

---

20 For a precedent see Appendix 4.
1 CCR Ord 13, r 6(3).
2 Personal service is desireable in case the respondent does not attend the hearing. CCR Ord 13, r 1(5) permits the court to proceed in the respondent's absence. Where the respondent has a solicitor on the record as acting, service on his solicitor is good service; CCR Ord 7, r 1(1)(b). An affidavit of service should be sworn and filed where personal service has been effected.
3 CCR Ord 13, r 1(2).
4 CCR Ord 3, r 4(4)(a).
5 CCR Ord 47, r 4(2) and see CCR Ord 13, r 6(2).
6 See Matrimonial Homes Act 1983, s 1(2)(a). (27 *Halsbury's Statutes* (4th edn) 585 MATRIMONIAL LAW).
7 CCR Ord 47, r 4(5).
8 CCR Ord, 47, r 4(1).
9 CCR Ord 13, r 6(6).
10 CCR Ord 13, r 6(6).
11 CCR Ord 13, r 6(7).
12 CCR Ord 29, rr 1(2),(3).
13 CCR Ord 29, rr 1(2),(3).
14 See further ch 12.
15 For a precedent see Appendix 4.
16 Defined by CCR Ord 47, r 4(7).
17 Under CCR Ord 13, r 1 by notice of application.
18 CCR Ord 47, r 4(4).

4   Applications to the High Court under the Domestic Violence and Matrimonial Proceedings Act 1976

The application made by a party to a marriages[19] to the High Court for an injunction under the Act of 1976 is, if no other relief is sought in the proceedings, made by originating summons[20] issued out of the Principal Registry[1] or out of a district registry[2] of the High Court.[3]

The originating summons should contain a concise statement of the relief or remedy claimed.[4] The parties to the originating summons are described as plaintiff and defendant.[5] On the issue of the originating summons, the plaintiff may apply for the date of the hearing to be fixed.[6]

The originating summons must be served not less than four clear days[7] before the date fixed for the hearing.[8] If the plaintiff wishes to adduce evidence in support at the hearing, he must do so by affidavit[9] which must be served on the defendant not less than four clear days before the hearing.[10]

The time for the defendant to acknowledge service of the originating summons expires on the next day but one before the date of hearing fixed.[11] Although the originating summons and memorandum of acknowledgment of service may be served by post[12] it is desirable that they should be served personally together with the affidavit in support.[13] The process server should swear an affidavit deposing to the fact of personal service and exhibiting any documents served upon the respondent.[14]

The defendant should swear an affidavit in answer to the application admitting or denying as appropriate, the allegations made by the plaintiff and, in addition, setting out any other relevant matters which the respondent will rely upon at the hearing of the application.

Unless directed otherwise by the judge, the application will be heard in chambers.[15]

If an injunction is granted then the order, duly endorsed with a penal

---

19 This includes a man and a woman who are living with each other in the same household as husband and wife. See Domestic Violence and Matrimonial Proceedings Act 1976, s 1(2). See also ch 1, section C, above, for unmarried couples.
20 RSC Ord 90, r 30(1). The originating summons is as in Form 10 in Appendix A of the Rules. For a precedent see Appendix 4, below.
1 This means the Principal Registry of the Family Division.
2 This means any district registry having a divorce county court within its district. Matrimonial Causes Rules 1977, r 2(2).
3 RSC Ord 90, r 30(1).
4 RSC Ord 7, r 3(1).
5 RSC Ord 7, r 2(2).
6 RSC Ord 28, r 2(2). This should be done so that the matter can be heard promptly.
7 The use of the word 'clear' has the result that both the date from which the period commences and the date when the act is done are excluded from the computation, see *Supreme Court Practice*, para 3/2/6.
8 RSC Ord 28, r 3(2).
9 RSC Ord 28, r 3(3).
10 RSC Ord 28, r 3(3).
11 RSC Ord 28, r 2(2).
12 RSC Ord 10, rr 1(2),5.
13 So that actual knowledge can be proved if the defendant fails to attend the hearing.
14 Stating by whom the document was served; the day of the week and the date on which it was served; where and how: RSC Ord 65, r 8, for a precedent see Appendix 4.
15 See Notice in Daily Cause List reproduced at Appendix 2, below, and *Practice Direction* [1974] 2 All ER 1119, [1974] 1 WLR 936.

notice[16] should be served personally on the defendant[17] so that the same may be enforced by committal.[18] The person serving the order thus endorsed with the penal notice, should, as a matter of practice swear an affidavit immediately following service in which he deposes to the circumstances of personal service and exhibits the documents served which should then be retained on the file of solicitors acting for the applicant so as to be available should the need arise for an application to commit the respondent for breach of the order.

5 Applications to the High Court for interlocutory relief in a matrimonial cause

The application is made by summons[19] supported by an affidavit. The application is made to a judge[20] and will be heard at the appropriate location.[1] The summons and supporting affidavit should be served personally[2] at least two clear days[3] before the date of hearing.[4] An affidavit of service of the summons and supporting affidavit should be sworn by the process server.[5]

The respondent should swear an affidavit in answer to the application admitting or denying as appropriate the allegations contained in the affidavit in support of the application[6] and furthermore setting out any other relevant matters which he intends to rely upon at the hearing of the application.

The application will be heard in chambers unless otherwise directed by the judge.[7]

If the judge grants the injunction then the same, duly endorsed with a penal notice[8] should be served personally[9] on the respondent so that the same may be enforced by committal.[10] The person serving the order

16 RSC Ord 45, r 7(4); the text of the penal notice is as at para 45/7/5 of the *Supreme Court Practice* and see Appendix 4, below.
17 RSC Ord 45, r 7(2).
18 See ch 12 below, for enforcement of injunctions by committal.
19 RSC Ord 29, r 1(2); Matrimonial Causes Rules 1977, r 122(1)(b). For a precedent see Appendix 4, below.
20 Supreme Court Act 1981, s 37(1); RSC Ord 32, r 11(1)(d). It is possible, but hardly ever done in practice, to make the application to the registrar where the parties are agreed as to the terms of the injunction, see RSC Ord 32, r 11(2).
1 Matrimonial Causes Rules 1977, r 123(1)(a).
2 Personal service is desirable in case the respondent does not attend the hearing. However, where a solicitor is on the record as acting, the summons may be served upon him by post: see Matrimonial Causes Rules 1977, r 119. Once a solicitor is on the record of the court as acting, service may be effected upon him until substitution of another solicitor on the record or if the party is acting in person has been effected: see *Supreme Court Practice*, para 67/1/5.
3 See *Supreme Court Practice*, para 3/2/6.
4 RSC Ord 32, r 3.
5 This is to prove personal service in case the respondent does not attend the hearing. The requirement is directory not mandatory; see *Savage* v *Savage*, [1979] CA Transcript 537. The effect is that if it becomes necessary to prove service, oral evidence is admissible in the event of an affidavit of service not being available to the court.
6 The affidavit of the applicant should contain the information set out in Appendix 4, below.
7 *Practice Direction* [1974] 2 All ER 1119, [1974] 1 WLR 936. See the Notice in the Daily Cause List reproduced as Appendix 2, below.
8 RSC Ord 45, r 7(4); *Supreme Court Practice* 45/7/5 and see Appendix 4, below.
9 RSC Ord 45, r 7(2).
10 See ch 12, below for enforcement of injunctions by commital.

endorsed with the penal notice should swear an affidavit of service immediately after the event of service which deposes to the circumstances in which service was effected on the respondent personally and which exhibits the documents that were served. The affidavit thus sworn should be retained by solicitors acting for the applicant for use in the event of an application to commit the respondent for breach of the order.

6 Applications to the High Court under the Matrimonial Homes Act 1983

The application is made by originating summons,[11] issued out of the divorce registry[12] or a district registry.[13] Unless otherwise directed,[14] at the time of issue, the applicant's affidavit[15] must be filed[16] together with a copy of the originating summons and affidavit for service on the respondent.[17]

The originating summons and supporting affidavit should be served personally on the respondent,[18] together with a form of acknowledgement of service.[19] The respondent should acknowledge service as directed. If the respondent intends to contest the application, he must, within 14 days after the time limited for giving notice of intention to defend,[20] file an affidavit in answer[1] setting out the grounds on which he relies.[2] If he does not do so the registrar may order him to do so[3] and, in default, debar him from defending.[4]

As the timetable prescribed does not provide for an early hearing of the application it is more appropriate to proceed in the county court.[5] Where proceedings are brought in the High Court an application may be made to the registrar, on issue of the originating summons, to reduce the time limits and to expedite the hearing.[6]

Where the application is for an ouster injunction it will be heard by a judge.[7] However, where it is sought to terminate the respondent's rights of occupation[8] and it appears to the registrar, on an ex parte application, that the respondent is not in occupation and that his whereabouts cannot, after

11 Matrimonial Causes Rules 1977 (SI 1977 344, r 104(1) as applied by r 107(1); see also Form 23 Appendix 1 to the Matrimonial Causes Rules 1977. For a precedent see Appendix 4.
12 This means the Principal Registry of the Family Division, Matrimonial Causes Rules 1977, r 2(2). Ibid, r 104(1) as applied by r 107(1).
13 This means any district registry having a divorce county court within its district, Matrimonial Causes Rules 1977 r 2(2). See 16 *Court Forms* 95 DIVORCE for a complete list of district registries. Matrimonial Causes Rules 1977, r 104(1) as applied by r 107(1).
14 Ibid r 104(1) as applied by r 107(1).
15 For a precedent see Appendix 4.
16 Matrimonial Causes Rules 1977, r 104(1) as applied by r 107(1).
17 Ibid. This is to prove service in case the respondent does not attend the hearing.
18 This is to prove service in case the respondent does not attend the hearing. An affidavit of service should be sworn and filed.
19 Matrimonial Causes Rules 1977, r 104(4) as applied by r 107(1).
20 Eight days, including the day of service. Ibid, rr 15(1),(2).
 1 Ibid, r 104(7) as applied by r 107(1).
 2 Ibid.
 3 Ibid, r 104(8) as applied by r 107(1).
 4 Ibid.
 5 See section B 3 above
 6 Matrimonial Causes Rules 1977, r 77(6) as applied by r 104(11) and as applied by r 107(1).
 7 Ibid, r 107(3).
 8 See Matrimonial Homes Act 1983, s 1(2)(a). (27 *Halsbury's Statutes* (4th edn) 585 MATRIMONIAL LAW).

reasonable inquiries, be ascertained, the registrar may dispense with service, and hear and determine the application.[9]

The application will be heard in chambers unless otherwise directed.[10]

If the judge grants the injunction then the same, duly endorsed with a penal notice,[11] should be served personally[12] on the respondent so that the same may be enforced by committal[13] if breached. It is good practice for an affidavit of service[14] to be made by the person serving the order and filed with the court so that it is ready in the event of an application to commit.

Where a cause[15] is pending between the parties in the High Court an application for relief under the Matrimonial Homes Act 1983 may be made by interlocutory summons[16] in those proceedings.[17]

7 Applications to the High Court in wardship proceedings

Wardship proceedings are commenced by originating summons[18] issued out of the Principal Registry or a district registry of the High Court.[19] Immediately on issue of the originating summons the minor becomes a ward.[20] An application for an injunction is made by summons[1] and may be made whether or not a claim for an injunction was included in the originating summons.[2]

The summons should be supported by an affidavit, both of which should be served personally,[3] not less than two clear days before the hearing.[4] The respondent to the application should file evidence in answer[5] as appropriate.

The application is made to a judge[6] and will be heard in chambers.[7] If the

---

9 Matrimonial Causes Rules 1977, r 107(4).
10 Ibid, r 107(1).
11 RSC Ord 49, r 7(4) and see Appendix 4.
12 RSC Ord 45, r 7(2).
13 See ch 12.
14 For a precedent see Appendix 4.
15 Ie a matrimonial cause (Matrimonial Causes Rules 1977, r 2(2)), begun by petition r 8(1) as defined by Matrimonial and Family Proceedings Act 1984, s 32 (27 *Halsbury's Statutes* (4th edn) 853 MATRIMONIAL LAW).
16 Under Matrimonial Causes Rules 1977, r 122(1)(b).
17 Ibid, r 107(2).
18 For a precedent see Appendix 4.
19 RSC Ord 90, r 3(1).
20 Supreme Court Act 1981, s 41. 756 11 *Halsbury's Statutes* (4th edn) (COURTS). The minor will cease to be a ward if no appointment for directions is taken out within 21 days of the issue of the originating summons (RSC Ord 90 r 4(1)) unless otherwise ordered.
1 RSC Ord 29, r 1(2).
2 RSC Ord 29, r 1(1). See also *Re N (infants)* [1967] Ch 512, [1967] 1 All ER 161.
3 Personal service is desirable in case the respondent does not attend the hearing. Where the respondent has solicitors on the record as acting for him service on them is good service, RSC Ord 65, r 5. Although the parties to an originating summons are described as *Plaintiff* and *Defendant* RSC Ord 7 r 2(2) the term *respondent* is used to indicate the respondent to the summons for the injunction who might be either plaintiff or defendant.
4 RSC Ord 32 r 3.
5 See *Practice Direction (Family Division: Filing Affidavits)* [1984] 1 All ER 684, [1984] 1 WLR 306.
6 RSC Ord 32, 11(1)(d), save that a registrar may grant an injunction by consent RSC Ord 32, r 11(2).
7 The court sits in chambers as a matter of practice; when wardship was assigned to the Chancery Division the practice was to hear matters in camera. The wardship jurisdiction is confidential. See Administration of Justice Act 1960, s 12, (11 *Halsbury's Statutes* (4th edn) 174 CONTEMPT OF COURT).

judge grants the injunction the same, duly endorsed with a penal notice[8] should be served personally[9] on the respondent so that the same may be enforced by committal[10] if breached. It is good practice for an affidavit of service[11] to be made by the person serving the order. The affidavit should then be filed with the court so that it is ready in the event of an application to commit.

8 Urgent applications procedure at the Royal Courts of Justice

A matrimonial cause pending in the divorce registry is treated as pending in a divorce county court, and not in the High Court,[12] and a particular procedure applies for making urgent applications for injunctions.[13] Under this procedure, the applicant selects any day at noon on which the court is sitting as the date and time on which the application is to be made; provided that two days notice can be given to the respondent. The applicant must serve a notice of application of such hearing on the respondent, giving him two days notice. The applicant must send at the same time, a copy of such notice to the Clerk of the Rules, giving the title and number of the proceedings. The matter is then listed in the Cause List for hearing on the day so selected by the applicant.[14]

This procedure does not apply to matrimonial causes pending in the High Court.[15] In such cases it is recommended that the applicant issues a summons specially fixed; the Clerk of the Rules will, on request fix the hearing for the earliest date available.[16]

9 Adjournments

As has already been seen[17] most applications, inter partes, for injunctions require only at least two clear days' notice. It frequently happens that a respondent is unable to instruct a solicitor to represent him at the hearing, that his solicitor is unable to obtain a grant of an emergency legal aid certificate, or that his solicitor is unable to draft a full affidavit in answer to the application. All these matters may give rise to an application to adjourn the hearing of the application.

The court has power to adjourn the hearing of the application either to a fixed date[18] or generally.[19] An adjournment may be granted on terms.[20]

---

8 RSC Ord 45, r 7(4) and see Appendix 4.
9 RSC Ord 45, r 7(2). For the importance of serving third parties affected by an injunction, see *Re L (a minor)* (1987) Times, 4 July.
10 See ch 12.
11 For a precedent see Appendix 4.
12 For the circumstances see Matrimonial Causes Rules 1977, r 4 See also Matrimonial and Family Proceedings Act 1984, s 42 (27 *Halsbury's Statutes* (4th edn) 853 MATRIMONIAL LAW).
13 *Practice Direction* 10 July 1972, [1972] 2 All ER 1360, [1972] 1 WLR 1047 and see Appendix 2, below. Further see the Notice in the Daily Cause List reproduced as Appendix 2, below.
14 For full details see the text of the *Practice Direction* reproduced at Appendix 2, below.
15 *Practice Direction* 10 July 1972, above.
16 *Practice Direction* 10 July 1972, above.
17 See above section B passim.
18 RSC Ord 32, r 4; CCR Ord 13, r 3.
19 Ibid. Such a course would probably only be taken where the parties wished to attempt to effect a reconciliation.
20 Such as by the grant of a non-molestation injunction or a re-entry injunction pending the full hearing. In many cases a respondent will offer undertakings in order to persuade the applicant to agree to an adjournment.

The power to grant an adjournment is a matter for the discretion of the judge.[1] As such the Court of Appeal will not interfere with the exercise on the judge's discretion unless it can be shown that he has exercised his discretion on improper grounds.[2]

Where there is no degree of urgency and an adjournment is sought to adduce evidence crucial to the issues to be decided by the court then an adjournment should be granted.[3] However where both parties are before the court and each has sworn a full affidavit the court may well feel that it has sufficient information to decide the issues, particularly as both parties may be cross-examined on their affidavits.

---

1 *Pearson* v *Pearson* (1982) 3 FLR 137 CA. See also *Joyce* v *King (1987)* Times 13 July, CA.
2 The appellant must show that the judge has considered an irrelevant matter, failed to consider a relevant matter or that the effect of his order is plainly wrong. See further ch 14, Appeals to the Court of Appeal.
3 *Pearson* v *Pearson* above.

Chapter 3
Restraint of molestation

1 Jurisdiction

The Domestic Violence and Matrimonial Proceedings Act 1976 gives the court power to grant an injunction restraining one party to a marriage (as therein defined) from molesting the other[1] and restraining one party from molesting a child living with the other.[2] In a matrimonial cause, the court has power to grant injunctions restraining molestation between spouses and to restrain either spouse from molesting any child of the family.[3] There is power in wardship[4] and guardianship[5] to restrain molestation of the minor or molestation of any person having care and control of the minor.[6] A husband has no right to discipline his wife by 'reasonable chastisement' or to confine her to enforce his rights to consortium.[7]

2 Meaning of molestation

The meaning of molestation was considered in *Vaughan* v *Vaughan*[8] where it was held that molestation has a very wide meaning. In the absence of any authority[9] the court considered definitions of molestation in the Concise Oxford Dictionary[10] and approved the definition in the Shorter Oxford Dictionary[11] which is in the following terms: 'To cause trouble; to vex; to annoy; to put to inconvenience'.

It is very difficult to lay down any conclusive definition of molestation but it should be recognised that it is very wide. It includes acts and threats of violence[12] and 'a multitude of other things'.[13] It could include attempted

---

1 S 1(1)(a).
2 S 1(1)(b).
3 Child of the family is defined by Matrimonial Causes Act 1973, s 52(1); see Appendix 1, below.
4 *Re V (a minor) (wardship)* (1979) 123 Sol Jo 201, Baker P.
5 *Re W (a minor)* [1981] 3 All ER 401, CA. See also *Ainsbury* v *Millington* [1986] 1 All ER 73 [1986] 1 FLR 331, CA.
6 For power to protect a person having care and control of a minor see *X County Council* v *A* [1985] 1 All ER 53, sub nom *Re X (a minor) (Wardship. Injunction)* [1984] 1 WLR 1422.
7 *R* v *Jackson* [1891] 1 QB 671, CA.
8 [1973] 3 All ER 449, [1973] 1 WLR 1159, CA.
9 Apart from one indirect authority *Phillips* v *Phillips* (1905) Times, 19 December.
10 5th edn, 'meddle hostilely or injuriously with (person)'.
11 3rd edn.
12 *Davis* v *Johnson* [1979] AC 264 at 341A, [1978] 1 All ER 1132 at 1150 d *per Lord Salmon*.
13 Ibid. See also *Horner* v *Horner* [1982] Fam 90, [1982] 2 All ER 495, CA, Harassment by sending threatening messages by post and making frequent pestering phone calls in molestation. Such *might* be criminal, see Post Office Act 1953, s 11 and Post Office Act 1969, s 78.

intercourse without consent of the other party[14] and would also include vexatious communication by one spouse towards another.

3 Principles on which the court acts

The court will not grant an injunction restraining molestation unless it is proved that the respondent has in the past committed acts of molestation.[15] The purpose of such injunctions is to protect the other spouse and children and to ensure that no undue pressure is put upon them while proceedings are pending and during the breakup of the marriage.[16]

It is unclear as to whether or not the court must, in addition to past acts of molestation, find that the respondent is likely to commit acts of molestation in the future. The seriousness or otherwise of past acts will assist the court in deciding whether or not future acts are likely to be committed. It is submitted that an applicant is entitled not to be molested and that it is unnecessary for the court to find that acts of molestation are likely to be committed in the future. This is particularly so where the application is for an order restraining molestation of a child where an important consideration is that of the child's welfare and as such, the court is concerned with the protection of the child. As the only remedy for breach of a non-molestation injunction is an order for committal, an application for an injunction should not be made lightly.[17]

4 Undertakings

The overwhelming majority of applications for injunctions restraining molestations are disposed of by one party giving an undertaking to the court not to molest the applicant or child[18] or by each party giving a cross-undertaking not to molest the other or the child as the case may be. An undertaking is a promise to the court which can be enforced in exactly the

---

14 *Paton* v *British Pregnancy Advisory Service Trustees* [1979] QB 276 at 280 E–F, [1978] 2 All ER 987 at 990h per Baker P. In order for sexual intercourse between husband and wife, without the consent of the wife, to constitute the crime of rape, the consent of the wife, by marriage, must be revoked. Filing a petition to commence a matrimonial cause does not, of itself, revoke such consent: *R* v *Miller* [1954] 2 QB 282. [1954] 2 All ER 529, Lynskey J. An order of a magistrates' court that a wife be no longer bound to cohabit with her husband does revoke such consent: *R* v *Clarke* [1949] 2 All ER 448. So, it is submitted would a decree of judicial separation. The pronouncement of a decree nisi revokes consent as the same effectively terminates the marriage: *R* v *O'Brien* [1974] 3 All ER 663, Park J. Where a husband and wife are living apart and there is an undertaking given by the husband to a court not to molest the wife then the matrimonial consent to intercourse is eliminated. *R* v *Steele* (1976) 65 Cr App Rep 22, CA. A non-molestation injunction would have similar effect but the effect of a personal protection order under the Domestic Proceedings and Magistrates' Courts Act 1978, s 16(2)(a) is unclear, although it is submitted that it would have the same effect as a non-molestation injunction.
15 *Spindlow* v *Spindlow* [1979] Fam 52, [1979] 1 All ER 169 CA.
16 *Paton* v *British Pregnancy Advisory Service Trustees* above at 280 C and at 990 e–f, per Baker P.
17 *Freedman* v *Freedman* [1967] 2 All ER 680n, [1967] 1 WLR 1102.
18 The usual wording of such an undertaking is '. . . not to assault, molest, or otherwise interfere with (the applicant or child or both, as the case may be)'. It is within the authors' experience that some judges have refused to add the words 'or otherwise interfere' on the basis that it adds nothing to the words 'assault or molest'.

same way as injunction, namely by committal.[19] The court must be satisfied that the undertaker is making a genuine promise.[20]

In general, an undertaking should be given if asked for as it does not involve the party giving the undertaking making any admission whatsoever that he or she has in the past assaulted or molested the applicant. Furthermore, it does not infringe the rights of the person giving the undertaking. If he or she intends in the future to assault or molest the applicant or the child, then he or she ought to be restrained; conversely, if he or she does not intend in the future to assault or molest the applicant or child then there is no harm in promising to the court not to do so. It is to be emphasised that a power of arrest cannot be attached to an undertaking.[1] It follows that where the applicant considers that it is necessary for a power of arrest to be attached to any order made it will be necessary for the respondent to submit to the injunction.

Disposing of such matters by way of undertakings has the advantage of saving costs and time, of easing the court lists and of avoiding bitter battles in court. Where an application for a non-molestation injunction is only part of the relief sought, as for example where the real issue is that of ousting a spouse from the matrimonial home, disposing of part of the application by way of undertakings has the additional advantage of clarifying the real issues before the court.

A party who has given an undertaking to the court may apply, on notice, for the same to be discharged or for the terms thereof to be varied, on good grounds, provided that there has not been a disposal of the application which gave rise to the giving of the undertaking.[2] An application is not disposed of where unertakings are given until further order, or where the application is adjourned generally. However, where the application which gave rise to the giving of the undertaking has been stood over, adjourned to a fixed date, or otherwise disposed of, the court will not, pending the adjourned hearing (if any), entertain an application for discharge from or to vary the terms of the undertaking.[3]

19 *Hipgrave* v *Hipgrave* [1962] P 91, [1962] 1 All ER 75 and see ch 12.
20 The court may well be reluctant to accept an undertaking not to drink from a person who is alleged to have serious drink problem: see *Ancliffe* v *Ancliffe* [1980] CA Transcript 520 (12 June), per Brandon LJ.
 1 *Carpenter* v *Carpenter* [1987] CA Transcript G25, CA.
 2 *Butt* v *Butt* (1987) Times, 27 June, CA.
 3 Ibid, and see *Chanel Ltd* v *FW Woolworth & Co Ltd* [1981] 1 All ER 745, [1981] 1 WLR 485, CA.

Chapter 4
Exclusion injunctions

1 General

Prior to the decision in *Richards* v *Richards*[1] it was thought that the power of the court to exclude a spouse from the matrimonial home was derived from the general jurisdiction of the court to grant injunctions.[2] An exclusion injunction was always regarded as a drastic remedy[3] and would not be granted where there was merely unpleasantness, tension and inconvenience[4] in the matrimonial home. The test was that a spouse should only be excluded where it was fair, just and reasonable that he or she should be so excluded.[5]

In several cases the court regarded the welfare of children of the family as the first and paramount consideration.[6] Furthermore where it was clear that the marriage had broken down irretrievably the problem was often one of 'who was to go' and the solution to that was to be found in the children[7] and on the balance of hardship.[8]

A conflict of authority, in decisions of the Court of Appeal, developed as to the test to be applied on an application for an exclusion injunction. In *Myers* v *Myers*[9] an injunction was refused as the applicant's unwillingness to return to the matrimonial home, while her husband remained, was unreasonable, although actuated by genuine fear. In *Samson* v *Samson*[10] it was held that the court should consider first the welfare of any children and then have regard to the interests of the parties. It was further held that a court should not consider whether the applicant was justified in leaving the matrimonial home (if that had happened) as such a consideration would often be based on inadequate material.

1 [1984] AC 174, [1983] 2 All ER 807, HL.
2 Supreme Court Act 1981, s 37 (11 *Halsbury's Statutes* (4th edn) 756 COURTS; County Courts Act 1984, s 38 (11 *Halsbury's Statutes* (4th edn) 411 COUNTY COURTS).
3 *Bassett* v *Bassett* [1975] Fam 76, [1975] 1 All ER 513, CA.
4 *Hall* v *Hall* [1971] 1 All ER 762, [1971] 1 WLR 404, CA.
5 *Walker* v *Walker* [1978] 3 All ER 141, [1978] 1 WLR 533, CA. Before such a conclusion could be reached all the circumstances of the case had to be examined including: (i) the behaviour of the applicant and the respondent, (ii) the effect on any children if the respondent stays or goes, (iii) the respondent's personal circumstances, and (iv) the likelihood of injury to the applicant, the respondent, their health either physical or mental; per Geoffrey Lane LJ.
6 *Renick* v *Renick* [1978] 1 All ER 817, [1977] 1 WLR 1455, CA; *Spindlow* v *Spindlow* [1979] Fam 52, [1979] 1 All ER 169, CA.
7 *Bassett* v *Bassett* , above.
8 Ibid.
9 [1982] 1 All ER 776, [1982] 1 WLR 247, CA; applying *Elsworth* v *Elsworth* (1978) 1 FLR 245, CA.
10 [1982] 1 All ER 780, [1982] 1 WLR 252, CA; following *Bassett* v *Bassett* above and *Walker* v *Walker* above.

This conflict has now been resolved, so far as spouses are concerned, by *Richards* v *Richards*[11] where it was held that during the subsistence of the marriage, applications for exclusion injunctions are to be brought under the provisions of the Matrimonial Homes Act 1983.[12]

2 Rights of occupation

Where a matrimonial home is owned by two spouses by virtue of the legal estate being vested in them jointly,[13] by virtue of a contract,[14] or by statute,[15] they are each entitled to occupy the property.[16]

A spouse, in whose sole name, the title to the matrimonial home is vested is entitled to occupy the same by virtue of his or her proprietary right.

Statutory rights of occupation are given to a spouse who has no proprietary rights in the matrimonial home.[17] Where:

(1) one spouse is entitled to occupy a dwelling house by virtue of any estate or interest or contract or by virtue of any enactment giving him or her the right to remain in occupation;[18] and

(2) the other spouse has no legal or equitable title to occupy the matrimonial home;[19] and

(3) the dwelling house is or has been the matrimonial home[20] of the parties; and

(4) the marriage subsists;[1]

the spouse without rights has statutory rights of occupation. These are: if in occupation, a right not to be evicted or excluded from the dwelling house or any part thereof except with the leave of the court[2] or, if not in occupation, a right with the leave of the court to enter and occupy the dwelling house.[3] Where one spouse has either of those rights, either spouse may apply to the court for an order declaring, enforcing, restricting or terminating those rights or prohibiting, suspending or restricting the exercise of the right to occupy the dwelling house by the other spouse; or requiring either spouse to permit the exercise by the other of that right.[4]

Where each spouse is entitled[5] to occupy such a dwelling house, either may apply, during the subsistence of the marriage, for an order prohibit-

11 [1984] AC 174, [1983] 2 All ER 807, HL
12 27 *Halsbury's Statutes* (4th edn) 585 MATRIMONIAL LAW.
13 It is immaterial whether they are, in equity, joint tenants or tenants in common.
14 Eg a contractual tenancy, whether protected or not.
15 Eg a statutory tenancy under the Rent Act 1977.
16 This is recognised by the Matrimonial Homes Act 1983 (27 *Halsbury's Statutes* (4th edn) 585 MATRIMONIAL LAW 59). See also *Gurasz* v *Gurasz* [1970] P 11 at 17, [1969] 3 All ER 822 at 824, CA.
17 Matrimonial Homes Act 1983, s 1. 'Dwelling house' includes any building or part thereof which is occupied as a dwelling, and any yard, garden or outhouse belonging to the dwelling house and occupied therewith: ibid, s 10(1). See *Kinzler* v *Kinzler* [1985] Fam Law 26, CA, where on the facts the whole of a hotel constituted the matrimonial home.
18 Matrimonial Homes Act 1983, s 1.
19 That spouse will have a common law right enforceable against the other; *Gurasz* v *Gurasz*, above. See also *Chaudhry* v *Chaudhry* [1987] 1 FLR 347, CA.
20 Matrimonial Homes Act 1983, s 1(10). See *S* v *S* (1980) 10 Fam Law 153, 124 Sol Jo 219 for the difficulties which may arise where the dwelling house has not been the matrimonial home. See section 8 below.
 1 Matrimonial Homes Act 1983, s 1(10).
 2 Ibid, s 1(1)(a).
 3 Ibid, s 1(1)(b).
 4 Ibid, s 1(2).
 5 By virtue of a proprietary, contractual or statutory right, see text and notes 13–15 above.

ing, suspending or restricting the exercise of the other's right to occupy,[6] or requiring the other to permit the applicant to exercise his or her rights.[7]

3 Matrimonial Homes Act 1983

The power of the High Court and county courts to grant injunctions requiring a party to a marriage, during the subsistence of the marriage, to vacate the matrimonial home or to restrain a spouse from returning to the matrimonial home, is derived from the Matrimonial Homes Act 1983[8] and the inherent jurisdiction[9] has been absorbed by statute.[10] An application for an exclusion injunction[11] should be drafted by reference to rights of occupation[12] rather than in terms of exclusion or ouster.

On an application for an exclusion injunction the court may make such order as it thinks just and reasonable,[13] having regard to:

(i)   the conduct of the spouses in relation to each other and otherwise;
(ii)   their respective needs and financial resources;
(iii) the needs of any children; and
(iv)   the circumstances of the case.[14]

The statute does not provide that any one factor is to be given any more weight than another;[15] the weight to be given to each factor is a matter for the judge depending on the facts of each individual case.[16] Decisions of appellate courts on exclusion injunctions given prior to *Richards* v *Richards*[17] should be regarded with extreme caution as such do not have regard to the criteria laid down by the Matrimonial Homes Act 1983,[18] although they have not necessarily erred on their own facts.[19]

An exclusion injunction is a drastic remedy[20] and should only be made where a judge is satisfied that no lesser measure will protect the applicant and any children sufficiently.[1] A lesser measure of protection would include an order whereby the parties would live separately under the same

---

6 Matrimonial Homes Act 1983, s 9(1),(3).
7 Ibid.
8 27 *Halsbury's Statutes* (4th edn) 585 MATRIMONIAL LAW, formerly the Matrimonial Homes Act 1967.
9 Supreme Court Act 1981, s 37 (11 *Halsbury's Statutes* (4th edn) 756 COURTS). County Courts Act 1984, s 38 (11 *Halsbury's Statutes* (4th edn) 411 COUNTY COURTS).
10 *Richards* v *Richards* [1984] AC 174, [1983] 2 All ER 807, HL.
11 Commonly called an ouster injunction.
12 See ch 2, Procedure, and Appendix 4, Precedents and Forms.
13 Matrimonial Homes Act 1983, s 1(3).
14 Ibid. The importance of applying the statutory criteria was emphasised in *Summers* v *Summers* [1986] 1 FLR 343, [1986] Fam Law 56, CA.
15 *Richards* v *Richards* [1984] AC 174 at 222, [1983] 2 All ER 807 at 830, HL, per Lord Brandon. The Guardianship of Minors Act 1971, s 1 (6 *Halsbury's Statutes* (4th edn) 305 CHILDREN) which provides, inter alia, that where the legal custody or upbringing of a minor is in question, the court, in deciding that question, must regard the welfare of the minor as the first and paramount consideration, does not apply on an application for an exclusion injunction; *Richards* v *Richards* above. On the facts of a particular case it may be that the welfare and needs of minor children should be given great weight; see *Lee* v *Lee* [1984] FLR 243, [1984] Fam Law 243 CA.
16 *Lee* v *Lee* above.
17 [1984] AC 174, [1983] 2 All ER 807, HL.
18 27 *Halsbury's Statutes* (4th edn) 585 MATRIMONIAL LAW.
19 *Richards* v *Richards* above, per Lord Hailsham LC.
20 *Burke* v *Burke* [1987] 2 FLR 71, CA; see also *Summers* v *Summers* (1987) Times, 19 May, CA: indeed it has always been regarded as drastic: see *Bassett* v *Bassett* [1975] Fam 76, [1975] 1 All ER 513, CA.
1 *Reid* v *Reid* (1984) Times, 30 July, CA. See also *Burke* v *Burke* above, exclusion should only be ordered in a case of real emergency.

roof,[2] although a realistic view must be taken of the possibility and practicality of parties living separately in the same home.[3] Involuntary violence[4] is not a ground for refusing an injunction,[5] the actual violence and the consequences to the applicant (and any children) are the important factors.[6] The fact that an applicant has been refused a personal protection order[7] in the magistrates' court does not fetter the judge's discretion on an application for an exclusion injunction.[8]

Often an application to exclude a party will be heard at the same time as an application for interim care and control.[9] It may be that a contested application for care and control should be adjudicated upon before the court considers an application to exclude one of the parties,[10] even if such means that the matter must be adjourned for a welfare report,[11] although where an interim order is made it may be appropriate to exclude the non-custodial parent pending the preparation of a court welfare report, if such is in the interests of the children.[12] Where applications for care and control, and exclusion, are listed for determination at the same hearing, the judge should decide the issue of care and control before dealing with the question of exclusion.[13]

It is inappropriate to decide the application on a partial view of the evidence[14] or to make an exclusion order where the evidence is limited to a single uncorroborated incident.[15] A spouse should not be excluded merely because the marriage has broken down and the matrimonial home has become a place of tension.[16] An exclusion order should not be made so as to 'allow the dust to settle' and thereby possibly lead to a reconciliation between the parties.[17] In considering the application the court should have

2 In an appropriate case coupled with a non-molestation injunction and, subject to the statutory criteria, a power of arrest (see ch 6).
3 *Anderson* v *Anderson* [1984] FLR 566, [1984] Fam Law 183 CA.
4 Eg caused by epilepsy.
5 *Wooton* v *Wooton* [1984] FLR 871, [1985] Fam Law 31, CA.
6 Ibid. Threats of violence are also important *Baggott* v *Baggott* [1986] 1 FLR 377, [1986] Fam Law 129, CA.
7 Under the Domestic Proceedings and Magistrates' Courts Act 1978 (27 *Halsbury's Statutes* (4th edn) 791 MATRIMONIAL LAW) See also ch 13 below.
8 *O'Brien* v *O'Brien* [1985] FLR 801, [1985] Fam Law 191, CA.
9 In interim proceedings relating to children it is preferable to make an order for interim care and control rather than for interim custody. Orders for interim custody often lead to psychological complications in that one parent may feel he has won, whereas the other parent may feel at a disadvantage at the substantive hearing. *Re B (a minor)* (1983) 4 FLR 683, 13 Fam Law 176, CA.
10 *Smith* v *Smith* (1979) 10 Fam Law 50, CA; *Wood* v *Wood* (1978) 9 Fam Law 254, [1978] CA Transcript 766, CA; *Mitchell* v *Mitchell* [1979] CA Transcript 221, CA.
11 A judge may order that the welfare report be expedited, but there must be special factors to justify expedition. Every case involving children is urgent and it must be remembered that the welfare officers are very busy. However an eight-month delay in the preparation of a welfare report is unacceptable *Elder* v *Elder* [1986] 1 FLR 610, [1986] Fam Law 190 CA. In most cases it should be possible to decide the question of exclusion without the assistance of a welfare report *Osborne* v *Osborne* [1982] CA Transcript 420, CA.
12 *D* v *D (Injunction: Exclusion Order)* (1983) 4 FLR 82, 12 Fam Law 150, CA.
13 *Re T (a minor: wardship); T* v *T (Ouster Order)* [1987] 1 FLR 181, [1986] Fam Law 298, CA.
14 *Reid* v *Reid* (1984) Times, 30 July, CA, and see ch 2 section B 9 as to adjournments.
15 *Reid* v *Reid* above.
16 *Burke* v *Burke* [1987] 2 FLR 71, CA, where it was said that an ouster injunction was not simply a routine stepping stone on the way to a divorce emphasised in *Summers* v *Summers* (1987) Times, 19 May, CA.
17 *Summers* v *Summers* [1986] 1 FLR 343, [1986] Fam Law 56, CA.

regard to the reasonableness or unreasonableness of the applicant's conduct.[18]

In considering the needs of the parties it is relevant to take into account the duty of the local authority to rehouse under Part III of the Housing Act 1985.[19] It is also relevant to take into account alternative accommodation available to the parties.[20]

Where, in the exercise of the court's discretion, it is decided to grant an exclusion injunction the same should take effect as soon as possible[1] unless there are very compelling reasons to the contrary.[2]

In making an exclusion order the court may except from a spouse's right of occupation a part of the dwelling house[3] and in particular, a part of the same used for or in connection with a trade, business or profession of the other spouse.[4]

Rights of occupation end on the death of a spouse,[5] or other termination of the marriage[6] unless, in the event of a matrimonial dispute or estrangement,[7] the court sees fit to direct otherwise[8] by order, during the subsistence of the marriage.[9]

Where an exclusion injunction is made it may be limited[10] or be expressed as being 'until further order'.[11] The court should, in every case, consider the imposition of a time limit on the operation of the injunction.[12] Where there are no matrimonial proceedings an order without limitation may have the consequence of being, in effect, a summary transfer of property order.[13]

---

18 *Harris* v *Harris* [1986] 1 FLR 12, [1986] Fam Law 16 CA. In some cases the court will not be able to decide the reasonableness of the applicant without cross-examination by the respondent.
19 21 *Halsbury's Statutes* (4th edn) 29 HOUSING. *Thurley* v *Smith* [1984] FLR 875, [1985] Fam Law 31, CA. However see *Warwick* v *Warwick* (1981) 3 FLR 393, CA, where it was held that it was manifestly wrong to make an exclusion order where the court had the express knowledge that the applicant would not, in the event of the exclusion injunction sought being granted, return to live in the matrimonial home, but wished to apply for re-housing by way of an exchange.
20 *Baggott* v *Baggott* [1986] 1 FLR 377, [1986] Fam Law 129, CA.
1 *Burke* v *Burke* [1987] 2 FLR 71, CA. It should normally take effect within a week or two and not be left hanging over a man's head 'to bring him to his senses'. There is no such creature as an 'ouster nisi', per Lloyd LJ. 'In *Burke* v *Burke* above the Court of Appeal substituted a two-week period for an eight week one. See also *Chadda* v *Chadda* (1980) 11 Fam Law 142, CA.
2 *Burke* v *Burke*, above.
3 Matrimonial Homes Act 1983, s 1(3)(a) (27 *Halsbury's Statutes* (4th edn) 585 MATRIMONIAL LAW.
4 Ibid.
5 Ibid, s 2(4)(a).
6 Ibid, s 2(4)(b).
7 The phrase 'matrimonial dispute or estrangement' is not defined but would include an application under the principles of the Matrimonial Homes Act 1983.
8 Matrimonial Homes Act 1983 ss 1, 2(4).
9 Ibid, s 2(4).
10 Ibid, s 1(4).
11 Ibid.
12 *Practice Note* [1978] 2 All ER 1056, sub nom *Practice Direction* [1978] 1 WLR 1123, see Appendix 2 below. Where an order suspends right of occupation a time limit is bound to be imposed. An order terminating rights of occupation is final and a time limit cannot be included. Where the order is prohibitive or restrictive in terms of exercise of rights of occupation a time limit should be considered. An order made as interlocutory relief in a matrimonial cause is often made until the hearing of the application for ancillary relief.
13 *Hopper* v *Hopper* [1979] 1 All ER 181, [1978] 1 WLR 1342n, CA.

4 Domestic Violence and Matrimonial Proceedings Act 1976

The procedure under the Domestic Violence and Matrimonial Proceedings Act 1976[14] is essentially designed to deal with emergencies.[15] The statute is purely procedural[16] and does not affect proprietary rights[17] although a person may be excluded notwithstanding that he or she has a proprietary interest in the home;[18] however, an injunction cannot be used permanently to deprive a property owner of his dwelling.[19]

On an application for an exclusion injunction under the Domestic Violence and Matrimonial Proceedings Act 1976, section 1(1)(c),[20] the court must make such order as is just and reasonable[1] having regard to the criteria set out in the Matrimonial Homes Act 1983,[2] the principles of which apply to applications between unmarried couples,[3] equally as to spouses.[4]

Where an exclusion order is made consideration should be given to imposing a time limit on the operation of the injunction.[5] If no time limit is given then the order may have the effect of being a summary transfer of property order.[6] Between married couples a limit on the injunction provides a period during which it will become clear whether or not the parties will reconcile, and if they do not it will allow time to commence matrimonial proceedings.

Between unmarried couples, where the property is in joint names and the parties are not going to reconcile, a time limit provides an opportunity for them to resolve the question of occupation of the home.[7] Where the property-owning party has been excluded there will be a 'cooling-off' period, during which the applicant can obtain permanent alternative accommodation. Where the non-property-owning party has been excluded it may be appropriate for the injunction to be expressed to last 'until further order'.[8]

---

14 27 *Halsbury's Statutes* (4th edn) 788 MATRIMONIAL LAW.
15 *Wooton* v *Wooton* [1984] FLR 871, [1985] Fam law 31, CA and see *Hopper* v *Hopper* [1979] 1 All ER 181 [1978] 1 WLR 1342n, CA.
16 *Davis* v *Johnson* [1979] AC 264, [1978] 1 All ER 1132, HL.
17 Ibid.
18 Ibid, overruling *B* v *B (Domestic Violence: Jurisdiction)* [1978] Fam 26, [1978] 1 All ER 821, CA, and *Cantliff* v *Jenkins* [1978] Fam 47, [1978] 1 All ER 836, CA.
19 *Davis* v *Johnson*, above.
20 27 *Halsbury's Statutes* (4th edn) 788 MATRIMONIAL LAW.
 1 Matrimonial Homes Act 1983, s 1(3) (27 *Halsbury's Statutes* (4th edn) 585 MATRIMONIAL LAW).
 2 Ibid, s 1(3). The statutory criteria are: (1) the conduct of the parties in relation to each other and otherwise; (2) their respective needs and financial resources; (3) the needs of any children; and (4) all the circumstances of the case.
 3 Persons who come within the meaning of the phrase 'living with each other in the same household as husband and wife': see Domestic Violence and Matrimonial Proceedings Act 1976, ss 1(2), 2(2).
 4 *Lee* v *Lee* [1984] FLR 243, [1984] Fam Law 243, CA.
 5 *Practice Note* [1978] 2 All ER 1056, [1978] 1 WLR 1123. See Appendix 2, below.
 6 *Hopper* v *Hopper* [1979] 1 All ER 181, [1978] 1 WLR 1352n, CA.
 7 Eg by commencing proceedings under Law of Property Act 1925, s 30. (37 *Halsbury's Statutes* (4th edn) REAL PROPERTY) or being rehoused by the local authority.
 8 *Spencer* v *Camacho* (1983) 4 FLR 662, 13 Fam Law 114, CA. See also *Hills* v *Bushby* [1977] CA Transcript 398B, CA, where it was held that the Domestic Violence and Matrimonial Proceedings Act 1976 gave the applicant a summary remedy in summary proceedings to enforce her legal rights as owner of her property against anyone going through the more complicated business of applying for a possession order. Per Ormrod LJ.

Where an injunction is limited in time the applicant may apply for an extension if he or she requires protection for a longer period. Likewise a respondent may apply for discharge of an order if the applicant no longer needs protection.

Where parties become reconciled the need for an injunction has gone, and the same should be discharged.[9]

5 Interlocutory relief in a matrimonial cause

Pending suit[10] an exclusion injunction may be made by way of interlocutory relief under the provisions of the Matrimonial Homes Act 1983.[11] There is no presumption that either spouse has the right to remain in the matrimonial home to the exclusion of the other.[12]

In almost every case there will, inevitably, be a degree of unpleasantness, inconvenience and tension consequent upon the break up of the relationship. In addition if there is to be a divorce[13] the parties must separate, sooner or later; however it is submitted that a court should not lose sight of the statutory criteria to be applied.[14] Where spouses are independent adults, without children, questions of occupation of the matrimonial home should be dealt with on an application for ancillary relief and not by way of injunction.[15] However where, pending suit, a spouse is in need of protection, the absence of children should not deter him or her from applying to exclude the other from the home.

After a decree absolute of divorce or nullity former spouses are unable to apply for relief under the Matrimonial Homes Act 1983[16] but may apply for an injunction under the inherent jurisdiction[17] in support of a legal right.[18]

The right of a spouse to apply for a transfer of property order[19] is not a proprietary right and therefore cannot be protected by a mandatory injunction requiring the other party to vacate the former matrimonial home.[20] The court has adequate powers to prevent the dissipation of assets

---

9 *Davis* v *Johnson* [1979] AC 264, [1978] 1 All ER 1132, HL. It is important that parties are advised that an injunction should be discharged on a reconciliation. A court may well refuse to enforce an injunction by committal after a reconciliation. Applicants whose feelings towards their partners are equivocal should be informed that the courts tend to discourage those who 'blow hot and cold'. The court's protection should not be sought lightly as orders are serious matters; see, by way of analogy, *Freedman* v *Freedman* [1967] 2 All ER 680n, [1967] 1 WLR 1102, Ormrod J.

10 Ie before decree absolute of divorce or nullity, or before a decree of judicial separation.

11 *Richards* v *Richards* [1984] AC 174, [1983] 2 All ER 807, HL; see section 3 above.

12 *Willmott* v *Willmott* [1921] P 143, 90 LJP 206.

13 Or a judicial separation or annulment.

14 Matrimonial Homes Act 1983, s 1(3) (27 *Halsbury's Statutes* (4th edn) 585 MATRIMONIAL LAW).

15 *Pearson* v *Pearson* (1981) 3 FLR 137, CA.

16 Matrimonial Homes Act 1983, s 2(4); unless in the event of a matrimonial dispute or estrangement the court sees fit to direct otherwise by order under ibid s 1 during the subsistence of the marriage. Spouses who are judicially separated may apply for relief under the Matrimonial Homes Act 1983.

17 Supreme Court Act 1981, s 37. (11 *Halsbury's Statutes* (4th edn) 756 COURTS.) County Courts Act 1984 s 38. (11 *Halsbury's Statutes* (4th edn) 411 COUNTY COURTS.) See also ch 1, section C, above.

18 *North London Rly Co* v *Great Northern Rly Co* (1883) 11 QBD 30, 52 LJQB 380, CA.

19 Under Matrimonial Causes Act, s 24(1)(a). (27 *Halsbury's Statutes* (4th edn) 700 MATRIMONIAL LAW).

20 *Brent* v *Brent* [1975] Fam 1, [1974] 2 All ER 1211, Dunn J obiter.

to frustrate the orders that a court might make for ancillary relief.[1] An application for an injunction, after decree absolute, as an attempt to set the scene for proceedings for ancillary relief is improper and an abuse of process.[2]

A former spouse, after decree absolute, who does not have a proprietary interest in the matrimonial home, has no more rights than an independent adult licensee and may not apply to exclude his or her former spouse under the inherent jurisdiction[3] unless it be in the interests of the children of the family.[4]

Where the title to the former matrimonial home is in the sole name of a former spouse it would seem that he or she would have a legal right to exclude the other. However an injunction to exclude a non-property-owning former spouse from the matrimonial home prior to the hearing of proceedings for ancillary relief might be regarded as molestation and refused in the exercise of the court's discretion. It should be noted that an injunction in matrimonial proceedings may not be used as a substitute for a possession action.[5]

6 Wardship and guardianship proceedings

There is no jurisdiction to make an ouster injunction in guardianship proceedings[6] where the title to the property is in the joint names of the parties.[7] If the applicant in the guardianship proceedings has a proprietary right in the property and the respondent does not, it may be that an exclusion injunction could be made, in the proceedings, ousting the respondent,[8] provided that the order was ancillary to an order for care and control.[9]

Exclusion injunctions have been made in wardship proceedings although the only reported decision[10] was made well before the decision in *Richards v Richards*[11] and the question of jurisdiction was not apparently investigated in any detail.

Where the circumstances of parties to wardship or guardianship proceedings are such that there is jurisdiction to make an application under the Matrimonial Homes Act 1983[12] or under the Domestic Violence and

---

1 Including under Matrimonial Causes Act 1973, s 37; and see ch 10 below.
2 *Waugh* v *Waugh* (1981) 3 FLR 375, CA. See also *Grace* v *Grace* [1980] CA Transcript 418, CA.
3 *O'Malley* v *O'Malley* [1982] 2 All ER 112, [1982] 1 WLR 244, CA.
4 *Quinn* v *Quinn* (1982) 4 FLR 394, CA; see also *Beard* v *Beard* [1981] 1 All ER 783, [1981] 1 WLR 369, CA.
5 *Delorey* v *Delorey* (1967) 111 Sol Jo 757 and *Jedfield* v *Jedfield* (1960) Times, 10 November.
6 Ie an application under the Guardianship of Minors Acts 1971 and 1973. (6 *Halsbury's Statutes* (4th edn) 305, 338 CHILDREN.)
7 *Ainsbury* v *Millington* [1986] 1 All ER 73, [1986] 1 FLR 331, CA, *Re W (a minor)* [1981] 3 All ER 401, 11 Fam Law 207, CA, distinguished. A further appeal in *Ainsbury* v *Millington* [1987] 1 All ER 929, [1987] 1 WLR 379, HL was dismissed without consideration of the merits.
8 *Re W (a minor)*, above.
9 As to the requirement that there must be a nexus between the substantive proceedings and an interlocutory injunction see ch 1, section A, above.
10 *Re V (a minor) (wardship)* (1979) 123 Sol Jo 201, Sir George Baker P.
11 [1984] AC 174, [1983] 2 All ER 807, HL.
12 27 *Halsbury's Statutes* (4th edn) 585 MATRIMONIAL LAW. See ch 1, section D, above.

Matrimonial Proceedings Act 1976[13] such proceedings may be heard at the same time as the wardship or guardianship application.

Where proceedings are heard together a judge may first deal with the question of care and control,[14] and then decide the issue of ouster taking into account his decision on care and control as one of the factors relevant to exclusion.[15] Such a process does not elevate the statutory criterion[16] of the needs of any children.[17] Indeed any other approach[18] would be illogical and might not result in any conclusion.[19]

7 Exclusion of third party

In a matrimonial cause[20] the court has power, to prevent molestation,[1] or for the protection of children, to exclude third parties from the matrimonial home.[2] Each of these cases was concerned with a wife applying to exclude her husband's mistress from the matrimonial home. In *Adams* v *Adams*[3] it was made clear that although an injunction would only be granted in support of a legal right or for the welfare of children,[4] and that the wife had no legal right against the husband's mistress[5] an injunction could be granted for the protection of children whose welfare was in jeopardy.

In *Jones* v *Jones*[6] the wife sought injunctions ordering the husband and his mistress (who was pregnant by the husband) to vacate the matrimonial home. The husband opposed the injunction on the ground that he was the sole tenant of the property. The court nevertheless held[7] that the husband and his mistress should vacate the home. In this case it should be noted that the children of the family consisted of a girl, aged eighteen, and a boy, aged seventeen. The decision appears to be based more on the conduct of the husband being so outrageous[8] as to make it impossible for the parties to live together than on the basis of the welfare of the children.

In *Hense* v *Hense and Churchill*[9] the court held that a wife should not be

---

13 27 *Halsbury's Statutes* (4th edn) 788 MATRIMONIAL LAW. See ch 1, sections B and G above.

14 Where the welfare of the child is the first and paramount consideration; Guardianship of Minors Act 1971, s 1 (6 *Halsbury's Statutes* (4th edn) 305 CHILDREN.) For the meaning of 'first and paramount' see *J* v *C* [1970] AC 668, [1969] 1 All ER 788, HL.

15 *Re T (a minor: wardship); T* v *T (Ouster Order)* [1987] 1 FLR 181, [1986] Fam Law 298, CA.

16 Matrimonial Homes Act 1983, s 1(3). (27 *Halsbury's Statutes* (4th edn) 585 MATRIMONIAL LAW).

17 *Re T; T* v *T*, above.

18 Such as deciding the question of ouster first.

19 *Re T; T* v *T*, above.

20 Ie an action for divorce, nullity or judicial separation; Matrimonial and Family Proceedings Act 1984, s 32 (27 *Halsbury's Statutes* (4th edn) 853 MATRIMONIAL LAW).

1 See ch 3 above.

2 *Adams* v *Adams* (1965) 109 Sol Jo 899, Baker J; *Jones* v *Jones* [1971] 2 All ER 737, [1971] 1 WLR 396, CA; *Pinckney* v *Pinckney* [1966] 1 All ER 121n, Ormrod J; *Hense* v *Hense and Churchill* [1976] CA Transcript 403, CA.

3 (1965) 109 Sol Jo 899, Baker J.

4 Following *Montgomery* v *Montgomery* [1965] P 46, [1964] 2 All ER 22, Ormrod J.

5 Except in an action for enticement, if the same could be proved. The cause of action of enticement was abolished by the Law Reform (Miscellaneous Provisions) Act 1970, s 5.

6 [1971] 2 All ER 737, [1971] 1 WLR 396 CA.

7 Following *Silverstone* v *Silverstone* [1953] P 174, [1953] 1 All ER 556 and *Gurasz* v *Gurasz* [1970] P 11 [1969] 3 All ER 822, CA.

8 And, therefore, it is submitted, molestation.

9 [1976] CA Transcript 403, CA.

expected to put up with the presence of the husband's mistress in the matrimonial home. Although the jurisdiction of the court does not appear to have been in dispute, the view was expressed[10] that the court might not have a discretion to refuse to grant an injunction in such circumstances.

Where a spouse is excluded from the matrimonial home[11] the court should not invite, or accept, any undertaking from the party remaining not to cohabit with another person therein;[12] if such an undertaking is offered it should not be accepted.[13] However, where an injunction to exclude the respondent has been refused, and there is tension in the matrimonial home, it is 'altogether reasonable' for a party to be asked to undertake not to invite his/her girlfriend/boyfriend to visit the matrimonial home.[14]

8 House other than the matrimonial home

The Matrimonial Homes Act 1983[15] does not apply to a dwelling house which has at no time been a matrimonial home of the spouses in question.[16] The Domestic Violence and Matrimonial Proceedings Act 1976[17] likewise only applies to a matrimonial home. In the case of an unmarried couple the term 'matrimonial home' would seem to mean the premises which contain the household in which they live with each other as husband and wife.[18]

An application to exclude a party from a property other than the matrimonial home must be based on a legal right that the applicant is entitled to occupy the same while the respondent is not. An injunction might be refused in the exercise of the court's discretion.[19]

In order for a spouse to be entitled to go to live in a property, other than the matrimonial home, owned by the other spouse, the applicant must prove an occupational licence.[20] Although a husband has a common law duty to provide a roof over his wife's head,[1] such duty may be limited to an existing matrimonial home.[2]

9 Financial consequences of exclusion

It is almost inevitable, pending suit, that where the parties to a marriage separate there is insufficient income to maintain two households. The spouse who leaves the matrimonial home needs to finance alternative accommodation; while the spouse who remains will be concerned to see that the outgoings on the matrimonial home are maintained. It is outside the scope of this work to consider, in detail, all the factors relevant on an application for ancillary relief.[3]

10 Per Sir John Pennycuick.
11 Or gives an undertaking to vacate.
12 *Holtom* v *Holtom* (1981) 11 Fam Law 249, CA.
13 Ibid.
14 *Miller* v *Miller* (1983) 4 FLR 115, CA per Sir John Arnold P at 117G–H.
15 27 *Halsbury's Statutes* (4th edn) 585 MATRIMONIAL LAW.
16 Ibid, s 1(10).
17 ss 1(1)(c), (d) and 2(1)(c) (27 *Halsbury's Statutes* (4th edn) 788 MATRIMONIAL LAW).
18 Ibid, ss 1(2), 2(2).
19 Eg where pending suit a husband living in the matrimonial home applied to exclude the wife from their 'holiday home' held in his sole name.
20 *S* v *S* (1980) 10 Fam Law 153, 124 Sol Jo 219, French J. Such a licence may be implied.
 1 *Gurasz* v *Gurasz* [1970] P 11, [1969] 3 All ER 822, CA.
 2 *S* v *S* above. See *Chaudhry* v *Chaudhry* [1987] 1 FLR 347, CA, for the position where the third party has a legal interest in the matrimonial home.
 3 See *Rayden on Divorce* (14 edn), chs 18–22; *Jackson's Matrimonial Finance and Taxation* (4th edn); and, *Distribution of Matrimonial Assets on Divorce* (2nd edn).

Where a court makes an exclusion injunction under the Matrimonial Homes Act 1983[4] it may order a spouse occupying the dwelling house, by virtue of a right of occupation, to make periodical payments to the other spouse in respect of the occupation[5] or impose on either spouse obligations as to the repair and maintenance of, or the discharge of liabilities in respect of, the dwelling house.[6] Orders may be limited for a period specified in the order, or have effect until further order.[7]

Any payment, tender or other thing made or done by a spouse entitled by virtue of this provision to occupy a dwelling house, towards satisfaction of the liability of the other spouse for any rent, rates,[8] mortgage payments, or other outgoings is as good as if made or done by the other spouse; and may be treated by the person to whom they are made as having been made by that other spouse.[9] The fact that a payment has been so treated does not affect any claim by that other spouse who made the payment to an interest in the property by virtue of the payment.[10] Occupation by one spouse by virtue of such a right of occupation or order is treated as possession by the other spouse for the purposes of the Rent (Agriculture) Act 1976,[11] the Rent Act 1977;[12] and treated as occupation by the other spouse for the purposes of the Housing Act 1985, Part IV.[13]

Liability for rates under the General Rate Act 1967[14] requires special consideration. A husband, although not in actual occupation of the matrimonial home, may be liable for rates if, by allowing his wife to remain in the matrimonial home, he is discharging his obligation to maintain her.[15] The fact that the wife is cohabiting in the matrimonial home does not, of itself, relieve the husband of his obligation to pay rates.[16] A separated husband, not in actual occupation of the matrimonial home, is only in rateable occupation if he has an interest in the home which he can pass on to his wife,[17] even if the fact that his wife owns the matrimonial home relieves him in part of his obligation to maintain her.[18] The fact that a wife has agreed to pay the rates and that the level of periodical payments has been agreed on that basis does not bind the rating authority who may assess the husband for rates,[19] if he would otherwise be liable.

4 27 *Halsbury's Statutes* (4th edn) 585 MATRIMONIAL LAW, and see section 3, above.
5 Ibid s 1(3)(b).
6 Ibid, s 1(3)(c).
7 Ibid, s 1(4). The court may make an interim order enforcing a spouses rights of occupation: *Baynham* v *Baynham* [1969] 1 All ER 305, [1968] 1 WLR 1890, CA.
8 See below.
9 Matrimonial Homes Act 1983, s 1(5) (27 *Halsbury's Statutes* (4th edn) 585 MATRIMONIAL LAW.)
10 Ibid, s 1(7).
11 1 *Halsbury's Statutes* (4th edn) 826 AGRICULTURE.
12 23 *Halsbury's Statutes* (4th edn) 405 LANDLORD AND TENANT, other than Part V and ss 103–106. This only applies to the matrimonial home, see *Hall* v *King* (1987) 131 Sol Jo 1186, CA.
13 21 *Halsbury's Statutes* (4th edn) 104 HOUSING.
14 36 *Halsbury's Statutes* (4th edn) RATING.
15 *Cardiff Corpn* v *Robinson* [1957] 1 QB 39, [1956] 3 All ER 56 and see *R* v *Harrow Magistrates' Court, ex p London Borough of Harrow* (1983) 147 JP 379, 4 FLR 678, where the husband had given an undertaking not to return to the matrimonial home. Where the husband, on the facts, no longer has a responsibility for the wife he is no longer in rateable occupation even though the house is in joint names. *Doncaster Metropolitan Borough Council* v *Lockwood* [1987] RA 29.
16 *R* v *Harrow, Magistrates' Court ex p London Borough of Harrow*, above.
17 *Brown* v *Oxford City Council* [1979] QB 607, [1978] 3 All ER 1113, CA.
18 Ibid.
19 *Charnwood Borough Council* v *Garner* [1979] RA 49. It would be open to the husband to apply for a downward variation of the order for periodical payments.

A wife who remains in the matrimonial home after separation is in rateable occupation of the matrimonial home if she has a legal interest in the property even though she has not brought any matrimonial proceedings.[20] Where a wife's occupation of the matrimonial home derives from a transfer of property order,[1] rather than being conferred by the husband in discharge of his common law obligation to maintain his wife and children, she is solely liable for rates.[2] In many circumstances a husband and wife should be jointly liable for rates.[3]

A transfer of property order[4] is, of course, available in respect of the former matrimonial home where the legal title is freehold or on a long lease. Such an order may also be made in respect of a private tenancy, where there is no covenant against assignment;[5] or, where there is a covenant against assignment, with the landlord's consent. Furthermore, a transfer of property order may be made in respect of a local authority tenancy.[6] Apart from the jurisdiction under the Matrimonial Causes Act 1973[7] there is an alternative procedure, in some ways more simple, under the Matrimonial Homes Act 1983.[8]

20 *Locker* v *Stockport Metropolitan Borough Council* [1985] FLR 771, [1984] Fam Law 189.
 1 Made under the Matrimonial Causes Act 1973, s 24(1)(a) (27 *Halsbury's Statutes* (4th edn) 700 MATRIMONIAL LAW) and see the works referred to in note 3 above on p 40 for the procedure and principles to be applied on such applications.
 2 *Routhan* v *Arun District Council* [1982] QB 502, [1981] 3 All ER 752, CA.
 3 Ibid.
 4 Made under the Matrimonial Causes Act 1973, s 24(1)(a).
 5 *Hale* v *Hale* [1975] 2 All ER 1090, [1975] 1 WLR 931, CA.
 6 *Thompson* v *Thompson* [1976] Fam 25, [1975] 2 All ER 208, CA, and see *Regan* v *Regan* [1977] 1 All ER 428, [1977] 1 WLR 84. See also Housing Act 1985, s 91(3)(b) (21 *Halsbury's Statutes* (4th edn) 29 HOUSING).
 7 Made under the Matrimonial Causes Act 1973, s 24(1)(a).
 8 S 7 and Sch 1 (27 *Halsbury's Statutes* (4th edn) 585 MATRIMONIAL LAW).

Chapter 5
Re-entry to the matrimonial home

The courts have power, under the Domestic Violence and Matrimonial Proceedings Act 1976[1] and as interlocutory relief in a matrimonial cause to grant a mandatory injunction under the principles of Matrimonial Homes Act 1983[2] requiring the respondent to permit the applicant to enter and remain in the matrimonial home or any specified part of it.

Where an applicant has been excluded from the home, either by being locked out or thrown out, it is proper to apply for re-entry relief ex parte[3] where the applicant has nowhere suitable to stay as the matter will then be one of urgency.

Where children have been excluded from the home it would seem that there is no power under the Domestic Violence and Matrimonial Proceedings Act 1976 to require a respondent to permit the children to re-enter the home;[4] there is power to make such an order in a matrimonial cause or under the Matrimonial Homes Act 1983[5] as the parental rights and duties include a duty to protect children.[6] This rather unfortunate lacuna in the statute can, it is submitted, be overcome if the court in addition to granting an order requiring the respondent to permit the applicant to re-enter the home, grants an order restraining the respondent from molesting the children. The meaning of molestation is very wide[7] and it is submitted that a respondent who did not, on request, permit the children to return to the home would be molesting them and therefore in breach of the order and in danger of being committed to prison for such breach on application.[8]

It has never been laid down by an appellate court as to the test to be applied on an application for a re-entry injunction although the matter was considered obiter by Lord Salmon in *Davis* v *Johnson*[9] in relation to applications under the Domestic Violence and Matrimonial Proceedings Act 1976. Lord Salmon's criteria are either that a party must have been driven from the home by serious[10] molestation or locked out of the home

---

1 S 1(1)(d) (27 *Halsbury's Statutes* (4th edn) 788 MATRIMONIAL LAW).
2 S 1(2)(c) (27 *Halsbury's Statutes* (4th edn) 585 MATRIMONIAL LAW).
3 See further ch 2, section A, above.
4 This would appear to be the result of the wording of s 1(1).
5 This would appear to be the result of the wording of s 1(2)(c).
6 See 24 *Halsbury's Laws* (4th edn) para 502 et seq.
7 See *Vaughan* v *Vaughan* [1973] 3 All ER 449, [1973] 1 WLR 1159, CA, and see ch 3, above.
8 See further ch 12, below.
9 [1979] AC 264 at 342A, [1978] 1 All ER 1132 at 1151b.
10 Lord Salmon does not seek to define 'serious'.

without reasonable justification,[11] before a judge could grant a re-entry injunction. The Matrimonial Homes Act 1983 sets out criteria to be considered.[12]

Furthermore Lord Salmon went on to say[13] that only in exceptional cases would a re-entry injunction be granted without the court, in addition, excluding the other party from the home. This may well be so on an inter partes application[14] but is not so where an application is made ex parte[15] as a party may only be excluded on an ex parte application in the most exceptional circumstances.[16] However merely because a party is entitled to a re-entry injunction the court should not lose sight of the principles to be applied on an application to exclude a party from the matrimonial home.[17]

11 There is no explanation of what would justify locking the other party out of the home. Where the parties are joint owners they each have a legal right to occupy the home. It is submitted that such justification might be more easily found between unmarried couples than between husband and wife. See also *Dennis* v *McDonald* [1982] Fam 63 at 70 B–E and 71 E–F, [1981] 2 All ER 632 at 637 g–j and 638 g–h, per Purchas J. The decision was upheld by the Court of Appeal [1982] Fam 63, [1982] 1 All ER 510, CA. The dicta were not considered.
12 S 1(3) see Appendix 1. The court may make such order as is just and reasonable having regard to the specified matters.
13 [1979] AC 264 at 343 B, [1978] 1 All ER 1132 at 1151c.
14 See ch 2, section B, above.
15 See ch 2, section A, above.
16 *Masich* v *Masich* (1977) 121 Sol Jo 645, CA. See further ch 2, section A 11, above.
17 See above, ch 4.

Chapter 6
Power of arrest
(High Court and county court)

1 Attachment of power of arrest

The Domestic Violence and Matrimonial Proceedings Act 1976[1] includes a provision which empowers a judge, in certain circumstances, to attach a power of arrest to certain injunctions. This provision was based on the recommendations of the Select Committee on Violence in Marriage.[2]

Section 2 (1) of the Act provides:

> Where, on the application by a party to a marriage,[3] a judge grants an injunction containing a provision (in whatever terms):
> (a) Restraining the respondent from using violence against the applicant, or
> (b) Restraining the respondent from using violence against a child living with the applicant, or
> (c) Excluding the respondent from the matrimonial home or from a specified area in which the matrimonial home is included, the judge may, if he is satisfied that the respondent has caused actual bodily harm to the applicant or, as the case may be, to the child concerned and considers that he is likely to do so again, attach a power of arrest to the injunction.

It should be noted that the Act does *not* provide for the attachment of a power of arrest to an injunction requiring the respondent to permit the applicant to enter and to remain in the matrimonial home or a part of the matrimonial home.

Before the judge can attach a power of arrest he must be satisfied first that the respondent has caused actual bodily harm to the applicant or to a relevant child; and, second must consider that he or she is likely to do so again. If those conditions are fulfilled then it is a matter for the judge's discretion as to whether or not the power should be imposed.[4]

Actual bodily harm, in this context, has the same meaning as in its normal usage, namely criminal law. Actual bodily harm includes[5] any hurt or injury calculated to interfere with the health or comfort of the victim.

1 27 *Halsbury's Statutes* (4th edn) 788 MATRIMONIAL LAW.
2 HC 553/1 July 1975.
3 The words 'party to a marriage' do not apply to parties whose marriage has been dissolved: *White* v *White* [1983] Fam 54, [1983] 2 All ER 51, CA. Thus a power of arrest cannot be attached to an injunction made against a former spouse unless they come within the meaning of the phrase 'living with each other in the same household as husband and wife'. It is submitted that a court is probably unable to extend the time of operation of a power of arrest, after decree absolute, which was attached to an injunction before decree absolute.
4 *Lewis* v *Lewis* [1978] Fam 60, [1978] 1 All ER 729, CA.
5 See Archbold *Criminal Pleading Evidence and Practice* (42nd edn) para 20–117; see also the Offences Against the Person Act 1861, s 47 (12 *Halsbury's Statutes*) (4th edn) 119 CRIMINAL LAW).

Furthermore, an injury to the state of the victim's mind for the time being, is within the definition of actual bodily harm.[6]

A power of arrest attached to an injunction is not to be regarded as a routine remedy, but is appropriate only in exceptional situations.[7]

The application for injunctions, where a power of arrest is sought, must include a request for a power of arrest to be attached to the injunction(s).[8] If the application for the injunction(s) does not include a request for a power of arrest a respondent, who would not oppose the grant of an injunction but would oppose the imposition of a power of arrest, might not attend the hearing.

Where a power of arrest is imposed without the respondent being present at the hearing the order should include a provision that the respondent be at liberty to apply on twenty-four hours notice to discharge that part of the injunction which relates to the power of arrest.[9]

Where a power of arrest is attached to an injunction a judge should consider for what length of time the power of arrest is a necessary for the protection of the applicant or the child.[10] In fixing a time limit, the judge, having found that the respondent is likely to cause actual bodily harm in the future either to the applicant or to a child, must consider for how long the applicant or child is likely to be in danger. Where a power of arrest is discharged, but the injunction remains in force, breach of the order can, of course, be enforced by applying for an order of committal.

A power of arrest may be attached to an injunction granted as interlocutory relief in matrimonial cause, pending in either the High Court or in a divorce county court, in the same way as it may be attached to an injunction granted in proceedings under the Act of 1976.[11]

It may also be attached to an injunction restraining trespass or assault in a common law action where the parties are husband and wife, or come within the meaning of the phrase 'living together in the same household as husband and wife'.[12]

A power of arrest may only be attached under its terms of the Domestic Violence and Matrimonial Proceedings Act 1976.[13] There is no jurisdiction to impose a power of arrest in wardship proceedings, as a means of enforcement, otherwise than under the statutory provision.[14]

It has never been considered by the Court of Appeal whether or not a respondent may consent to the attachment of a power of arrest to injunctions made against him. It is within the authors' experience that such has occurred. It is submitted that the court should always be asked to approve

---

6 *R* v *Miller* [1954] 2 QB 282 at 292 [1954] 2 All ER 529 at 534c, per Lynsky J. Tenderness and pain is sufficient to constitute actual bodily harm *R* v *Reigate Justices, ex p Counsell* (1983) 148 JP 193.

7 See *Lewis* v *Lewis*, above, *per curiam* Ormrod LJ, at 63 and 731, Roskill LJ at 64B and 732c. See also *McLean* v *Nugent* (1980) 1 FLR 26, CA, per Ormrod LJ.

8 See *Lewis* v *Lewis*, above and *McLean* v *Nugent*, above.

9 See *McLean* v *Nugent*, above.

10 See *Practice Note* [1981] 1 All ER 224, [1981] 1 WLR 27 which states: 'Unless a judge is satisfied that a longer period is necessary in a particular case, the period should not exceed 3 months'. If there is power to extend the operation of a power of arrest, a judge must decide the same by reference to the statutory criteria which apply to the initial attachment, *Carpenter* v *Carpenter* [1987] CA Transcript G25, CA the court was split as to whether there must be fresh actual bodily harm since the incidents which led to the initial attachment.

11 See *Lewis* v *Lewis*, above.

12 See *McLean* v *Nugent* above.

13 27 *Halsbury's Statutes* (4th edn) 788 MATRIMONIAL LAW.

14 *Re G (Wardship) (Jurisdiction: Power of Arrest)* (1983) 4 FLR 538, 13 Fam Law 50, CA.

such an agreement and that approval may only be given if the statutory pre-conditions have been satisfied.

Where an order is made which includes a power of arrest in the county court the power of arrest is in Form N110[15] There is no prescribed form for use in the High Court, in practice however, the same form of wording is used.

Where a power of arrest is attached to an injunction the same should nonetheless be endorsed with a penal notice so that it may be enforced by committal if the same should be necessary.[16]

A copy of an injunction containing a power of arrest must be delivered to the applicant's local police station.[17] The court will send a copy of the order to the police station. Where the proceedings are heard at the Royal Courts of Justice a copy of the order will be accompanied by Form D462 which gives the police information about the parties' names, addresses and solicitors.

While a power of arrest is in force, if an order is made varying or discharging the injunction, an officer of the court[18] must immediately inform the senior officer at the applicant's local police station. Furthermore, if the applicant's address has changed since the order was made the local police station for the new address must be informed, and a copy of the order must be delivered to them.[19] A power of arrest cannot be attached to an undertaking.[20]

2 Arrest for breach

Where a power of arrest has been attached to an injunction then a constable may, without warrant, arrest a person whom he has reasonable cause for suspecting of being in breach of that injunction. Where the injunction restrains the use of violence, the breach must be the use of violence; and, where the injunction excludes a party from the matrimonial home or an area including the matrimonial home, the breach must be entry into the excluded area.[21]

Thus, where an injunction restrains a respondent from 'assaulting, molesting or otherwise interfering with the applicant' and the judge attaches a power of arrest, a person can be in breach of order without using violence. However, it is only for a *violent* breach that he can be arrested. In this respect it is to be regretted that the wording of Form N110 does not make this clear.[1]

15 County Court (Forms) Rules 1982 (S 1 1982/586).
16 RSC Ord 45, r 7(4); CCR Ord 29 rr 1(2), (3).
17 RSC Ord 90, r 30(2); CCR Ord 47, r 8(5).
18 In the High Court this is done by a registrar of the Family Division.
19 RSC Ord 90, r 30(3); CCR Ord 47, r 8(6).
20 *Carpenter* v *Carpenter* [1987] CA Transcript G25, CA.
21 Domestic Violence and Matrimonial Proceedings Act 1976, s 2(3). It is of note that at common law, a licence to enter premises granted by a wife in a domestic dispute cannot be unilaterally revoked by the husband (the subject of the complaint made to the police) so as to make the police officers trespassers from the moment they are told to go (or as soon afterwards as they can reasonably be expected to leave). It is implied that when a request is made to police in such circumstances, the licence extends to a right not only to enter the home, but also to remain there long enough to take reasonable steps to inquire as to the whereabouts and safety of the complainant and any children, and for the police to be satisfied that there was no reasonable fear of a breach of the peace: *R* v *Thornley* (1980) 72 CR App Rep 302.
1 See also the form used in magistrates' courts which does make this clear. 1, *Stone's Justices Manual* (1987) para 5–1745 and see Appendix 4.

3 Committal for breach

A person arrested under a power of arrest must be brought before a judge within twenty-four hours of his arrest (without taking into account Christmas Day, Good Friday or any Sunday), and may not be released within the twenty-four hours except on the direction of a judge; but the Act does not authorise detention after the expiry of twenty-four hours.[2]

The arresting constable must forthwith after arrest seek the directions of the court which granted the injunction as to the time and place at which the arrested person is to be brought before the judge.[3] A person arrested for breach of an injunction made in the High Court, when brought before the judge, may be committed to prison notwithstanding that he has not been served with a copy of the injunction under Order 45, rule 7(2) and that there is no application for a committal order under Order 53, rule 4.[4] A person arrested and brought before a judge in breach of a county court injunction may be committed to prison notwithstanding that he has not been served with a copy of the injunction under CCR Order 29 rule 1(4) and that he has not been served with a notice in Form N78.[5]

The power of the court to commit a person to prison, who has been arrested under a power of arrest, is to be used with great care because it is a very draconian provision, intended to get rid of all technicalities and to streamline the procedure so that judges can deal with domestic emergencies.[6] The effect of CCR Order 47 rules 8(7) and (8) when read together is exactly the same as the provisions of RSC Order 90, rule 30(4).[7] In consequence a judge in the county court has exactly the same power as a judge of the High Court to deal with breaches of injunctions granted under the Domestic Violence and Matrimonial Proceedings Act 1976.[8]

Where a judge in the county court orders the committal to prison of a person before him under section 2 of the Act of 1976 the order and warrant for committal must be in Form N111.[9]

In the High Court there is no prescribed form for an order of committal of a person before the court under section 2 of the Domestic Violence and Matrimonial Proceedings Act 1976. It is submitted that the order should be drawn up as an order for committal, reciting that the person committed was before the court under the provisions of section 2 of the Act of 1976.[10]

There is no necessity to commit someone to prison merely because he has breached an order.[11] In a domestic context all the facts must be examined, and it is doubtful whether a judge is justified in sending a spouse to prison without finding out the views of the other spouse.[12] A judge has a very wide discretion as to whether or not to make a committal order where there has been a breach of an injunction.[13]

2 Domestic Violence and Matrimonial Proceedings Act 1976, s 2(4). See *Practice Direction* (23 January 1980, unreported) Appendix 2, below.
3 Domestic Violence and Matrimonial Proceedings Act 1976. S 2(5).
4 RSC Ord 90, r 30(4).
5 CCR Ord 47, r 8(7).
6 *Boylan v Boylan* (1980) 11 Fam Law 76, CA, per Ormrod LJ.
7 Ibid.
8 Ibid.
9 County Court (Forms) Rules 1982 (S 1 1983/586).
10 For the principles upon which orders for committal are made, suspended committal orders are made and applications for discharge of a person in custody see ch 12, below.
11 See *Smith v Smith* (1987) Times, 20 June, CA.
12 See *Boylan v Boylan*, above, per Ormrod LJ.
13 See *McLean v Nugent* (1980) 1 FLR 26, CA.

Chapter 7
Wardship and children

1 Restraint of removal from the jurisdiction

In this context 'jurisdiction' means England and Wales. It does not include Scotland, Northern Ireland, the Isle of Man, the Channel Islands, or anywhere else. It is uncertain as to whether it includes territorial waters up to the three mile limit.

Wardship
Immediately on becoming a ward of court the minor may not go out of the jurisdiction, even temporarily, without the leave of the court. This restriction is automatic[1] and applies by operation of the inherent jurisdiction. This rule of law has been modified by statute[2] to allow a ward, in certain circumstances,[3] to travel from England or Wales to another part of the United Kingdom,[4] or outside the United Kingdom with the leave of a court in another part of the United Kingdom.[5]

Removal of a ward from the jurisdiction may be restrained, by injunction, where there is danger of unlawful removal or such is threatened. The application may be made ex parte,[6] on affidavit,[7] and before the issue of proceedings[8] on the usual undertaking to commence such forthwith.[9]

Matrimonial causes
In any cause begun by petition[10] either party may apply at any time, after presentation of the petition,[11] for an order prohibiting the removal of any child of the family[12] under eighteen from England and Wales without the leave of the court except on such terms as may be specified in the order.[13]

1 The restriction is very long standing. See *Mountstuart v Mountstuart* (1801) 6 Ves 363.
2 Family Law Act 1986, s 38. *Not in force at the date of writing.*
3 Ibid, s 38(2). *Not in force at the date of writing.*
4 Ibid, s 38(3) (a). *Not in force at the date of writing.*
5 Ibid, s 38(3) (b). *Not in force at the date of writing.*
6 See ch 2 above.
7 RSC Ord 29, r 1.
8 *L v L* [1969] P 25, [1969] 1 All ER 852.
9 In this context 'forthwith' and 'as soon as reasonably practical' have the same meaning and effect. It is important that there should be no default in compliance with such an undertaking. See *PS Refson & Co Ltd v Saggers* [1984] 3 All ER 111, [1984] 1 WLR 1025.
10 These are suits for divorce, nullity or judicial separation: Matrimonial Causes Rules 1977, r 8(1).
11 In a case of urgency an application could be made ex parte on an understanding to issue a petition and supporting documents either forthwith or within a very short time, usually not more than 24 hours. See ch 2, above. See also *PS Refson & Co Ltd v Saggers* above.
12 Definition of child of the family, see Matrimonial Causes Act 1973, s 52(1); see Appendix 1, below. see *W(RJ) v W(SJ)* [1972] Fam 152, [1971] 3 All ER 303 and *A v A (Family: Unborn Child)* [1974] Fam 6, [1974], All ER 755; see also *Rowe v Rowe* [1980] Fam 47 [1979] 2 All ER 1123, CA. A child may be a 'child of the family' in respect of more than one family: *Newman v Newman* [1971] P 43, [1970] 3 All ER 529.
13 Matrimonial Causes Rules 1977, r 94 (1).

Unless otherwise directed an application for such injunction may be made ex parte.[14] Very often such applications are made ex parte because if there are fears that a child would be removed from the jurisdiction, without the consent of the other party, service of an application seeking an order preventing removal from the jurisdiction of the child might well result in the child being removed from the jurisdiction before the hearing of the application!

The application should be made by notice of application[15] or by summons.[16] The application should be supported by affidavit. If the application is made inter partes a copy of the notice of application or summons, as the case may be, and affidavit must be served on the other party to the cause at least two clear days before the return date.

The application, may be made to the registrar and in London should be made to the registrar of the day.[17]

In deciding the application the welfare of the child is the first and paramount consideration;[18] neither parent has a claim superior to that of the other.[19]

An injunction restraining removal of a child from the jurisdiction should be endorsed with penal notice[20] and served personally on the other party[1] so that the same may be enforced by committal[2] if necessary.

An order for custody, care and control of a child will provide that the child may not be removed from England and Wales without leave of the court except on such terms as are specified in the order.[3] Such orders, if breached, cannot be enforced immediately by committal unless they are endorsed with a penal notice[4] and served personally on the disobedient party.[5]

Guardianship

Where, in guardianship proceedings, the High Court,[6] a county court[7] or a magistrates' court[8] makes an order,[9] or an interim order,[10] regarding the legal custody of a minor the court, on making the order, or at any time

14 Ibid. See also ch 2, above.
15 If the cause is a county court matter: Matrimonial Causes Rules 1977, r 122 (1)(b), CCR Ord 13, r 1(2).
16 If the cause is pending in the High Court: Matrimonial Causes Rules 1977, r 122 (1)(b).
17 Matrimonial Causes Rules 1977, rr 94(1), 122(1)(a); *Practice Direction* [1973] 2 All ER 400, [1973] 1 WLR 657.
18 Guardianship of Minors Act 1971, s 1.
19 *J v C* [1970] AC 668, [1969] 1 All ER 788, HL.
20 RSC Ord 45, r 7(4); CCR Ord 29 rr 1(2), (3).
 1 RSC Ord 45, r 7(2); CCR Ord 29 rr 1(2), (3).
 2 See further ch 12, above.
 3 Matrimonial Causes Rules 1977, r 94(2). The terms usually specified in an order are: that the child be not removed from England and Wales without leave of the court until he or she attain the age of 18 years; provided that if either parent do give written undertaking to the court to return the child to England and Wales when called upon to do so, and, unless otherwise directed, with the written consent of the other parent, that parent may remove the child from England and Wales for any period specified in such written consent. See Divorce Registry Form. D 325, Custody Order and Form D 559 Order on hearing pursuant to Matrimonial Causes Act 1973, s 41. For a precedent see Appendix 4 below.
 4 See fn 11, above,
 5 See fn 12, above.
 6 Guardianship of Minors Act 1971, s 15(1)(a) (6 *Halsbury's Statutes* (4th edn) 305 CHILDREN).
 7 Ibid, s 15(1)(b) as limited by s 15(3)
 8 Ibid, s 15(1)(c) as limited by s 15(3).
 9 Under ibid ss 9(1), 10(1)(a) or 11(a).
10 Under Guardianship Act 1973, s 2(4) (6 *Halsbury's Statutes* (4th edn) 338 CHILDREN).

while the same is in force, may, on application,[11] make an order directing that no person shall take the minor out of England and Wales without the leave of the court.[12]

Such order may subsequently be varied or discharged.[13] It would seem that leave to remove a minor temporarily would take effect as a variation and that leave to remove a minor permanently could take effect either as a variation or as a discharge.

An order of the High Court or a county court under the Guardianship of Minors Act 1971, section 13A takes effect as an injunction[14] and may be enforced by committal.[15] An order of a magistrates' court may be enforced by a fine[16] or committal.[17]

Custodianship

Where an authorised court[18] makes a custodianship order[19] or an interim order[20] containing a provision regarding legal custody[1] the court may, at any time while the order is in force, on application,[2] direct by order, that no person shall take the child out of England and Wales except with the leave of the court.[3] An order may be varied or revoked.[4]

Magistrates' courts

Apart from the powers in guardianship and custodianship proceedings[5] a magistrates' court has power[6] in matrimonial proceedings to restrict the removal of a child of the family from England and Wales.

Where a magistrates' court makes an order[7] regarding the legal custody of a child[8] or makes an interim custody order[9] in respect of a child,[10] the court, on making the order, or while the order is in force, may on application[11] direct by order that no person shall take the child out of England and

---

11 An application may be made by a party to the proceedings: Guardianship of Minors Act 1971, s 13A(3).

12 Ibid, s 13A(1) added by the Domestic Proceedings and Magistrates' Courts Act 1978, s 39, in force from 1 February 1981 by SI 1980/1479. For 'England and Wales' there will be substituted 'the United Kingdom or any part specified in the order' as from a date to be appointed: Family Law Act 1986, s 35(1)(a).

13 Guardianship of Minors Act 1971, s 13A(2).

14 See ch 2 above.

15 See ch 12 below.

16 Magistrates' Courts Act 1980, s 63(3)(a) (27 *Halsbury's Statutes* (4th edn) 157 MAGISTRATES) and see ch 13 below. The fine may be £50 per day but may not exceed £1,000.

17 Ibid, s 63(3)(b) and see ch 13 below. Imprisonment may be until the default is remedied but may not exceed two months.

18 As defined by the Children Act 1975, s 100(2) (6 *Halsbury's Statutes* (4th edn) 355 CHILDREN); see Appendix 1.

19 Ibid, s 43A(1A)(a).

20 Under ibid, s 34(5).

 1 Ibid, s 43A(1A)(b).

 2 Application may be made by the father, mother or custodian, ibid, s 43A(3).

 3 Ibid, s 43A(1). For 'England and Wales' there will be substituted 'the United Kingdom or any part specified in the order' as from a date to be appointed: Family Law Act 1986, s 35(1)(b).

 4 Ibid, s 43A(2).

 5 See above.

 6 Domestic Proceedings and Magistrates' Courts Act 1978 s 34.

 7 Under ibid s 8(2).

 8 Ibid s 34(1)(a).

 9 Under ibid, s 19.

10 Under ibid, s 34(1)(b).

11 An application may be made by a party to the marriage in question or by a parent of the child who is not a party to the marriage in question: ibid, s 34(3).

Wales except with the leave of the court.[12] Such order may be varied or revoked.[13]

An order may be enforced by a fine[14] or committal.[15]

Leave to remove

Once an order has been made, whether ex parte or inter partes, preventing the removal of a child from the jurisdiction the onus is then on the respondent to the application to apply for leave to remove the child from the jurisdiction; it is not open for the respondent to seek discharge of the order on the basis that he does not intend to remove the child from the jurisdiction.

An application for temporary removal of a minor from the jurisdiction is often opposed on the ground that the child will not be returned. The applicant can usually show his *bona fides* if he has a substantial connection with England and Wales, if he has a job or a home in the jurisdiction. The applicant must explain on affidavit the purpose of the visit abroad giving details of where the minor will stay and setting out the relevant travel arrangements.[16]

An application for permanent removal is to be decided by considering first the welfare of the minor. The court is unlikely to refuse leave to a party with care and control where the foreign mode of life proposed[17] is reasonable having regard to the welfare of the minor.[18] Leave may be granted on terms[19] and an undertaking to return the child to the jurisdiction, if called upon to do so, is usually required.

2 Kidnapping from the jurisdiction

It is a criminal offence[20] for a person connected with a child[1] to take or send[2] such child under the age of 16 out of the United Kingdom[3] without the appropriate consent,[4] unless he believes that the other person has

---

12 Ibid, s 34(1). For 'England and Wales' there will be substituted 'the United Kingdom or any part specified in the order' as from a date to be appointed: Family Law Act 1986, s 35(1)(c).
13 Ibid, s 34(2).
14 Magistrates' Courts Act 1980 s 63(3)(a), and see fn 16 on p 51 above.
15 Ibid, s 63(3)(b), and see fn 17 on p 51 above.
16 Airline and other tickets frequently cause problems. The applicant (or his family) may have already purchased the tickets and they are produced to the court to show that because they are return tickets the child will return. Respondents often feel that this presents the court with a *fait accompli*. It is submitted that if an application is made in good time an order for leave can be made subject to the production to the court of return tickets. This saves the applicant from wasting money yet provides a safeguard.
17 The affidavit must be full and explain all aspects of the proposed way of life abroad.
18 *P(LM)(otherwise E) v P(GE)* [1970] 3 All ER 659, [1970] 1 WLR 1469 CA. See also *A v A (child: removal from the jurisdiction)* (1979) 1 FLR 380, 10 Fam Law 116, CA
19 Eg providing a deposit of money for the child's return fare in case it should be necessary for the child to return; *P(LM)(otherwise E) v P(GE)* above.
20 Child Abduction Act 1984, s 1(1) (12 *Halsbury's Statutes* (4th edn) 933 CRIMINAL LAW). See Appendix 1.
1 As defined by ibid, s 1(2).
2 See ibid, s 3.
3 Defined by Interpretation Act 1978, s 5 and Sch 1(41*Halsbury's Statutes* (4th edn) STATUTES) as Great Britain and Northern Ireland.
4 Defined by Child Abduction Act 1984, s 1(3).

consented,[5] would consent if aware of all relevant circumstances,[6] or he has been unable to communicate with the other person despite having taken all reasonable steps,[7] or the other person has unreasonably refused to consent.[8]

Where a child is removed from England and Wales in breach of an order it is appropriate to make an immediate application[9] for an order that the child be returned to the jurisdiction.[10] It may be appropriate to obtain an order for press publicity.[11] Where the order breached was made by a magistrates' court it may be advantageous to apply in wardship proceedings for an order for return of the child by reason of the wider powers of the High Court; although, any court may make a declaration in custody proceedings that the removal of a child from the United Kingdom is unlawful.[12]

An injunction requiring the return of a child to the jurisdiction must be enforced once it has been obtained. This may not be easy and will often depend largely on the attitude of a foreign court to an order granted in proceedings in England and Wales.

If the child has been wrongfully taken to a country[13] where the Hague Convention[14] is in force, application may be made under Article 8 for the return of the child, which must be ordered[15] unless, inter alia, the provisions of Article 13[16] apply.

If the child has been improperly taken to a country[17] where the European Convention[18] is in force, a decision relating to custody[19] made by a court in the United Kingdom may, on application,[20] be recognised[1] and enforced[2] in the other country unless refusal is justified under the terms of the convention.[3]

5 Ibid, s 1(5)(a)(i).
6 Ibid, s 1(5)(a)(ii).
7 Ibid, s 1(5)(b).
8 Ibid, s 1(5)(c) save as provided by s 1(5).
9 The application may be made ex parte although the respondent's solicitors (if any) may be notified of the hearing.
10 The order will be that the offending party return the child either forthwith or within a specified time. See *Fabbri v Fabbri* [1962] 1 All ER 35, [1962] 1 WLR 13.
11 *Practice Note (Child: Abduction: Press Publicity)* [1980] 2 All ER 806.
12 Child Abduction and Custody Act 1985, s 23(2). Such a declaration may be important under the European Convention, see fn 18 below.
13 Australia, France, Hungary, Portugal, Switzerland and parts of Canada, namely: Ontario, New Brunswick, British Columbia, Manitoba, Nova Scotia, Newfoundland, Prince Edward Island, Quebec and Yukon Territory. See Child Abduction and Custody (Parties to Conventions) Order 1986 (SI 1986/1159), art 2(2)(a) and Sch 1, as amended by SI 1987/163.
14 The Convention on the Civil Aspects of International Child Abduction signed at the Hague on 25 October 1980. See Child Abduction and Custody Act 1985, Sch 1; Appendix 1, below. It is outside the scope of this work to give detailed consideration to the Convention.
15 Hague Convention, art 12.
16 See Child Abduction and Custody Act 1985, Sch 1.
17 Austria, Belgium, Cyprus, France, Luxembourg, Portugal, Spain and Switzerland. See Child Abduction and Custody (Parties to Conventions) Order 1986 (SI 1986/1159), art 3(2)(a) and Sch 2.
18 The European Convention on Recognition and Enforcement of Decisions concerning Custody of Children and on the Restoration of Custody signed in Luxembourg on 20 May 1980. See Child Abduction and Custody Act 1985, Sch 2; Appendix 1, below. It is outside the scope of this work to give detailed consideration to the convention.
19 European Convention, art 1(c).
20 Ibid, art 4.
1 Ibid, art 7.
2 Ibid, art 7 where the decision is enforceable in the United Kingdom.
3 Ibid, inter alia, arts 9 and 10.

The Family Law Act 1986[4] provides for recognition[5] and enforcement[6] of custody orders,[7] made in one part of the United Kingdom, by the courts of other parts of the United Kingdom.

A person who removes a child from the jurisdiction in breach of a court order, or who fails to comply with an order for return of the child is in contempt of court and, in general, may not make any application until his contempt has been purged[8] although he may appeal or apply to set aside the order which founds his contempt.[9]

A party who returns a child to the jurisdiction in compliance with an order should deliver the child as directed by the order, or, if no directions are given in the order should forthwith seek the direction of the court.[10]

3 Kidnapping to the jurisdiction

Where a child is brought to the jurisdiction in breach of an order of a foreign court, or by the unilateral decision of a parent, the court, usually in wardship, has to choose between making an order for the child's immediate return or having, at a later date, a full investigation of the merits.[11] In deciding between the two courses of action the welfare of the child is first and paramount.[12]

The court will give great weight to, but is not bound by, orders of a foreign court,[13] where the order is inconsistent with the child's welfare.[14] Kidnapping is to be strongly discouraged by the swift, realistic and un-sentimental assessment of the welfare of the child.[15] To remove a child from his native land with disruption of his life by leaving his home, school and friends, and being faced with the social system[16] of a different country may be very disturbing.[17] In such a case, on a prompt application for immediate return, a judge may conclude that it is in the best interests of the child for the disturbing factors to be removed speedily by making such an order for immediate return.[18]

Where a court orders a child to return to another jurisdiction it is undesirable to make an order in terms which suggest that it has formed a concluded view as to which parent should have custody.[19] The concept of *forum conveniens* has no place in the wardship jurisdiction.[20]

---

4 *Not in force at the date of writing.*
5 Family Law Act 1986, s 25. *Not in force at the date of writing.*
6 Ibid, s 29. *Not in force at the date of writing.*
7 Ibid, s 32. *Not in force at the date of writing.*
8 *Hadkinson v Hadkinson* [1952] P 285, [1952] 2 All ER 567, CA.
9 Ibid and see *Maynard v Maynard* [1984] FLR 85, [1984] Fam Law, 87, CA.
10 For procedure in some circumstances see *Practice Direction (Child: Airport Arrival)* [1980] 1 ALL ER 288, [1980] 1 WLR 73.
11 *Re L (Minors)(Wardship: Jurisdiction)* [1974] 1 All ER 913, [1974] 1 WLR 250, CA.
12 Ibid and see Guardianship of Minors Act 1971, s 1 (6 *Halsbury's Statutes* (4th edn) 305 CHILDREN).
13 *McKee v Mckee* [1951] AC 352, [1951] 1 All ER 942, PC.
14 *Re R (minors)(Wardship: Jurisdiction)* (1981) 2 FLR 416, 11 Fam Law 57, CA.
15 Ibid. It is important that the application is made promptly.
16 And maybe a new language.
17 *See Re L (Minors)(Wardship: Jurisdiction)*, above, and fn 14.
18 Ibid. See also *Re C (minors)(Wardship: Jurisdiction)* [1978] Fam 105, [1978] 2 All ER 230, CA.
19 *Re L (Minors)(Wardship: Jurisdiction)*, above.
20 *Re R (Minors)(Wardship: Jurisdiction)*, above.

Where a child is wrongfully[1] brought to the jurisdiction from a country[2] where the Hague Convention[3] is in force, application may be made to the High Court,[4] by originating summons,[5] for an order[6] for the return of the child[7] which, unless an exception applies,[8] is mandatory.[9]

Where a child is improperly[10] brought to the jurisdiction from a country[11] where the European Convention[12] is in force, application[13] may be made by a person on whom rights of custody[14] are conferred for registration[15] and enforcement[16] of a decision relating to custody[17] made by an authority[18] in another Contracting State.

While an application is pending for registration or enforcement the court may give interim directions[19] for the purpose of securing the welfare of the child or for preventing a change of relevant circumstances. Application for such directions may, in a case of urgency, be made ex parte on affidavit,[20] but otherwise must be made by summons.[1]

Where an application is pending under the Hague Convention and an application as to the merits of the rights of custody[2] is pending before a court in the jurisdiction, a concise statement of the nature of the application must be filed in the principal registry of the Family Division.[3] Notifica-

1 See Hague Convention. Art 3.
2 Australia, France, Hungary, Portugal, Switzerland and parts of Canada namely: Ontario, New Brunswick, British Columbia, Manitoba, Nova Scotia, Newfoundland, Prince Edward Island, Quebec and Yukon Territory. See Child Abduction and Custody (Parties to Conventions) Order 1986 (SI 1986/1159), art 2(2)(a) and Sch 1, as amended by SI 1987/163.
3 The Convention on the Civil Aspects of International Child Abduction signed at the Hague on 25 October 1980. See Child Abduction and Custody Act 1985, Sch 1: Appendix 1, below. It is outside the scope of this work to give detailed consideration to the Convention.
4 Child Abduction and Custody Act 1985, s 4(a).
5 RSC Ord 90, rr 33, 34 and 35. See Appendix 3, below.
6 Pending a final decision the court may give interim directions for the purpose of securing the welfare of the child or for preventing a change of relevant circumstances. See the Child Abduction and Custody Act 1985, s 5. The application may be made ex parte on affidavit in a case of urgency, but otherwise must be made by summons; RSC Ord 90, r 44.
7 Hague Convention, art 12.
8 See inter alia Hague Convention, art 13. See *A v A, In re A (a Minor)* (1987) Times 13 June, CA. 'Psychological harm' in art 13 (b) means substantial and not trivial psychological harm, *A v A, In re A (a minor)*, above.
9 Ibid, art 12.
10 See European Convention, art 1(d).
11 Austria, Belgium, Cyprus, France, Luxembourg, Portugal, Spain and Switzerland. See Child Abduction and Custody (Parties to Conventions) Order 1986 (SI 1986/1159), art 3(2)(a) and Sch 2.
12 The European Convention on Recognition and Enforcement of Decisions concerning Custody of Children and on the Restoration of Custody signed in Luxembourg on 20 May 1980. See Child Abduction and Custody Act 1985, Sch 2; Appendix 1, below. It is outside the scope of this work to give detailed consideration to the Convention.
13 By originating summons to the High Court. See RSC Ord 90, rr 33, 34 and 35; see Appendix 3, below.
14 Child Abduction and Custody Act, s 16(1).
15 Ibid, s 16.
16 Ibid, s 18.
17 European Convention, art 1(c).
18 Which may be judicial or administrative. European Convention, art 1(b).
19 Child Abduction and Custody Act, s 19.
20 RSC Ord 90 r 44:
1 Ibid.
2 Child Abduction and Custody Act 1985, s 9.
3 RSC Ord 90, r 42(1).

tion is then given by the proper officer[4] to the relevant authority[5] of the proceedings and subsequently, the result.[6]

Where notification is received by the High Court from the Court of Session or the High Court in Northern Ireland that application is pending under the Hague Convention in either of those courts, the High Court must stay[7] custody proceedings[8] unless and until the proceedings under the Hague Convention are dismissed and the High Court has been notified.[9]

Where notification is received by a county court[10] or a magistrates' court[11] of proceedings under the Hague Convention, custody proceedings[12] must be stayed[13] unless and until the proceedings under the Hague Convention have been dismissed and the county court[14] or the magistrates' court[15] have been notified.

Similar provisions apply for the suspension of custody proceedings where an application for recognition and enforcement under the European Convention is pending in the High Court.[16]

The Family Law Act 1986[17] provides for the recognition[18] and enforcement[19] of custody orders,[20] made in one part of the United Kingdom, by the courts of other parts of the United Kingdom.

4 Restraint of removal from custody, care and control

An order for custody, care and control, cannot be enforced by committal unless it has been endorsed with a penal notice.[1] Such orders are not generally endorsed with a penal notice but in appropriate circumstances, such as where it is feared that one party may flout the order, the court may well endorse such order with a penal notice.

Where an order for custody, care and control[2] has been made the party having care and control may apply to the court for an injunction restraining the other party to the cause or matter from removing the child or children

4 As defined by RSC Ord 90, r 32(c).
5 Which includes the High Court, county courts and magistrates' courts; see RSC Ord 90, r 42(5).
6 RSC Ord 90, r 42(3).
7 RSC Ord 90 r 42(4).
8 Child Abduction and Custody Act 1985, s 27 and Sch 3.
9 RSC Ord 90, r 42(4).
10 CCR Ord 47, r 10(2).
11 Magistrates' Courts (Child Abduction and Custody) Rules 1986 (SI 1986/1141), r 3.
12 Child Abduction and Custody Act 1985, s 27 and Sch 3.
13 CCR Ord 47, r 10(2), Magistrates' Courts (Child Abduction and Custody) Rules 1986 r 3.
14 CCR Ord 47, r 10(2).
15 Magistrates' Courts (Child Abduction and Custody) Rules 1986, r 5.
16 Child Abduction and Custody Act 1985, s 20, RSC Ord 90, r 42(2), CCR Ord 47, r 10(3), Magistrates' Courts (Child Abduction and Custody) Rules 1986, r 7.
17 *Not in force at the date of writing.*
18 Family Law Act 1986, s 25. *Not in force at the date of writing*
19 Ibid, s 29. *Not in force at the date of writing.*
20 Ibid, s 32. *Not in force at the date of writing.*
1 RSC Ord 45, r 7(4); CCR Ord 29 rr 1(2),(3).
2 Where a 'split' order has been made (that is, where one parent has custody and the other has care and control, or both parents have joint custody but one has care and control) the parent with care and control of the child has the day-to-day responsibility for the child and the child will be living with that parent. In such cases the parent with care and control may require an injunction restraining removal of the child from his or her care and control. It is no answer to such application that the respondent spouse has custody or joint custody, without care and control.

from his or her care and control. The fact that an order has been made in the applicant's favour shows prima facie[3] that he or she is entitled to such an injunction subject to satisfying the court that there is a danger that the party against whom the order is sought may flout the original order.

Such application may be made ex parte[4] where there is a real risk that the child may immediately be snatched; otherwise the application should be made on notice[5] for a prompt hearing.

Where the applicant does not have an order for care and control in his or her favour but has de facto care and control[6] then the applicant will have to satisfy the court not only that there is a danger that the child may be removed from his or her care and control but also that it is proper for him or her to have, in effect, interim care and control of the child.

If the injunction is opposed on the basis that custody is in issue, then there must, of necessity, be some hearing on the merits and an interim order may be made pending a full hearing when the court would have the benefit of a welfare officer's report.[7] An interim order should always be made pending a full hearing where it is alleged that a child may be in danger. Where an interim order is made it is preferable for the same to be made in respect of care and control rather than custody.[8] Where an order for interim care and control is made the Court of Appeal will only interfere if there are the clearest possible indications for so doing.[9]

Where an applicant not only does not have an order for custody, care and control in his favour but also care and control is at large, as where husband and wife are living with the children in the same house, then an applicant must not only prove that it is appropriate for him or her to have, in effect, interim care and control of the child but in addition that there was a danger that the child might be removed from his or her care and control. If the parties were at the time of the application living with the children in the same house then application would probably be made, at the same time, to exclude the other spouse from the home.[10]

An injunction should not be used as a summary method of obtaining care and control.[11]

In any case where there are children of the family and an application is made to exclude one or other of the parties from the home then the court will have to decide, if the circumstances warrant the exclusion of one of the parties, which of the parties should be excluded and which should remain with the children.[12] This process requires consideration of the merits of

3 Unless circumstances have materially changed since the order was made.
4 See ch 2, above.
5 See ch 2, above,
6 As, for example, where the spouses have separated, one being left with the children or where one has left the home with the children.
7 Matrimonial Causes Rules 1977, r 95 empowers the court at any time to seek investigation and report by a court welfare officer. It is submitted that the words 'at any time' in the rule mean exactly that and would cover an ex parte application made before the issue of substantive proceedings.
8 *Re B (a Minor) (Interim Custody)* (1983) 4 FLR 683, 13 Fam Law 176, CA.
9 *G v G (interim Custody: Appeal)* (1982) 4 FLR 327, 12 Fam Law 185, CA.
10 See further ch 4.
11 In the same way that an injunction should not be used as a summary method of obtaining a transfer of property order. See *Grace v Grace* [1980] CA Transcript No 418, CA.
12 See *Bassett v Bassett* [1975] Fam 76, [1975] 1 All ER 513, CA; *Walker v Walker* [1978] 3 All ER 141, [1978] 1 WLR 533, CA; *Spindlow v Spindlow* [1979] Fam 52, [1979] 1 All ER 169, CA; *Harding v Harding* (1979) 10 Fam Law 146, CA and see ch 4, above.

each party as the potential custodial parent of the child or children.[13] Furthermore where an application for an injunction restraining the removal of children from care and control is opposed, especially where care and control is in issue, then the application should be adjourned pending a welfare officer's report.[14] However in all cases where children are in danger or where the circumstances demand immediate action then the court should hear the merits and make an interim order.

An application for an injunction restraining the removal of children from care and control may be made ex parte[15] before the commencement of proceedings[16] on the usual undertakings to issue proceedings[17] forthwith.

Where a child is unlawfully removed from a person who has custody[18] an injunction will be granted for the return of the child; if necessary the court will seek the assistance of press publicity.[19] Where in proceedings for, or relating to, a custody order[20] the court does not have available adequate information as to the whereabouts of the child concerned, the court may order[1] any person[2] reasonably believed to have relevant information to disclose it to the court.

Where an existing custody order has been breached[3] a judge, making an interim order, pending the hearing of an application to vary the original order, ought to restore the status quo[4] in the absence of particular reasons to the contrary.[5] Such reasons should be strong otherwise, in the long term, uncertainty may well be brought about by the consolidation of a position that was initially unlawful.[6]

A local authority may not remove a child from its parents[7] without a place of safety order[8] or an order of the court;[9] removal without authority is wholly illegal.

5 Restraint of removal from custodianship

Where an application is made for a custodianship order in respect of a child who has had his home[10] with the applicant for at least three years,[11] while

13 *Harding v Harding* [1979] CA Transcript 639.
14 By analogy with exclusion cases; *Smith v Smith* (1979) 10 Fam Law 50; CA; *Mitchell v Mitchell* [1979] CA Transcript 221, CA; *Wood v Wood* [1978] CA Transcript 766, CA.
15 See ch 2, above.
16 L v L [1969] P 25, [1969] 1 All ER 852.
17 See ch 2, above.
18 Or care and control.
19 *Practice Note (Child: Abduction: Press Publicity)* [1980] 2 All ER 806. See Appendix 2.
20 See Family Law Act 1986, s 40(1). *Not in force at the date of writing.* It is submitted that an application for an injunction for the return of a child would be 'a proceeding relating to a custody order.'
 1 Family Law Act 1986, s 33(1). *Not in force at the date of writing.*
 2 Who need not be a party to the proceedings.
 3 Eg a parent who refuses to return a child at the end of an access visit.
 4 *Townson v Mahon* [1984] FLR 690, [1984] Fam Law 204, CA.
 5 *Townson v Mahon* above and see *W v D (Interim Custody Order)* (1979) 1 FLR 393, 10 Fam Law 149, CA.
 6 *Townson v Mahon*, above.
 7 Children Act 1975, s 85(1) (6 *Halsbury's Statutes* (4th edn) 355 CHILDREN), or, in the case of an illegitimate child, the mother, who has all the parental rights and duties; see ibid, s 85(7).
 8 See Children and Young Persons Act 1969, s 28(1) (6 *Halsbury's Statues* (4th edn) 227 CHILDREN).
 9 *Havering London Borough Council v S* [1986] 1 FLR 489, [1986] Fam Law 157.
10 See Children Act 1975, s 87(3) (6 *Halsbury's Statues* (4th edn) 355 CHILDREN).
11 Ie an application under ibid, s 33(3)(c).

the application is pending, the child may not be removed from the applicant,[12] against his will, without the leave of a court,[13] or by statute,[14] or on the arrest of the child.[15] Where such a child was in care before he had his home with the applicant and remains in care, the local authority may not remove the child from the applicant's actual custody without the applicant's consent or the leave of a court.[16]

A person who removes a child in breach of the terms of the Children Act 1975, section 41 commits an offence[17] which is punishable by up to three months' imprisonment or a fine not exceeding level 5 on the standard scale.

Where a child has been removed from the applicant in breach of the Children Act 1975, section 41, an authorised court[18] may order the person who removed the child to return him or her to the applicant.[19] Where a person has reasonable grounds[20] for believing that another is intending to remove the child from the applicant's actual custody[1] an authorised court[2] may restrain such intended removal.[3]

Where the High Court[4] or a county court[5] has made an order[6] for the return of a child and the child has not been returned the court may make an order authorising an officer of the court[7] to search specified premises for the child; and, if the child is found, authorising the return of the child to the applicant.[8] Such an order may be enforced in the same way as a warrant for committal.[9]

If a justice of the peace is satisfied[10] that there are reasonable grounds for believing that a child, in respect of whom an order for return[11] has been made, is in specified premises, he may issue a search warrant[12] authorising a constable[13] to search such premises as may be specified in the warrant;[14] and, if the constable finds the child he must return him or her to the applicant.[15]

12 Ibid, s 41(1).
13 Ibid.
14 Eg under a place of safety order; see Children and Young Persons Act 1969, s 28(1) (6 *Halsbury's Statutes* (4th edn) 227 CHILDREN).
15 This makes it clear that such a child is subject to the ordinary law.
16 Children Act 1975, s 41(2).
17 Ibid, s 41(3); the offence is triable summarily only.
18 See ibid, s 100(2).
19 Ibid, s 42(1).
20 It would seem that a person must not only have reasonable grounds for the belief but must also have actual belief. See *R v Banks* [1916] 2 KB 621, CCA, and see *R v Harrison* [1938] 3 All ER 134, CCA.
 1 Ie in breach of Children Act 1975, s 41.
 2 See ibid, s 100(2).
 3 Ibid, s 42(2).
 4 Ibid, s 42(3).
 5 Ibid.
 6 Under ibid, s 42(1).
 7 In the High Court this will be the tipstaff and, in county courts, the bailiff.
 8 Ibid, s 42(3).
 9 Ibid, s 42(5).
10 By information on oath.
11 Under ibid, s 42(1).
12 Under the Magistrates' Courts Act 1980, s 125(2) (27 *Halsbury's Statutes* (4th edn) 157 MAGISTRATES).
13 This means any person holding the office of constable (see 36 *Halsbury's Laws* (4th edn) paras 201 et seq), not a member of a police force holding the rank of constable.
14 Children Act 1975, s 42(4).
15 Ibid.

A custodianship order vests the legal custody of the child in the applicant[16] who is called the custodian.[17] Where the custodianship order was made by the High Court or a county court, the custodian may, while entitled to actual custody, apply to restrain by injunction threatened or actual removal of the child from his custody.

Where a custodian is entitled to actual custody of a child, by virtue of a custodianship order made by a magistrates' court, and, another person has actual custody of the child, the order may be enforced[18] as if it were an order requiring that other person to give up the child to the custodian,[19] provided a copy of the custodianship order has been served on that other person.[20]

6 Undesirable associations and communications

Access is the right of the child[1] not the right of the parent.[2] A court should not refuse a parent access unless it is wholly satisfied that it is in the interests of the child for access to cease.[3] Where a court denies access to a party it may reinforce the order with an injunction restraining the party from communicating[4] with or approaching the child.[5] There is no power to attach a power of arrest to an injunction restraining a party from approaching a child who is a ward.[6]

The court may restrain a non-custodial parent from communicating with his child[7] where past communications have been, or proposed communications would be, contrary to the child's welfare.[8]

In wardship the court may restrain contact and communication between the ward and a third party.[9] An injunction will be granted to restrain the

---

16 Ibid, s 33(1).
17 Ibid, s 33(2).
18 Under the Magistrates' Courts Act 1980, s 63(3) (27 *Halsbury's Statutes* (4th edn) 157 MAGISTRATES).
19 Children Act 1975, s 43(1).
20 Ibid.
1 *M v M (Child: Access)* 2 All ER 81, DC.
2 Ibid.
3 Ibid. A court should be slow to come to such a conclusion, per curiam. See also *S v S and P* [1962] 2 All ER 1, [1962] 1 WLR 445, CA; and see *B v B* [1971] 3 All ER 682, [1971] 1 WLR 1486, CA.
4 *R v R and I* [1961] 3 All ER 461, [1961] 1 WLR 1334.
5 If such were necessary for the protection or welfare of the child.
6 *Re G (Wardship) (Jurisdiction: Power of Arrest)* (1982) 4 FLR 538, 13 Fam Law 50, CA. There is a fundamental difference between the almost unlimited powers of the High Court in wardship to make orders and the power of the court to enforce its orders. A power of arrest may only be attached to an injunction in accordance with the criteria set out in the Domestic Violence and Matrimonial Proceedings Act 1976, s 2 (27 *Halsbury's Statutes* (4th edn) 788 MATRIMONIAL LAW).
7 *R v R and I* above.
8 In *R v R and I* above the letter was described as 'most disturbing and unhappy' per Scarman J at 462.
9 *Roach v Garvan* (1748) 1 Dick 88, *Beard v Travers* (1749) 1 Ves Sen 313. In the early cases the injunctions were granted, ultimately, to prevent a marriage of a ward without leave. It would seem that an undesirable relationship or liaison may be restrained; especially if the ward is a female under the age of 16, who is therefore unable to consent to sexual intercourse. Sexual Offences Act 1956, s 6 (12 *Halsbury's Statutes* (4th edn) 271 CRIMINAL LAW). For procedure see *Practice Direction (Wardship: Parties to Proceedings)* [1983] 2 All ER 672, [1983] 1 WLR 790; see Appendix 2 below.

proposed marriage of a ward[10] where leave has been refused or has not been sought.[11] Marriage of or with a ward without leave is a serious contempt.[12]

7 Harmful publications

Publication of information about wardship[13] proceedings, heard[14] in private,[15] constitutes contempt of court, unless publication is with the leave of the court. However there is no restriction on publication of other information about the ward himself[16] unless such is specifically restrained.[17]

Where leave is sought to use information which forms part of the proceedings[18] the interest of the ward[19] is the first and most important consideration,[20] and a judge may, in the exercise of discretion, grant leave.[1]

In *Re X (a Minor) (Wardship: Jurisdiction)*[2] a 14-year-old girl was made a ward of court for the sole purpose of preventing publication of a book, ready for publication, which contained passages in one chapter, describing alleged aberrant private activities and sexual predelictions of the ward's deceased father. Although publication was restrained at first instance[3] the Court of Appeal[4] discharged the injunction on the ground that the court must hold a proper balance between protection of the ward and the free right of publication enjoyed by outside parties,[5] and hesitate long before interfering with that free right[6] but might do so in an exceptional case.[7]

Exceptional circumstances were found in *X County Council v A*[8] to enable the court to restrain a newspaper from publishing the identity of a ward,[9] her mother or father because, on the evidence, publication of their

10 A ward may not marry without the leave of the court. *Eyre v Countess of Shaftesbury* (1725) 2 P Wms 102. The restraint is automatic on the institution of proceedings.
11 *Smith v Smith* (1745) 3 Atk 304. The injunction may be granted against the other party to the proposed marriage or his parents. *Lord Raymond's Case* (1734) Cas temp Talb 58.
12 *Re H's Settlement, H v H* [1909] 2 Ch 260, 78LJ ch 745.
13 Also adoption, guardianship and custody proceedings. See the Administration of Justice Act 1960, s 12(1)(a) (11 *Halsbury's Statutes* (4th edn) 174 CONTEMPT OF COURT) and see Appendix 1.
14 This does not merely refer to the oral evidence but includes affidavit evidence and confidential reports. *Re F (otherwise A) (a Minor) (Publication of Information)* [1977] Fam 58, [1977] 1 All ER 114, CA.
15 It is the practice of the court in such proceedings to sit in chambers.
16 *Re F (otherwise A) (a Minor) (Publication of Information)*, above. The existence of wardship does not give a ward a privilege over and above other young people who are not wards; per Lord Denning MR. The effect of the Administraton of Justice Act 1960, s 12(4) is that a ward enjoys no greater protection against unwelcome publicity than other children; per Scarman LJ.
17 *X County Council v A* [1985] 1 All ER 53, sub nom *Re X (a Minor (Wardship: Injunction)* [1984] 1 WLR 1422.
18 See note 14 above.
19 Or a child in adoption, guardianship or custody proceedings, see Administration of Justice Act 1960, s 12(1)(a).
20 *Re R (MJ) (a Minor) (Publication of Transcript)* [1975] Fam 89, [1975] 2 All ER 749.
 1 See ch 11, section 2, Confidentiality of discovery and evidence. See also *Practice Direction (Infants: Transcript)* [1972] 1 All ER 1056, [1972] 1 WLR 442.
 2 [1975] Fam 47 and 54, [1975] 1 All ER 697 and 702, Latey J and CA.
 3 [1975] Fam 47, [1975] 1 All ER 697.
 4 [1975] Fam 54, [1975] 1 All ER 702, CA.
 5 Per Sir John Pennycuick at 61 and 706.
 6 Ibid.
 7 Ibid.
 8 [1985] 1 All ER 53, sub nom *Re X (a Minor) (Wardship: Injunction)* [1984] 1 WLR 1422.
 9 Then aged two months.

identities would, by reason of the mother's criminal past, be very likely to disturb the fragile stability which she had achieved and that would rebound on the ward's welfare.[10] It is probably significant that the wardship was not instituted for the purpose of preventing publication. The injunction was not a complete ban on publishing facts about the ward's mother but only facts which disclosed her identity or whereabouts, thereby revealing the identity and whereabouts of the ward.[11] Such an injunction is binding on the world at large[12] although a person who breached it would only be in contempt of court if the breach was committed with knowledge of the injunction.[13]

8 Restraint of change of surname

A custody order, in whatever proceedings, does not entitle the custodial parent unilaterally to change the child's surname.[14] A custody order[15] in a matrimonial cause[16] contains a provision expressly restricting the change of surname of a child named in the order without the leave of the court or the written consent of the other parent.[17]

As change of surname is an important matter for a minor[18] it would be contempt of court for the surname of a ward to be changed without the leave of the court. The court in wardship must be consulted about every important decision about the future of a ward.[19]

Change of surname of a minor is generally effected by the custodial parent (or the minor if over 16) executing a deed poll which can then be enrolled in the Central Office of the Supreme Court.[20] However, informal changes of surname may take place whereby for example the child is known by a different surname only at school. It is to be emphasised that no change (formal or informal) may take place without the leave of the court or the consent of the other parent, as appropriate.

On an application to change a surname the court should regard the child's welfare as first and paramount and consider the issue as important.[1]

An actual or threatened change of surname may be restrained by injunction, although the ultimate sanction of committal for breach would be used sparingly.[2] A court might be very reluctant to refuse an application for change of surname after a long period of unauthorised use.

---

10 Ibid at 57 and 1427.
11 Following the balancing exercise, as required by *Re X (a Minor) (Wardship: Jurisdiction)* above, between the protection of the ward and the rights of free publication by outside parties.
12 *X County Council v A*, sub nom *Re X (a Minor) (Wardship: Injunction)*, above. See also *Scott v Scott* [1913] AC 417, 82 LTP 74, HL.
13 *X County Council v A*, sub nom *Re X (a Minor) (Wardship: Injunction)* above at 56 and 1426.
14 *Y v Y (Child: surname)* [1973] Fam 147, [1973] 2 All ER 574.
15 For a precedent see Appendix 4.
16 But not in guardianship or other proceedings.
17 Matrimonial Causes Rules 1977 (SI 1977/344), r 92(8). The restriction only applies while the child is under the age of 18 except a girl may change her surname if she marries under that age.
18 *W v A (Minor: surname)* [1981] Fam 14, [1981] 1 All ER 100, CA.
19 *Surrey County Council v W* (1982) 3 FLR 167, 12 Fam Law 91, CA.
20 See RSC Ord 63 r 10 and see *Practice Direction (Minor: Change of Surname)* [1977] 3 All ER 451, [1977] 1 WLR 1065; see Appendix 2.
 1 *W v A (Minor: surname)*, above.
 2 See *R v R* (1979) 10 Fam Law 56, CA.

Chapter 8
Trespass and assault

In general, where an injunction is sought in the matrimonial or domestic context it is not necessary to bring an action relying on the torts of trespass or assault unless the parties have never been married *and* do not come within the meaning of the phrase 'living with each other in the same household as husband and wife'.[1]

1 Trespass

A trespass is an unlawful entry by one person on land in the lawful possession[2] of another.[3] An action will lie even if no damage is done.[4] A landowner, whose title is not in issue, is prima facie entitled to an interlocutory injunction restraining trespass, even where no damage has been done.[5] Examples of trespass range from setting foot on land to taking possession of it[6] and would include one tenant in common excluding the other.[7]

2 Assault

An assault is the intentional use of force or violence to another. It is also an assault for one person to threaten another with violence if the person making the threat is immediately able to carry out the threat. The threat must be accompanied by intent to use violence or the person threatened must actually fear violence.[8]

A battery is any act which directly and either intentionally or negligently causes some physical contact with the victim without consent.[9] An action for assault or battery may be brought without proof of damage.

A conviction for common assault[10] or the dismissal of such a complaint may be a bar to civil proceedings for the same cause.[11]

---

1 See further ch 1, section G, above.
2 Ie in possession by virtue of being the freehold or leasehold owner, or the tenant at the time of the trespass. See further 45 *Halsbury's Laws* (4th edn) para 1396 TORT.
3 45 *Halsbury's Laws* (4th edn) para 1384 TORT.
4 Ibid.
5 *Patel v WH Smith (Eziot) Ltd* [1987] 2 All ER 569, [1987] 1 WLR 853, CA.
6 45 *Halsbury's Laws* (4th edn) para 1384 TORT.
7 Ibid and see *Dennis v McDonald* [1982] Fam 63, [1981] 2 All ER 632, Purchas J, and [1982] Fam 63, [1982] 1 All ER 590, CA.
8 45 *Halsbury's Laws* (4th edn) para 1310 TORT.
9 45 *Halsbury's Laws* (4th edn) para 1311 TORT.
10 Under Offences Against the Person Act 1861, s 42. (12 *Halsbury's Statutes* (4th edn) 115 CRIMINAL LAW.)
11 Offences Against the Person Act 1861, s 45. (12 *Halsbury's Statutes* (4th edn) 118 CRIMINAL LAW.)

An action for assault or battery will fail if the defendant shows that he was acting in self defence or that he was defending his land or chattels against a threatened or actual trespass provided in each case he used no more force than was reasonably necessary.[12]

3 Procedure

The action should be commenced in the county court[13] for the district in which the defendant resides or in which the cause of action arose.[14] The action is a default action[15] and is commenced by filing a request for issue of a summons together with particulars of claim[16] which will seek damages[17] and also permanent injunctions. As permanent injunctions will only be granted at the trial[18] of the action it is necessary, in order to give more immediate protection to the plaintiff, to apply for interlocutory injunctions in the same terms as the permanent injunctions sought.

Application for such interlocutory injunctions is made by notice of application[19] unless made ex parte. It is not strictly necessary for the application to be supported by an affidavit[20] but in practice the application should be supported by affidavit served personally,[1] at least two days before the hearing.[2]

Where the application is one of urgency it may be made ex parte on affidavit[3] and before the issue of the summons.[4] It may be that a plaintiff should give the usual undertaking as to damages, as a condition of being granted an injunction, even though the injunction sought would regulate personal conduct.[5]

In order to decide whether or not to grant an injunction the court must consider whether there is a serious issue to be tried and, if there is, will then decide whether an interlocutory injunction is appropriate on the balance of convenience[6] or more properly the balance of justice.[7]

12 45 *Halsbury's Laws* (4th edn) paras 1317 and 1318 TORT.
13 Unless there is any special reason for commencing the proceedings in the High Court as where the damages claimed exceed the county court limit as defined by County Courts Act 1984, s 147 (11 *Halsbury's Statutes* (4th edn) COUNTY COURTS). The limit is currently £5,000 in tort, County Courts Jurisdiction Order 1981 (SI 1981/1123). See also County Courts Act 1984, s 22 (injunctions and declarations relating to land) which applies where the rateable value does not exceed £1,000; ibid, ss 22(2) and 147.
14 CCR Ord 4, r 2(1).
15 CCR Ord 3, r 2(2).
16 CCR Ord 3, r 3(1) for a precedent of particulars of claim see Appendix 4 below.
17 In some circumstances relating to land it is not obligatory to claim damages. County Courts Act 1984, s 22 and see below.
18 Before the trial can take place various procedural steps must be carried out. It is not possible in a work of this size to include all such procedure in an action. It has been assumed that the reader will have at least a basic knowledge of county court procedure. See generally *County Court Practice* 1987 and *Atkin's Encyclopedia of Court Forms in Civil Proceedings*.
19 CCR Ord 13, rr 1, 6. For a precedent see Appendix 4 below.
20 CCR Ord 13, rr 1, 6.
 1 This is to prove service in case the defendant does not attend the hearing. An affidavit of service should be sworn; see further ch 2 above.
 2 CCR Ord 13, r 1(2).
 3 CCR Ord 13, r 6(3).
 4 CCR Ord 13, r 6(4) see further ch 2 above.
 5 *Practice Direction* [1974] 2 All ER 400, [1974] 1 WLR 576 does not extend to civil proceedings. The Practice varies widely between individual county courts.
 6 *American Cyanamid Co v Ethicon Ltd* [1975] AC 396, [1975] 1 All ER 504, HL.
 7 *Francome v Mirror Group Newspapers Ltd* [1984] 2 All ER 408, [1984] 1 WLR 892, CA at 413 h and 898 F-G, per Sir John Donaldson MR.

Whether or not an interlocutory injunction is granted it is necessary to continue the action to trial in order for the court to determine if the plaintiff is entitled to the permanent injunctions and damages.[8] A plaintiff who obtains an interlocutory injunction and then does not proceed with the action may have to resist an application that the action dismissed for want of prosecution,[9] or be faced with an application by the defendant to discharge the injunction. The practice in the Queen's Bench and Chancery Divisions of the High Court whereby the parties may consent to the hearing of an application for an injunction being treated as the hearing of the action is followed in some county courts but not in others. It would seem that, where no objection is made by either of the parties, such practice is appropriate[10] as the saving of time and costs[11] can be considerable.

Injunctions restraining trespass and assault are by no means confined in the domestic context, to quasi-matrimonial relationships but may also be employed between parent and child[12] or vice versa. It should be noted that a court may order that a person be deprived of his right to live in or to visit his own home, if that be the only way to protect his neighbour from frequent and repetitive acts of nuisance.[13]

There is no tort of harassment in law[14] and consequently no common law power[15] to restrain by injunction, a party entering an 'exclusion area' around a specified property.[16] Merely approaching premises cannot give rise to a cause of action and therefore cannot be restrained by an injunction at common law because it cannot constitute an actual or reasonably anticipated tort.[17]

---

8 Often it appears that while legal aid is available for an application for an interlocutory injunction the scope of the certificate prevents continuance of the action to trial; furthermore it seems that the legal aid authorities are very reluctant to extend certificates to bring such an action to trial.

9 CCR Ord 13, r 2(1).

10 The county court has the same jurisdiction to grant an injunction in respect of land as the High Court, County Courts Act 1984, s 22. Thus it is not necessary to claim damages as well. Where the action is brought for (or includes) assault there must be a claim for damages in the particulars of claim. A claim for nominal damages is sufficient to give the county court jurisdiction where the real relief sought is an injunction, provided the claim for damages is bona fide. *Hatt & Co (Bath) Ltd v Pearce* [1978] 2 All ER 474, [1978] 1 WLR 885, CA.

11 Often to the legal aid fund.

12 *Egan v Egan* [1975] Ch 218, [1975] 2 All ER 167, Oliver J.

13 *Liburd v Cork* (1981) Times, 4 April.

14 *Patel v Patel* (1987) Times 21 August, CA.

15 But see Domestic Violence and Matrimonial Proceedings Act 1976; s 1(1)(c) (27 *Halsbury's Statutes* (4th edn) 788 MATRIMONIAL LAW).

16 *Patel v Patel* above.

17 Ibid.

Chapter 9
Judicial proceedings

1 Restraint of foreign proceedings

An injunction ordering a party to take, or to omit to take, a step, or steps, in proceedings in a foreign court is directed to the party, not to the foreign court.[1]

Although the court has jurisdiction to restrain a party to a matrimonial cause[2] from instituting, or continuing, similar proceedings in a foreign country[3] it will not do so as a matter of course[4] but only if the institution, or continuance, of the foreign suit would be oppressive or vexatious so as to cause serious, if not irreparable, damage to the applicant.[5] It is a jurisdiction to be exercised with great caution[6] because such an injunction indirectly affects the foreign court.[7]

The jurisdiction to restrain a party from instituting or from continuing foreign proceedings is to be exercised when the 'ends of justice' require it.[8] An injunction will only be granted where the party restrained is amenable to the jurisdiction of the court, and therefore against whom an injunction would prove to be an effective remedy.[9]

The principles governing the exercise of the court's discretion to grant an injunction restraining foreign proceedings are not the same as those in relation to the staying of proceedings commenced within the jurisdiction on the ground of *forum non conveniens*.[10]

1 *Lord Portarlington v Soulby* (1834) 3 My & K 104, *Bushby v Munday* (1821) 5 Madd 297, and see *Ellerman Lines Ltd v Read* [1928] 2 KB 144, CA where the earlier authorities are reviewed.
2 'Matrimonial cause' means an action for divorce, nullity of marriage or judical separation. Matrimonial and Family Proceedings Act 1984, s 32 (27 *Halsbury's Statutes* (4th edn) 869 MATRIMONIAL LAW), as amended by Family Law Act 1986, Sch 1, para 28.
3 *Orr-Lewis v Orr-Lewis* [1949] P 347, [1949] 1 All ER 504, based on *Cohen v Rothfield* [1919] 1 KB 410, CA.
4 *Vardopulo v Vardopulo* (1909) 25 TLR 518, CA.
5 *Orr-Lewis v Orr-Lewis*, above.
6 Ibid and *Ellerman Lines Ltd v Read*, above.
7 *Société Nationale Industrielle Aerospatiale v Lee Kui Jak* [1987] 3 WLR 59, PC.
8 Ibid.
9 Ibid and see *The Siskina* [1979] AC 210 at 256, [1977] 3 All ER 803 at 824 HL, per Lord Diplock; see the quotation at page ii above.
10 *Société Nationale Industrielle Aerospatiale v Lee Kui Jak* above. For the staying of proceedings on the ground of *forum non conveniens* see *Castanho v Brown and Root (UK) Ltd* [1981] AC 557, [1981] 1 All ER 143, HL; *MacShannon v Rockware Glass* [1978] AC 795, [1978] 1 All ER 625, HL; and *Spiliada Maritime Corpn v Cansulex Ltd* [1986] 3 All ER 843, [1986] 3 WLR 972, HL.

The Domicile and Matrimonial Proceedings Act 1973[11] provides for the staying of proceedings[12] commenced in England or Wales where there are proceedings in foreign countries.[13] Where the proceedings are in a related jurisdiction[14] the stay will be obligatory;[15] where the proceedings are in another jurisdiction[16] the stay will be discretionary.[17] Such discretion is to be exercised in favour of a stay if the balance of fairness (including convenience) as between the parties to the marriage is such that it is appropriate for the proceedings in another jurisdiction to be disposed of before further steps are taken in the proceedings within the jurisdiction.[18] It is outside the scope of this work to deal comprehensively with the law and practice relating to the staying of matrimonial proceedings.[19]

Where the courts of another country clearly provide the appropriate forum to resolve a matrimonial dispute English proceedings in respect of the marriage should be stayed where it is not unfair to confine the parties to their rights and obligations as regards maintenance under that foreign law.[20]

In *Thyssen-Bornemisza v Thyssen-Bornemisza*[1] the judge, at first instance, having refused the application of the wife to stay the husband's cross-petition, restrained her, by injunction, from taking any step in the foreign proceedings.[2] Apart from delay and expense in having two sets of concurrent proceedings in different countries there does not seem to have been any suggestion that the continuance of the foreign suit would have been oppressive or vexatious, or that any serious, let alone irreparable damage would have been caused to the husband.[3] Unfortunately, the

---

11 27 *Halsbury's Statutes* (4th edn) 777 MATRIMONIAL LAW.

12 The Domicile and Matrimonial Proceedings Act 1973, s 5(6) and Sch 1, para 2, defines 'matrimonial proceedings' as proceedings for divorce, judicial separation, nullity of marriage, a declaration as to the validity of the marriage of the petitioner and a declaration as to the subsistence of such marriage.

13 Ibid, s 5(6) and Sch 1, paras 8 and 9.

14 Ibid, Sch 1, para 3(2) 'related jurisdiction' means Scotland, Northern Ireland, Jersey, Guernsey and the Isle of Man (the reference to Guernsey being treated as including Alderney and Sark).

15 Ibid, Sch 1, para 8.

16 Ibid, Sch 1, para 3(1), 'another jurisdiction' means any country outside England and Wales.

17 Ibid, Sch 1, para 9.

18 Ibid, Sch 1, para 9(1)(b). In considering the balance of fairness and convenience the court must have regard to all factors appearing to be relevant, including the convenience of witnesses and any delay or expense which may result from the proceedings being stayed, or not being stayed. Ibid, Sch 1, para 9 (2).

19 For a full analysis of the law and practice see *Rayden on Divorce* (14th edn) ch 3, section IV.

20 *De Dampierre v de Dampierre* [1987] 2 All ER 1, [1987] 2 WLR 1006, HL. This is so even where the petitioner has a clear legitimate personal or juridicial advantage in England; such advantage cannot be decisive. It might be unfair to stay English proceedings where orders for ancillary relief would be enforced against assets in England or Wales, or where the petitioner remained within the jurisdiction. Ibid.

1 [1985] FLR 670 Eastham J, affirmed on different grounds [1986] Fam 1, [1985] 1 All ER 328, CA.

2 The precise terms were that she was restrained 'from taking any step in any proceedings in respect of or arising out of the marriage (save in the English proceedings) either in Switzerland or elsewhere without the leave of the court'.

3 See *Orr-Lewis v Orr-Lewis* above. It seems that the injunction was thought to be a natural consequence of the refusal of the stay even though the wife had a clear personal or juridical advantage in the Swiss proceedings.

precise reasons for the grant of the injunction do not appear in the judgment.[4]

2 Restraint of domestic proceedings

Although it is possible to restrain the institution of proceedings in the High Court, by injunction,[5] once commenced proceedings in the High Court and the Court of Appeal can not be restrained by injunction.[6] The institution and continuance of proceedings in county courts may be restrained.

An injunction may be granted, as interlocutory relief, in a matrimonial cause, to restrain the institution or continuance of proceedings where such proceedings would cause the applicant to suffer irreparable harm.[7]

While a separation deed[8] does not prevent either party from petitioning for divorce[9] or judicial separation[10] the institution of proceedings may be a breach of a non-molestation clause if the purpose is to annoy the respondent rather than to obtain relief[11] and might be restrained by injunction.[12]

Where there are concurrent proceedings in different courts[13] between parties who for practical purposes are the same in each, and the same issue will have to be determined in each, the court has jurisdiction to stay one set of proceedings if it is just and convenient to do so or if the circumstances are such that one set of proceedings is vexatious and an abuse of the process of the court.[14]

A court is not bound to stay proceedings under the Married Women's Property Act 1882[15] where divorce proceedings are pending[16] but has a discretion to do so.[17] Likewise where there are concurrent proceedings

---

4 In *K v K* [1986] 2 FLR 411, [1986] Fam Law 329, Hollis J, having refused the husband's application for a discretionary stay, refused the wife's oral application for an injunction to restrain the husband from taking any steps in the Dutch divorce proceedings as there was no formal application, the merits of such an application were not considered.

5 *Besant* v *Wood* (1879) 12 Ch D 605 at 630.

6 Supreme Court of Judicature (Consolidation) Act 1925, s 41, repealed by Supreme Court Act 1981, s 152(4) and Sch 7 (11 *Halsbury's Statutes* (4th edn) 756 COURTS), but the effect is retained by ibid ss 19 and 49.

7 *Murcutt v Murcutt* [1952] P 266, [1952] 2 All ER 427, Willmer J, where the court refused to restrain a husband from proceeding with an action to evict the adult children of the family from the matrimonial home; the position might be different if the children were children to whom the Matrimonial Causes Act 1973, s 41 (27 *Halsbury's Statutes* (4th edn 700 MATRIMONIAL LAW) applied.

8 See ch 11, section 4, below.

9 *Yeatman v Yeatman and Rummell* (1870) 21 LT 733.

10 *Brown v Brown and Shelton* (1874) LR 3 P & D 202; doubted in *Besant* v *Wood* above.

11 *Hunt v Hunt* [1897] 2 QB 547, CA (divorce); see also *Thomas v Everard* (1861) 6 H & N 448 (judicial separation); *Welch v Welch* (1916) 85 LJP 188, CA (proceedings in the magistrates' court for maintenance).

12 *Besant v Wood* above.

13 Or, it is submitted, in the same court.

14 *Imperial Tobacco Ltd v A-G* [1981] AC 718, [1980] 1 All ER 866, HL.

15 27 *Halsbury's Statutes* (4th edn) 566 MATRIMONIAL LAW.

16 *Hickson v Hickson* [1953] 1 QB 420, [1953] 1 All ER 382, CA.

17 *Short v Short* [1960] 3 All ER 6, [1960] 1 WLR 833, CA. Unless there are particular circumstances which justify an application under the Married Women's Property Act 1882, s 17, all financial issues should be dealt with in the matrimonial cause on the application for ancillary relief. *Fielding v Fielding* [1978] 1 All ER 267, [1977] 1 WLR 1146n, CA.

between spouses for divorce[18] in the High Court or county court and under the Domestic Proceedings and Magistrates' Courts Act 1978[19] for maintenance and/or custody the magistrates' court will usually adjourn the application to allow the proceedings in the superior court to be determined[20] but where there are urgent matters of custody or maintenance an interim order may be made.[1]

It is submitted that where there are concurrent proceedings in respect of molestation or occupation of the matrimonial home in both the High Court or county court[2] and the magistrates' court,[3] that the magistrates' court should, in general, allow the matter to be heard by the High Court or county court, subject to granting relief in cases of urgency. The reason is that the powers of the High Court and county court are wider.[4] A refusal of relief in the magistrates' court does not fetter the grant of relief in the High Court or county court[5] and the High Court and county court may in some circumstances direct that an order of the magistrates' court cease to have effect.[6]

3 Restraint of applications within proceedings

There is jurisdiction in wardship proceedings to invoke the very wide powers[7] of the court to protect children, and consequently those looking after them, to restrain a party from making an application without leave.[8] There is no jurisdiction to make a blanket prohibition on applications.[9] An injunction restraining a party from making an application without leave is quite separate from the power of the courts concerning vexatious litigants.[10]

On an application for leave to make an application the test is probably for the court to consider whether or not the proposed application is likely to succeed.[11]

---

18 Or judicial separation or nullity.
19 27 *Halsbury's Statutes* (4th edn) 791 MATRIMONIAL LAW.
20 *Kaye v Kaye* [1965] P 100, [1964] 1 All ER 620.
 1 Under Domestic Proceedings and Magistrates' Courts Act 1978; *Lanitis v Lanitis* [1970] 1 All ER 466, [1970] 1 WLR 503; and see *Jones v Jones* [1974] 3 All ER 702, [1974] WLR 1471, CA.
 2 Under the Matrimonial Homes Act 1983 (27 *Halsbury's Statutes* (4th edn) 585 MATRIMONIAL LAW) or the Domestic Violence and Matrimonial Proceedings Act 1976 (27 *Halsbury's Statutes* (4th edn) 788 MATRIMONIAL LAW).
 3 Under the Domestic Proceedings and Magistrates' Courts Act 1978, s 16, 17 and 18.
 4 *Horner v Horner* [1982] Fam 90, [1982] 2 All ER 495, CA.
 5 *O'Brien v O'Brien* [1985] FLR 801, [1985] Fam Law 191, CA.
 6 Domestic Proceedings and Magistrates' Courts Act 1978, s 28(2). See also RSC Ord 90, r 31 and CCR Ord, 47 r 9.
 7 The scope of the powers of the court in the wardship jurisdiction were considered in *Re X (a minor) (Wardship: Restriction on Publication)* [1975] Fam 54, [1975] 1 All ER 702, CA. See also ch 1 section B 5 above.
 8 *Re P (Wardship: Prohibition on Applications)* (1982) 3 FLR 420, CA.
 9 Ibid.
10 See Supreme Court Act 1981, s 42 (11 *Halsbury's Statutes* (4th edn) 756 COURTS).
11 *F v S* [1973] Fam 203, [1973] 1 All ER 722, CA.

Chapter 10
Preservation of assets

1 Matrimonial Causes Act 1973

The court has very wide powers to grant an injunction to restrain a person against whom proceedings for financial relief[1] are brought from disposing of his assets for the purpose of defeating or restricting the claim. Those powers, which are granted to the court by section 37 of the Matrimonial Causes Act 1973 also extend to setting aside dispositions which have already been made. The latter powers are not within the scope of this book.[2]

There are three prerequisites to the court exercising its power to grant an injunction under this section. First, an application for financial relief must have been made by one party against another.[3] If the person seeking the injunction has filed a petition or answer it is sufficient that such pleading includes a prayer for the form of financial relief which it is sought to protect.[4] If no pleading has been filed application in the prescribed form must have been made.[5]

Second, the court must be satisfied[6] that the person against whom the proceedings for financial relief are brought is about to make a disposition, transfer assets out of the jurisdiction or otherwise deal with his assets.[7] It is sufficient to show that such person is, for instance, about to charge assets in his possession. A disposition by will is, however, expressly excluded from the ambit of the section.[8]

Third, the court must be satisfied that such disposition is intended[9] to

---

1 S 37(1) defines 'financial relief' as meaning relief under ibid, ss 22, 23, 24, 27, 31 (except sub-s (6)) and 35. Proceedings under Matrimonial Causes Act 1973, s 27, failure to provide reasonable maintenance, the court has limited jurisdiction to make orders for custody: ibid, s 47(2); but there is no jurisdiction to grant injunctions restraining molestaton or regulating the occupation of the matrimonial home: *Des Salles d'Epinoix v Des Salles d'Epinoix* [1967] 2 All ER 539. [1967] 1 WLR 553, CA.

2 For avoidance of dispositions see *Jackson's Matrimonial Finance and Taxation* (4th edn), ch 17.

3 Matrimonial Causes Act 1973, s 37(2).

4 *Jackson v Jackson* [1973] Fam 99, [1973] 2 All ER 395.

5 Form 11, Appendix 1, Matrimonial Causes Rules 1977 (SI 1977/344); see also r 68(2), (3).

6 *Smith v Smith* (1973) 117 Sol Jo 525. Whether or not a dealing is about to take place is a question of fact proof of which is on the civil standard, namely a preponderance of probability: *K v K* (1983) 4 FLR 31, 12 Fam Law 143, CA. The statute uses the word 'satisfied' therefore the standard of proof where fraud is alleged is inappropriate. Ibid.

7 Matrimonial Causes Act 1973, s 37(2).

8 Matrimonial Causes Act 1973, s 37(6).

9 Absence of direct purpose, malignant design or spite does not rebut the presumption. *Jordan v Jordan (Jordan intervening)*(1965) 109 Sol Jo 353.

defeat or reduce the claim[10] for financial relief.[11] Where the statutory criteria are not fulfilled there may be power to freeze an asset by reference to the inherent jurisdiction.[12]

Where a disposition or other dealing is about to take place, and the court is satisfied[13] that if the same took place it would have the effect of defeating[14] the claim then there is a rebuttable[15] presumption that the disposition was intended to have that consequence.[16] Dispositions or dealings in the ordinary course of business will not, therefore, normally be restrained.[17] Further, if the person against whom the proceedings are brought will, after the disposition is made, still have more than sufficient assets to meet the claim an injunction is unlikely to be granted. A disposition for valuable consideration to a person who acted in good faith and without notice of the claim for financial relief will not be set aside although it may be restrained if it has not yet taken place.[18] The court may make any order it thinks fit to restrain the person against whom the proceedings are brought from carrying out his intentions and to protect the claim.[19] So, for example, orders may be made preventing a sale; freezing bank and other accounts; requiring monies to be held in the names of solicitors and generally restraining a person from dealing with his assets.

The application is made ex parte in the first instance since otherwise the assets may be beyond the jurisdiction of the court by the time the matter is heard, and should be made to the registrar.[20] It must be supported by affidavit. Such affidavit must give details of the applicant's claim for ancillary relief. It may be possible merely to refer to an affidavit, already sworn, in support of the application for ancillary relief.[1] Where the applicant has not yet sworn an affidavit in ancillary relief proceedings details should be given of the likely claim, identifying the respondent's assets; such as property in respect of which a transfer is sought, or the funds out of which a lump sum is sought. The applicant should give particulars of his contribution to the family assets. A respondent to an application for ancillary relief is under a duty to file an

---

10 Or that such would frustrate or impede the enforcement of any order made on the claim. Matrimonial Causes Act 1973, s 37(1).
11 *Quartermain v Quartermain* (1974) 4 Fam Law 156. For the standard of proof see *K v K* above.
12 *Roche v Roche* (1981) 11 Fam Law 243, CA where the judge had purported to freeze an asset under the Matrimonial Causes Act 1973, s 37, although he made no finding as to the respondent's intentions and on the facts no dealing could have been about to take place. The Court of Appeal upheld the order by reference to the inherent jurisdiction saying that the freeze would not cause the respondent hardship and the more he protested and refused to give an undertaking the more anxious the court would be.
13 See *K v K*, above; 'satisfied' means on a balance of probability.
14 'Defeating' a claim for financial relief means preventing financial relief from being granted to the applicant for the benefit of a child of the family; or reducing the amount of financial relief which might be granted, or frustrating or impeding the enforcement of any order which might be or has been made. Matrimonial Causes Act 1973, s 37(1).
15 See *Jordan v Jordan, (Jordan intervening)*, above.
16 Matrimonial Causes Act 1973, s 37(1).
17 *A v C (No 2)* [1981] QB 961, [1981] 2 All ER 126.
18 Matrimonial Causes Act 1973, s 37(4).
19 Ibid s 37(2)(a).
20 Matrimonial Causes Rules 1977, r 84.
 1 See Matrimonial Causes Rules 1977 (SI 1977/344) r 73(2).

affidavit of means;[2] therefore the full extent of the applicant's claim may not become clear until the evidence has been filed or in some cases until discovery[3] has taken place.

The affidavit should identify all bank, building society and other accounts to be frozen. In many cases it will be possible to give the actual account number as well as the branch name. If the branch or account is not known the applicant may require the bank or other institution to search all of its branches to trace the respondent's assets.[4] The affidavit[5] must disclose all relevant matters fully and frankly.[6] Failure to give the court all relevant matters may disentitle the applicant to the relief sought.[7]

An applicant will normally be required to give an undertaking as to damages. Such is an undertaking to pay any damages suffered by the respondent by reason of the order if, on full investigation, it appears that the injunction ought not to have been granted and that damages should be paid.[8]

The court may, on the application, make such order as it thinks fit restraining the respondent from disposing[9] of his assets or otherwise for protecting the claim.[10] On an ex parte application it may be appropriate to freeze all the respondent's capital assets; but, when the matter is heard inter partes the amount of the respondent's assets to be frozen can be determined by balancing the potential claim of the applicant against the potential, or actual, hardship to the respondent. On the breakdown of many marriages there is not enough money to go round and, while the court should avoid over-protection of the applicant it should also avoid allowing the disposal of capital which would have the effect of tying the same up in such a manner that would not leave sufficient free capital to make a reasonable order for a lump sum; or that could impede the court in making an order for ancillary relief in accordance with the statutory criteria.[11]

The court may make an order restraining dealings with assets outside the jurisdiction[12] although it would not exercise its jurisdiction to do so where there is an order in respect of foreign property, where the same could not be

2 An affidavit must contain full particulars of the deponent's property and income. See ibid, r 73(3).
3 Discovery frequently takes place pursuant to the provisions of ibid, r 77(4) under which a party may require the other to give further information on any matter contained in an affidavit or any other relevant matter; and may require a list of documents or inspection of documents.
4 *Z Ltd v A – Z and AA-LL* [1982] QB 558, [1982] 1 All ER 556, CA. If such a search is required the applicant must undertake to pay the costs of the same *Z Ltd v A* above per Lord Denning MR. In 1982 such a search could cost £2,000 in respect of every branch of one of the clearing banks, and could cost even more today. In only a few cases will the cost of such a search be justified.
5 For a precedent, see Appendix 4 below.
6 *Third Chandris Corp v Unimarine SA* [1979] QB 645, [1979] 2 All ER 972.
7 *R v Kensington Income Tax General Comrs, ex parte Princess Edmond de Polignac* [1917] 1 KB 486, CA.
8 See *Practice Direction (Injunction: Undertaking as to damages)* [1974] 2 All ER 400, [1974] 1 WLR 576; see Appendix 2 below. While the Practice Direction suggests that an undertaking is more to be required where a claim of a proprietary right is made than where the application is in connection with a discretionary order such as a transfer of property order. However, the court may well require an undertaking as to damages where the potential consequences of a freezing order are drastic. See *Z Ltd v A* above.
9 Or transferring out of the jurisdiction or otherwise dealing with; for a precedent of an order see Appendix 4, below.
10 Matrimonial Causes Act 1973, s 37(2)(a).
11 Ibid, s 25.
12 *Hamlin v Hamlin* [1986] Fam 11, [1985] 2 All ER 1037, CA.

enforced.[13] Service pay, grants and pensions have a special statutory status[14] and a court may not make an order under Matrimonial Causes Act 1973 to prevent a serviceman from receiving such entitlement.[15] It may be that once the serviceman has received his pay etc it loses its protected status and the court may then make an order in respect of cash[16] that represents the pay, grant or pension.

When freezing a cash sum or fund due to the respondent the court may direct that the respondent pay the same into an account in the joint names of the parties' solicitors.[17] It is unclear whether there is power to require a sum to be paid into court.[18]

Whilst it may be necessary to join third parties to the application if a specific direction as to the payment of monies is sought as, for instance, sums due to the person against whom the proceedings are brought under a contract with a third party, joinder is not necessary if all that is required is that a bank account be frozen. Once the bank has notice of the injunction it will be guilty of contempt if it aids or abets a breach.[19]

2 Mareva injunction

The Mareva injunction[20] is an interlocutory order which restrains the respondent from removing from the jurisdiction or otherwise dealing with,[1] in whole or in part, his assets within the jurisdiction. An order will not be made in respect of assets outside the jurisdiction.[2] An order may be made against a person who is domiciled, resident or present within the jurisdiction[3] as well as against a party who is not so domiciled, resident or present.[4]

A Mareva injunction will only be granted where it appears likely that the applicant will obtain judgment[5] against the respondent for a certain or approximate amount and, that while the respondent has assets, within the jurisdiction, sufficient to meet the likely judgment, in whole or in part, there is reason to believe that he may well take steps to attempt to see that such assets are not available or traceable at the time of judgment.[6]

13 Ibid.
14 Army Act 1955, s 203; Air Force Act 1955, s 203; see also Naval and Marine Pay and Pensions Act 1865, s 4.
15 *Walker v Walker* [1983] Fam 68, [1983] 2 All ER 909, CA. See also *Ransom* v *Ransom* (1987) Times 12 August, CA.
16 Or funds in an account.
17 *Roche v Roche* (1981) 11 Fam Law 243, CA.
18 *Walker v Walker*, above.
19 *Acrow (Automation) Ltd v Rex Chainbelt Inc* [1971] 3 All ER 1175, [1971] 1 WLR 1676, CA See also ch 11 section 11, below. See also *Seaward v Paterson* [1897] 1 Ch 545, CA. and *Thorne RDC v Bunting (No 2)* [1972] 3 All ER 1084, CA. It may be that the order operates in rem; see *Z Ltd v A* above.
20 So called after *Mareva Cia Naviera SA v International Bulkcarriers SA* [1980] 1 All ER 213n, [1975] 2 Lloyds Rep 509, CA.
 1 The words '. . . or otherwise dealing with . . .' are not to be construed *ejusdem generis* with the words '. . . remove out of the jurisdiction . . .' *Z Ltd v A – Z and AA – LL* [1982] QB 558, [1982] 1 All ER 556, CA.
 2 *The Bhoja Trader* [1981] 2 Lloyds Rep 256, CA. See however *Hamlin v Hamlin* [1986] Fam 11, [1985] 2 All ER 1037, CA on an application under Matrimonial Causes Act 1973 (27 *Halsbury's Statutes* (4th edn) 700 Matrimonial Law), s 37(2)(a) an order may be made in respect of property outside the jurisdiction; see section 1 above.
 3 Supreme Court Act 1981 (11 *Halsbury's Statutes* (4th edn) 756 COURTS). Originally a Mareva injunction could only be granted against a foreign based defendant.
 4 Ibid. Clarifying doubts expressed in *The Agrabele* [1979] 2 Lloyd's Rep 117.
 5 In the matrimonial context 'judgment' would include an order for a lump sum of for transfer of property.
 6 *Z Ltd v A*, above.

An applicant will normally be required to give the usual undertaking as to damages[7] and the court may require security to be given in support of the undertaking; although security may not be required where the applicant is legally aided.[8] It is submitted that security is unlikely to be required in matrimonial cases except where there is need to provide protection for third parties.

An application should be made ex parte in the first instance otherwise if the respondent had notice of the application, assets might be dissipated before the hearing, thus making any order worthless. The application must be supported by an affidavit which must disclose fully and completely all matters which it is relevant for the court to know.[9] Failure by the applicant to make such disclosure may disentitle him to the relief sought.[10] The affidavit must set out the matters in support of the applicant's claim for ancillary relief, and depose to the nature and extent of the respondent's assets.[11] The affidavit must also give particulars of all bank and other accounts which it is sought to freeze.

The order, which operates in rem, takes effect as soon as it is made.[12] A bank must freeze all the respondent's accounts as soon as it receives notice of the injunction. While the applicant may require a bank to search all of its branches to locate the respondent's assets, the bank is entitled to require the applicant to pay for such a search.[13] The effect of freezing a bank account has very serious consequences for the respondent. The bank may not pay any cheque presented, while the order is in force, unless supported by a cheque guarantee card.[14] Likewise credit card transactions must be honoured by the credit card company, who may debit the respondent's account in respect of sums incurred by him.[15] It is submitted that it would be a serious contempt for a respondent, with knowledge of a Mareva injunction, to continue to write cheques supported by a guarantee card or to use a credit card as the result would be that the applicant's protection would be circumvented.

In a proper case the injunction is granted to freeze assets of the respondent to protect the applicant; however the extent of the freeze will only be such as is sufficient to meet the applicant's claim. In the commercial use of the Mareva a plaintiff will be able to quantify the extent of his claim. In matrimonial cases it is frequently difficult to assess the likely extent of the applicant's claim for ancillary relief until there has been discovery.[16] It is submitted that it is often appropriate on an ex parte application to freeze

---

7 Such is an undertaking to pay any damages suffered by the respondent by reason of the order if, on full investigation, it appears that the injunction should not have been granted and that damages should be paid. See also *Practice Direction (Injunction: Undertaking as to Damages)* [1974] 2 All ER 400, [1974] 1 WLR 576; see Appendix 2 below. While the practice direction suggests that an undertaking as to damages should not be required where a claim is made for a discretionary order it is submitted that an order freezing assets is so drastic that the undertaking should be required; see *Z Ltd v A*, above.

8 *Allen v Jambo Holdings Ltd* [1980] 2 All ER 502, [1980] 1 WLR 1252, CA.

9 *Third Chandris Corp v Unimarine SA* [1979] QB 645, [1979] 2 All ER 972, CA.

10 Ibid and see *R v Kensington Income Tax General Comrs, ex p Princess de Polignac* [1917] 1 KB 486.

11 See section 1 above for the contents of the affidavit in support.

12 *Z Ltd v A – Z and AA – LL* [1982] QB 558, [1982] 1 All ER 556, CA.

13 Ibid.

14 Ibid.

15 Ibid.

16 There is a duty on both parties to make full and frank disclosure of all their capital and income. See Matrimonial Causes Rules 1977 (SI 1977/344), rr 73, 75, 98, 100 and 101.

all the respondent's capital assets, until the return date, which should be as soon as possible.[17] It is important that a respondent should not be restrained from spending his income. On the return date the extent (if any) to which the respondent's assets should be frozen can be determined by balancing the applicant's potential claim against the potential hardship to the respondent. A Mareva injunction should not have the effect of preventing the respondent from carrying out a transaction or other dealing in the ordinary course of business.[18]

In deciding the extent to which assets should be frozen pending the hearing of the application for ancillary relief the court should have regard to the likely outcome of such application, although without full discovery it may be difficult to make even a provisional assessment. On the breakdown of many marriages there is frequently not enough money to go round. While the court should avoid over-protection of the applicant it should also avoid allowing the disposal of capital which would have the effect of tying the same up in such a manner that would not leave sufficient free capital to make a reasonable order for a lump sum; or, allowing a disposal which could, impede the court, at the hearing of the application for ancillary relief, from making an order in accordance with the statutory criteria.[19]

3 Anton Piller order

An Anton Piller order[20] is a most exceptional ex parte order which orders the respondent to permit the applicant to enter specified premises occupied by the respondent and to look for, inspect and remove into solicitors' custody, for the purpose of copying, relevant documents;[1] or, to look for, inspect and value or remove for the purpose of valuation, relevant items of value.[2]

The jurisdiction was first invoked in support of an injunction restraining infringement of copyright.[3] Originally, an Anton Piller order was only granted in respect of property which was the subject matter of the action.[4] However, an order may also be made in respect of documents which, although not the subject matter of the proceedings, are sought to be used in evidence in the case.[5] Such an order is, in effect, a summary order for immediate discovery and before making such an order the court should be satisfied that the documents sought are properly the subject of discovery.

A party is under a duty to give discovery of all documents which are or have been in his possession, custody or power relating to all matters in question in the proceedings.[6] In matrimonial cases relating to ancillary

---

17 *Ansah v Ansah* [1977] Fam 138, [1977] 2 All ER 638, CA. Despite some remarks in *Z Ltd v A*, above, it is submitted that in a matrimonial case a return date should always be given.
18 *A v C (No 2)* [1981] QB 961, [1981] 2 All ER 126.
19 Matrimonial Causes Act 1973 (27 *Halsbury's Statutes* (4th edn) 700 Matrimonial Law), ss 25, 25A.
20 So called after *Anton Piller KG v Manufacturing Processes Ltd* [1976] Ch 55, [1976] 1 All ER 779, CA.
 1 *Emanuel v Emanuel* [1982] 2 All ER 342, [1982] 1 WLR 669.
 2 *Kepa v Kepa* (1982) 4 FLR 515.
 3 *EMI Ltd v Pandit* [1975] 1 All ER 418, [1975] 1 WLR 302, approved and followed by *Anton Piller KG v Manufacturing Processes Ltd*, above.
 4 *Kepa v Kepa* above is an example of an Anton Piller order in matrimonial proceedings where the order related to the subject matter of the proceedings.
 5 *Yousif v Salama* [1980] 3 All ER 405, [1980] 1 WLR 1540, CA.
 6 RSC Ord 24, r 1(1), CCR Ord 14, r 1(1).

relief[7] and some similar matters[8] there is a requirement that both parties disclose full particulars of their property and income on affidavit.[9] If a party does not comply an affidavit may be ordered.[10] A party may require discovery on any matter contained in an affidavit, or in respect of any relevant matter.[11] Full and frank disclosure of assets and relevant matters is very important.[12]

There are three essential preconditions to the grant of an Anton Piller order. First, there must be an extremely strong prima facie case.[13] Second, the damage, potential or actual, must be very serious to the applicant.[14] Third, there must be clear evidence that the respondent has in his possession incriminating documents or things, and there must be a real possibility that such might be destroyed (or concealed) before an application inter partes could be made.[15]

It is to be emphasised that such an order is an exceptional remedy.[16] On an application the court must balance the potential harm to the applicant, if an order is not made; against the potential harm to the respondent by infringement of his privacy, if an order is made.[17] Where the potential harm to the applicant is that the court may be unable to make an appropriate order for ancillary relief by not having full knowledge of the respondent's means an order should be made[18] as the potential harm to the applicant is great and long term whereas the potential harm to the respondent is relatively minor.[19]

Full disclosure must be made by the applicant in his affidavit in support of the application of all relevant facts.[20] Failure to make such disclosure will result in the order being discharged, without consideration of the merits.[1] Where a respondent alleges that an applicant has not disclosed material facts the court must decide that question: not whether a judge with all the facts would have come to the same conclusion.[2]

---

7 Defined as (a) an avoidance of disposition order, (b) a financial provision order, (c) an order for maintenance pending suit, (d) a property adjustment order, and (d) a variation order. See Matrimonial Causes Rules 1977 (SI 1977/344), r 2(2).

8 Eg an application on the ground of failure to provide reasonable maintenance; see Matrimonial Causes Act 1973 (27 *Halsbury's Statutes* (4th edn) 700 MATRIMONIAL LAW), s 27.

9 Matrimonial Causes Rules 1977, rr 73, 75, 98, 100 and 101; and see *Kepa v Kepa* (1982) 4 FLR 515 at 519.

10 Matrimonial Causes Rules 1977, rr 73, 75, 98, 100 and 101. Although the requirement is obligatory the sanction is discretionary, see *Thyssen-Bornemisza v Thyssen-Bornemisza (No 2)* [1985] FLR 1069, [1985] Fam Law 283, CA.

11 Matrimonial Causes Rules 1977 (SI 1977/344), r 77(4); and see *B v B (Matrimonial Proceedings: Discovery)* [1978] Fam 181, [1979] 1 All ER 801.

12 See *Livesey v Jenkins* [1985] AC 424, [1985] 1 All ER 106, HL, and see *Kepa v Kepa*, above, at 519.

13 *Emanuel v Emanuel* [1982] 2 All ER 342, [1982] 1 WLR 669, *Kepa v Kepa*, above.

14 *Anton Piller KG v Manufacturing Processes Ltd* [1976] Ch 55, [1976] 1 All ER 779, CA and see *Kepa v Kepa*, above.

15 Ibid.

16 *Emanuel v Emanuel*, above, at 349a and 677C, see also *Kepa v Kepa*, above, at 520.

17 *Kepa v Kepa*, above.

18 Provided that the criteria are satisfied.

19 See *Kepa v Kepa*, above.

20 *Thermax Ltd v Schott Industrial Glass Ltd* [1981] FSR 289.

 1 Ibid.

 2 *Wardle Fabrics Ltd v G Myristis Ltd* [1984] FSR 263. Where there has been non disclosure the applicant may make a fresh application with full disclosure, *Yardley & Co Ltd v Higson* [1984] FSR 304, CA.

The court should not make an ex parte order for delivery up of documents where the respondent, by delivering them up, would be in danger of incriminating himself[3] and would be able to claim privilege.[4] However an order may be made where there is prima facie evidence that the respondent has committed perjury.[5]

The applicant must give the usual undertaking as to damages.[6] In addition, the applicant must undertake to serve the injunction by a solicitor (an officer of the court) together with copies of the affidavit evidence and copiable exhibits.[7] The solicitor serving the order must explain the meaning of the order in everyday language and, save in special cases, warn the respondent of his right to seek legal advice. The applicant's solicitors must give an undertaking that documents or property obtained as a result of the order will be retained by them in safe custody.

A respondent may refuse to comply with an Anton Piller order in which case the applicant may not force entry to the respondent's premises.[8] Failure to comply with an order is, of course, contempt[9] even it would seem where the respondent refuses to comply for the purpose of making an immediate application to set the order aside. The consequences to the respondent of using an application to set aside an ex parte order to gain time to destroy incriminating documents would be extremely grave.[10] A court should not set aside an order on the respondent's ex parte application[11] but only inter partes and on the basis of sworn evidence.[12] A respondent should apply to set aside[13] an ex parte order, to which he objects, and should not appeal[14] unless his inter partes application is unsuccessful.

An applicant may not use an Anton Piller order as a means of finding out whether he has a case against the respondent.[15]

4 Financial relief after overseas divorce

The Matrimonial and Family Proceedings Act 1984[16] empowers the High Court to make orders for financial relief[17] between parties whose marriage

---

3 *Rank Film Distributors Ltd v Video Information Centre* [1982] AC 380, [1981] 2 All ER 76, HL.
4 Privilege against self incrimination has been withdrawn in some circumstances in the field of intellectual property, see Supreme Court Act 1981 (11 *Halsbury's Statutes* (4th edn) 756 COURTS), s 72.
5 *Emanuel v Emanuel*, above, following *Rice v Gordon* (1843) 13 Sim 580. See also *Thorn EMI Video Programmes Ltd v Kitching and Busby* [1984] FSR 342.
6 For a precedent, see Appendix 4, below.
7 *International Electronics Ltd v Weigh Data Ltd* [1980] FSR 423.
8 *Anton Piller KG v Manufacturing Processes Ltd* [1976] Ch 55, [1976] 1 All ER 779, CA following *Entick v Carrington* (1765) 2 Wils 275.
9 See ch 11 below.
10 *WEA Records Ltd v Visions Channel 4 Ltd* [1983] 2 All ER 589, [1983] 1 WLR 721, CA.
11 *Hallmark Cards Inc v Image Arts Ltd* [1977] FSR 150.
12 Ibid.
13 RSC Ord 32, r 6.
14 *WEA Records Ltd v Visions Channel 4 Ltd* above.
15 *Hytrac Conveyors Ltd v Conveyors International Ltd* [1982] 3 All ER 415, [1983] 1 WLR 44, CA. However in the Family Division an application for discovery in an application for ancillary relief cannot be refused as a 'fishing' application, see *B v B (Matrimonial Proceedings: Discovery)* [1978] Fam 181, [1979] 1 All ER 801. The mere fact that a party is entitled to have full disclosure about the means of the other does not make such orders any less exceptional.
16 (27 *Halsbury's Statutes* (4th edn) 853 MATRIMONIAL LAW), Part III.
17 As defined by ibid, s 12(4).

has been dissolved or annulled, or who have been legally separated, by means of judicial or other proceedings[18] in an overseas country;[19] provided that such divorce, annulment or legal separation is entitled to be recognised in England and Wales.[20] It is outside the scope of this work to give detailed consideration to financial relief after overseas divorce.[1]

Such an application for financial relief may only be made with the leave of the court.[2] Leave will only be granted where the court considers that there is substantial ground for the making of the application;[3] this would seem to involve some consideration of the likely outcome if leave were granted.[4] An application for leave is made by an ex parte originating summons issued out of the divorce registry.[5]

The court has jurisdiction to entertain an application for an order for financial relief where (i) either of the parties is domiciled in England and Wales on the date of the application for leave, or was so domiciled on the date when the overseas divorce, annulment or legal separation took effect;[6] or (ii) either of the parties was habitually resident[7] in England and Wales for a period of one year ending with the date of the application for leave, or was habitually resident in England and Wales for a period of one year ending with the date on which the overseas divorce, annulment or legal separation took effect;[8] or (iii) either or both parties had, at the date of the application for leave, a beneficial interest, in possession, in a dwelling house, situate in England or Wales, which was at some time during the marriage, a matrimonial home of the parties.[9]

Where leave is granted to make an application for financial relief, an application may be made, by summons,[10] on behalf of the applicant, for an order restraining the other party from making any disposition, transfer out of the jurisdiction, or any other dealing with property.[11] In a case of urgency, or where it is feared that the respondent, if he had notice, would make such disposition, transfer or dealing, the application may be made ex parte, on affidavit. Before making such an order the court must be satisfied that the respondent is, with the intention of defeating the claim for financial relief, about to make[12] such a disposition, transfer or dealing.[13] In

---

18 See *Quazi v Quazi* [1980] AC 744, [1979] 3 All ER 897, HL, and see *Chaudhary v Chaudhary* [1985] Fam 19, [1984] 3 All ER 1017, CA.
19 In a country outside the British Islands, Matrimonial and Family Proceedings Act 1984, s 27. British Islands means the United Kingdom, the Channel Islands and the Isle of Man, Interpretation Act 1978 (41 *Halsbury's Statutes* (4th edn) STATUTES) Sch 1.
20 See Recognition of Divorces and Legal Separations Act 1971 (27 *Halsbury's Statutes* (4th edn) 899 MATRIMONIAL LAW) repealed and replaced by Family Law Act 1986, Part II, as from a date to be appointed.
 1 See *Jackson's Matrimonial Finance and Taxation* (4th edn), ch 22.
 2 Matrimonial and Family Proceedings Act 1984, s 13(1).
 3 Ibid.
 4 See the matters to be considered in ibid, ss 16 and 18.
 5 Matrimonial Causes Rules 1977 (SI 1977/344), r 111A(1).
 6 Matrimonial and Family Proceedings Act 1984, s 15(1)(a).
 7 For the meaning of habitually resident see *Kapur v Kapur* [1984] FLR 920, [1985] Fam Law 22 and see *Shah v Barnet London Borough Council* [1983] 1 All ER 226, sub nom *R v Barnet Londom Borough Council, ex p Shah* [1983] 2 AC 309, HL.
 8 Matrimonial and Family Proceedings Act 1984, s 15(1)(b).
 9 Ibid, s 15(1)(c).
10 Matrimonial Causes Rules 1977, r 112(1)(b).
11 Matrimonial and Family Proceedings Act 1984, s 23(2)(a).
12 This is a question of fact, see *Smith v Smith* (1973) 4 Fam Law 80, 117 Sol Jo 525.
13 Matrimonial and Family Proceedings Act 1984, s 23(2)(a).

respect of a disposition, transfer or dealing which is about to take place, where the court is satisfied, that if the same were to take place, it would have the consequence of defeating the claim for financial relief, there is a rebuttable presumption that the person making the disposition, transfer or other dealing intends that it should have that consequence.[14] The onus of rebutting the presumption is on the respondent.[15]

In this context 'defeating a claim for financial relief' means preventing financial relief from being granted, reducing the amount of relief which might be granted, or frustrating or impeding the enforcement of any order which might be or has been granted.[16]

Where the jurisdiction of the court to entertain the application for financial relief is by reason only of the fact that either or both of the parties had[17] a beneficial interest[18] in a dwelling house, situated in England or Wales, which was at some time during the marriage, their matrimonial home[19] an injunction[20] may only be made in respect of such dwelling house.[1]

The application must be supported by an affidavit[2] and is made to a judge.[3] The court is highly likely to require the applicant to give the usual undertaking as to damages as a precondition to the grant of such injunction.[4]

Where there has been an overseas divorce, annulment or legal separation[5] and a party to that marriage intends to apply for leave[6] to make an application for financial relief[7] as soon as he or she has been habitually resident[8] in England or Wales for a period of one year[9] and the other party is, with the intention of defeating[10] the claim for financial relief, about to make[11] any disposition, transfer out of the jurisdiction or otherwise deal with any property[12] the court may make such order as it thinks fit for restraining the disposition, transfer or other dealing.[13] The presumption

---

14 Ibid, s 23(7).
15 Ibid; and see *Jordan v Jordan, Jordan intervening* (1965) 109 Sol Jo 353.
16 Matrimonial and Family Proceedings Act 1984, s 23(1).
17 At the date of the application for leave.
18 In possession.
19 In jurisdiction by reason of Matrimonial and Family Proceedings Act 1984, s 15(1)(c).
20 Under ibid, s 23(4).
 1 Under ibid, s 19(4).
 2 For the strict requirements of the affidavit in support see section 1 above.
 3 Matrimonial Causes Rules 1977 (SI 1977/344), r 111B(8).
 4 See section 1 above.
 5 Matrimonial and Family Proceedings Act 1984, s 24(1)(a).
 6 Under ibid, s 13.
 7 Under ibid, s 17.
 8 See *Kapur v Kapur* [1984] FLR 920 1 [1985] Fam Law 22; and see *Shah v Barnet London Borough Council* [1983] 1 All ER 226, sub nom *R v Barnet London Borough Council, ex p Shah* [1983] 2 AC 309, HL.
 9 Matrimonial and Family Proceedings Act 1984 (27 *Halsbury's Statutes* (4th edn) 853 MATRIMONIAL LAW), s 24(1)(b).
10 In this context 'defeating' means preventing financial relief from being granted, reducing the amount of relief which might be granted, or frustrating or impeding the enforcement of any order which might be granted. See ibid, s 23(1) as applied by s 24(2)(a).
11 See *Smith v Smith* (1973) 4 Fam Law 80, 117 Sol Jo 525; whether or not a dealing is about to take place is a question of fact.
12 Matrimonial and Family Proceedings Act 1984, s 24(1)(c).
13 Ibid, s 24(1).

that a disposition, which is about to take place, is intended to defeat the claim if it would have the consequence of defeating the claim, unless restrained applies[14] and may be rebutted.[15]

The application is made by originating summons[16] issued out of the divorce registry[17] supported by an affidavit.[18] In a case of urgency the application may be made ex parte on affidavit,[19] especially where it is feared that assets would be dissipated before the inter partes hearing; and may, in a case of urgency, be made before the issue of the originating summons,[20] on an undertaking to issue the same forthwith.[1]

After issue of the originating summons the applicant must serve the same on the respondent together with a copy of the affidavit in support and a notice of proceedings and acknowledgment of service.[2] The respondent must acknowledge service within 31 days[3] and if he intends to contest the application he must, within 28 days thereafter, file an affidavit in answer and serve a copy on the applicant.[4] The application is made to a judge.[5]

Dispositions by will are excluded from restraint by injunction.[6] The powers of the High Court to restrain dispositions in connection with an application for financial relief after overseas divorce[7] are very similar to those available to the High Court and divorce county courts in matrimonial causes[8] are in addition to the powers of the High Court under the inherent jurisdiction.[9]

5 Married Women's Property Act 1882

Under this Act[10] the court, on an application by a husband or a wife,[11] may determine the title or possession to any property of either or both of them. A party[12] may also make an application in respect of money[13] or other

---

14 Ibid, s 24(2)(b).
15 See *Jordan v Jordan (Jordan intervening)* (1965) 109 Sol Jo 353.
16 Matrimonial Causes Rules 1977, r 111C(1). For a precedent see Appendix 4, below.
17 Ibid, r 111C(1).
18 Ibid.
19 RSC Ord 29, r 1(2).
20 Ibid, Ord 29, r 1(3).
 1 It is important that this be complied with; see *PS Refson & Co Ltd v Saggers* [1984] 3 All ER 111, [1984] 1 WLR 1025.
 2 Matrimonial Causes Rules 1977, r 111C(2).
 3 Ibid, r 15 as applied by r 111C(2).
 4 Ibid, r 111C(3).
 5 Ibid, r 111C(4).
 6 Matrimonial and Family Proceedings Act 1984, ss 23(8) and 24(2)(b).
 7 Ibid, ss 23 and 24.
 8 See Matrimonial Causes Act 1973 (27 *Halsbury's Statutes* (4th edn) 700 MATRIMONIAL LAW), s 37. See also section 1 above.
 9 Matrimonial and Family Proceedings Act 1984, ss 23(9) and 24(3). For the inherent jurisdiction of the High Court see Supreme Court Act 1981 (11 *Halsbury's Statutes* (4th edn) 756 COURTS), s 37; and see sections 2 and 3 above.
10 s 17 (27 *Halsbury's Statutes* (4th edn) 566 MATRIMONIAL LAW); see Appendix 1 below.
11 The parties need not be married at the time of the application which may be made within three years of divorce or annulment, Matrimonial Proceedings and Property Act 1970, s 39 (27 *Halsbury's Statutes* (4th edn) 652 MATRIMONIAL LAW) Application may also be made by either of a couple who were formerly engaged, Law Reform (Miscellaneous Provisions) Act 1970, s 2.
12 Matrimonial Causes (Property and Maintenance) Act 1958 s. 7(5) (27 *Halsbury's Statutes* (4th edn) 576 MATRIMONIAL LAW).
13 Including proceeds of sale of property in which a beneficial interest is claimed.

property in which a beneficial interest is claimed and which the applicant alleges that the respondent has had in his possession or under his control.[14] The court may order a sale of property[15] and will determine the application on the basis of proprietary rights[16] giving credit for improvements to property.[17]

The application may be made to the High Court by originating summons[18] or to the county court by originating application.[19] Where a matrimonial cause[20] has been commenced between the parties the application should be made to the court in which the cause is pending,[1] and so far as possible the application should be heard at the same time as the substantive application for ancillary relief.[2]

Where it is feared that the subject matter of the application will be dissipated or disposed of before the hearing of the matter either party may apply[3] for an interlocutory injunction to preserve the property, or the proceeds of sale thereof, pending the hearing of the matter.

The applicant must show that there is a serious issue to be tried and the court will decide whether or not to grant the injunction on the balance of convenience[4] or as it is better called the balance of justice.[5] The applicant must adduce evidence that there is a real danger of dissipation of assets.[6]

In the High Court the registrar may grant an injunction by consent[7] or where the injunction is ancillary or incidental to the relief sought.[8] In a county court only a judge may grant the injunction.[9] The applicant is normally required to give an undertaking as to damages.[10]

6 Writ of *ne exeat regno*

The writ of *ne exeat regno* originated in about the thirteenth century as a prerogative writ used for the political purposes of the Crown, but by the nineteenth century had developed into an equitable counterpart to arrest on mesne process at law.[11]

---

14 Matrimonial Causes (Property and Maintenance) Act 1958, s 7.
15 Married Women's Property Act 1882, s 17.
16 *Pettitt v Pettitt* [1970] AC 777, [1969] 2 All ER 385, HL and *Gissing v Gissing* [1971] AC 886, [1970] 2 All ER 780, HL.
17 Matrimonial Proceedings and Property Act 1970, s 37. For a full consideration of the principles see *Jackson's Matrimonial Finance and Taxation* (4th edn), ch 16.
18 See Matrimonial Causes Rules 1977 (SI 1977/344), r 104.
19 CCR Ord 47, r 2.
20 See Matrimonial and Family Proceedings Act 1984, s 32 (27 *Halsbury's Statutes* (4th edn) 869 MATRIMONIAL LAW).
1 CCR Ord 47, r 2(2).
2 *Button v Button* [1968] 1 All ER 1064 at 1067, CA, approved in *Pettit v Pettitt*, above.
3 In the High Court by summons, RSC Ord 32, r 1, Matrimonial Causes Rules 1977, r 122(1)(b). In the county court by notice of application, CCR Ord 13, r 1(2). See ch 2 above.
4 *American Cyanamid Co v Ethicon Ltd* [1975] AC 396, [1975] 1 ALL ER 504, HL.
5 *Francome v Mirror Group Newspaper Ltd* [1984] 2 All ER 408, [1984] 1 WLR 892, CA.
6 See as to Mareva injunctions, above.
7 RSC Ord 32, r 11(2).
8 Matrimonial Causes Rules 1977, r 104(9).
9 CCR Ord 13, r 6(2).
10 *Practice Direction (Injunction: Undertaking as to Damages)* [1974] 2 All ER 1119, [1974] 1 WLR 936; see Appendix 2 below.
11 For a full account of the history of the writ of *ne exeat regno* see *Fenton v Callis* [1969] 1 QB 200, [1968] 3 All ER 673, Megarry J.

The writ takes the form of a command addressed to the tipstaff[12] that, if the respondent[13] should seek or attempt to leave the jurisdiction of the High Court[14] without having paid to the applicant[15] a specified sum, he shall arrest the respondent and bring him before a judge of the High Court forthwith or as soon as is reasonably practical, unless he provides security for the specified sum.[16] When the respondent is brought before a judge, the writ may be left in force, discharged or varied and the judge may make such further or supplemental order as the circumstances dictate.[17]

The court has a discretion[18] to grant leave to a party to issue a writ of *ne exeat regno* at any time before final judgment where the four conditions laid down in Debtors Act 1869, section 6,[19] are satisfied.[20] These conditions are:

(1) The action is one in which the respondent would have been liable to arrest at law[1] prior to 1869;

(2) there is a good cause of action[2] for at least fifty pounds,

(3) there is probable cause for believing that the respondent is about to leave the jurisdiction unless apprehended; and,

(4) the absence of the respondent from the jurisdiction will materially prejudice the applicant in the prosecution of the action.[3]

An applicant for a writ of *ne exeat regno* must give an undertaking as to damages as the issue of a writ is a severe matter.[4] The standard of proof on the applicant is high[5] the court must be convinced.[6]

A writ of *ne exeat regno* may be issued, subject to the requirements of Debtors Act 1869,[7] in support of a Mareva injunction.[8]

---

12 *Al Nahkel for Contracting and Trading Ltd v Lowe* [1986] QB 235, [1986] 1 All ER 729. The writ used to be addressed to the sheriff but now should be addressed to the tipstaff, his deputy, all constables and other peace officers.

13 The term 'respondent' is used to mean the party against whom the application is made, who may be petitioner or plaintiff, respondent or defendant in the action.

14 Ie England and Wales.

15 The term 'applicant' is used to mean the party who applied for the order. See fn 13, above.

16 For a precedent see Appendix 4, below.

17 *Al Nahkel for Contracting and Trading Ltd v Lowe*, above.

18 A writ of *ne exeat regno* is always in the discretion of the court; see *Fenton v Callais*, above, following *Re Lehman, exp Hasluck* (1890) 6 TLR 376. See also *Thaha v Thaha* [1987] Fam Law 234, Wood J.

19 4 *Halsbury's Statutes* (4th edn) 480 BANKRUPTCY AND INSOLVENCY.

20 *Hands v Hands* (1881) 43 LT 750, *Fenton v Callis* [1969] 1 QB 200, [1968] 3 All ER 673.

1 The most obvious example is debt, see *Fenton v Callis*, above, at 215B–C and 682C–D. The debt must be due and payable, not a future debt; see *Coverson v Bloomfield* (1885) 29 Ch D 341, CA. This requirement will prevent the issue of a writ of *ne exeat regno* where eg the claim is for a lump sum under the ,Matrimonial Causes Act 1973, s 23(1)(c) (27 *Halsbury's Statutes* (4th edn) 700 MATRIMONIAL LAW) as such is a future debt.

2 The standard of proof is high: *Fenton v Callis*, above.

3 The application in *Fenton v Callis*, above was dismissed because there was no evidence that the defendant's absence from the jurisdiction would materially prejudice the plaintiff in the prosecution of the action. The defendant's presence was not necessary to obtain judgment against him.

4 *Fenton v Callis*, above at 206G and 676G–H and see the authorities cited therein for the circumstances in which a defendant could claim under the undertaking.

5 *Fenton v Callis*, above.

6 Ibid and see *Thaha v Thaha* [1987] 2 FLR 142 [1987] Fam Law 234. See also *In re Underwood* (1903) 51 WR 335 at 336.

7 S 6 (4 *Halsbury's Statutes* (4th edn) 480 BANKRUPTCY AND INSOLVENCY).

8 *Al Nahkel for Contracting and Trading Ltd v Lowe* [1986] QB 235, [1986] 1 All ER 729. For Mareva injunctions generally see section 2, above.

In the Family Division of the High Court the use of the writ is greatly limited by the requirements that a writ may only be issued before final judgment[9] and that it must be in respect of a debt that is due and payable.[10] The writ has, it would seem, only been issued once in the Family Division in *Thaha v Thaha*[11] in support of an application for a judgment summons.[12]

Apart from the power of the High Court to issue a writ of *ne exeat regno* there is power under the inherent jurisdiction[13] for the High Court to grant an injunction restraining a party from leaving the jurisdiction and for delivery up of his passport.[14]

---

9 Debtors Act 1896, s 6.
10 Ibid and see *Colverson v Bloomfield* (1885) 29 Ch D 341, CA.
11 [1987] 2 FLR 142 [1987] Fam Law 234, Wood J.
12 Ie a summons under Debtors Act 1869, s 5 that the defendant appear and be examined on oath as to his means. See *Rayden on Divorce* (14th edn) ch 24, section II.
13 Supreme Court Act 1981, s 37 (11 *Halsbury's Statutes* (4th edn) 756 COURTS).
14 *Bayer AG v Winter* [1986] 1 All ER 733, [1986] 1 WLR 497, CA where such orders were made in support of Mareva and Anton Piller orders; see also *In re I (a minor)* (1987) Times, 22 May.

Chapter 11
Miscellaneous injunctions

1 Personal family relationships

In general, personal family relationships in marriage cannot be enforced by order of a court.[1] Legal effect will not be given to domestic agreements without intention to create a legal relations.[2]

A husband has no rights enforceable, either at law or in equity, to prevent his wife from having a legal abortion nor to prevent doctors from carrying out a legal abortion.[3] It is unclear whether or not a husband could obtain an injunction to prevent his wife undergoing an illegal abortion.[4] It is unlikely that an injunction would be granted to prevent an abortion even if it was alleged that the doctors did not hold their views in good faith or had not come to their conclusions in good faith.[5]

A father of an illegitimate child has no rights other than those granted to him by statute.[6] A prospective father of an illegitimate child has no *locus standi* to bring proceedings for an injunction to restrain an abortion based on his personal interest by alleging that the proposed abortion would be criminal under the Infant Life (Preservation) Act 1929[7] where the court has no proof that an offence is about to be committed.[8]

A foetus, *en ventre sa mère*, is incapable of maintaining an action, through the father as next friend,[9] to seek an injunction against the mother to prevent termination of the pregnancy.[10] A foetus has no rights in law until it has been born and has an existence separate from its mother.[11] The

1 *Paton v British Pregnancy Advisory Service Trustees* [1979] QB 276, [1978] 2 All ER 987, per Sir George Baker P.
2 *Balfour v Balfour* [1919] 2 KB 571, CA, and see *Spellman v Spellman* [1961] 2 All ER 498, [1961] 1 WLR 921, CA.
3 *Paton v BPAST* above. For the circumstances in which an abortion is legal see the Abortion Act 1967 (12 *Halsbury's Statutes* (4th edn) 414 CRIMINAL LAW). See also the Abortion Regulations 1968, (SI 1968/390).
4 It might be difficult for the husband to show that he had *locus standi*. See *Paton v BPAST* above, and see *Gouriet v Union of Post Office Workers* [1978] AC 435, [1977] 3 All ER 70, HL.
5 *Paton v BPAST* above at 281B and 991d per Sir George Baker, obiter; and see *R v Smith (John)* [1974] 1 All ER 376, [1973] 1 WLR 1510, CA.
6 *Paton v BPAST* above at 279H–280A and 990c–d. See also the Children Act 1975, s 85(7) (6 *Halsbury's Statutes* (4th edn) 402 CHILDREN).
7 12 *Halsbury' Statutes* (4th edn) 222 CRIMINAL LAW. S 1(1) provides: '. . . any person who, with intent to destroy the life of a child, capable of being born alive, by any wilful act causes the child to die before it has an existence independent of its mother, shall be guilty of felony . . .'.
8 *C v S* [1987] 1 All ER 1230, [1987] 2 WLR 1108 Heilbron J; the Court of Appeal did not rule on this point.
9 See RSC Ord 80. It might be difficult for the solicitor for the plaintiff to certify that the father (the proposed next friend) had no interest in the case adverse to that of the foetus (the 'person' under the disability). See RSC Ord 80, r 3.
10 *C v S* above, Heilbron J; the Court of Appeal did not decide this point.
11 *Paton v BPAST* above at 279D and G, and at 989h and 990b.

question of whether or not a foetus is 'capable of being born alive'[12] depends on the facts of each case, but as it is a matter of statutory interpretation it is a question of law for the court.[13]

Even in a suit for restitution of conjugal rights[14] the court could never compel matrimonial intercourse to take place[15] and would not do so today in any proceedings.

The court would refuse to grant an injunction sought to restrain a proposed operation for sterilisation or a proposed vasectomy.[16] Unfortunately, it is not clear whether the basis of the decision was that the court does not have jurisdiction to grant such an injunction *or* whether it was that the court, whilst having jurisdiction to grant such an injunction, would never, as a matter of public policy, exercise the jurisdiction. It is submitted that the court does have jurisdiction to grant such injunctions[17] but would only exercise the same to restrain a proposed sterilisation, vasectomy or abortion in respect of a ward of court[18] even if the ward was married, where the leave of the court has not been granted.[19] The court, in considering such an application, would be bound to have regard to the welfare of the ward[20] and where the operation is for a non-therapeutic purpose it is clear that the decision as to whether or not the operation should be carried out is not a matter exclusively for the clinical judgment of the medical profession.[1] Nevertheless, the court will give great weight to the evidence and opinions expressed by medical witnesses.

Where a minor is a ward of court, even in the care of the local authority, no major decision about the child's future may be made without the sanction of the court.[2] A major decision would include whether or not the ward should have an abortion,[3] and any major operation.[4] An order is often given providing general leave for routine physical examination and treatment.[5]

---

12 Infant Life (Preservation) Act 1929, s 1(1). Contraction of the cardiac muscle and primitive movement is insufficient. *C v S* above, CA. It would seem that the foetus must be capable of breathing naturally, *C v S* above, CA, or possibly with the aid of a ventilator: *C v S* above, CA.
13 *C v S* [1987] 1 All ER 1230, [1987] 3 WLR 1108, Heilbron J and CA.
14 A remedy abolished by Matrimonial Proceedings and Property Act 1970, s 20.
15 *Forster v Forster* (1790) 1 Hag Con 144, cited with approval in *Paton v BPAST* above. Disobedience to a decree for restitution was punishable by attachment until abolished by the Matrimonial Causes Act 1884, s 2. Thereafter, by ibid, s 5, disobedience was deemed to be desertion, giving the other spouse a right to petition for divorce or judicial separation, as the case may be. A decree for restitution could not be enforced by committal: *Weldon v Weldon* (1885) 54 LJP 60, CA.
16 *Paton v BPAST* above.
17 Supreme Court Act 1981, s 37(1); County Courts Act 1984, s 38.
18 *Re D (a minor) (Wardship: Sterilisation)* [1976] Fam 185, [1976] 1 All ER 326, Heilbron J.
19 Leave would only be given to sterilise a ward as a last resort when all other forms of contraception had been considered and were unsuitable. *In Re B (a minor) (Sterilisation)* [1987] 2 All ER 206, [1987] 2 WLR 1213, CA and HL.
20 Guardianship of Minors Act 1971, s 1 (6 *Halsbury's Statutes* (4th edn) 306 CHILDREN).
1 *Re D (a minor) (Wardship: Sterilisation)*, above.
2 *Surrey County Council v W* (1982) 3 FLR 167, 12 Fam Law 91, CA and see *Re B (a minor) (Sterilisation)* [1987] 2 All ER 206, [1987] 2 WLR 1213, CA and HL.
3 *Re G-U (a minor) (Wardship)* [1984] FLR 811, [1984] Fam Law 248.
4 *Re B* (1982) 3 FLR 117, 12 Fam Law 25, Ewbank J and CA [1981] 1 WLR 1421, CA, which involved the most fundamental question of all as to whether the ward should live or die.
5 Psychiatric examination or treatment always requires the specific leave of the court. *Re R (PM) (an infant)* [1968] 1 All ER 691, [1968] 1 WLR 385.

2 Confidentiality

Marital confidences

The relationship of husband and wife depends upon mutual trust and confidence. This is recognised by the law with the object of preserving marriages. If, after the break-down of the marriage, one spouse intends to break this confidence, or does so, the general jurisdiction of equity is wide enough to restrain such a breach of confidence by injunction.[6] Not only will a spouse, or a former spouse, be restrained from breaching the confidence, but any other person, such as a newspaper, who has received the information may also be restrained.[7]

Not every disclosure of a matrimonial communication will be restrained, but only disclosure of confidential communications within the marriage.[8] Whether or not a marital communication is a confidential one, entitled to protection from disclosure, will be a question of fact to be determined in each and every particular case. An application for such injunction may be made either as interlocutory relief in a matrimonial cause or by a separate action.[9]

It would seem probable that an applicant for an injunction to prevent disclosure of marital confidences must 'come to court with clean hands'. In *Argyll v Argyll*[10] this defence was raised on the ground that the plaintiff had published some marital secrets and that the defendant had been granted a decree of divorce on the ground of the plaintiff's adultery. The defence failed because the defendant proposed to disclose far more intimate matters than the plaintiff had disclosed; furthermore adultery, however reprehensible,[11] did not, retrospectively, release the defendant from his duty of confidence.

However, where a married couple have regarded their relationship as in the public domain, rather than their own private business, the court may well refuse to grant an injunction to restrain publication of marital confidences.[12]

Confidentiality of discovery and evidence

Documents obtained by a party on discovery[13] may be used by that party only for the proper purposes of the litigation in which they were obtained.[14] There is an implied undertaking by a party who obtains discovery not to use documents so obtained for any collateral or ulterior motive.[15]

If documents, obtained on discovery, are misused[16] such misuse may be restrained, by injunction,[17] or punished as a contempt of court.[18]

---

6 *Duchess of Argyll v Duke of Argyll* [1967] Ch 302, [1967] 1 All ER 611, Ungoed-Thomas J.
7 Ibid.
8 Ibid at pp 330 and 625 respectively.
9 See ch 2 above.
10 Above.
11 Adultery was a matrimonial offence prior to the passage of the Divorce Reform Act 1969.
12 *Lennon v News Group Newspapers Ltd and Twist* [1978] FSR 573, CA.
13 Discovery takes place under RSC Ord 24 and CCR Ord 14.
14 *Distillers Co (Biochemicals) Ltd v Times Newspapers Ltd* [1975] QB 613, [1975] 1 All ER 41.
15 Ibid, and see *Alterskyte v Scott* [1948] 1 All ER 469. In this context 'collateral or ulterior purpose' means some purpose different from that which was the only reason why the party was accorded the advantage, which he would not otherwise have had, of having in his possession copies of another person's documents. *Harman v Home Office* [1983] AC 280 at 302, [1982] 1 All ER 532 at 536 HL per Lord Diplock.
16 Ie used for a collateral or ulterior purpose.
17 *Distillers Co (Biochemicals) Ltd v Times Newspapers Ltd*, above.
18 See further ch 12.

Confidentiality of documents obtained on discovery is based on the ground that a party, compelled by process of law to make what may be damaging disclosures for the purposes of a particular suit, should not be required to be at risk of their use for other purposes.[19]

Although a matrimonial cause is heard in open court[20] applications for ancillary relief or concerning children are heard in chambers.[1] The court file is not generally open to inspection.[2] Applications to the magistrates' court in its domestic jurisdiction are heard in private.[3]

On an application for ancillary relief, and some analogous applications, both parties are required to swear affidavits containing full particulars of their property and income.[4] In default of compliance such an affidavit may be ordered.[5] Full and frank disclosure of all relevant matters is very important.[6] Discovery may be required on any matter contained in an affidavit or in respect of any relevant matter.[7] In consequence, where an affidavit of means has come into the possession of a third party he may be restrained, by injunction, from using such document, even in legal proceedings[8] and may be ordered to deliver up all copies in his possession.[9] An application for such relief can conveniently be brought in the Chancery Division or as interlocutory relief in a matrimonial cause.

On such an application the judge must balance two differing and competing applications of the same public interest, ie it is important for the administration of justice that the truth is disclosed.[10]

The balance in *Medway v Doublelock Ltd*[11] was in favour of the confidentiality of the affidavits of means but this will not necessarily be so in every case. The importance of the proceedings in which the third party wishes to use the affidavits or documents must be balanced against the importance of full and frank disclosure in the matrimonial proceedings.[12]

In wardship and adoption proceedings publication of information relating to proceedings held in private is a contempt of court;[13] the court has a discretion to give leave in proper cases.[14] Where it is proposed to use such

19 *Medway v Doublelock Ltd* [1978] 1 All ER 1261, [1978] 1 WLR 710 explaining *Distillers Co (Biochemicals) Ltd v Times Newspapers Ltd* above and *Riddick v Thames Board Mills Ltd* [1977] QB 881, [1977] 3 All ER 677, CA. The court may release a party from, or modify, the implied undertaking where such would not cause injustice nor detract from the solemnity or importance of the undertaking: *Crest Homes plc v Marks* [1987] 2 All ER 1074, [1987] 3 WLR 293, HL.
20 In some circumstances the hearing may be in camera.
1 Exceptionally part of the case, often the judgment, may be in open court.
2 Matrimonial Causes Rules 1977, SI 1977 344, r 130.
3 Magistrates' Courts Act 1980, s 69(2) (27 *Halsbury's Statutes* (4th edn) 157 MAGISTRATES) provides who may be admitted. As to reporting see ibid, s 71. For the position of witnesses see *Tomlinson v Tomlinson* [1980] 1 All ER 593, [1980] 1 WLR 322, DC.
4 Matrimonial Causes Rules 1977, rr 73, 75, 98, 100 and 101.
5 Ibid. Although the rule is mandatory the sanction is discretionary; see *Thyssen-Bornemisza v Thyssen-Bornemisza (No 2)* [1985] FLR 1069, [1985] Fam Law 283, CA.
6 *Livesey v Jenkins* [1985] AC 424, [1985] 1 All ER 106, HL.
7 Matrimonial Causes Rules 1977, r 77(4) and see *B v B (Matrimonial Proceedings: Discovery)* [1978] Fam 181, [1979] 1 All ER 801.
8 *Medway v Doublelock Ltd*, above.
9 Ibid.
10 *D v NSPCC* [1978] AC 171, [1977] 1 All ER 589, HL applied in *Medway v Doublelock Ltd*, above.
11 Above.   12 Ibid.
13 Administration of Justice Act 1960, s 12(1)(a) (11 *Halsbury's Statutes* (4th edn) 174 CONTEMPT OF COURT).
14 See eg *Practice Direction* [1972] 1 All ER 1056, sub nom *Practice Note* (Infants: Transcript) [1972] 1 WLR 443.

information in judicial proceedings the court will consider foremost the interests of the minor and will balance the public interest in ensuring that frankness should prevail by preserving confidentiality, against the public interest in upholding the law by providing relevant evidence for use in legitimate proceedings.[15]

3 Use of surnames and titles

On marriage it is customary for a wife to use her husband's surname; a woman who marries a peer or a knight is entitled, by custom, to assume the name, title and rank of her husband. She is entitled to continue to use his name, and any title, after divorce or other termination of the marriage,[16] even if she has remarried.[17] A former husband is not entitled to an injunction, restraining his former wife from using his name or title,[18] except probably where she is doing so with the intention of defrauding him[19] or where her use is infringing other of his rights.[20]

Although the right to petition for jactitation of marriage[1] has been abolished[2] if a former wife is, directly or indirectly, holding herself out as the present wife of her ex-husband such conduct is probably molestation[3] and would be restrained by injunction on the application of the former husband. Such an application could conveniently be made in the divorce proceedings, notwithstanding the pronouncement of decree absolute.[4]

It should be noted that if, after a former husband has remarried, his ex-wife holds herself out to be his wife, she may commit libel or slander if the reasonable inference is that he is not lawfully married to his subsequent wife or that they are committing adultery and have illegitimate children.

4 Separation deeds

A separation deed is an agreement, under seal, whereby two parties to a marriage agree to live separate and apart by releasing each other from the marital duty of cohabitation. An agreement is void, as contrary to public policy, unless it is followed by an immediate separation.[5]

---

15 *In Re R (MJ) (a minor) (Publication of Transcript)* [1975] Fam 89, [1975] 2 All ER 749. See also *Re J (a minor) (Wardship)* [1984] FLR 535, [1984] Fam Law 308 and *In Re H (a minor) (Wardship: Applications)* [1985] 3 All ER 1, [1985] 1 WLR 1164, CA.
16 *Cowley v Cowley* [1900] P 305, CA, affd [1901] AC 450, HL.
17 In *Cowley v Cowley* the former wife had remarried.
18 *Cowley v Cowley*, above.
19 For example by pledging his credit. Marriage in itself does not give the wife authority to pledge her husband's credit, but where they are living together the wife is presumed to have her husband's authority to pledge his credit for necessaries suitable to their style and standard of living. A wife living separate from her husband is not presumed, in the absence of evidence to the contrary, to have authority to pledge his credit.
20 *Cowley v Cowley* above; see also *Du Boulay v Du Boulay* (1869) LR 2 PC 430, PC, at 441.
 1 A decree of jactitation of marriage was granted in the form of an injunction restraining the respondent from making false assertions that he or she is married to the petitioner.
 2 Family Law Act 1986, s 61 *not in force at the date of writing*.
 3 Molestation has a very wide meaning. See *Vaughan v Vaughan* [1973] 3 All ER 449, [1973] 1 WLR 1159, CA; see also ch 3, above.
 4 *Webb v Webb* [1986] 1 FLR 541, CA and see cases therein cited.
 5 *Wilson v Wilson* (1848) 1 HL Cas 538, HL. A reconciliation deed which provides for a future separation is not void. *Re Meyrick's Settlement* [1921] 1 Ch 311.

It is standard for such deeds to contain terms which regulate the spouses' lives during the separation.[6] Almost invariably a separation deed will contain covenants that each spouse will not molest or interfere with the other.

Valuable consideration is given by the covenants to live separate and apart.[7] A separation deed generally ceases to be effective if the parties resume cohabitation, having reconciled.[8]

While an agreement is in force the remedy for a refusal, by either party, to carry out its terms is by way of an action for specific performance.[9] The performance sought will be that of the covenants contained in the deed in question, as, for example, the usual covenants by a husband to permit his wife to live separate and apart without molestation or interference by him.[10] Damages may be obtained for breach of a non-molestation clause.[11]

An injunction may be granted restraining either party from molesting the other, or otherwise committing a breach of an enforceable provision of the deed.[12] Pending the trial of the action an interlocutory injunction may be granted depending upon the balance of convenience.[13]

Where a spouse is in breach of a non-molestation clause of a separation deed (but no other provision) the other spouse may well find it procedurally more convenient to make an application under the Domestic Violence and Matrimonial Proceedings Act 1976[14] rather than to commence an action for specific performance. An added advantage is that, if the offending spouse has committed actual bodily harm on the other, a power of arrest may be attached to the injunction,[15] which is probably not available in an action for specific performance. Furthermore, the proceedings will be heard in chambers[16] unless the court otherwise directs.

6 For example dealing with custody of children and with maintenance.
7 See 22 *Halsbury's Laws* (4th edn) para 1146.
8 This depends upon the terms of the agreement, the intention of the parties and all the circumstances of the case: *Nicol v Nicol* (1886) 31 Ch D 524, CA: see also 22 *Halsbury's Laws* (4th edn) para 1150.
9 *Besant v Wood* (1879) 12 Ch D 605.
10 For precedents see 21 *Atkin's Court Forms* (1985 Issue) HUSBAND AND WIFE, Forms 33–38.
11 *Fearon v Earl of Aylesford* (1884) 14 QBD 792, CA.
12 *Besant v Wood*, above.
13 *American Cyanamid Co v Ethicon Ltd* [1975] AC 396, [1975] 1 All ER 504, HL. It is submitted that if the validity of the separation deed was not disputed the balance of convenience would almost always be in favour of granting the injunction.
14 27 *Halsbury's Statutes* (4th edn) MATRIMONIAL LAW 788; see also ch 3 above.
15 Domestic Violence and Matrimonial Proceedings Act 1976, s 2(1).
16 CCR Ord 47, r 8(4).

Chapter 12
Enforcement

1 Committal to prison

Where the High Court or county court has granted an applicant a prohibitory or mandatory injunction, or the respondent has given the court a formal undertaking[1] other than an undertaking to pay a sum or sums of money[2] which is recorded by the court, then the injunction or undertaking, if breached, may be enforced by applying to the court for an order that the party in breach of the injunction or undertaking be committed to prison or fined.

Orders that the respondent do not assault or molest the applicant or that a respondent do not return to the matrimonial home are examples of prohibitory injunctions. An order that the respondent do vacate the matrimonial home is an example of a mandatory injunction. However, before an injunction or undertaking can be enforced by committal, the applicant for the committal order must satisfy the court that the correct procedure has been followed. Committal to prison is a drastic order involving the liberty of the subject and as such the court will not make an order of committal unless the procedure as laid down by Rules of Court has been followed strictly.[3] It does not matter how disobedient the party against whom the order is directed may have been because unless the process of committal has been carried out strictly in accordance with the Rules he is entitled to his freedom. The Rules of Court have statutory force and where there are no express exceptions, the court has no power to dispense with their requirements.[4]

Injunctions

The court will not enforce an order by committal unless the order to be enforced has been endorsed with a penal notice.[5] The order, duly endorsed with the penal notice, must have been served personally upon the party against whom it is sought to enforce the order in the case of a mandatory injunction[6] but not necessarily in the case of a prohibitory injunction. Where a prohibitory injunction has not been served, it is necessary to prove knowledge of the injunction as where the party who is the respondent to the application for the order was in court at the time the order was pronounced.[7]

---

1 *Hipgrave v Hipgrave* [1962] P 91, [1962] 1 All ER 75, Scarman J.
2 Debtors Act 1869, s 4.
3 *Gordon v Gordon* [1946] P 99, [1946] 1 All ER 247, per Lord Greene MR.
4 See for example *Husseyin v Husseyin* (1982) 12 Fam Law 154, CA.
5 RSC Ord 45, r 7(4); CCR Ord 29, r 1(3); see Appendix 3, below.
6 RSC Ord 45, r 7(2); CCR Ord 29, r 1(2).
7 *Husson v Husson* [1962] 3 All ER 1056, [1962] 1 WLR 1434.

At one time it was not necessary to effect personal service of an order granted as interlocutory relief in a matrimonial cause. Such an order could be delivered to the solicitor acting for the party to whom the order was directed.[8] However, as from 5 January 1981, it has been necessary to serve such orders personally.[9]

The person who serves the order should swear an affidavit stating that he served the order personally;[10] the affidavit should explain how the server knew that he was delivering the order to the person named therein and should exhibit a copy of the order served.[11] Notwithstanding these requirements for personal service, on an application to commit, the court may waive personal service in the following circumstances:

(a) Where pending service of a prohibitory order, the party against whom the order was made was present when the order was made by the court or had been notified of the order and of its terms by telephone, telegram or otherwise.[12]

(b) Where, in the case of both prohibitory or mandatory orders it is just to do so.[13]

Both the Rules of the Supreme Court and the County Court Rules are silent on the time at which the court should be invited to exercise its discretion to dispense with personal service. However, it may be appropriate to apply to the judge for dispensation at the time the injunction is granted.

Non-service of an order does not prevent the court from committing to prison a person arrested under a power of arrest attached to an order of the court.[14]

Undertakings
An undertaking given by a party to the court is as solemn, binding and effective as an injunction.[15] There is no requirement in the Rules[16] either for the indorsement of a penal notice or for personal service[17] as a precondition to committal. Nevertheless, it is highly desirable that an undertaking should be recorded in an order of the court and served personally on the giver.[18] It is also desirable that the order, recording the undertaking, should contain a notice indicating to the giver the consequences of breach of the terms of the undertaking, in terms which show that the notice applies to the undertaking rather than the order.[19]

---

8 Pursuant to Matrimonial Causes Rules 1977, r 60.
9 R 60 of the Matrimonial Causes Rules 1977 having been revoked by r 2 of the Matrimonial Causes (Amendment) Rules 1980.
10 RSC Ord 65, r 8; CCR Ord 7, r 2.
11 For a precedent see Appendix 4.
12 RSC Ord 45, r 7(6); CCR Ord 29, r 1(6)
13 RSC Ord 45, r 7(7); CCR Ord 29, r 1(7); the power to waive personal service of a prohibitive order is only to be exercised in cases of deliberate evasion of service: *Hill Samuel & Co Ltd v Littaur* (1985) Times, 13 April, CA.
14 RSC Ord 90, r 30(4); CCR Ord 47, r 8(7).
15 *Hussain v Hussain* [1986] Fam 134, [1986] 1 All ER 961, CA. See also *Hipgrave v Hipgrave* [1962] P 91, [1962] 1 All ER 75, Scarman J.
16 RSC Ord 45, r 7, Ord 52, CCR Ord 29, r 1.
17 *Hussain v Hussain* [1986] Fam 134, [1986] 1 All ER 961, CA, dicta in *Williams v Fawcett* [1986] QB 604, [1985] 1 All ER 787, CA, qualified.
18 *Hussain v Hussain*, above.
19 *Hussain v Hussain*, above.

2 The application to commit

In the High Court, where proceedings are under the Domestic Violence and Matrimonial Proceedings Act 1976 or the Matrimonial Homes Act 1983, the application to commit is made by motion supplied by an affidavit.[20] Where the order it is sought to enforce was made by the High Court as an interlocutory order in a matrimonial cause, the application to commit is by summons supported by an affidavit.[1]

In the county court where the order it is sought to enforce was made pursuant to the Domestic Violence and Matrimonial Proceedings Act 1976 or the Matrimonial Homes Act 1983, the proper officer on application of the applicant, issues a notice[2] to the respondent to attend the court to show cause why an order of committal should not be made against him. The notice should not be signed by the applicant's solicitors unless it is qualified by showing that the notice is issued on their application.[3] The Rules do not require that the application be supported by an affidavit although the universal practice is to support an application in the first instance with an affidavit which should be served on the respondent to an application to commit at the same time as the notice is sent to the respondent by the registrar. Where it is sought to enforce an order made by a divorce county court as interlocutory relief in a matrimonial cause, application to commit is made in exactly the same way as if it was sought to enforce by committal an order made pursuant to the Act of 1976.

3 Contents of the application

The application must state the grounds upon which it is sought to have the respondent committed to prison. Where an injunction or undertaking is in prohibitory terms, as for example that the respondent be restrained from assaulting, molesting or otherwise interfering with the applicant having recited the order, should state each and every act relied upon as a breach of the order and should give particulars of dates, times and places.[4] It is important and it must be emphasised that the application to commit should specify each and every breach relied upon as, in general, only the grounds specified in the application may be relied upon at the hearing.[5]

In the case of a mandatory injunction or undertaking as for example an order or undertaking that the respondent do vacate the former matrimonial home, the application, having recited the terms of the injunction or undertaking, should state that the respondent has failed to carry out the terms of the order within the time specified for carrying the same out.

The specific and particular requirements of an application for committal are to enable the respondent to the application to know exactly what he is alleged to have done, which constitutes contempt of court, with sufficient

---

20 RSC Ord 52, r 4(1). See Appendix 4, below, for a notice of motion.
1 RSC Ord 52, r 4(1) as applied by Matrimonial Causes Rules 1977, r 90.
2 In Form N 78 – Notice to show cause why Order of Committal should not be made: CCR Ord 29, r 1(4). See Appendix 4, below, for a precedent.
3 *Williams v Fawcett* [1986] QB 604, [1985] 1 All ER 787, CA.
4 RSC Ord 52, r 4(2); CCR Ord 29, r 1(4) and see *Woolley v Woolley* (1974) 124 NLJ 768 Bagnall J. See also *Williams v Fawcett* [1986] QB 604, [1985] 1 All ER 787, CA, *Chiltern District Council v Keane* [1985] 2 All ER 118, [1985] 1 WLR 619, CA.
5 RSC Ord 52, r 6(3). There is no corresponding provision in the CCR.

particularity so that he can defend himself.[6] It is unclear whether it is sufficient for the alleged breaches to be particularised in the supporting affidavit.[7] Where the application fails to specify the breaches but the affidavit evidence does specify them a judge might well allow the application to proceed, dispensing with the requirements,[8] on the ground that the respondent has not been prejudiced by the fact that the breaches are contained in an affidavit rather than in an application.

Where an application to commit has been dismissed by reason of the defects in the application a second application may be brought in respect of the same alleged contempt without offending the rule against double jeopardy.[9]

4 The affidavit in support

The affidavit in support of the application should set out in detail the circumstances of the breaches relied upon to support the application to commit. The purpose of this is so that the person whose committal is sought knows exactly what is being alleged against him.[10] Furthermore, it enables the court to decide, subject to oral evidence at the hearing, just how serious and wilful the alleged contempt is. It is good practice to ensure that the respondent to an application to commit is served with any affidavit in support well before the hearing so that an affidavit from the respondent in answer may be prepared and filed with the court prior to the hearing. Failure so to serve may result in an application by the respondent for an adjournment of the hearing in order to prepare evidence in answer which application is likely to be treated sympathetically by the court.

5 Service of the application and affidavit in support

Applications to commit must be served personally[11] upon the respondent to such application together with affidavits in support. The court does, however, have a power to waive personal service if it thinks it just to do so.[12]

The Family Division of the High Court has an inherent jurisdiction to make a committal order on an application ex parte[13] and may dispense with service of the notice of motion or summons[14] if it thinks it just to do so. The

---

6 *Woolley v Woolley* (1974) 124 NLJ 768 Bagnall J. *Williams v Fawcett* [1986] 1 QB 604, [1985] 1 All ER 787, CA, *Chiltern District Council v Keane* [1985] 2 All ER 118, [1985] 1 WLR 619, CA.

7 *Chanel Ltd v FGM Cosmetics Ltd* [1981] FSR 471, Whitford J states that the breaches must be made clear in the application not the affidavit. *Chakravorty v Braganza* (1983) Times, 12 October, Comyn J states that the application and supporting affidavit had to identify specifically the alleged breaches. *Chiltern District Council v Keane* above does not deal with this conflict but refers to the notice of motion as having to state the breaches.

8 RSC Ord 52, rr 4(3), 6(3); CCR Ord 29, r 1(7).

9 *Jelson (Estates) Ltd v Harvey* [1984] 1 All ER 12, [1983] 1 WLR 1401, CA.

10 *Woolley v Woolley*, above, and cases cited above.

11 RSC Ord 52, r 4(2); CCR Ord 29, r 1(4). It should be noted that an application for committal for failure to give discovery of documents may be served on the respondent's solicitors; see RSC Ord 24, r 16(3), CCR Ord 14, r 10(3).

12 RSC Ord 52, r 4(3); CCR Ord 29, r 1(7).

13 *Hipgrave v Hipgrave* [1962] P 91, [1962] 1 All ER 75, Scarman J following *Gilbert v Gilbert* (1961) Times, 15 September, Plowman J; *Pearce v Pearce* (1959) Times, 30 January; *Devaux v Devaux* (1959) Times, 4 September; and *Moran v Moran* (1959) Times, 25 September. It must be emphasised that a committal order ex parte is a most exceptional remedy which will only be granted where delay by applying on notice might cause irreparable or serious mischief.

14 RSC Ord 52, r 4(3).

county court may hear an application to commit ex parte, by dispensing with service of the notice in Form 78.[15] For an order of committal to be made ex parte the circumstances must be exceptional.[16] A judge has a discretion to hear the application ex parte, and must balance the desirability of an immediate hearing and the urgency of the matter against the possibility that the evidence may not be complete.[17]

There must, on an ex parte application, be a notice[18] although the judge may take account of breaches alleged to have been committed after the issue of the notice.[19] Personal service should only be waived where the matter is grave, the need for relief is urgent and the respondent has knowledge of the application.[20] Personal service will probably be waived where the applicant could show that the person whose committal was sought was deliberately evading service.[1] Where the hearing of an application to commit is adjourned, notice of the adjourned hearing must be served personally on the alleged contemnor,[2] subject to the power to dispense with service.[3]

An affidavit of service of these documents should be sworn and filed, in case the respondent does not attend at the hearing of the application for the committal order when the court would then need to be satisfied that the documents have been served.[4] The affidavit of service should include details of how the respondent was identified by the person serving the document; the circumstances in which the documents were served and exhibiting to the affidavit copies of all the documents that were served.[5]

6 The affidavit in answer

Having been served with the application for committal, it is, of course, open to the respondent to file affidavit evidence in answer to the application. In his affidavit, the respondent should admit or deny whether or not he admits each and every alleged breach. If the breach or breaches are admitted, then any mitigating circumstances should be put forward in the affidavit no doubt coupled with a sincere apology to the court and a promise to abide by the order in the future. If the breaches are denied, then the affidavit will take the form of denying what is alleged in the applicant's affidavit and, indeed, the respondent may file affidavits sworn by such persons as can support his denial. It would seem that an alleged contemnor may not be required to file an affidavit as he cannot be compelled to give evidence against his will.[6]

---

15 CCR Ord 29, r 1(7).
16 *Wright v Jess* [1987] 2 All ER 1067 [1987] 1 WLR 1076, CA. The very essence of a case being exceptional is that one is unlikely to find a precisely parallel set of facts in some other reported authority. *Harben v Harben* [1957] 1 All ER 379, [1957] 1 WLR 261, Sachs J, at p 381 and p 265.
17 *Lamb v Lamb* [1984] FLR 278, [1984] Fam Law 60, CA.
18 Specifying the alleged breaches; *Wright v Jess* above.
19 *Wright v Jess*, above.
20 *Spooner v Spooner* (1962) Times, 4 December.
1 Ibid.
2 *Chiltern District Council v Keane* [1985] 2 All ER 118, [1985] 1 WLR 619, CA. See also *Phonographic Performance Ltd v Tsang* [1985] LS. Gaz R 2331, CA.
3 RSC Ord 52, r 4(3), CCR Ord 29, r 1(7).
4 Oral evidence of service may be given: *Savage v Savage* [1979] CA Transcript 537.
5 For a precedent see Appendix 4.
6 *Comet Products UK Ltd v Hawkex Plastics Ltd* [1971] 2 QB 67, [1971] 1 All ER 1141, CA.

7 The hearing of the application to commit

In the High Court, the application will, subject to certain exceptions, be heard in open court.[7] In any event, the order must be made in open court.[8] In the High Court an application for a committal order may not, without leave of the court, be made which relies on grounds other than those contained in the application for the committal order.[9] This practice is in general followed in the county court. It would seem that there is no power in the county court to hear the application except in open court.

All persons who have sworn affidavits either in support of or in opposition to the application for committal should attend the hearing so that they can be cross-examined upon their respective affidavits. In the High Court the alleged contemnor has a right to give evidence at the hearing if he so wishes.[10] This is generally followed in the county court.

During the course of the hearing, the applicant for an order for committal must prove:

(a) An injunction embodied in an order of the court endorsed with a penal notice, or that an undertaking has been given;

(b) That the order but not an undertaking mentioned in (a) above has been duly served personally upon the respondent or that such service has been dispensed with;

(c) That the respondent has wilfully disobeyed the order or that he has wilfully failed to obey the order;[11]

(d) If the respondent does not attend the hearing of the application to commit, that service of the application to commit together with the affidavit in support has been effected upon the respondent or that such service has been dispensed with.[12]

An application to commit is quite separate from any criminal proceedings which might arise from the same facts.[13] Therefore an application to commit should not be adjourned pending the outcome of a criminal trial.[14] It is important for committal proceedings to be dealt with swiftly and decisively.[15]

---

7 RSC Ord 52, r 6(1). For the purposes of this work the only really relevant exception is r 6(1)(a); see Appendix 2.

8 RSC Ord 52, r 6.

9 RSC Ord 52, r 6(5).

10 RSC Ord 52, r 6(4).

11 Proof of which must be beyond reasonable doubt: *Re Bramblevale* [1970] Ch 28, [1969] 3 All ER 1062, CA and see *Dean v Dean* (1986) Times, 13 November, CA, overruling *West Oxfordshire District Council v Beratec Ltd* (1986) Times, 30 October.

12 In general this will be by affidavit of service, though oral evidence of service is admissible – see *Savage v Savage*, above.

13 *Szczepanski v Szczepanski* [1985] FLR 468, [1985] Fam Law 120, CA, and see *Caprice v Boswell* (1985) 149 JP 703, [1986], Fam Law 52, CA. The question of double jeopardy was not considered.

14 Ibid, and see *Jefferson Ltd v Bhetcha* [1979] 2 All ER 1108, [1979] 1 WLR 898, CA, where it was held that a plaintiff in civil proceedings is not to be debarred from pursuing an action merely because to do so might result in the defendant, if he wished to defend, having to disclose his defence thereby giving an indication of his likely defence in contemporaneous criminal proceedings.

15 *Szczepanski v Szczepanski*, above, and *Caprice v Boswell*, above.

8   Court orders upon proof of breach

Breach of an injunction[16] or undertaking to the court[17] is a contempt of court. It follows that it is a matter for the court to decide whether or not imprisonment is the appropriate order to make upon the application to commit. The real purpose of bringing matters back to court on applications to commit, certainly in the context of orders made in family cases, is often not so much to punish disobedience of court orders as to secure compliance with the injunction in the future with the result that committal orders are and must be regarded as orders of the very last resort.[18] A judge has a very wide discretion as to whether or not to make a committal order where there has been a breach of an injunction.[19] Whilst the views of the applicant for the committal order are very relevant[20] it should be remembered by judges when exercising their discretion that orders to commit are potentially damaging to complainant spouses as to offending spouses particularly where children are concerned with the result that orders should be made very reluctantly and only when every other effort to bring the situation under control has failed or is almost certain to do so.[1] In particular, the power to order imprisonment is one which should be used very sparingly indeed in proceedings for contempt of custody and access orders.[2]

Nevertheless and notwithstanding the foregoing, it must be remembered that unless the courts are prepared ultimately to exercise the power to commit in cases of breach, the purpose of making orders ousting parties from the matrimonial home and/or orders not to molest other spouses will be defeated. A short term of immediate imprisonment may be appropriate even where there has only been one breach of the order or undertaking if that breach is sufficiently serious and flagrant.[3] Where an application to commit has been adjourned generally, it is very similar to a deferment of sentence in criminal proceedings. Accordingly further breaches of the injunction or undertaking are likely to justify a custodial sentence.[4] Consecutive terms of imprisonment may be appropriate where there have been several different breaches.[5]

A committal order is not appropriate where there is a satisfactory alternative method of enforcing the order.[6] The High Court[7] and county courts[8] have power to punish contempt by a sentence of imprisonment of up to two years, or by an unlimited fine, or both. The sentence of imprisonment must be expressed as a fixed term.[9]

16 *Ansah v Ansah* [1977] Fam 138, [1977] 2 All ER 638, CA, per Ormrod LJ.
17 *Hipgrave v Hipgrave*, [1962] P 91, [1962] 1 All ER 75.
18 *Ansah v Ansah*, above, at 144 (1980) 1 FL R 26, CA, per Ormrod LJ.
19 *McLean v Nugent* and at 643, per Ormrod LJ. Committal should never be ordered in respect of a purely technical breach of an injunction or undertaking; see *Marshall v Marshall* (1966) 110 Sol Jo 112, CA. See also *Smith v Smith* (1987) Times, 20 June, CA.
20 See *Boylan v Boylan* (1980) 11 Fam Law 76, CA.
 1 *Ansah v Ansah*, above, at 144 and 643, per Ormrod LJ.
 2 *R v R* (1979) 10 Fam Law 56, CA, per Orr LJ.
 3 *Pickering v Pickering* [1980] Transcript 193, CA, and see *Re H* (1985) Times, 7 November, CA.
 4 *George v George* [1986] 2 FLR 347, [1986] Fam Law 294, CA.
 5 *Lee v Walker* [1985] QB 1191, [1985] 1 All ER 781, CA.
 6 *Danchevsky v Danchevsky* [1975] Fam 17, [1974] 3 All ER 934.
 7 Contempt of Court Act 1981, s 14(1).
 8 Ibid, s 14(4A), added by the County Courts (Penalties for Contempt) Act 1983 reversing the decision of *Whitter v Peters, Peart v Stewart* [1983] 2 AC 109, [1983] 1 All ER 859, HL.
 9 *Westcott v Westcott* [1985] FLR 616, [1985] Fam Law 278, CA and see *Re C (a minor)* [1986] 1 FLR 578, [1986] Fam Law 187, CA.

The court has jurisdiction to enforce orders or binding undertakings made or given even where they are made or given after the decree has been made absolute.[10] Indeed, the court has jurisdiction to make an order even after the decree absolute has been pronounced.[11] An absurd situation would result if the court was able to make injunctions but unable to enforce them.[12]

9 Orders for committal

If an order for committal is made by the court, the order as drawn up by the court staff must reflect exactly the order that is made by the judge.[13] In particular, any order which is drawn up by the court staff must reflect the period of imprisonment which has been imposed by the judge.

Where a committal order is made on an ex parte application the contemnor should be shown a copy of the order (whether or not he is shown the warrant) either before or shortly after his arrest.[14] An ex parte order should contain a proviso that the contemnor should apply for his release three days (a period necessary for practical purposes) after being taken into custody.[15] An ex parte committal order is not an interim order and if a judge on a later occasion hears evidence from the contemnor he may not increase the sentence[16] as a person may only be sentenced once for each contempt.[17] Where a contemnor applies for an order of committal, made in his absence, to be set aside the whole matter should be reheard.[18] The judge should not merely hear the contemnor's evidence.[19] However, it is important to distinguish between an application to set aside a committal order and an application for release, which is on the ground that the contemnor has purged, or is desirous of purging, his contempt.[20]

The prescribed forms[1] must be drawn up accurately by the court staff. However defects in the formal parts of an order do not affect its validity.[2] If the court has exercised its powers to dispense with service of the injunction[3] or the application to commit[4] then the order must state the same.[5] An order of a county court must state the evidence that has been given.[6]

An order of the High Court or a county court must state each and every contempt proved[7] although it would seem that where a breach is admitted

---

10 *Stewart v Stewart* [1973] Fam 21, [1973] 1 All ER 31.
11 See ch 1, section A.2, above.
12 *Stewart v Stewart*, above.
13 *Danchevsky v Danchevsky* [1975] Fam 17, [1974] 3 All ER 934.
14 *Egan v Egan* (1971) 115 Sol Jo 673 Lane J.
15 *Egan v Egan*, above.
16 *Lamb v Lamb* [1984] FLR 278, [1984] Fam Law 60, CA.
17 *Church's Trustee v Hibbard* [1902] 2 Ch 784, CA.
18 *Aslam v Singh* [1987] 1 FLR 122, [1986] Fam Law 362, CA.
19 *Aslam v Singh* above.
20 RSC Ord 52, r 8(1), CCR Ord 29, r 3(1).
 1 RSC App A Form 85, County Court (Forms) Rules 1982, Form 79.
 2 *Palmer v Townsend* (1979) 123 Sol Jo 570, *Burrows v Iqbal* (No 2) [1985] Fam Law 188, CA.
 3 RSC Ord 45, rr 7(6) and (7), CCR Ord 29, r 1(7).
 4 RSC Ord 52, r 4(3), CCR Ord 29, r 1(7).
 5 *Nguyen v Phung* [1984] FLR 773, [1985] Fam Law 54, CA, and see *Williams v Fawcett* [1986] QB 604, [1985] 1 All ER 787, CA.
 6 See County Court (Forms) Rules 1982, Form 79, and see *Cinderby v Cinderby*, *Pekesin v Pekesin* (No 2) (1978) 8 Fam Law 244, CA.
 7 *McIlrath v Grady* [1968] 1 QB 468, [1967] 3 All ER 625, CA.

by the contemnor it need not be particularised,[8] nevertheless it is submitted that breaches should be specified in orders so that the court record is clear for the future.

Where a period of imprisonment is ordered the term must be stated in the order,[9] and imprisonment can only be for a fixed term.[10] The fact that the prescribed form in the High Court[11] seems to provide for an indefinite period of imprisonment does not alter the position.[12]

A person can only be sentenced once for each contempt[13] therefore a judge may not increase a term of imprisonment imposed ex parte once he has heard from the contemnor[14] nor can a sentence be increased, once made, because of the effect of remission.[15]

It would seem that an invalid order cannot be rectified by the court of first instance substituting a valid order.[16] However, on appeal, while an invalid order must be quashed,[17] a valid order may be substituted.[18] If there has been a fair hearing without any material irregularity in the proceedings but merely an irregularity in drawing up the order there is no reason why the Court of Appeal may not substitute a just sentence,[19] which could in an exceptional case be a longer one.[20] A court should hesitate long before increasing a sentence. [1]

10 Suspended committal orders

If the court is of the opinion that immediate imprisonment is not appropriate, it has power to make an order of committal suspended upon terms. [2] Care must be taken however when making a suspended committal order, to ensure that the terms upon which the committal is suspended do not have the effect of removing the respondent's liberty from the judge's discretion and control. [3] In particular, orders which are expressed to take effect upon the filing of the document the veracity of which has been untested and without a further review by the court are bad orders.

In general, a suspended committal order is only appropriate where a mandatory injunction has been breached and the purpose of the committal order is to secure future compliance. It is often, for example, used where its purpose is to secure compliance with an order for discovery or for directions. If an affidavit is filed which states that the respondent has failed

---

8 *Kavanagh v Kavanagh* (1978) 128 NLJ 1007, CA.
9 See the wording of the prescribed forms; RSC App A, Form 85, County Court (Forms) Rules 1982, Form 79.
10 Contempt of Court Act 1981, s 14 (11 *Halsbury's Statutes* (4th edn) 181 CONTEMPT OF COURT). *Linnett v Coles* [1987] QB 555, [1986] 3 All ER 652, CA.
11 RSC App A, Form 85.
12 In *Re C (a minor)* [1986] 1 FLR 578, [1986] Fam Law 187, CA. RSC Ord 1, r 9 is ultra vires the statute: Contempt of Court Act 1981, s 14, and the statute must prevail.
13 *Church's Trustee v Hibbard* [1902] 2 Ch 784.
14 *Aslam v Singh* [1987] 1 FLR 122, [1986] Fam Law 362, CA.
15 *Westcott v Westcott* [1985] FLR 616, [1985] Fam Law 278, CA.
16 *Hegarty v O'Sullivan* [1985] NLJ Rep 557, CA, but this decision must be read subject to *Linnett v Coles* [1987] QB 555, [1986] 3 All ER 652, CA.
17 *Linnett v Coles*, above.
18 *Linnett v Coles*, above, applying Administration of Justice Act 1960, s 13(3) (11 *Halsbury's Statutes* (4th edn) 174 CONTEMPT OF COURT.)
19 *Linnett v Coles*, above.
20 Ibid.
 1 Ibid.
 2 RSC Ord 52, r 7 and see *Lee v Walker* [1985] QB 1191, [1985] 1 All ER 781, CA.
 3 *Ansah v Ansah* [1977] Fam 138, [1977] 2 All ER 638, CA at 144C and 643g.

to vacate the matrimonial home, it is dealing with fact (and not with opinion) which will either be true or false. For that reason, it is frequently used to enforce such orders. Breaches of molestation orders are by their nature far from clear cut. [4] Molestation varies considerably in degree and what constitutes molestation in any given circumstances may well be in a grey area between fact and opinion. Indeed, it would seem to be dangerous to commit a person to prison suspended on terms that he did not assault or molest the applicant and to provide that the suspension will be removed upon filing an affidavit that he had in fact assaulted or molested the applicant. In this context, it should be noted that under the power of arrest, a person can only be arrested if he is suspected of being in breach of non molestation injunctions by reason of his use of violence. [5] Where terms are imposed on fulfilment of which a suspended committal order is to come into operation for breach of a non molestation order, the terms should be as particularly drafted as it is possible to do in the circumstances of the case.,

At the hearing of a committal application, if the application were not to be adjourned with liberty to restore, the court could attach powers of arrest to an injunction as this is in general an effective way of securing future compliance of a prohibitory injunction. [6] However, before the power of arrest can be attached, the statutory conditions must be fulfilled. [7] Where a power of arrest is imposed, control is maintained by the court in that the person arrested must be brought before the court within twenty-four hours. [8]

11 Applications to commit non-parties

Not only may an application be made to commit a party in breach of an injunction or his undertaking to the court, but application may also be made to commit to prison any person who with knowledge [9] of such injunction or undertaking to the court aids and abets a party to breach the injunction or undertaking. [10] A stranger to an action who is required, by an order in such action, to do or to refrain from doing something will be amenable to proceedings for contempt if he refuses to comply or obstructs compliance with the order. [11] This is so even if the stranger is not, in law, bound by the order. [12]

The principle is indeed well established and is a power accepted and used by the court because it is not for the public benefit that the course of justice

4 *Vaughan v Vaughan* [1973] 3 All ER 449, [1973] 1 WLR 1159, CA, and see ch 3 above.
5 Domestic Violence and Matrimonial Proceedings Act 1976, s 2(3).
6 *Ansah v Ansah*, above, per Ormrod LJ.
7 See *Lewis v Lewis* [1978] Fam 60, [1978] 1 All ER 729, CA, and ch 6, above.
8 Domestic Violence and Matrimonial Proceedings Act 1976, s 2, as amended by the Domestic Proceedings and Magistrates' Courts Act 1978, Sch 2.
9 See *Seaward v Paterson* [1897] 1 Ch 545.
10 *Thorne v Bunting* (No 2) [1972] 3 All ER 1084, CA, and see the cases cited therein.
11 *Bawden v Bawden* (Note) [1979] 1 QB 419, [1978] 3 All ER 1216 at 420H–421B and at 1218d per Goff LJ obiter.
12 *Bawden v Bawden* above. It should be noted that an order which is good on its face remains in force and valid unless and until it is set aside by a court of competent jurisdiction on a proper application to do so. *McLean v Nugent* (1980) 1 FLR 26, CA.

should be obstructed in a deliberate manner by strangers to the action. Indeed, if the court were not to take this power a very grave weakness in the battery of court powers would be revealed.

To enforce an order against a non-party, it is necessary to prove firstly knowledge[13] and secondly aiding or abetting a breach of the order by a party to the order.

The application to commit, however, must be served personally as required by the Rules[14] and should be made in the same manner and as if the application were to commit a party. The application should be supported by an affidavit to be served personally. In general, the order for breach of which it is proposed to apply to commit a stranger will have come to the stranger's notice one way or another at some stage prior to the application to commit being served since otherwise there would be little or no point in proceeding with the application. In general, it is submitted that a legal adviser when faced with breaches by a stranger should send an open letter to the stranger concerned enclosing a copy of the order by recorded delivery and inviting him to desist from breaching the order. Failure to comply with that letter when enclosing a copy of the order will be the most vital evidence to be exhibited to any affidavit in support of an application to commit a stranger.

12 Discharge from prison of person committed for contempt

A person committed to prison for contempt may apply to the court to be released from prison.[15] This application is normally made to the judge who made the committal order but may be made to any other judge of the court and in certain circumstances as set out in the Rules may be made to a registrar of the court.

There is no requirement in the High Court that the application for release should be supported by an affidavit. In the county court, the application must be supported by an affidavit in support showing that the applicant has purged or is desirous of purging his contempt and it must be served with a copy of his application on the party who applied for his committal in the first place.[16] The general practice is to file such an affidavit in the High Court. Not only can the affidavit deal with the purging of the contempt, but furthermore it can deal fully with any change of circumstances since the order was made.

Where someone has been committed to prison for a fixed term, as it must be, it is perhaps difficult to argue (in the absence of a change of circumstances) that he should be released from prison because his contempt has been purged. Often, it is not the length of the imprisonment that is important but the fact of imprisonment itself. Certainly, no order should be made which prevents a person applying to the court for this purpose.[17]

Once an application to discharge has been made, the question is one purely for the discretion of the judge to whom the application is made.

---

13 Ibid. There may be a requirement that the order should have been served on the non-party where committal is sought. *In re L (a Minor)* (1987) Times 4 July.
14 See above.
15 RSC Ord 52, r 8; CCR Ord 29, r 3; and MCR 1977, r 90(2).
16 CCR Ord, 29, r 3(1).
17 *Yager v Musa* [1961] 2 QB 214 at 219, [1961] 2 All ER 561 at 564, per Devlin. See also *Raymond v Honey* [1983] 1 AC 1, [1982] 1 All ER 756, HL.

Chapter 13
Magistrates' courts

1 General

With the coming into force of sections 16 to 18 of the Domestic Proceedings and Magistrates' Courts Act 1978 (the Act of 1978) magistrates' courts were, for the first time, given powers hitherto reserved for the higher courts. In particular they were given the power to exclude a party to a marriage from the matrimonial home as well as to make orders in the nature of injunctions to restrain violence or threatened violence towards spouses and children of the family. Despite these new powers, the indications are that the popularity of magistrates' courts as a forum for matrimonial disputes is declining. Since the powers that are available to magistrates in the sphere of domestic violence, whilst wider than ever before, are nevertheless far narrower[1] than those possessed by the (divorce) county court and the Family Division of the High Court this is not altogether surprising. In particular, the power of magistrates to act upon evidence of domestic violence is confined to people who are married and before magistrates can act there must be evidence of violence or threatened violence. Neither of these restrictions apply to the jurisdiction exercised by the higher courts under the Domestic Violence and Matrimonial Proceedings Act 1976 nor does the latter restriction apply when the courts are invited to make interlocutory orders in divorce and judicial separation proceedings. It follows that whenever a magistrates' court is empowered to act a divorce county court could also act. It is likely that by the time a marriage has reached the stage of violence or threatened violence whether towards a spouse or to a child or to the children of the family the spouse who is applying for protection will also wish to terminate the marriage by way of a divorce or to take judicial separation proceedings. In that case, there is little point and much duplication of costs involved in applying to a magistrates' court for an order which can be obtained and speedily in the court which would have jurisdiction to deal with the divorce or judicial separation proceedings. It has been noted by some commentators[2] that the attitude of the legal aid authorities will be crucial. In practice it seems that applications under the Domestic Violence and Matrimonial Proceedings Act 1976 are preferred.

---

1 See *Horner v Horner* [1982] Fam 90, [1982] 2 All ER 495, CA, in which the powers of county courts and magistrates' courts were compared. See also *O'Brien v O'Brien* [1985] FLR 801, [1985] Fam Law 191, CA.
2 Notably Alec Samuels 'The New Matrimonial Law in Magistrates' Courts, (1981) 11 Fam Law 60.

2 Procedure

Proceedings within sections 16 to 18 are defined as 'domestic pro-ceedings'.[3] However, proceedings for the enforcement of any order made, confirmed or registered under, inter alia, the Act of 1978 are not to be regarded as domestic proceedings unless the court before which the enforcement proceedings are to be heard, in its discretion, orders the proceedings to be treated as domestic proceedings[4]. If the parties to the enforcement proceedings are also parties to domestic proceedings which are to be heard together then the whole of those proceedings are to be treated as domestic proceedings for the purposes of the Act.[5]

The effect of these provisions, it is submitted, is that an application for an order under section 16 of the Act of 1978 is deemed domestic pro-ceedings and as such is subject to the restrictions which apply to such hearings whereas proceedings for enforcement (whether on the hearing following the issue of a warrant for breach or following the arrest of a respondent under the power of arrest) are not and so should be held under normal magistrates' courts conditions unless either:

(a) the enforcement proceedings are being heard at the same time as other domestic proceedings between the parties; or

(b) the magistrates have exercised their discretion under section 65(2) of the Act of 1980.

There is no appeal from the making of or refusal to make an order under section 65.[6]

Whilst there appears to be no authority on the point, the discretion which is accorded to the magistrates under section 65(2) would have to be exercised judicially and so, possibly, would be open to judicial review in the event, for example, of a failure to hear both parties to the application before making a decision.

Domestic proceedings and matters to be treated as domestic proceedings must be heard by a court consisting of magistrates selected from the domestic panel.[7]

A specific exception is created by section 16(5) of the Act of 1978 where, on an application for a personal protection and/or exclusion order, the court considers it is essential that the application be heard without delay, the court may hear the application notwithstanding:

(a) the court does not include a man and a woman; or

(b) any member of the court is not a member of the domestic panel; or

(c) the proceedings on the application are not separated from the hearing and determination of proceedings which are not domestic proceedings.

It would appear that any Court before which an application comes can decide in its discretion that 'it is essential that the application be heard without delay' and can thereupon proceed to hear it. However, advocates appearing in such circumstances should point out to the court hearing the application, if it falls within any of the three sections set out above,

---

3 Magistrates' Courts Act 1980, s 65(1) (27 *Halsbury's Statutes* (4th edn) 223 MAGISTRATES).

4 Ibid, s 65(2).

5 Ibid, s 65(3).

6 See ibid, s 65(4).

7 See ibid, s 67(2).

therefore before the court has jurisdiction to entertain the application it must first adopt jurisdiction. It is submitted that in practice, courts before which such applications come will almost always accept jurisdiction under this provision given the restricted circumstances in which magistrates' courts are empowered to make orders.

Applications for orders under section 16 of the Act of 1978 must always take place under the conditions prescribed by section 66 of the Magistrates' Courts Act 1980 since an application remains domestic proceedings even though heard by a court which is not a domestic court under the exception referred to above. Section 69(2) of that Act requires that no one should be present during the application except the officers of the court; parties to the application; their legal representative and 'other persons directly concerned with the case'. In addition, representatives of the press may remain, but all other persons seeking to be present may be admitted only at the discretion of the magistrates who are sitting who, however, must not exclude anyone who appears to them to have adequate grounds for being present.

So far as 'other persons directly concerned in the case' are concerned, this would include doctors, social workers or probation officers involved with the family concerned in the application. However, the witnesses of fact should, in general, be excluded until they have given their evidence and persons such as doctors, social workers and probation officers, if they are to give evidence of fact as well as to expert evidence, should be excluded until their evidence has been given. In such circumstances, if a person has not been excluded and is called as a witness, the magistrate should not refuse to hear the witness unless he or she had remained in court in defiance of an order that all witnesses should leave when the magistrates have a discretion whether to admit his or her evidence.[8]

Section 69(6) Magistrates' Court Act 1980 provides that nothing in the section is to affect the exercise by a magistrates' court of the power to direct that witnesses shall be excluded until their call for examination.

Although the Act permits the presence of newspaper representatives[9] what they can report is limited by section 71 of the Act of 1980. These provisions apply irrespective of whether the court hearing the application is the Domestic Court or not. Breach of the provisions of section 71 carries the maximum penalty, on summary conviction, of a fine of level 4 of the standard scale.[10]

When the court is hearing proceedings for the enforcement of an order under section 16 (whether following an arrest on warrant issued for alleged breach at the instance of the applicant or following the arrest of the respondent under a power of arrest) all hearings (including all remand hearings) are 'proceedings for the enforcement' of an order made under Part I of the Act of 1978. It follows that unless section 65(2) or (3) applies, proceedings are not domestic proceedings; that any bench of magistrates may hear the case and none of the restrictions to which reference has been made would apply. This is consistent with the approach of the higher courts which hear proceedings that may result in depriving a person of his

---

8 See *Tomlinson v Tomlinson* [1980] 1 All ER 593, [1980] 1 WLR 322, per Sir John Arnold P.

9 See Magistrates' Courts Act 1980, s 69(1)(c).

10 Ibid, s 71(3) as amended by Criminal Justice Act 1982, s 46(1) (27 *Halsbury's Statutes* (4th edn) 229 MAGISTRATES); the current maximum is £1,000.

liberty in public. Since the enforcement proceedings may well result in depriving a person of his liberty, it is submitted that a magistrates' court should be slow to exercise its discretion under section 65(2).

3 Applications

Applications for an order under section 16 of the 1978 Act should be made to the magistrates' courts for the commission area where either the applicant or the respondent ordinarily reside.[11] The test is purely residential and the domicile of either of the parties is wholly irrelevant.[12] Either party to a marriage may apply for an order under section 16.[13] The application is by summons which must be served upon the respondent personally.[14] Where a summons is served by an officer of the court he will endorse on the document served a certificate of service. Such certificate is no more than evidence which the justices may take into account in coming to a decision as to whether or not the rules as to service have been obeyed.[15] Service of the summons by leaving it with some person at the respondent's last known address or usual place of abode[16] or by sending it by post in a letter addressed to him at such address[17] may only be adopted where a justice of the peace is satisfied by evidence on oath that prompt personal service of the summons is impracticable and allows service in such manner.[18] Such an application may be made conveniently at the making of the complaint in order to obtain the issue by the magistrate of the summons.

4 Expedited orders

Although there is no jurisdiction in the magistrates to make an order under section 16 ex parte, the court may make an 'expedited order' where the court is satisfied that 'there is imminent danger of physical injury to the applicant or to a child of the family' and the summons has not been served on the respondent or has not been served within a reasonable time of the hearing of the application or the summons is returnable at some other place or time.[19] Such an order may be made by a single magistrate.[20]

However, even if the court is satisfied that there is an imminent danger of physical injury it is only empowered to make a protection order of non molestation under section 16(2) so that the value of an expedited order is very limited. In order to get an application for an expedited order before the court, the applicant or the applicant's solicitors should deliver a written statement, signed by the applicant to the effect that there is imminent danger of physical injury to the applicant or a child of the family, to the clerk of the appropriate magistrates' court. The clerk of the court then has

---

11 See Domestic Proceedings and Magistrates' Courts Act 1978, s 30(1) (27 *Halsbury's Statutes* (4th edn) 791 MATRIMONIAL LAW.)
12 Ibid, s 30(5).
13 Ibid, s 16(1).
14 Magistrates' Courts Rules 1981, rr 99(1)(a) (SI 1981/552).
15 *Maher v Gower (formerly Kubilius)* (1982) 3 FLR 287, 12 Fam Law 32, DC, where it was pointed out there is no provision in either the Magistrates' Courts Act 1980 or the Magistrates' Courts Rules 1981 which makes such a certificate binding on the justices. See also *Hawkins v Crown Prosecution Service* (1987) Times, 24 August, DC.
16 Ibid, r 99(1)(b).
17 Ibid, r 99(1)(c).
18 Ibid, r 99(7).
19 See Domestic Proceedings and Magistrates' Courts Act 1978, s 16(6).
20 See ibid, s 16(7).

to bring the matter before a court as soon as practicable.[1] Where a magistrates' court makes an expedited order, the clerk of the court must notify the respondent personally unless a magistrate has been satisfied by evidence on oath that prompt personal service is impractical, when the magistrate may give the clerk leave to serve a copy of the order by leaving or posting it to his last known address.[2] Prudent practitioners are likely to advise their clients to seek an ex parte order in the county court rather than an expedited order in the magistrates' court since in such a case an ouster injunction is within the court's powers even though application is made ex parte.[3]

An expedited order, which will not take effect until service[4] upon the respondent or such later date as the court may specify, will expire after twenty-eight days from making of the order or commencement of the hearing of the application for an order under section 16[5] or earlier if so provided.[6] A spouse who has the benefit of an expedited order may apply for another one to take effect on the expiry of the subsisting one.[7] An expedited order may be subject to conditions or exceptions as may be specified.[8] Whilst the power exists, it is hard to see how it can be satisfactorily put into effect within the context of a protection order whether or not it is expedited. It may be for example that an order under the terms of section 16(2)(b) may be made subject to an exception of lawful chastisement, but it is submitted that such an exception would create problems of enforcement which is highly desirable to avoid.

The court has power to attach to an expedited order a power of arrest since that power is exercisable upon the making of an order under section 16 subject to the statutory criteria. Whilst it is the case that on a full hearing of an application under section 16 of the Act of 1978 it is inconsistent with the refusal of an exclusion order to grant a power of arrest[9] and whilst it is the case that if an application for a power of arrest is to be made notice should be given to the other side in the summons[10] it is going too far to suppose that the court hearing an application for an expedited order under the Domestic Proceedings and Magistrates' Courts Act 1978 should always refuse a power of arrest.[11] Evidence that a wife is too frightened to go back is evidence that may justify the use of a power of arrest even on an expedited application.[12] Indeed, *McCartney v McCartney*[13] is to be confined strictly to cases where the court is hearing a full application under section 16. The wording of section 16(6) is more, not less, emphatic in terms than section 16(3) so that the inconsistency noted in the case of

1 Magistrates' Courts (Matrimonial Proceedings) Rules 1980, r 13(1) (SI 1980/1582).
2 Magistrates' Courts (Matrimonial Proceedings) Rules 1980, r 19(1).
3 See further ch 2, section A, above.
4 Where the order is served by an officer of the court he will complete the certificate of service endorsed on the reverse of the copy. Such a certificate is not conclusive; it is no more than evidence which the court may take into account in coming to a decision as to whether or not there has been compliance with the rules as to service; *Maher v Gower (formerly Kubilius)* (1982) 3 FLR 287, 12 Fam Law 32, DC.
5 See the Domestic Proceedings and Magistrates' Courts Act 1978, s 16(8).
6 See ibid, s 16(9).
7 See ibid, s 17(1).
8 See ibid, s 16(9).
9 *McCartney v McCartney* [1981] Fam 59, [1981] 1 All ER 597, DC.
10 See *Lewis v Lewis* [1978] Fam 60 at 63C [1978] 1 All ER 729 at 731, per Ormrod J.
11 See *Morgan v Morgan* [1978] CA Transcript 423, CA.
12 See *Lewis v Lewis*, above.
13 [1981] Fam 59, [1981] 1 All ER 597, DC.

McCartney in respect of a refusal of an order under section 16(3) does not exist. In addition, as has already been noted, the magistrates' court hearing an expedited order has no power to make an exclusion order. The weakness of the magistrates' powers on an expedited hearing is that they have no power to exclude. If the court is satisfied that there is 'imminent danger of physical injury' then providing the respondent has committed acts of violence against the applicant and the child, there is nothing inconsistent and indeed it is entirely consistent that a power of arrest should be imposed. Often the imposition of a power of arrest will be the only way a magistrates' court will be able to persuade a spouse who has been subjected to violence to return if he or she has not the benefit of an exclusion order and indeed even the imposition of a power of arrest may not have this effect.

The inability of a magistrates' court to impose an exclusion order on an expedited hearing is a fundamental weakness in their powers which can only dissuade litigants from using the magistrates' court. Where a magistrates' court makes an order to which a power of arrest is attached, the clerk of the court shall cause a copy of the order to be sent to the officer for the time being in charge of any police station for the address at which the person who applied for the order resides.[14]

One matter which courts, on expedited applications, must be wary of is the marital status of the parties. Unlike the Domestic Violence and Matrimonial Proceedings Act 1976, the Domestic Proceedings and Magistrates' Courts Act 1978 gives the magistrates powers to act only where the parties are in fact married.[15] In practice, on full hearings, the court can satisfy itself of the marital status of the parties before it by admissions by the respondent. However, where the applicant only is before the court on an expedited hearing they must be satisfied of the marital status of the parties before they act. Whilst the court could act on the oral testimony from the applicant alone that she is married to the respondent, practitioners should obtain a certified copy of the marriage certificate if at all possible and have it available as such is evidence of the marriage without further or other proof.[16] Since any order obtained by a person against another to whom they are not married is bound to be void and any arrest which follows, unlawful,[17] a court should take every step to satisfy itself with the marital status of the parties before acting.

In many of the cases which a magistrates' court would hear on an expedited hearing, the party applying would have been driven from the matrimonial home and be too frightened to return. In those circumstances, it may well be impossible for him or her to obtain a certified copy of the marriage certificate and the time which has elapsed between them leaving and the court hearing the expedited hearing may be too short to obtain documentary evidence. In addition, it is unlikely that unrepresented parties would have such documentation available at the court. Magistrates should, therefore, be willing in appropriate cases to act on oral testimony as to the marital status of the parties but practitioners should if at all possible have a certified copy of the marriage certificate available at the hearing.

14 Magistrates' Courts (Matrimonial Proceedings) Rules 1980, r 19(2)(a).
15 See s 16(1).
16 Marriage Act 1949, s 65(3) (37 *Halsbury's Statutes* (4th edn) REGISTRATION CONCERNING THE INDIVIDUAL).
17 See Samuels (1981) 11 Fam Law 60.

5 Powers under section 16

Where a magistrates' court is satisfied the respondent to an application is:
(a) a spouse of the applicant;[18] and
(b) has used or threatened to use violence against the person of the applicant or a child of the family[19] and;
(c) that an order is necessary for the protection of a child of the family or the applicant;[20]
a magistrates' court may:
(1) order the respondent not to use or threaten to use violence against the person of the applicant and/or
(2) order the respondent not to use or threaten to use violence against the person of a child of the family.

Before a magistrates' court can order the respondent to leave the matrimonial home[1] and/or prohibit him from returning thereto[2] the court must be satisfied that:
(a) the respondent is the applicant's spouse;[3] and
(b)　(i) the respondent has used violence against the person of the applicant or a child of the family;[4] or
　　(ii) that the respondent has threatened to use violence against the person of the applicant or a child of the family; and has used violence against some other person,[5] or
(c) the respondent in contravention of an order made under section 16(2) threatened to use violence against the person of the applicant or a child of the family,[6] and
(d) that the applicant or a child of the family is in danger of being physically injured by the respondent or would be if either were to enter the matrimonial home.

It will be seen that before the court can even consider making either a protection or exclusion order against a respondent various conditions precedent have to be satisfied. Even if those conditions are satisfied, the magistrates' court is not obliged to make either a protection or an exclusion order. They have a discretion whether or not an order is to be made and that discretion should be exercised according to the principles discernible from cases decided under the Domestic Violence and Matrimonial Proceedings Act 1976.[7]

It is very important to realise that the magistrates' courts have no jurisdiction over cohabitees. The Domestic Proceedings and Magistrates' Courts Act 1978 does not contain any provision similar to sections 1(2) or 2(2) of the Domestic Violence and Matrimonial Proceedings Act 1976.[8] Section 16(1) of the Act of 1978 refers to 'either party to a marriage' and not to 'a man and woman while living with each other in the same household as husband and wife' so applications by cohabitees are excluded. It is

18 Domestic Proceedings and Magistrates' Courts Act 1978, s 16(1).
19 Ibid, s 16(2).
20 Ibid.
 1 Ibid, s 16(3)(i).
 2 Ibid, s 16(3)(ii).
 3 Ibid, s 16(1).
 4 Ibid, s 16(3)(a).
 5 Ibid, s 16(3)(b).
 6 Ibid, s 16(3)(c).
 7 See chs 3 and 4 above.
 8 See ch 1, section G, above.

necessary that an applicant for an order under section 16 could establish before closing his or her case that she is or he is in fact married to the respondent. The better practice is to have a certified copy of a marriage certificate available at the hearing. However, it is open to the court to act upon the oral evidence of an applicant alone but it is submitted that where a respondent denies that he is married to the petitioner the better course is to insist upon the production of a certified copy of the marriage certificate and adjourn the application pending its production.

'Used or threatened to use violence'

Before the court can proceed to consider whether to grant either an exclusion or a protection order under the Act of 1978 they must be satisfied that the respondent either used or threatened to use violence against either the applicant or a child of the family. It follows that whilst section 1 of the Act of 1976 is not in any way limited by violence or other adverse conduct by the respondent, section 16 of the Act of 1978 is.

Since the statute refers to 'violence . . . against the person of, violence towards property will not give the court jurisdiction to act. Mental illness brought about by the behaviour of the respondent is capable of being actual bodily harm in criminal law[9] but such behaviour is not capable of being violence within the context of section 16 of the Act. It is 'violence against the person' which is actionable under the Act. However, threats of violence against the person of either the applicant or a child of the family is actionable irrespective of whether or not mental anguish is caused by such threats to either the applicant or the child. In other words, threats against the applicant or a child of the family will be actionable irrespective of the effect of these threats on either the child or the applicant.

Violence receives no statutory definition within the terms of the Act.

6 Child of the family

This is defined by section 88 of the Act of 1978 as:
(a) a child of both parties;
(b) any other child, not being a child who is being boarded out with those parties by a local authority or voluntary organisation, who has been treated by both those parties as a child of their family.

This brings the definition of children of the family into line with the Matrimonial Causes Act 1973.[10] Such a child need not be a child of either spouse and it is sufficient if it is treated as a member of the family. Whether a child is being treated as a member of the family is a question of fact. Belief by either party to the marriage as to the status of the child is not relevant to the question of whether it has been treated as a child of the family, providing the child has been so treated.[11] Before a child can be treated as a child of the family it must be alive.[12] Treatment involves behaviour towards a person who must be in existence.

It is important to note the use of the words 'a child of the family' throughout section 16. If violence or the threat of violence has been

---

9 *R v Miller* [1954] 2 QB 282, [1954] 2 All ER 529.
10 S 52(1) (27 *Halsbury's Statutes* (4th edn) 700 MATRIMONIAL LAW).
11 See *W (RJ) v W (SJ)* [1972] Fam 152, [1971] 3 All ER 303 and see *M v M (Child of the Family* (1980) 2 FLR 39 CA and *D v D (Child of the Family)* (1980) 2 FLR 93, CA.
12 See *A v A* [1974] Fam 6, [1974] 1 All ER 755.

directed towards one child of the family who for some reason had ceased to be present in the matrimonial home at the time of the application there is nothing to prevent the court finding that an order is necessary for the protection of another child of the family and making an order. This might arise where one child has been removed to hospital, taken into care or been sent to a detention centre, prison or even a boarding school.[13]

Indeed the court could, having been satisfied of a threat or actual violence towards a child of the family, be satisfied that an order was necessary for the protection of the applicant or vice versa. Whether a court would make an order would of course depend on the evidence before it and whether they were justified in exercising their discretion according to established principles. Nonetheless, a finding in such terms would overcome the initial hurdle which would allow the magistrates to consider whether they ought or ought not to exercise their discretion.

7 Exclusion orders

Before an exclusion order can be made by a magistrates' court, it has to be satisfied that the respondent has used violence against the applicant or a child of the family or has threatened such violence or used violence against some other person or uttered the threat in contravention of an order under section 16(2) of the Domestic Proceedings and Magistrates' Courts Act 1978 in any of which cases the court may exclude the respondent from the matrimonial home if either the applicant or a child of the family is in danger of physical injury. In essence, before a magistrates' court can exclude a party from the matrimonial home it has to be satisfied not only of the conditions precedent but also that either the applicant or a child of the family is in danger of physical injury and then they merely have a discretion to exclude which has to be exercised in accordance with the established principles to which reference has already been made.

'Used violence against some other person'
If reliance is placed upon this condition precedent, it will usually be proved by oral evidence given by the victim of the violence which is relied upon. Within the matrimonial context, violence against mothers-in-law, fathers-in-law, brothers and sisters are perhaps the most common examples. However, it is submitted, that an equally convenient and appropriate way of dealing with this requirement if it is relied upon, is by proof of a conviction for violence in previous criminal proceedings. Since a respondent to any application will be entitled to submit that there was no case in matter of law[14] for failure to prove this aspect of the case, if a conviction is to be relied upon it will have to be proved strictly. In the case of a conviction for an offence of violence, proof will be by way of certified extract of the crown court record[15] or of a certificate containing the substance and effect of the indictment and conviction and signed by the clerk or other authorised officer.[16] However, it is also necessary to prove that the

---

13 Cf *Surrey County Council v S* [1974] QB 124, [1973] 3 All ER 1074, CA.
14 See *McCartney v McCartney* [1981] Fam 59 at 63, [1981] 1 All ER 597 at 600, per Ewbank J, but see *Bond v Bond* [1967] P 39, [1964] 3 All ER 346.
15 Under Evidence Act 1851, s 13 (17 *Halsbury's Statutes* (4th edn) 82 EVIDENCE).
16 Under Prevention of Crimes Act 1871, s 18 (12 *Halsbury's Statutes* (4th edn) 146 CRIMINAL LAW).

respondent before the court is the person named in the indictment. This identity aspect of the case can be proved by calling as a witness, a person who was in court at the time of the conviction. A police officer, prison warder, solicitor or solicitor's clerk, reporter, usher or indeed within the context of the matrimonial applicant, a husband or wife, would suffice. If it is sought to rely upon a summary conviction for a crime of violence, a certificate[17] or alternatively the production of a certified extract from the magistrates' court records[18] will suffice. However, evidence of identity of the sort to which reference has already been made will be required.

An applicant for an order under section 16 of the Domestic Proceedings and Magistrates' Court Act 1978 is entitled to rely upon a conviction for an offence of violence by the respondent by virtue of the Civil Evidence Act 1968,[19] since the fact that such an offence was committed is plainly relevant to the issue of whether he has used violence against any other person.

Before an exclusion order can be made (and whether it is made is always discretionary) the court must be satisfied that the 'applicant or a child of the family is in danger of being physically injured'. Subjective belief by the applicant is not sufficient. The applicant must demonstrate an objective observable danger, that is, 'one which the justices think to exist and not one which the complainant thinks to exist'.[20]

The statutory words 'physical danger' should not be judicially qualified so that where magistrates refused an exclusion order on the grounds that the applicant had not demonstrated an '*immediate* physical danger' they acted upon a wrong principle.[1]

Once it has been established that there is a risk of physical injury the court then has jurisdiction to grant an order excluding the husband from the matrimonial home. However before they do so they must exercise their discretion judicially and according to the principles enunciated in cases decided in higher courts.[2]

It should be noted that exclusion orders in the magistrates' court (unlike exclusion injunctions) can only exclude a respondent from a matrimonial home. There is no power under the Domestic Proceedings and Magistrates' Courts Act 1978 to prevent a respondent from returning to a given area for example within 100 yards of the matrimonial home.

8 Conditions, exceptions and duration

By section 16(9) an order may be made subject to such exceptions and conditions as may be specified in the order and may be for such term as may be so specified.

Though the Practice Direction which recommends limitation of time of exclusion orders to three months does not specifically apply to orders made in the magistrates' court under the 1978 Act,[3] it is submitted that the better

17 Ibid.
18 Magistrates' Courts Rules 1981, r 68.
19 S 11. (17 *Halsbury's Statutes* (4th edn) 155 EVIDENCE).
20 *McCartney v McCartney* [1981] Fam 59 at 63H, [1981] 1 All ER 597 at 600F, per Sir John Arnold P.
 1 See *McCartney v McCartney*, above, at 62 and 599, per Ewbank J.
 2 See ch 4, above. See *Richards v Richards* [1984] AC 174, [1983] 2 All ER 807, HL. It should be remembered that as the parties will be married that the provisions of the Matrimonial Homes Act 1983 (27 *Halsbury's Statutes* (4th edn) 585 MATRIMONIAL LAW) will apply.
 3 See *Practice Note* [1978] 2 All ER 1056, [1978] 1 WLR 1123; see Appendix 2, below.

practice is to limit the orders for such a period. There is nothing to prevent an applicant applying for a variation by extension should the need arise.[4] As the legislation is designed to complement other emergency jurisdictions, since it is limited to parties who are married and, if an exclusion order is obtained, the parties will either divorce (where proceedings will have to be commenced in a divorce county court in which case it is submitted the correct procedure is to apply for interlocutory relief and for an order under section 28 of the Act of 1978 discharging the magistrates' court order) or the parties will reconcile, in which case it is right that the order should be discharged. If at the expiry of three months, the situation remains in a state of flux, an extension can be granted, again limited in time, to provide temporary protection.

If an order which was not limited in time were made and the parties reconciled it would, of course, be open to a respondent to apply for re-vocation of the order under section 17(1) but it is submitted that in practice, unless he is represented, a respondent to an order made in the magistrates' court is unlikely to do so. It is not in the interests of sound administration of justice that orders continue to exist which have been superseded by the passage of time and events.[5]

The use of the phrase 'exceptions' may allow the court to exclude a husband from the matrimonial home under section 16(3) but at the same time permit him to remain partially in residence under section 16(9). So for an example, like the higher courts, a magistrates' court in an appropriate case can exclude the husband from a matrimonial home save, for instance, a bedroom; the bathroom between certain hours; the kitchen between certain hours and the stairs and hallways of the home. The circumstances in which an order of this sort should be made do not differ in the magistrates' court from those which apply in the higher court. It should be noted however that before an order of the sort in question is contemplated the matrimonial home must be of sufficient size to make it practical. Equally, if the house were also used for business purposes by a respondent it would be right to permit him limited access to it if his livelihood is not to be ruined.[6]

Equally, section 16(9) would permit an order that the respondent be excluded from the matrimonial home save for the purposes of enjoying such access to the children of the family as may be ordered or agreed between the parties. This is a common exception frequently built into county court orders and there is no legal or logical reason why such an exception should not be built into a magistrates' court order. Finally, section 16(9) permits the magistrates when making an order to build into it such provisions as they consider desirable or necessary for the efficient administration of it. For example, an order may be expressed to take effect within so many days of its being made or as subject to unlimited access to the property for a fixed number of hours on a fixed date in order to allow the respondent to remove his belongings or to find alternative accommodation or indeed the magistrates may consider it desirable to build into the order a condition that he has access to the matrimonial home for so many hours on a fixed date in each week or

---

4 Under the Domestic Proceedings and Magistrates' Courts Act 1978, s 17(1).
5 See *Hopper v Hopper* [1979] 1 All ER 181, [1978] 1 WLR 1342n, CA.
6 See *Walker v Walker* [1978] 3 All ER 141, [1978] 1 WLR 533, CA.

month to permit him to pay bills or carry out repairs. The circumstances in which such an order would be appropriate will necessarily be rare but may arise where he is the tenant of the property and is subject to a repairing covenant with which it is necessary to comply. In normal circumstances, the limiting in time of the order will obviate the necessity for building in access times of this sort.

Reference has already been made to the exercise by the magistrates of a discretion whether or not to exclude a husband once all the conditions precedent set out in the statute have been satisfied. They should in particular be aware of the general desirability of deciding any questions of custody, care and control of the children before deciding who if anyone should have occupation of the matrimonial home,[7] where the same is in issue.[8]

9 Attachment of power of arrest

Reference to the power to attach a power of arrest to an order made under section 16 of the Act of 1978 conferred by section 18 has already been made in the discussion of expedited orders. Whilst there is nothing inconsistent with imposing a power of arrest to an expedited order, different considerations apply on the full hearing of an application under section 16. In particular, where a court decides the case is not the sort that warrants an exclusion order, by definition it follows that the case is not a suitable one for the attachment of a power of arrest.[9]

Before the court attaches a power of arrest to an order made under section 16, it must be satisfied that:

(a) The respondent has physically injured the applicant or a child of the family, and

(b) Considers that he is likely to do so again.

By analogy with the decided cases on powers of arrest under the Domestic Violence and Matrimonial Proceedings Act 1976, it follows that both these prerequisites must be satisfied before a power of arrest is attached.[10]

Where an exclusion order is refused, to attach a power of arrest to a protection order is inconsistent, but it does not follow that the making of an exclusion order under section 16(3) means that a power of arrest should follow automatically.

The use of the power is an exceptional remedy[11] to be used only in the strongest of cases. Quite apart from that, if an exclusion order is made under section 16(3)(b) or (c) (which concerns threats without actual violence towards either the applicant or a child of the family) the attachment of a power for arrest would appear to be wholly wrong. Parliament has decided that sufficient protection in such cases is given by excluding the respondent. Only where he has used actual violence on them or any of them is a power of arrest deemed expedient. Even then, a distinction is drawn in the Act between 'violence' and 'physical injury' which suggests that assaults short of those which cause actual bodily harm are not sufficient to justify the imposition of a power of arrest where a power of arrest

7 See ch 4, above.
8 By pending proceedings under the Guardianship of Minors Acts 1971 and 1973 (6 *Halsbury's Statutes* (4th edn) 305 and 338 CHILDREN) or under the Domestic Proceedings and Magistrates' Courts Act, s 1 (27 *Halsbury's Statutes* (4th edn) 791 MATRIMONIAL LAW).
9 See *McCartney v McCartney* [1981] Fam 59 at 62, [1981] 1 All ER 597 at 599.
10 See *Lewis v Lewis* [1978] Fam 60, [1978] 1 All ER 729, CA, followed in *Widdowson v Widdowson* (1983) 4 FLR 121, 12 Fam Law 153, DC, which emphasises that a power of arrest is not a routine remedy. See also *Horner v Horner* [1982] Fam 90, [1982] 2 All ER 495, CA.
11 Ibid.

is attached the court should state why the same is considered to be appropriate.[12] The practical utility of such assumption is much to be doubted but
until the Act is amended or replaced it remains the law.

10 Enforcement – generally

Getting the respondent to court
The mechanism by which a respondent who has disobeyed an order made
by the magistrates' court under section 16 of the Act of 1978 is got to court
depends upon whether he has been arrested pursuant to a power of arrest
or whether he is alleged to be in breach of an order to which a power of
arrest has not been attached or which, if attached, has not been exercised.

11 Enforcement by power of arrest

The effect of attaching a power of arrest to a section 16 order is to
empower a police officer to arrest, without warrant, a person he has
reasonable cause to believe to be in breach of an order made under section
16.[13]

When a person is arrested pursuant to a power of arrest he must be
brought before a justice of the peace within twenty-four hours from the
time of his arrest.[14]

The justice of the peace before whom he is brought may remand the
person so arrested[15] which means that he may be either remanded in
custody (in which case he must be produced within three clear days of the
remand if he is remanded in the custody of a police officer)[16] or within eight
clear days if remanded to prison[17] or he may be bailed.[18]

12 Enforcement by the applicant

If no power of arrest has been attached to an order made under section 16
of the Act of 1978 or if such power has been attached but not exercised, if
at any time the applicant considers the other party to the marriage in
question to have disobeyed the order he or she may apply for issue of a
warrant against the respondent. The application is made to a justice of the
peace for the commission area where either party ordinarily resides but
before a warrant is issued the applicant must substantiate the application
on oath and the justice of the peace granting the warrant must have
reasonable grounds for believing that the other party to the marriage has
disobeyed the order.[19]

The court before whom any person is brought pursuant to such a warrant
may remand him[20] in which case the same provisions as to remand apply
here as they do to a person arrested pursuant to a power of arrest.[1]

---

12 *Widdowson v Widdowson* above. The giving of reasons will avoid any suggestion that the
    power is used indiscriminately.
13 See Domestic Proceedings and Magistrates' Courts Act 1978, s 18(2).
14 No account being taken of Christmas Day, Good Friday or any Sunday by ibid, s 18(3)(a).
15 Ibid, s 18(3)(b).
16 Magistrates' Courts Act 1980, s 128(7).
17 Ibid, s 128(6).
18 Ibid, s 128(4).
19 See Domestic Proceedings and Magistrates' Courts Act 1978, s 18(4).
20 See ibid, s 18(5).
 1 See above.

13 Powers of the court to deal with disobedience

A magistrates' court may deal with a respondent who is brought before it in either of the ways mentioned above by fine or committal.[2]

Section 63(3) of the Act of 1980 provides for the punishment of continuing breaches by fine not exceeding £50 for every day which the respondent is in default up to a maximum of £2,000 or committal in custody until the default is remedied for a period not exceeding two months.

In cases where committal is contemplated, procedural steps must be scrupulously followed or any committal which results is bad and must be quashed on appeal. In particular, a failure to bring a respondent before a justice of the peace within 24 hours of his arrest would deprive the court of power to either commit or fine him.

Justices have no power to commit a person to prison for consecutive periods in respect of different breaches of a family protection order.[3] A committal must take effect on the day on which it is ordered.[4]

In committal proceedings a full note of the evidence must always be taken.[5]

14 Appeals

Appeals from the making of or refusal to make or to vary or to revoke an order made under Part 1 of the Domestic Proceedings and Magistrates' Courts Act 1978 (which includes orders made under sections 16, 17 and/or 18) lie to the High Court[6]. The appeal is by notice of motion,[7] in accordance with the procedure set out in the Rules of Court.[8]

It is essential that apeals against exclusion orders are heard promptly, particularly as it is unlikely that a stay pending appeal would be granted.[9] If necessary, an application may be made to expedite the hearing of an appeal.[10]

Where an appeal is against an order which is in the discretion of the magistrates the Divisional Court should only interfere where it considers that the decision of the court below exceeds the ambit in which judicial disagreement is reasonably possible and plainly wrong; not merely where the appellate court prefers a different solution from that adopted below.[11]

---

2 Magistrates' Courts Act 1980, s 63.
3 *Head v Head* [1982] 3 All ER 14, [1982] 1 WLR 1186, DC.
4 Ibid.
5 Ibid and see *Tilmouth v Tilmouth* [1985] FLR 239, [1985] Fam Law 92, DC. Indeed the clerk to the justices has a duty to record the oral evidence in all domestic proceedings: *Gray v Gray* [1987] 1 FLR 16, [1986] Fam Law 267, DC.
6 See Domestic Proceedings and Magistrates' Courts Act 1978, s 29(1).
7 See *Practice Direction* [1977] 2 All ER 543, [1977] 1 WLR 609, and Appendix 2, below. For a precedent of a Notice of Motion see Appendix 4, below.
8 See RSC Ord 90, rr 9 and 29 and Ord 104, r 11.
9 *Widdowson v Widdowson* (1983) 4 FLR 121, 12 Fam Law 153, DC.
10 Ibid. The application is to a single judge: RSC Ord 90, r 29(8).
11 *G v G* [1985] 2 All ER 225, [1985] 1 WLR 647, HL.

Chapter 14
Appeals to the Court of Appeal

1 From the High Court (Family Division) – procedure

An appeal from an order made by a judge of the Family Division is to the Court of Appeal.[1] Where an appeal is against the grant or the refusal of an interlocutory injunction, leave to appeal is not required.[2]

An appeal does not operate as a stay of the order appealed against unless the court of first instance or the Court of Appeal so order.[3] An application for a stay should first be made to the judge who heard the matter, at the time of judgment, or, subsequently on notice; if refused by the court of first instance application may be made, on notice, to the Court of Appeal.[4] The grant of a stay is in the discretion of the court[5] and will only be granted where there are special circumstances[6] for example, where the refusal of a stay would cause irreparable injury.[7] The court will balance the prejudice which would be caused to each party by the grant or refusal of a stay. If a judge orders a stay, there is no power to vary the same once the order is passed and entered.[8]

In many injunction cases[9] the practicalities may mean that the grant of a stay is effectively to allow the appeal; whereas to refuse a stay is effectively to dismiss the appeal. In such circumstances the positions of both parties may be preserved by an early hearing of the appeal. The judge might therefore refuse to stay the order, thus requiring the unsuccessful party to apply to the Court of Appeal for a stay and for an early hearing of the appeal.

Where an exclusion injunction has been made for a limited period it is in the last degree improbable that any court would, in any circumstances, grant a stay.[10] The appropriate remedy is for the appeal to be heard promptly, if necessary after an application to expedite the hearing of the appeal.[11]

The appeal is made by way of notice of motion, referred to as a notice of appeal,[12] which must specify the grounds of appeal and the orders sought

---

1 Supreme Court Act 1981 s 16(1) (11 *Halsbury's Statutes* (4th edn) 756 COURTS).
2 Ibid, s 18(1)(h)(iii).
3 RSC Ord 59, r 13(1)(a).
4 See *Supreme Court Practice*, para 59/13/4.
5 *The Ratata* [1897] P 118, HL.
6 Ibid.
7 *Chester v Powell* (1885) 1 TLR 390, CA.
8 *Re VGM Holdings Ltd* [1941] 3 All ER 417.
9 Especially in relation to exclusion injunctions.
10 *Widdowson v Widdowson* (1982) 4 FLR 121, per Sir John Arnold P at 125 E–H, DC.
11 Ibid.
12 RSC Ord 59, r 3(1). For a precedent see Appendix 4, below.

from the Court of Appeal.[13] An appellant is not entitled, without the leave of the court, to rely on any grounds not specified in the notice of appeal; or, to apply for any relief which is not so specified.[14] The notice of appeal must specify the list in which the appellant proposes that the appeal should be set down.[15]

The notice of appeal must be served on all parties to the proceedings in the court of first instance who are directly affected by the appeal[16] within four weeks from the date on which the judgment or order of the court below was signed, entered or otherwise perfected.[17] The Court of Appeal[18] or the court below[19] may extend the time for serving the notice of appeal; although the court of first instance may only extend the time for appealing if the application for an extension is made before the expiry of the time for appealing.[20] The court has a broad discretion to extend time where the justice of the case so demands.[1] Where there is an acceptable reason for a short delay in serving the notice of appeal, an extension of time will not be refused on the merits, unless the appeal is hopeless.[2]

Within twenty-one days[3] after service of the notice of appeal the respondent, himself, may serve a notice (called a respondent's notice) contending that the order of the court below should be varied or affirmed on grounds different from those given in the judgment of the court of first instance.[4] Such notice must specify the grounds of the contentions[5] and the precise order sought from the Court of Appeal.[6] The respondent is not entitled, without the leave of the court, to rely on any contention, seek any variation of the order, or seek to uphold the order on any ground, save one contained in the judgment of the court, unless it is specified in his notice.[7]

The notice of appeal or a respondent's notice may be amended at any time, with the leave of the Court of Appeal[8] or without leave by a supplemental notice, served before the date on which the appeal first appears in the List of Forthcoming Appeals.[9] If notice of intention to amend is given to the other party and no objection is taken, there is no need to apply for leave; the court should be informed at the hearing.[10]

Within seven days after the later of the service of the notice of appeal and the date on which the judgment or order appealed against was sealed

---

13 RSC Ord 59, r 3(2). Grounds of appeal should be short and not too elaborate: *Sansom* v *Sansom* [1956] 3 All ER 446, [1956] 1 WLR 945, CA.
14 RSC Ord 59, r 3(3).
15 RSC Ord 59, r 3(4). The relevant list is Family Division (Interlocutory List); see *Supreme Court Practice*, para 59/3/8.
16 RSC Ord 59, r 3(5).
17 RSC Ord 59, 4(1).
18 RSC Ord 3, r 5.
19 RSC Ord 59, r 15(1).
20 Ibid, and see *Supreme Court Practice*, para 59/15/1.
 1 *Re J Wigfull & Sons' Trade Marks* [1919] 1 Ch 52, at 59, CA.
 2 *Allette v Allette* [1986] 2 FLR 427, [1986] Fam Law 333, CA following *Palata Investments Ltd v Burt & Sinfield Ltd* [1985] 2 All ER 517, [1985] 1 WLR 942, CA.
 3 RSC Ord 59, r 6(3).
 4 RSC Ord 59, r 6(1).
 5 Ibid.
 6 Ibid.
 7 RSC Ord 59, r 6(2).
 8 RSC Ord 59, r 7(1)(a).
 9 RSC Ord 59, r 7(1)(b).
10 *Gelberg v Vivian* [1952] 2 All ER 746, CA.

or otherwise perfected, the appellant must lodge with the Registrar of Civil Appeals a copy of the order appealed against and two copies of the notice of appeal[11] whereupon the registrar will cause the appeal to be set down in the appropriate list.[12] A respondent who has served a respondent's notice, must lodge with the registrar two copies of the notice within four days of the later of the date of service of the notice and the date of notification of setting down the appeal.[13] A party who has served a supplemental notice must lodge two copies of it with the registrar within two days of service.[14]

Not more than fourteen days after the appeal first appears in the List of Forthcoming Appeals the appellant must lodge three copies of certain documents.[15] It is to be emphasised that failure to comply with the time limits for setting down and lodging documents in proper form[16] may result in the appeal being struck out.[17] Solicitors unable to comply with the time limits are under a duty to apply for an extension of time.[18]

An appeal concerning children or which is otherwise urgent[19] is likely to enter the List of Forthcoming Appeals within a week of setting down. Appeals concerning children should be heard within two or exceptionally three months of judgment.[20]

2 From county courts – procedure

The procedure is substantially the same as an appeal from the Family Division of the High Court, although there are some very significant and important differences, explained below.

Advocates appearing in the county court have a duty to raise all questions of law[1] and request the judge to take a note of each question of law and the facts in evidence in relation to the same.[2] Advocates must take a

---

11 RSC Ord 59, r 5(1).
12 RSC Ord 59, r 5(2).
13 RSC Ord 59, r 6(4).
14 RSC Ord 59, 7 (2).
15 RSC Ord 59, r 9. In some circumstances two copies of the documents will be sufficient: RSC Ord 59, r 9(2)(a). See RSC Ord 59, r 9(1) set out in Appendix 3 below for the documents required. See *Practice Direction (Appeals: Documentation)* [1986] 3 All ER 630, [1986] 1 WLR 1318, CA, and see Appendix 2 below, for the requirements of bundles. See also *R v R and H (Harrow London Borough Council Intervening)* (1987) Times, 6 July, CA, as to the undesirability of excessive documents.
16 For the exact requirements see *Practice Note (Appeal: Documents)* [1983] 2 All ER 416 and *Practice Note (Appeal: Documents)* [1985] 1 All ER 841, CA, as consolidated and expanded in *Practice Direction (Appeals: Documentation)* above.
17 *Hollis v R B Jenkins (a firm)* (1986) Times, 31 January, CA and see *C M van Stillevoldt BV v EL Carriers Inc* [1983] 1 All ER 699, [1983] 1 WLR 207, CA at 703 and 212.
18 *Practice Note (Documentation in Appeals)* (1986) Times, 13 June, and see *Supreme Court Practice*, para 59/9/1.
19 This would apply to most injunctions sought in the matrimonial and domestic context, and especially to orders of committal.
20 *Ridgway v Ridgway* [1986] Fam Law 363, CA. See also *Re W (A Minor)* [1984] 3 All ER 58n, [1984] 1 WLR 1125, CA; an appeal should be heard within a maximum of 28 days where it involves the postponement of the implementation of a judge's order that a child should be transferred from one parent to the other or from a local authority to a parent.
 1 An appeal on a point of law is confined to points of law raised at the hearing unless the court has done something illegal or acted outside its jurisdiction. See *Balchin v Buckle* (1982) 126 Sol Jo 412, CA.
 2 County Courts Act 1984 s 80(1) (11 *Halsbury's Statutes* (4th edn) 411 COUNTY COURTS); see Appendix 1 below.

note of the judgment[3] and for the purposes of an appeal it is essential that an agreed note of the judgment, approved by the judge, is provided for the Court of Appeal.[4]

There is a right of appeal against an order which includes or preserves an interlocutory injunction[5] but leave may be required where an application for an interlocutory injunction has been refused.[6] Where leave to appeal is necessary, the application should be made to the judge,[7] at the time of judgment, or subsequently on notice,[8] unless the time for appealing has expired. Where the judge who tried the case is not available, or for some other reason it is not practical to apply to him, the subsequent application for leave may be made to any other judge of that court.[9] Where the time for appealing has expired, any application for leave to appeal must be made to the Court of Appeal.[10]

The notice of appeal must be served within four weeks from the date on which judgment was given or order made,[11] not from the date on which the order was drawn up. Where leave to appeal is required and is granted by the Court of Appeal on an application, made within four weeks from the date of the judgment or order, the notice of appeal may be served within seven days after the date on which the order for leave was obtained.[12] The notice of appeal must be served on the registrar of the county court[13] in addition to all parties directly affected by the appeal.

Where the grounds of appeal, in whole or in part, allege some misconduct on the part of the trial judge at the hearing, the notice of appeal must be submitted to the trial judge for him to have the opportunity of making comments and observations on the matter and communicating them to the parties and to the Court of Appeal.[14] If the appellant intends to rely on

---

3 *Practice Direction (Appeals: Documentation)* [1986] 3 All ER 630, [1986] 1 WLR 1318, CA, and see *Letts* v *Letts* (1987) Times, 8 April, CA.

4 Such agreed and approved note is necessary to comply with County Courts Act 1984, s 80(1)(c) and see *Practice Direction (Appeals: Documentation)* above; see Appendix 2 below.

5 County Court Appeals Order 1981 (SI 1981/1749 Art 3(a), made under County Courts Act 1984, s 77(2).

6 County Court Appeals Order 1981 Art 3(a). Although it might appear that Supreme Court Act 1981, s 18(1)(h)(iii) (11 *Halsbury's Statutes* (4th edn) 756 COURTS) would provide a right of appeal where an interlocutory injunction is refused, the terms of County Courts Act 1984, s 77(2) clearly restrict the rights of appeal in addition to the restrictions contained in Supreme Court Act 1981, s 18. Leave is only required against the refusal of an application for an interlocutory injunction where the proceedings come within one of the classes specified in County Court Appeals Order 1981, Art 2; see *County Court Practice 1987* at p 65.

7 County Courts Act 1984, s 77(2). RSC Ord 59, r 14(4).

8 Where an application for leave is made ex parte some time after judgment the court should, if it is minded to grant leave, adjourn the matter to be heard on notice; but may dismiss the ex parte application for leave. *Aveyard* v *Aveyard* [1984] 1 All ER 159, [1984] 1 WLR 467, CA.

9 *Moberly* v *Hughes* 11 March 1985 (unreported) [1985] CA Transcript 101, CA. See also *Warren* v *T Kilroe & Sons Ltd* (1987) Times, 3 July, CA, a decision on the meaning of the word 'court' in Supreme Court Act 1981, s 18(1)(h).

10 *Supreme Court Practice*, para 59/14/2.

11 RSC Ord 59, rr 4, 19(3)(a).

12 RSC Ord 59, r 4(3).

13 RSC Ord 59, r 19(2).

14 *Re R (A Minor) (Adoption: Parental Agreement)* [1987] 1 FLR 391, CA.

notes of evidence[15] such should be agreed with the respondent and sub-mitted to the judge with the notice of appeal.[16]

The appeal will be set down in either the County Courts (Interlocutory List) or the County Courts (Divorce) (Interlocutory List).[17]

The party entitled to the benefit of the order of the Court of Appeal must lodge the order or an office copy in the office of the county court.[18]

3 Powers of the Court of Appeal

Generally

The appeal is by way of rehearing.[19] The court may draw any inference of fact[20] and may order a new trial on such terms as it thinks just,[1] order judgment to be entered for any party,[2] or make a final or other[3] order on such terms as it thinks proper to ensure a determination on the merits of the real questions of controversy between the parties.[4] The Court of Appeal may reverse or vary, in favour of a party seeking to support the decision appealed from, any appealable determination of the judge on a question of fact or a point of law.[5]

Fresh evidence

The Court of Appeal has power to receive further evidence, in its dis-cretion.[6] The court, particularly in children's cases, may receive evidence as to events which have occurred since the order appealed from

---

15 Other than the judge's own note.
16 *Re R (A Minor)(Adoption: Parental Agreement)* above.
17 See *Supreme Court Practice*, para 59/2/8.
18 CCR Ord 22, r 13.
19 RSC Ord 59, r 3(1). The matter will not be tried afresh but the Court of Appeal is not limited to the alleged defects but may review the evidence as a whole, including events which have occurred since the hearing, in order to do justice between the parties. See eg *Sales v Sales* (1979) 10 Fam Law 115, CA, the appeal was decided largely on the basis of a letter from the local authority which was not in evidence below.
20 County Courts Act 1984, s 81(1) (11 *Halsbury's Statutes* (4th edn) 411 COUNTY COURTS;) RSC Ord 59, r 10(3).
 1 County Courts Act 1984, s 81(1)(a); RSC Ord 59, r 11. In general orders for new trials are rare as the Court of Appeal has power to draw inferences of fact from the material before it. New trials were ordered in *Tribe v Dainton* (6 June 1980, CA Unbound Transcript 464). The judge at first instance held that the events which gave rise to the application were nothing more than a 'lovers' tiff' and dismissed the application. On appeal a new trial was ordered as the respondent's evidence should have been heard. 'It is impossible to assess the relationship of the parties in a matrimonial or quasi-matrimonial situation except by oral evidence on both sides', per Brandon LJ. *Dirir v Dirir* (1987) 9 Fam Law 20, CA; the judge decided the issues on the affidavit evidence without cross-examination. On appeal a new trial was ordered as the judge should have allowed cross-examination as it was requested by the parties. It should be noted that *Bassett v Bassett* [1975] Fam 76, [1975] 1 All ER 513, CA, was decided on affidavit evidence, untested by cross-examination, but although the point was taken on appeal it was rejected because no application was made to adjourn for cross-examination and because, even though practically every word of the wife's affidavit was challenged, there was sufficient common ground for the court to reach a proper decision. *M v M* (1987) 23 June, CA, a new trial was ordered because of a lack of findings of fact by the trial judge. See also *Summers v Summers* [1986] 1 FLR 343, [1986] Fam Law 56, CA.
 2 County Courts Act 1984, s 81(1)(b); RSC Ord 59, r 10(3).
 3 Eg interlocutory.
 4 County Courts Act 1984, s 81(1)(c); RSC Ord 59, r 10(4).
 5 County Courts Act 1984, ss 81(1), (2); RSC Ord 59, r 10(4).
 6 RSC Ord 59, r 10(2).

was made.[7] However, further evidence about matters which occurred before the hearing will only be admitted on special grounds[8] namely: that it could not have been obtained with reasonable diligence for use at the trial;[9] that such evidence, if given, would probably have had an important influence on the result of the case;[10] and, that evidence must be apparently credible.[11]

Contempt

On an appeal against an order of committal to prison for contempt[12] the Court of Appeal may release the appellant on bail pending appeal.[13] At the hearing of the appeal the court may vary or reverse the order of the court below[14] and may make such other order as may be just,[15] which can, in an exceptional case, mean the imposition of a longer sentence.[16]

Ex parte orders

Where an ex parte application has been refused at first instance an application for a similar purpose may be made to the Court of Appeal within seven days after the refusal.[17] The application to the Court of Appeal is to some extent more in the nature of a renewed application than an appeal.[18]

The Court of Appeal will not normally exercise its jurisdiction to hear an appeal against the grant of an ex parte injunction[19] or against an injunction granted at an 'opposed ex parte' hearing.[20] A respondent aggrieved by an ex parte injunction should apply for the same to be set aside.[1] A respondent aggrieved by an injunction granted at an 'opposed ex parte' hearing should allow the matter to be stood over to a hearing inter partes.[2]

Undertakings

Frequently applications for interlocutory injunctions are compromised on the basis of one or both parties giving undertakings. It is not possible to appeal against the giving of an undertaking[3] even where such undertaking is given 'without prejudice to the right of appeal'.[4] A party should in such circumstances refuse to give the undertaking and appeal against the injunction, if

---

7 Eg *Sales v Sales* (1979) 10 Fam Law 115, CA.
8 RSC Ord 59, r 10(2).
9 *Ladd v Marshall* [1954] 3 All ER 745, [1954] 1 WLR 1489, CA, approved in *Skone v Skone* [1971] 2 All ER 582, [1971] 1 WLR 812, HL.
10 *Ladd v Marshall*, above and *Skone v Skone*, above. The fresh evidence need not be decisive.
11 *Ladd v Marshall*, above and *Skone v Skone*, above. The fresh evidence need not be incontrovertible.
12 See ch 12, above.
13 Administration of Justice Act 1960, s 13(3) (11 *Halsbury's Statutes* (4th edn) 174 CONTEMPT OF COURT); RSC Ord 109, r 3. ·
14 Administration of Justice Act 1960, s 13(3).
15 Ibid.
16 *Linnett v Coles* [1986] 3 All ER 652, [1986] 3 WLR 843, CA. See also RSC Ord 59, r 10(3) and *Linkletter v Linkletter* (1987) Times, 13 June, CA.
17 RSC Ord 59, r 14(3).
18 *Webb v Webb* [1986] 1 FLR 541, CA, is an example of such an application.
19 *WEA Records Ltd v Visions Channel 4 Ltd* [1983] 2 All ER 589, [1983] 1 WLR 721, CA.
20 *Hunter & Partners v Welling & Partners* (1986) 131 Sol Jo 75, CA.
1 RSC Ord 32, r 6; CCR Ord 37, r 2(1); *Becker v Noel* [1971] 2 All ER 1248, [1971] 1 WLR 803, CA.
2 *Hunter & Partners v Welling & Partners*, above.
3 *McConnell v McConnell* (1980) 10 Fam Law 214, [1980] Civil Appeal Transcript 194, CA.
4 Ibid.

such be ordered. Alternatively, a respondent may apply to be discharged from his undertaking. Where an application for an interlocutory injunction is adjourned generally on the basis of undertakings by the respondent there is no restriction on the right of the respondent to apply to be discharged from the terms of the undertaking.[5] If an application is stood over to a substantive hearing, or otherwise disposed of, on the basis of undertakings given by the respondent no application may be made by the respondent to be discharged from such undertakings.[6]

4 Principles on which the Court of Appeal acts

An injunction is a discretionary remedy[7] and as such the Court of Appeal will interfere with the judge's exercise of discretion if and only if:

(a) the discretion has been exercised on a wrong principle of law,
(b) an irrelevant matter has been taken into consideration,
(c) a relevant matter has not been taken into consideration, or,
(d) the decision is so plainly wrong that somewhere there must have been a wrong method in the exercise of discretion.[8]

An appeal will not succeed merely on the ground that insufficient weight, or too much weight, was given by the judge to a particular category of admissable evidence.[9] Accordingly, where a decision involves the exercise of a judge's discretion the Court of Appeal will not interfere unless the decision exceeds the generous ambit within which reasonable disagreement is possible.[10]

5 *Butt v Butt* (27 June 1987, unreported), CA.
6 Ibid, see also *Chanel Ltd v FW Woolworth & Co* [1981] 1 All ER 745, [1981] 1 WLR 485, CA.
7 Supreme Court Act 1981, s 37(1) (11 *Halbury's Statutes* (4th edn) 756 COURTS).
8 *McLean v Burke* (1980) 3 FLR 70, CA at 73 H per Sir John Arnold P. There are many authorities for this proposition; see eg *Evans v Bartlam* [1937] AC 473, [1937] 2 All ER 646, HL.
9 *Harewood Hotels Ltd v Harris* [1958] 1 All ER 104, [1958] 1 WLR 108, CA.
10 *Bellenden (formerly Satterthwaite) v Satterthwaite* [1948] 1 All ER 343, CA. See also *G v G (Minors: Custody Appeal)* [1985] 2 All ER 225, [1985] 1 WLR 647, HL. This decision has been emphasised, see *In re G (A Minor) (Role of the Appelate Court)* [1987] 1 FLR 164, CA; see also *R v R and H (Harrow London Borough Council Intervening)* (1987) Times, 6 July, CA.

Appendix 1
Statutes

Contents

Family Law Act 1986 (1986 c 55)
(6 *Halsbury's Statutes* (4th edn) 43 S CHILDREN)

Married Women's Property Act 1882

Questions between husband and wife as to property to be decided in a summary way.
17[1]. In any question between husband and wife as to the title to or possession of property, either party, may apply by summons or otherwise in a summary way to the High Court or such county court as may be prescribed and the court may, on such application (which may be heard in private), make such order with respect to the property as it thinks fit. In this section 'prescribed' means prescribed by rules of court and the rules made for the purposes of this section may confer jurisdiction on county courts whatever the situation or value of the property in dispute.

Administration of Justice Act 1960

Publication of information relating to proceedings in private
12. (1) The publication of information relating to proceedings before any court sitting in private shall not of itself be contempt of court except in the following cases, that is to say—
   (a) where the proceedings relate to the wardship or adoption of an infant or wholly or mainly to the guardianship, custody, maintenance or upbringing of an infant, or rights of access to an infant;
   (b) where the proceedings are brought under Part VIII of the Mental Health Act 1959, or under any provision of that Act authorising an application or reference to be made to a Mental Health Review Tribunal or to a county court;
   (c) where the court sits in private for reasons of national security during that part of the proceedings about which the information in question is published;
   (d) where the information relates to a secret process, discovery or invention which is in issue in the proceedings;

1 As amended by Matrimonial and Family Proceedings Act 1984 (27 *Halsbury's Statutes* (4th edn) 853 MATRIMONIAL LAW), s 43.

(e) where the court (having power to do so) expressly prohibits the publication of all information relating to the proceedings or of information of the description which is published.

(2) Without prejudice to the foregoing subsection, the publication of the text or a summary of the whole or part of an order made by a court sitting in private shall not of itself be contempt of court except where the court (having power to do so) expressly prohibits the publication.

(3) In this section references to a court include references to a judge and to a tribunal and to any person exercising the functions of a court, a judge or a tribunal; and references to a court sitting in private include references to a court sitting in camera or in chambers.

(4) Nothing in this section shall be construed as implying that any publication is punishable as contempt of court which would not be so punishable apart from this section.

Appeal in cases of contempt of court
13. (1) Subject to the provisions of this section, an appeal shall lie under this section from any order or decision of a court in the exercise of jurisdiction to punish for contempt of court (including criminal contempt); and in relation to any such order or decision the provisions of this section shall have effect in substitution or any other enactment relating to appeals in civil or criminal proceedings.

(2) An appeal under this section shall lie in any case at the instance of the defendant and, in the case of an application for committal or attachment, at the instance of the applicant; and the appeal shall lie—
  (a) from an order or decision of any inferior court not referred to in the next following paragraph, to a Divisional Court of the High Court;
  (b) from an order or decision of a county court or any other inferior court from which appeals generally lie to the Court of Appeal, and from an order or decision, of a single judge of the High Court, or of any court having the powers of the High Court or of a judge of that court, to the Court of Appeal;
  (bb) from an order or decision of the Crown Court to the Court of Appeal
  (c) from an order or decision of a Divisional Court or the Court of Appeal (including a decision of either of those courts on an appeal under this section), and from an order or decision of the Court of Criminal Appeal or the Courts-Martial Appeal Court, to the House of Lords.

(3) The court to which an appeal is brought under this section may reverse or vary the order or decision of the court below, and make such other order as may be just; and without prejudice to the inherent powers of any court referred to in subsection (2) of this section, provision may be made by rules of court for authorising the release on bail of an appellant under this section.

(4) Subsections (2) to (4) of section one and section two of this Act shall apply to an appeal to the House of Lords under this section as they apply to an appeal to that House under the said section one, except that so much of the said subsection (2) as restricts the grant of leave to appeal shall apply only where the decision of the court below is a decision on appeal to that court under this section.

(5) In this section 'court' includes any tribunal or person having power

to punish for contempt; and references in this section to an order or decision of a court in the exercise of jurisdiction to punish for contempt of court include references—

(a) to an order or decision of the High Court, the Crown Court or a county court under any enactment enabling that court to deal with an offence as if it were contempt of court;

(b) to an order or decision of a county court, or of any court having the powers of a county court, under section 14, 92 or 118 of the County Courts Act 1984;

(c) to an order or decision of a magistrates' court under subsection (3) of section 63 of the Magistrates' Courts Act 1980,

but do not include references to orders under section 5 of the Debtors Act 1869, or under any provision of the Magistrates' Courts Act 1980 or the County Courts Act 1984, except those referred to in paragraphs (b) and (c) of this subsection and except sections 38 and 142 of the last mentioned Act so far as those sections confer jurisdiction in respect of contempt of court.

(6) This section does not apply to a conviction or sentence in respect of which an appeal lies under Part I of the Criminal Appeal Act 1968, or to a decision of the criminal division of the Court of Appeal under that Part of that Act.

Divorce Reform Act 1969

2. *(5) For the purpose of this Act a husband and wife shall be treated as living apart unless they are living with each other in the same household.*
3. *(6) References in this section to the parties to a marriage living with each other shall be construed as references to their living with each other in the same household. (Repealed by Matrimonial Causes Act 1973, s 54 and Sch 3.)*

Guardianship of Minors Act 1971

Restriction on removal of minor from England and Wales
13A. (1) Where the court makes—

(a) an order under section 9(1), 10(1)(a) or 11(a) of this Act regarding the legal custody of a minor, or

(b) an interim order under section 2(4) of the Guardianship Act 1973 containing provision regarding the legal custody of a minor, the court, on making the order or at any time while the order is in force, may, if an application is made under this section, by order direct that no person shall take the minor out of England and Wales while the order made under this section is in force, except with the leave of the court.

(2) An order made under subsection (1) above may be varied or discharged by a subsequent order.

(3) An application for an order under subsection (1) above, or for the variation or discharge of such an order, may be made by any party to the proceedings, in which the order mentioned in paragraph (a) or (b) of that subsection was made.

Matrimonial Causes Act 1973

2.(6) For the purposes of section 1(2)(d) and (e) above and this section a husband and wife shall be treated as living apart unless they are living with each other in the same household and references in this section to the parties to a marriage living with each other shall be construed as references to their living with each other in the same household.

Avoidance of transactions intended to prevent or reduce financial relief
37.(1) For the purposes of this section 'financial relief' means relief under any of the provisions of sections 22, 23, 24, 27, 31 (except subsection (6)) and 35 above, and any reference in this section to defeating a person's claim for financial relief is a reference to preventing financial relief from being granted to that person, or to that person for the benefit of a child of the family, or reducing the amount of any financial relief which might be so granted, or frustrating or impeding the enforcement of any order which might be or has been made at his instance under any of those provisions.

(2) Where proceedings for financial relief are brought by one person against another, the court may, on the application of the first mentioned person—

    (a) if it is satisfied that the other party to the proceedings is, with the intention of defeating the claim for financial relief, about to make any disposition or to transfer out of the jurisdiction or otherwise deal with any property, make such order as it thinks fit for restraining the other party from so doing or otherwise for protecting the claim;

    (b) if it is satisfied that the other party has, with that intention, made a reviewable disposition and that if the disposition were set aside financial relief or different financial relief would be granted to the applicant, make an order setting aside the disposition;

    (c) if it is satisfied, in a case where an order has been obtained under any of the provisions mentioned in subsection (1) above by the applicant against the other party, that the other party has, with that intention, made a reviewable disposition, make an order setting aside the disposition.

and an application for the purposes of paragraph (b) above shall be made in the proceedings for the financial relief in question.

(3) Where the court makes an order under subsection 2(b) or (c) above setting aside a disposition it shall give such consequential directions as it thinks fit for giving effect to the order (including directions requiring the making of any payments or the disposal of any property).

(4) Any disposition made by the other part to the proceedings for financial relief in question (whether before or after the commencement of those proceedings) is a reviewable disposition for the purposes of subsection (2)(b) and (c) above unless it was made for valuable consideration (other than marriage) to a person who, at the time of the disposition, acted in relation to it in good faith and without notice of any intention on the part of the other party to defeat the applicant's claim for finanical relief.

(5) Where an application is made under this section with respect to a disposition which took place less than three years before the date of the application or with respect to a disposition or other dealing with property which is about to take place and the court is satisfied—

(a) in a case falling within subsection (2)(a) or (b) above, that the disposition or other dealing would (apart from this section) have the consequence, or

(b) in a case falling within subsection (2)(c) above, that the disposition has had the consequence,

of defeating the applicant's claim for financial relief, it shall be presumed, unless the contrary is shown, that the person who disposed of or is about to dispose of or deal with the property did so or, as the case may be, is about to do so, with the intention of defeating the applicant's claim for financial relief.

(6) In this section 'disposition' does not include any provision contained in a will or codicil but, with that exception, includes any conveyance, assurance or gift of property of any description, whether made by an instrument or otherwise.

(7) This section does not apply to a disposition made before 1st January 1968.

52.(1) . . . 'child', in relation to one or both of the parties to a marriage, includes an illegitimate . . . child of that party or as the case may be of both parties;

'Child of the family', in relation to the parties to a marriage means—

(a) a child of both parties; and

(b) any other child, not being a child who has been boarded out with those parties by a local authority or voluntary organisation, as being treated by both those parties as a child of that family; . . .

Children Act 1975

Custodianship orders

33. (1) An authorised court may on the application of one or more persons qualified under subsection (3) make an order vesting the legal custody of a child in the applicant or, as the case may be, in one or more of the applicants if the child is in England or Wales at the time the application is made.

(2) An order under subsection (1) may be referred to as a custodianship order, and the person in whom legal custody of the child is vested under the order may be referred to as the custodian of the child.

(3) The persons qualified to apply for a custodianship order are—

(a) a relative or step-parent of the child—

(i) who applies with the consent of a person having legal custody of the child, and

(ii) with whom the child has had his home for the three months preceding the making of the application;

(b) any person—

(i) who applies with the consent of a person having legal custody of the child, and

(ii) with whom the child has had his home for a period or periods before the making of the application which amount to at least twelve months and include the three months preceding the making of the application;

(c) any person with whom the child has had his home for a period or periods before the making of the application which amount to at least three years and include the three months preceding the making of the application.

(4) The mother or father of the child is not qualified under any paragraph of subsection (3).

(5) A step-parent of the child is not qualified under any paragraph of subsection (3) if in proceedings for divorce or nullity of marriage the child was named in an order made under paragraph (b) or (c) of section 41(1) (arrangements for welfare of children of family) of the Matrimonial Causes Act 1973.

(6) If no person has legal custody of the child, or the applicant himself has legal custody or the person with legal custody cannot be found, paragraphs (a) and (b) of subsection (3) apply with the omission of subparagraph (i).

(7) The Secretary of State may by order a draft of which has been approved by each House of Parliament amend subsection (3)(c) to substitute a different period for the period of three years mentioned in that paragraph (or the period which, by a previous order under this subsection, was substituted for that period).

(8) Subsection (5) does not apply—
  (a) if the parent other than the one the step-parent married is dead or cannot be found, or
  (b) if the order referred to in subsection (5) was made under subsection (1)(c) of section 41 of the Matrimonial Causes Act 1973 and it has since been determined that the child was not a child of the family to whom that section applied.

(9) For the avoidance of doubt, it is hereby declared that the provisions of section 1 of the Guardianship of Minors Act 1971 apply to applications made under this Part of this Act.

(10) This section and sections 34 to 46 do not apply to Scotland.

Restriction on removal of child where applicant has provided home for three years
41. .(1) While an application for a custodianship order in respect of a child made by the person with whom the child has at the time the application is made had his home for a period (whether continuous or not) amounting to at least three years is pending, another person is not entitled, against the will of the applicant, to remove the child from the applicant's actual custody except with the leave of a court or under authority conferred by any enactment or on the arrest of the child.

(2) In any case where subsection (1) applies, and
  (a) the child was in the care of a local authority before he began to have his home with the applicant, and
  (b) the child remains in the care of a local authority,
the authority in whose care the child is shall not remove the child from the applicant's actual custody except with the applicant's consent or the leave of a court.

(3) Any person who contravenes subsection (1) commits an offence and shall be liable on summary conviction to imprisonment for a term not exceeding three months or a fine not exceeding level 5 on the standard scale or both.

(4) The Secretary of State may by order a draft of which has been approved by each House of Parliament amend subsection (1) to substitute a different period for the period mentioned in that subsection (or the period which, by a previous order under this subsection, was substituted for that period).

Return of child taken away in breach of section 41

42. (1) An authorised court may on the application of a person from whose actual custody a child has been removed in breach of section 41 order the person who has so removed the child to return the child to the applicant.

(2) An authorised court may on the application of a person who has reasonable grounds for believing that another person is intending to remove a child from the applicant's actual custody in breach of section 41 by order direct that other person not to remove the child from the applicant's actual custody in breach of that section.

(3) If, in the case of an order made by the High Court under subsection (1), the High Court or, in the case of an order made by a county court under subsection (1), a county court is satisfied that the child has not been returned to the applicant, the court may make an order authorising an officer of the court to search such premises as may be specified in the order for the child and, if the officer finds the child, to return the child to the applicant.

(4) If a justice of the peace is satisfied by information on oath that there are reasonable grounds for believing that a child to whom an order under subsection (1) relates is in premises specified in the information, he may issue a search warrant authorising a constable to search the premises for the child; and if a constable acting in pursuance of a warrant under this section finds the child, he shall return the child to the person on whose application the order under subsection (1) was made.

(5) An order under subsection (3) may be enforced in like manner as a warrant for committal.

Courts

100. (1) In this Act 'authorised court', as respects an application for an order relating to a child, shall be construed as follows.

(2) If the child is in England or Wales when the application is made, the following are authorised courts—

 (a) the High Court;
 (b) the county court within whose district the child is and, in the case of an application under section 14, any county court within whose district a parent or guardian of the child is;
 (c) any other county court prescribed by the rules made under section 75 County Courts Act 1984;
 (d) a magistrates' court within whose area the child is and, in the case of an application under section 14, a magistrates' court within whose area a parent or guardian of the child is.

(3) . . .
(4) . . .
(5) . . .
(6) . . .

(7) Subsection (2) applies in the case of an application for an order under section 34, 35 or 38 relating to a child who is subject to a custodianship order whether or not the child is in England or Wales and for the purposes of such an application the following are also authorised courts—

 (a) the court which made the custodianship order and, where that court is a magistrates' court, any other magistrates' court acting for the same petty session area;

(b) the county court within whose district the applicant is;

(c) a magistrates' court within whose area the applicant is;

(d) where the application is made under section 35 and the child's mother or father or custodian is the petitioner or respondent in proceedings for a decree of divorce, nullity or judicial separation which are pending in a court in England or Wales, that court.

(8) Subsection (2) does not apply in the case of an application under section 30 or 42 but for the purposes of such an application the following are authorised courts—

(a) if there is pending in respect of the child an application for an adoption order or an order under section 14 or a custodianship order, the court in which that application is pending;

(b) in any other case, the High Court, the county court within whose district the applicant lives and the magistrates' court within whose area the applicant lives.

(9) . . .

(10) Any court to which the proceedings are transferred under any enactment is, as regards the transferred proceedings, an authorised court if it is not an authorised court under the preceding provisions of this section.

Domestic Violence and Matrimonial Proceedings Act 1976

Matrimonial injunctions in the county court

1. (1) Without prejudice to the jurisdiction of the High Court, on an application by a party to a marriage a county court shall have jurisdiction to grant an injunction containing one or more of the following provisions namely—

(a) a provision restraining the other party to a marriage from molesting the applicant;

(b) a provision restraining the other party from molesting a child living with the applicant;

(c) a provision excluding the other party from the matrimonial home or a part of the matrimonial home or from a specified area in which the matrimonial home is included;

(d) a provision requiring the other party to permit the applicant to enter and remain in the matrimonial home or a part of the matrimonial home;

whether or not any relief is sought in the proceedings.

(2) Sub-section (1) above shall apply to a man and a woman who are living with each other in the same household as husband and wife as it applies to the parties to a marriage and any reference to the matrimonial home shall be construed accordingly.

Arrest for breach of injunction

2. (1) Where, on the application by a party to a marriage, a judge grants an injunction containing a provision (in whatever terms)—

(a) restraining the other party to the marriage from using violence against the applicant, or

(b) restraining the other party from using violence against a child living with the applicant, or

(c) excluding the other party from the matrimonial home or from a specified area in which the matrimonial home is included,

the Judge may, if he is satisfied that the other party has caused actual bodily harm to the applicant or, as the case may be, to the child concerned and considers that he is likely to do so again, attach a power of arrest to the injunction.

(2) References in sub-section (1) above to the parties to a marriage include references to a man and a woman who are living with each other in the same household as husband and wife and any reference in that sub-section to the matrimonial home shall be construed accordingly.

(3) If by virtue of sub-section (1) above, a power of arrest is attached to an injunction, a constable may arrest without warrant a person who he has reasonable cause for suspecting of being in breach of such a provision of that injunction as falls within paragraphs (a) to (c) of sub-section (1) above by reason of that person's use of violence or, as the case may be, of his entering into any premises or area.

(4) Where a power of arrest is attached to an injunction and the person to whom the injunction is addressed is arrested under subsection (3) above—

(a) he shall be brought before a judge within the period of 24 hours beginning at the time of his arrest, and

(b) he shall not be released within that period except on the direction of the judge,

but nothing in this section shall authorise his detention at any time after the expiry of that period. In reckoning for the purposes of this sub-section any period of 24 hours, no account shall be taken of Christmas Day, Good Friday or any Sunday.

(5) Where by virtue of a power of arrest attached to an injunction a constable arrests any person under sub-section (3) above, the constable shall forthwith seek the directions—

(a) in a case where the injunction was granted by the High Court of that court and

(b) in any other case, of the county court,

as to the time and place at which the person is to be brought before a judge.

Domestic Proceedings and Magistrates' Courts Act 1978

POWERS OF COURT TO MAKE ORDERS FOR THE PROTECTION OF A PARTY TO A MARRIAGE OR A CHILD OF THE FAMILY

Powers of court to make orders for the protection of a party to a marriage or a child of the family

16. (1) Either party to a marriage may, whether or not an application is made by that party for an order under section 2 of this Act, apply to a magistrates' court for an order under this section.

(2) Where on an application for an order under this section the court is satisfied that the respondent has used or threatened to use violence against the person of the applicant or a child of the family and that it is necessary for the protection of the applicant or child of the family that an

order should be made under this sub-section, the court may make one or both of the following orders that is to say—

    (a) an order that the respondent shall not use, or threaten to use, violence against the person of the applicant;

    (b) an order that the respondent shall not use, or threaten to use, violence against the person of the child of the family.

(3) Where on an application or an order under this section the court is satisfied—

    (a) that the respondent has used violence against the person of the applicant or a child of the family, or

    (b) that the respondent has threatened to use violence against the person of the applicant or a child of the family and has used violence against some other person, or

    (c) that the respondent has in contravention of the order made under sub-section (2) above threatened to use violence against the person of the applicant or a child of the family,

and that the applicant or child of the family is in danger of being physically injured by the respondent or would be in such danger if the applicant or child were to enter the matrimonial home the court may make one or both of the following orders that is to say—

    (i) an order requiring the respondent to leave the matrimonial home;

    (ii) an order prohibiting the respondent from entering the matrimonial home.

(4) Where the court makes an order under sub-section (3) above, the court may, if it thinks fit, make a further order requiring the respondent to permit the applicant to enter and remain in the matrimonial home.

(5) Where on an application for an order under this section the court considers that it is essential that the application shall be heard without delay, the court may hear the application notwithstanding—

    (a) that the court does not include both a man and a woman,

    (b) that any member of the court is not a member of a domestic court panel, or

    (c) that the proceedings on the application are not separated from the hearing and determination proceedings which are not domestic proceedings.

(6) Where on an application for an order under this section the court is satisfied that there is imminent danger of physical injury to the applicant or to a child of the family, the court may make an order under sub-section (2) above notwithstanding—

    (a) that the summons has not been served on the respondent or has not been served on the respondent within a reasonable time before the hearing of the application, or

    (b) that the summons requires the respondent to appear at some other time or place.

and any order made by virtue of this sub-section is in this section and in section 17 of this Act referred to as an 'expedited order'.

(7) The power of the court to make, by virtue of sub-section (6) above, an expedited order under sub-section (2) above may be exercised by a single justice.

(8) An expedited order shall not take effect until the date on which notice of the making of the order is served on the respondent in such manner as may be prescribed or, if the court specified a later date as the

date on which the order is to take effect, that later date, and an expedited order shall cease to have effect on whichever of the following dates occurs first, that is to say—

    (a) the date of the expiration of the period of 28 days beginning with the date of the making of the order; or

    (b) the date of the commencement of the hearing, in accordance with the provisions of Part II of the Magistrates' Court Act 1952, of the application for an order under this section.

(9) An order under this section may be made subject to such exceptions or conditions as may be specified in the order and, subject in the case of an expedited order to sub-section (8) above, may be made for such a term as may be so specified.

(10) The court in making an order under sub-section (2)(a) or (b) above may include provision that the respondent shall not incite or assist any other person to use, or threaten to use, violence against the person of the applicant or, as the case may be, the child of the family.

Supplementary provisions with respect to orders under s 16

17. (1) A magistrates' court shall, on an application made by either party to the marriage in question, have power by order to vary or revoke any order made under section 16 of this Act.

(2) Rules may be made for the purpose of giving effect to the provision of section 16 of this Act and any such rules may in particular, but without prejudice to the generality of this sub-section, make provision for the hearing without delay of any application for an order under sub-section 3 of that section.

(3) The expiry by virtue of sub-section (8) of section 16 of this Act of an expedited order shall not prejudice the making of a further expedited order under that section.

(4) Except so far as the exercise by the respondent of a right to occupy the matrimonial home is suspended or restricted by virtue of an order made under sub-section (3) of section 16 of this Act an order made under that section shall not affect any estate or interest in the matrimonial home of the respondent or any other person.

Powers of arrest for breach of s 16 order

18. (1) Where a magistrates' court makes an order under section 16 of this Act which provides that the respondent—

    (a) shall not use violence against the person of the applicant, or

    (b) shall not use violence against a child of the family, or

    (c) shall not enter the matrimonial home,

the court may, if it is satisfied that the respondent has physically injured the applicant or a child of the family and considers that he is likely to do so again, attach a power of arrest to the order.

(2) Where by virtue of sub-section (1) above the power of arrest is attached to an order, a constable may arrest without warrant a person who he has reasonable cause for suspecting of being in breach of any such provision of the order as is mentioned in paragraph (a), (b) or (c) of sub-section (1) above by reason of that person's use of violence or, as the case may be, his entry into the matrimonial home.

(3) Where a power of arrest is attached to an order under sub-section (1) above and the respondent is arrested under sub-section (2) above—

    (a) he shall be brought before a justice of the peace within a period of 24 hours beginning at the time of his arrest and

(b) the justice of the peace before who he is brought may remand him.

In reckoning for the purposes of this sub-section any period of 24 hours, no account shall be taken of Christmas Day, Good Friday or any Sunday.

(4) Where a court has made an order under section 16 of this Act that has not attached to the order a power of arrest under sub-section (1) above, then, if at any time the applicant for that order considers that the other party to the marriage in question has disobeyed the order he may apply for the issue of a warrant for the arrest of that other person to a justice of the peace for the commission area in which either party to the marriage ordinarily resides; but a justice of the peace shall not issue a warrant on such an application unless—

(a) the application is substantiated on oath, and

(b) the justice has reasonable grounds for believing that the other party to the marriage has disobeyed the order.

(5) The magistrates' court before whom any person is brought by virtue of the warrant issued under sub-section (4) above may remand him.

Powers of High Court and county court in relation to certain orders under Part I

28. (1) Where after the making by a magistrates' court of an order under this part of this Act proceedings between, and relating to the marriage of, the parties to the proceedings in which that order was made have been commenced in the High Court or a county court then except in the case of an order for the payment of a lump sum, the court in which the proceedings or any application made therein is pending may, if it thinks fit direct that the order made by a magistrates' court shall cease to have effect on such date as may be specified in the direction.

(2) Where after the making by a magistrates' court of an order under sub-section (3) of section 16 of this Act in relation to a matrimonial home, one of the parties to the marriage in question applies for an order to be made in relation to that matrimonial home under—

(a) section 1(2) of the Matrimonial Homes Act 1967 (which enables an application to be made for an order relating to rights of occupation under that act or relating to the exercise by either spouse of a right to occupy a dwellinghouse), or

(b) section 4 of the Domestic Violence and Matrimonial Proceedings Act 1976 (which enables an application to be made for an order relating to the exercise of the right to occupy a dwellinghouse where both spouses have joint rights),

the High Court or county court by which the application is heard may, if it thinks fit, direct that the order made under sub-section (3) of section 16 of this Act, and any order made under sub-section (4) of that section in relation to that matrimonial home, shall cease to have effect on such date as may be specified in the direction.

(3) Nothing in this section shall be taken as prejudicing the effect of any order made by the High Court or a county court so far as it implicitly supersedes or revokes an order or part of any order made by a magistrates' court.

Appeals

29. (1) Subject to section 27 of this Act, where a magistrates' court makes or refuses to make, varies or refuses to vary, revokes or refuses to revoke an order (other than an interim maintenance order) under this Part of this Act, an appeal shall lie to the High Court.

(2) On an appeal under this section the High Court shall have power to make such orders as may be necessary to give effect to its determination of the appeal, including such incidental or consequential orders as appear to the court to be just, and, in the case of an appeal from a decision of a magistrates' court made on an application for or in respect of an order for the making of periodical payments, the High Court shall have power to order that its determination of the appeal shall have effect from such date as the court thinks fit, not being earlier than the date of the making of the application to the magistrates' court.

(3) Without prejudice to the generality of subsection (2) above, where, on an appeal under this section in respect of an order of a magistrates' court requiring any person to make periodical payments, the High Court reduces the amount of those payments or discharges the order, the High Court shall have power to order the person entitled to payments under the order of the magistrates' court to pay to the person liable to make payments under that order such sum in respect of payments already made in compliance with the order as the court thinks fit and, if any arrears are due under the order of the magistrates' court, the High Court shall have power to remit the payment of those arrears or any part thereof.

(4) Where on an appeal under this section in respect of an interim custody order made by a magistrates' court the High Court varies or revokes that order, the High Court shall have power to vary or revoke any interim maintenance order made in connection with that order by the magistrates' court.

(5) Any order of the High Court made on an appeal under this section (other than an order directing that an application shall be reheard by a magistrates' court) shall for the purposes of the enforcement of the order and for the purposes of sections 14(3), 20 and 21 of this Act be treated as if it were an order of the magistrates' court from which the appeal was brought and not of the High Court.

Restriction on removal of child from England and Wales

34. (1) Where a magistrates' court makes—
  (a) an order under section 8(2) of this Act regarding the legal custody of a child, or
  (b) an interim custody order under section 19 of this Act in respect of a child,
the court, on making the order or at any time while the order is in force, may, if an application is made for an order under this section, by order direct that no person shall take the child out of England and Wales while the order made under this section is in force, except with the leave of the court.

(2) A magistrates' court may by order vary or revoke any order made under this section.

(3) An application for an order under subsection (1) above, or for the variation or revocation of such an order, may be made by either party to the marriage in question and also, in the case of an order made under section 8(2) or 19 of this Act with respect to a child of the family who is not a child of both the parties to the marriage, by any person who, though not one of the parties to the marriage, is a parent of that child.

Interpretation Act 1978

References to service by post
7. Where an Act authorises or requires any document to be served by post (whether the expression 'serve' or the expression 'give' or 'send' or any other expression is used) then, unless the contrary intention appears, the service is deemed to be effected by properly addressing, pre-paying and posting a letter containing the document and, unless the contrary is proved, to have been effected at the time at which the letter would be delivered in the ordinary course of post.

Magistrates' Courts Act 1980

Issue of summons on complaint
51. Subject to the provisions of this Act, where a complaint is made to a justice of the peace acting for any petty sessions area upon which a magistrates' court acting for that area has power to make an order against any person, the justice may issue a summons directed to that person requiring him to appear before a magistrates' court acting for that area to answer to the complaint.

Jurisdiction to deal with complaints
52.   Where no express provision is made by any Act or the rules specifying what magistrates' courts shall have jurisdiction to hear a complaint, a magistrates' court shall have such jurisdiction if the complaint relates to anything done within the commission area for which the court is appointed or anything left undone that ought to have been done there, or ought to have been done either there or elsewhere, or relates to any other matter arising within that area.

   In this section 'commission area' has the same meaning as in the Justices of the Peace Act 1979.

HEARING OF COMPLAINT

Procedure on hearing
53. (1) On the hearing of a complaint, the court shall, if the defendant appears, state to him the substance of the complaint.

   (2) The court, after hearing the evidence and the parties, shall make the order for which the complaint is made or dismiss the complaint.

   (3) Where a complaint is for an order for the payment of a sum recoverable summarily as a civil debt, or for the variation of the rate of any periodical payments ordered by a magistrates' court to be made, or for such other matter as may be prescribed, the court may make the order with the consent of the defendant without hearing evidence.

Adjournment
54. (1) A magistrates' court may at any time, whether before or after beginning to hear a complaint, adjourn the hearing, and may do so, notwithstanding anything in this Act, when composed of a single justice.

   (2) The court may when adjourning either fix the time and place at

which the hearing is to be resumed or, unless it remands the defendant under section 55 below, leave the time and place to be determined later by the court; but the hearing shall not be resumed at that time and place unless the court is satisfied that the parties have had adequate notice thereof.

Non-appearance of defendant

55. (1) Where at the time and place appointed for the hearing or adjourned hearing of a complaint the complainant appears but the defendant does not, the court may, subject to subsection (3) below, proceed in his absence.

(2) Where the court, instead of proceeding in the absence of the defendant, adjourns, or further adjourns, the hearing, the court may, if the complaint has been substantiated on oath, and subject to the following provisions of this section, issue a warrant for his arrest.

(3) The court shall not begin to hear the complaint in the absence of the defendant or issue a warrant under this section unless either it is proved to the satisfaction of the court, on oath or in such other manner as may be prescribed, that the summons was served on him within what appears to the court to be a reasonable time before the hearing or adjourned hearing or the defendant has appeared on a previous occasion to answer to the complaint.

(4) Where the defendant fails to appear at an adjourned hearing, the court shall not issue a warrant under this section unless it is satisfied that he has had adequate notice of the time and place of the adjourned hearing.

(5) Where the defendant is arrested under a warrant issued under this section, the court may, on any subsequent adjournment of the hearing, but subject to the provisions of subsection (6) below, remand him.

(6) The court shall not issue a warrant or remand a defendant under this section or further remand him by virtue of section 128(3) below after he has given evidence in the proceedings.

(7) Where the court remands the defendant, the time fixed for the resumption of the hearing shall be that at which he is required to appear or be brought before the court in pursuance of the remand.

(8) A warrant under this section shall not be issued in any proceedings for the recovery or enforcement of a sum recoverable summarily as a civil debt or in proceedings in any matter of bastardy.

Non-appearance of complainant

56. Where at the time and place appointed for the hearing or adjourned hearing of a complaint the defendant appears but the complainant does not, the court may dismiss the complaint or, if evidence has been received on a previous occasion, proceed in the absence of the complainant.

Non-appearance of both parties

57. Where at the time and place appointed for the hearing or adjourned hearing of a complaint neither the complainant nor the defendant appears, the court may dismiss the complaint.

Orders other than for payment of money

63. (1) Where under any Act passed after 31st December 1879 a magistrates' court has power to require the doing of anything other than the payment of money, or to prohibit the doing of anything, any order of the court for the purpose of exercising that power may contain such provisions for the manner in which anything is to be done, for the time within which anything is to be done, or during which anything is not to be done, and generally for giving effect to the order, as the court thinks fit.

(2) The court may by order made on complaint suspend or rescind any such order as aforesaid.

(3) Where any person disobeys an order of a magistrates' court made under an Act passed after 31st December 1879 to do anything other than the payment of money or to abstain from doing anything the court may—

    (a) order him to pay a sum not exceeding £50 for every day during which he is in default or a sum not exceeding £2,000; or

    (b) commit him to custody until he has remedied his default or for a period not exceeding 2 months;

but a person who is ordered to pay a sum for every day during which he is in default or who is committed to custody until he has remedied his default shall not by virtue of this section be ordered to pay more than £2,000 or be committed for more than 2 months in all for doing or abstaining from doing the same thing contrary to the order (without prejudice to the operation of this section in relation to any subsequent default).

(4) Any sum ordered to be paid under subsection (3) above shall for the purposes of this Act be treated as adjudged to be paid by a conviction of a magistrates' court.

(5) The preceding provisions of this section shall not apply to any order for the enforcement of which provision is made by any other enactment.

Reasons for decisions in domestic proceedings
74. (1) The power to make rules conferred by section 144 below shall, without prejudice to the generality of subsection (1) of that section, include power to make provision for the recording by a magistrates' court, in such manner as may be prescribed by the rules, of reasons for a decision made in such domestic proceedings or class of domestic proceedings as may be so prescribed, and for making available a copy of any record made in accordance with those rules of the reasons for a decision of a magistrates' court to any person who requests a copy thereof for the purposes of an appeal against that decision or for the purpose of deciding whether or not to appeal against that decision.

(2) A copy of any record made by virtue of this section of the reasons for a decision of a magistrates' court shall, if certified by such officer of the court as may be prescribed, be admissible as evidence of those reasons.

Contempt of Court Act 1981

Proceedings in England and Wales
14. (1) In any case where a court has power to commit a person to prison for contempt of court and (apart from this provision) no limitation applies to the period of committal, the committal shall (without prejudice to the power of the court to order his earlier discharge) be for a fixed term, and that term shall not on any occasion exceed two years in the case of committal by a superior court, or one month in the case of committal by an inferior court.

(2) In any case where an inferior court has power to fine a person for contempt of court and (apart from this provision) no limit applies to the amount of the fine, the fine shall not on any occasion exceed £500.

(3) In relation to the exercise of jurisdiction to commit for contempt of court or any kindred offence, subsection (1) of section 19 of the Powers of Criminal Courts Act 1973 (prohibition of imprisonment of persons under seventeen years of age) shall apply to all courts having that jurisdiction as it applies to the Crown Court and magistrates' courts.

(4) Each of the superior courts shall have the like power to make a hospital order or guardianship order under section 60 of the Mental Health Act 1959 in the case of a person suffering from mental illness or severe subnormality who could otherwise be committed to prison for contempt of court as the Crown Court has under that section in the case of a person convicted of an offence.

(4A) For the purposes of the preceding provisions of this section a county court shall be treated as a superior court and not as an inferior court.

(5) The enactments specified in Part III of Schedule 2 shall have effect subject to the amendments set out in that Part, being amendments relating to the penalties and procedure in respect of certain offences of contempt in coroners' courts, county courts and magistrates' courts.

Supreme Court Act 1981

Restrictions on appeals to the Court of Appeal
18. (1) No appeal shall lie to the Court of Appeal—
. . .
(h) without the leave of the court or tribunal in question or of the Court of Appeal, from any interlocutory order or interlocutory judgment made or given by the High Court or any other court or tribunal, except in the following cases, namely—
(i) where the liberty of the subject or the custody, education or welfare of a minor is concerned;
(ii) . . .
(iii) where an injunction . . is granted or refused.
(iv) . . .
(v) . . .
(vi) in such other cases as may be prescribed.

Powers of High Court with respect to injunctions and receivers
37. (1) The High Court may by order (whether interlocutory or final) grant an injunction or appoint a receiver in all cases in which it appears to the court to be just and convenient to do so.

(2) Any such order may be made either unconditionally or on such terms and conditions as the court thinks just.

(3) The power of the High Court under subsection (1) to grant an interlocutory injunction restraining a party to any proceedings from removing from the jurisdiction of the High Court, or otherwise dealing with, assets located within that jurisdiction shall be exercisable in cases where that party is, as well as in cases where he is not, domiciled, resident or present within that jurisdiction.

(4) . . .
(5) . . .

Matrimonial Homes Act 1983

Rights concerning matrimonial home where one spouse has no estate, etc
1. (1) Where one spouse is entitled to occupy a dwelling house by virtue of a beneficial estate or interest or contract or by virtue of any enactment giving him or her the right to remain in occupation, and the other spouse is not so entitled, then, subject to the provisions of this Act, the spouse not so entitled shall have the following rights (in this Act referred to as 'rights of occupation')—

(a) if in occupation, a right not to be evicted or excluded from the dwelling house or any part thereof by the other spouse except with the leave of the court given by an order under this section;

(b) if not in occupation, a right with the leave of the court so given to enter into and occupy the dwelling house.

(2) So long as one spouse has rights of occupation, either of the spouses may apply to the court for an order—

(a) declaring, enforcing, restricting or terminating those rights, or

(b) prohibiting, suspending, or restricting the exercise by either spouse of the right to occupy the dwelling house, or

(c) requiring either spouse to permit the exercise by the other of that right.

(3) On an application for an order under this section, the court may make such order as it thinks just and reasonable having regard to the conduct of the spouses in relation to each other and otherwise, to their respective needs and financial resources, to the needs of any children and to all the circumstances of the case, and, without prejudice to the generality of the foregoing provision—

(a) may except part of the dwelling house from a spouse's rights of occupation (and in particular a part used wholly or mainly for or in connection with the trade, business or profession of the other spouse),

(b) may order a spouse occupying the dwelling house or any part thereof by virtue of this section to make periodical payments to the other in respect of the occupation,

(c) may impose on either spouse obligations as to the repair and maintenance of the dwelling house or the discharge of any liabilities in respect of the dwelling house.

(4) Orders under this section may, in so far as they have a continuing effect, be limited so as to have effect for a period specified in the order or until further order.

(5) Where a spouse is entitled under this section to occupy a dwelling house or any part thereof, any payment or tender made or other thing done by that spouse in or towards satisfaction of any liability of the other spouse in respect of rent, rates, mortgage payments or other outgoings affecting the dwelling house shall, whether or not it is made or done in pursuance of an order under this section, be as good as if made or done by the other spouse.

(6) A spouse's occupation by virtue of this section shall, for the purposes of the Rent (Agriculture) Act 1976, and of the Rent Act 1977 (other than Part V and sections 103 to 106), be treated as possession by the other spouse and for purposes of Chapter II of Part I of the Housing Act 1980 be treated as occupation by the other spouse.

(7) Where a spouse is entitled under this section to occupy a dwelling

house or any part thereof and makes any payment in or towards satisfaction of any liability of the other spouse in respect of mortgage payments affecting the dwelling house, the person to whom the payment is made may treat it as having been made by that other spouse, but the fact that that person has treated any such payment as having been so made shall not affect any claim of the first-mentioned spouse against the other to an interest in the dwelling house by virtue of the payment.

(8) Where a spouse is entitled under this section to occupy a dwelling house or part thereof by reason of an interest of the other spouse under a trust, all the provisions of subsections (5) to (7) above shall apply in relation to the trustees as they apply in relation to the other spouse.

(9) The jurisdiction conferred on the court by this section shall be exercisable by the High Court or by a county court, and shall be exercisable by a county court notwithstanding that by reason of the amount of the net annual value for rating of the dwelling house or otherwise the jurisdiction would not but for this subsection be exercisable by a county court.

(10) This Act shall not apply to a dwelling house which has at no time been a matrimonial home of the spouses in question; and a spouse's rights of occupation shall continue only so long as the marriage subsists and the other spouse is entitled as mentioned in subsection (1) above to occupy the dwelling house, except where provision is made by section 2 of this Act for those rights to be a charge on an estate or interest in the dwelling house.

(11) It is hereby declared that a spouse who has an equitable interest in a dwelling house or in the proceeds of sale thereof, not being a spouse in whom is vested (whether solely or as a joint tenant) a legal estate in fee simple or a legal term of years absolute in the dwelling house, is to be treated for the purpose only of determining whether he or she has rights of occupation under this section as not being entitled to occupy the dwelling house by virtue of that interest.

Effect of rights of occupation as charge on dwelling house
2. (1) Where, at any time during the subsistence of a marriage, one spouse is entitled to occupy a dwelling house by virtue of a beneficial estate or interest, then the other spouse's rights of occupation shall be a charge on that estate or interest, having the like priority as if it were an equitable interest created at whichever is the latest of the following dates, that is to say—
    (a) the date when the spouse so entitled acquires the estate or interest,
    (b) the date of the marriage, and
    (c) the 1st January 1968 (which is the date of commencement of the Act of 1967).
    (2) . . .
    (3) . . .
    (4) Notwithstanding that a spouse's rights of occupation are a charge on an estate or interest in the dwelling house, those rights shall be brought to an end by—
    (a) the death of the other spouse, or
    (b) the termination (otherwise than by death) of the marriage,
unless in the event of a matrimonial dispute or estrangement the court sees fit to direct otherwise by an order made under section 1 above during the subsistence of the marriage.

(5) . . .
(6) . . .
(7) . . .
(8) . . .
(9) . . .
(10) . . .
(11) . . .

Rights concerning matrimonial home where both spouses have estate, etc
9. (1) Where each of two spouses is entitled, by virtue of a legal estate vested in them jointly, to occupy a dwelling house in which they have or at any time have had a matrimonial home, either of them may apply to the court, with respect to the exercise during the subsistence of the marriage of the right to occupy the dwelling house, for an order prohibiting, suspending or restricting its exercise by the other or requiring the other to permit its exercise by the applicant.

(2) In relation to orders under this section, section 1(3), (4) and (9) above shall apply as they apply in relation to orders under that section.

(3) Where each of two spouses is entitled to occupy a dwelling house by virtue of a contract, or by virtue of any enactment giving them the right to remain in occupation, this section shall apply as it applies where they are entitled by virtue of a legal estate vested in them jointly.

(4) . . .

Interpretation
10. (1) In this Act—
'Act of 1967' means the Matrimonial Homes Act 1967;
'Act of 1981' means the Matrimonial Homes and Property Act 1981;
'dwelling house' includes any building or part thereof which is occupied as a dwelling, and any yard, garden, garage or outhouse belonging to the dwelling house and occupied therewith;
'mortgage' includes a charge and 'mortgagor' and 'mortgagee' shall be construed accordingly;
'mortgagor' and 'mortgagee' includes any person deriving title under the original mortgagor or mortgagee;
'rights of occupation' has the meaning assigned to it in section 1(1) above.

(2) It is hereby declared that this Act applies as between a husband and a wife notwithstanding that the marriage in question was entered into under a law which permits polygamy (whether or not either party to the marriage in question has for the time being any spouse additional to the other party).

(3) . . .

County Courts Act 1984

General ancillary jurisdiction
38. (1) Every county court, as regards any cause of action for the time being within its jurisdiction—

    (a) shall grant such relief, redress or remedy or combination of remedies, either absolute or conditional; and

    (b) shall give such and the like effect to every ground of defence or counterclaim equitable or legal, as ought to be granted or given in the like case by the High Court and in as full and ample a manner.

(2) For the purposes of this section it shall be assumed (notwithstanding any enactment to the contrary) that any proceedings which can be commenced in a county court could be commenced in the High Court.

Ancillary powers of judge
39. A judge shall have jurisdiction in any pending proceedings to make any order or exercise any authority or jurisdiction which, if it related to an action or proceeding pending in the High Court, might be made or exercised by a judge of the High Court in chambers.

Application of practice of High Court
76. In any case not expressly provided for by or in pursuance of this Act, the general principles of practice in the High Court may be adopted and applied to proceedings in a county court.

Appeals: general provisions
77. (1) Subject to the provisions of this section and the following provisions of this Part of this Act, if any party to any proceedings in a county court is dissatisfied with the determination of the judge or jury, he may appeal from it to the Court of Appeal in such manner and subject to such conditions as may be provided by the rules of the Supreme Court.

(2) The Lord Chancellor may by order prescribe classes of proceedings in which there is to be no right of appeal under this section without the leave either of the judge of the county court or of the Court of Appeal.

(3) . . .

(4) . . .

(5) . . .

(6) . . .

(7) This section shall not—
   (a) confer any right of appeal from any judgment or order where a right of appeal is conferred by some other enactment; or
   (b) take away any right of appeal from any judgment or order where a right of appeal is so conferred,

and shall have effect subject to any enactment other than this Act.

(8) . . .

Agreement not to appeal
79. (1) No appeal shall lie from any judgment, direction, decision or order of a judge of county courts if, before the judgment, direction, decision or order is given or made, the parties agree, in writing signed by themselves or their solicitors or agents, that it shall be final.

(2) No such agreement shall require a stamp.

Judge's note on appeal
80. (1) At the hearing of any proceedings in a county court in which there is a right of appeal or from which an appeal may be brought with leave, the judge shall, at the request of any party, make a note—
   (a) of any question of law raised at the hearing; and
   (b) of the facts in evidence in relation to any such question; and

    (c) of his decision on any such question and of his determination of the proceedings.

(2) Where such a note has been taken, the judge shall (whether notice of appeal has been served or not), on the application of any party to the proceedings, and on payment by that party of such fee as may be prescribed by the fees orders, furnish him with a copy of the note, and shall sign the copy, and the copy so signed shall be used at the hearing of the appeal.

Powers of Court of Appeal on appeal from county court
81. (1) On the hearing of an appeal, the Court of Appeal may draw any inference of fact and either—
    (a) order a new trial on such terms as the court thinks just; or
    (b) order judgment to be entered for any party; or
    (c) make a final or other order on such terms as the court thinks proper to ensure the determination on the merits of the real question in controversy between the parties.

(2) Subject to any rules of the Supreme Court, on any appeal from a county court the Court of Appeal may reverse or vary, in favour of a party seeking to support the judgment or order of the county court in whole or in part, any determinations made in the county court on questions of fact, notwithstanding that the appeal is an appeal on a point of law only, or any such determinations on points of law, notwithstanding that the appeal is an appeal on a question of fact only.

(3) Subsection (2) shall not enable the Court of Appeal to reverse or vary any determination, unless the party dissatisfied with the determination would have been entitled to appeal in respect of it if aggrieved by the judgment or order.

Issue and execution of orders of committal
119. (1) Whenever any order or warrant for the committal of any person to prison is made or issued by a county court (whether in pursuance of this or any other Act or of county court rules), the order or warrant shall be directed to the registrar of the court, who shall thereby be empowered to take the body of the person against whom the order is made or warrant issued.

(2) It shall be the duty of every constable within his jurisdiction to assist in the execution of every such order or warrant.

(3) The governor of the prison mentioned in any such order or warrant shall be bound to receive and keep the person mentioned in it until he is lawfully discharged.

Child Abduction Act 1984

Offence of abduction of child by parent, etc
1. (1) Subject to subsections (5) and (8) below, a person connected with a child under the age of sixteen commits an offence if he takes or sends the child out of the United Kingdom without the appropriate consent.

(2) A person is connected with a child for the purposes of this section if
    (a) he is a parent or guardian of the child; or
    (b) there is in force an order of a court in the United Kingdom awarding custody of the child to him, whether solely or jointly with any other person; or

(c) in the case of an illegitimate child, there are reasonable grounds for believing that he is the father of the child.

(3) In this section 'the appropriate consent', in relation to a child, means

    (a) the consent of each person—
        (i) who is a parent or guardian of the child; or
        (ii) to whom custody of the child has been awarded (whether solely or jointly with any other person) by an order of a court in the United Kingdom; or
    (b) if the child is the subject of such a custody order, the leave of the court which made the order; or
    (c) the leave of the court granted on an application for a direction under section 7 of the Guardianship of Minors Act 1971 or section 1(3) of the Guardianship Act 1973.

(4) In the case of a custody order made by a magistrates' court, subsection (3)(b) above shall be construed as if the reference to the court which made the order included a reference to any magistrates' court acting for the same petty sessions area as that court.

(5) A person does not commit an offence under this section by doing anything without the consent of another person whose consent is required under the foregoing provisions if—

    (a) he does it in the belief that the other person
        (i) has consented; or
        (ii) would consent if he was aware of all the relevant circumstances; or
    (b) he has taken all reasonable steps to communicate with the other person but has been unable to communicate with him; or
    (c) the other person has unreasonably refused to consent,

but paragraph (c) of this subsection does not apply where what is done relates to a child who is the subject of a custody order made by a court in the United Kingdom, or where the person who does it acts in breach of any direction under section 7 of the Guardianship of Minors Act 1971 or section 1(3) of the Guardianship Act 1973.

(6) Where, in proceedings for an offence under this section, there is sufficient evidence to raise an issue as to the application of subsection (5) above, it shall be for the prosecution to prove that that subsection does not apply.

(7) In this section—

    (a) 'guardian' means a person appointed by deed or will or by order of a court of competent jurisdiction to be the guardian of a child; and
    (b) a reference to a custody order or an order awarding custody includes a reference to an order awarding legal custody and a reference to an order awarding care and control.

(8) This section shall have effect subject to the provisions of the Schedule to this Act in relation to a child who is in the care of a local authority or voluntary organisation or who is committed to a place of safety or who is the subject of custodianship proceedings or proceedings or an order relating to adoption.

Offence of abduction of child by other persons
2. (1) Subject to subsection (2) below, a person not falling within section 1(2)(a) or (b) above commits an offence if, without lawful authority or reasonable excuse, he takes or detains a child under the age of sixteen—

(a) so as to remove him from the lawful control of any person having lawful control of the child; or

(b) so as to keep him out of the lawful control of any person entitled to lawful control of the child.

(2) In proceedings against any person for an offence under this section, it shall be a defence for that person to show that at the time of the alleged offence—

(a) he believed that the child had attained the age of sixteen; or

(b) in the case of an illegitimate child, he had reasonable grounds for believing himself to be the child's father.

Construction of references to taking, sending and detaining

3. For the purposes of this Part of this Act—

(a) a person shall be regarded as taking a child if he causes or induces the child to accompany him or any other person or causes the child to be taken;

(b) a person shall be regarded as sending a child if he causes the child to be sent; and

(c) a person shall be regarded as detaining a child if he causes the child to be detained or induces the child to remain with him or any other person.

Penalties and prosecutions

4. (1) A person guilty of an offence under this Part of this Act shall be liable—

(a) on summary conviction, to imprisonment for a term not exceeding six months or to a fine not exceeding the statutory maximum, as defined in section 74 of the Criminal Justice Act 1982, or to both such imprisonment and fine;

(b) on conviction on indictment, to imprisonment for a term not exceeding seven years.

(2) No prosecution for an offence under section 1 above shall be instituted except by or with the consent of the Director of Public Prosecutions.

Restriction on prosecutions for offence of kidnapping

5. Except by or with the consent of the Director of Public Prosecutions no prosecution shall be instituted for an offence of kidnapping if it was committed

(a) against a child under the age of sixteen; and

(b) by a person connected with the child, within the meaning of section 1 above.

Matrimonial and Family Proceedings Act 1984

Avoidance of transactions intended to defeat applications for financial relief

23. (1) For the purposes of this section 'financial relief' means relief under section 14 or 17 above and any reference to defeating a claim by a party to a marriage for financial relief is a reference to preventing financial relief from being granted or reducing the amount of relief which might be granted, or frustrating or impeding the enforcement of any order which might be or has been made under either of those provisions at the instance of that party.

(2) Where leave is granted under section 13 above for the making by a

party to a marriage of an application for an order for financial relief under section 17 above, the court may, on an application by that party—

(a) if it is satisfied that the other party to the marriage is, with the intention of defeating the claim for financial relief, about to make any disposition or to transfer out of the jurisdiction or otherwise deal with any property, make such order as it thinks fit for restraining the other party from so doing or otherwise for protecting the claim;

(b) if it is satisfied that the other party has, with that intention, made a reviewable disposition and that if the disposition were set aside financial relief or different financial relief would be granted to the applicant, make an order setting aside the disposition.

(3) Where an order for financial relief under section 14 or 17 above has been made by the court at the instance of a party to a marriage, then, on an application made by that party, the court may, if it is satisfied that the other party to the marriage has, with the intention of defeating the claim for financial relief, made a reviewable disposition, make an order setting aside the disposition.

(4) Where the court has jurisdiction to entertain the application for an order for financial relief by reason only of paragraph (c) of section 15(1) above, it shall not make any order under subsection (2) or (3) above in respect of any property other than the dwelling-house concerned.

(5) Where the court makes an order under subsection (2)(b) or (3) above setting aside a disposition it shall give such consequential directions as it thinks fit for giving effect to the order (including directions requiring the making of any payments or the disposal of any property).

(6) Any disposition made by the other party to the marriage (whether before or after the commencement of the application) is a reviewable disposition for the purposes of subsections (2)(b) and (3) above unless it was made for valuable consideration (other than marriage) to a person who, at the time of the disposition, acted in relation to it in good faith and without notice of any intention on the part of the other party to defeat the applicant's claim for financial relief.

(7) Where an application is made under subsection (2) or (3) above with respect to a disposition which took place less than three years before the date of the application or with respect to a disposition or other dealing with property which is about to take place and the court is satisfied—

(a) in a case falling within subsection (2)(a) or (b) above, that the disposition or other dealing would (apart from this section) have the consequence, or

(b) in a case falling within subsection (3) above, that the disposition has had the consequence,

of defeating a claim by the applicant for financial relief, it shall be presumed, unless the contrary is shown, that the person who disposed of or is about to dispose of or deal with the property did so or, as the case may be, is about to do so, with the intention of defeating the applicant's claim for financial relief.

(8) In this section 'disposition' does not include any provision contained in a will or codicil but, with that exception, includes any conveyance, assurance or gift of property of any description, whether made by an instrument or otherwise.

(9) The preceding provisions of this section are without prejudice to any power of the High Court to grant injunctions under section 37 of the Supreme Court Act 1981.

Prevention of transactions intended to defeat prospective applications for financial relief
24. (1) Where, on an application by a party to a marriage, it appears to the court—

(a) that the marriage has been dissolved or annulled, or that the parties to the marriage have been legally separated, by means of judicial or other proceedings in an overseas country; and

(b) that the applicant intends to apply for leave to make an application for an order for financial relief under section 17 above as soon as he or she has been habitually resident in England and Wales for a period of one year; and

(c) that the other party to the marriage is, with the intention of defeating a claim for financial relief, about to make any disposition or to transfer out of the jurisdiction or otherwise deal with any property,

the court may make such order as it thinks fit for restraining the other party from taking such action as is mentioned in paragraph (c) above.

(2) For the purposes of an application under subsection (1) above—

(a) the reference to defeating a claim for financial relief shall be construed in accordance with subsection (1) of section 23 above (omitting the reference to any order which has been made); and

(b) subsections (7) and (8) of section 23 above shall apply as they apply for the purposes of an application under that section.

(3) The preceding provisions of this section are without prejudice to any power of the High Court to grant injunctions under section 37 of the Supreme Court Act 1981.

Directions as to distribution and transfer of family business and proceedings
37. The President of the Family Division may, with the concurrence of the Lord Chancellor, give directions with respect to the distribution and transfer between the High Court and county courts of family business and family proceedings.

Child Abduction and Custody Act 1985

Part I—International child abduction

The Hague Convention
1. (1) In this Part of this Act 'the Convention' means the Convention on the Civil Aspects of International Child Abduction which was signed at The Hague on 25 October 1980.
(2) Subject to the provisions of this Part of this Act, the provisions of that Convention set out in Schedule 1 to this Act shall have the force of law in the United Kingdom.

Contracting States
2. (1) For the purposes of the Convention as it has effect under this Part of this Act the Contracting States other than the United Kingdom shall be those for the time being specified by an Order in Council under this section.

(2) An Order in Council under this section shall specify the date of the coming into force of the Convention as between the United Kingdom and

any State specified in the Order; and, except where the Order otherwise provides, the Convention shall apply as between the United Kingdom and that State only in relation to wrongful removals or retentions occurring on or after that date.

(3) Where the Convention applies, or applies only, to a particular territory or particular territories specified in a declaration made by a Contracting State under Article 39 or 40 of the Convention references to that State in subsections (1) and (2) above shall be construed as references to that territory or those territories.

Central Authorities

3. (1) Subject to subsection (2) below, the functions under the Convention of a Central Authority shall be discharged—

   (a) in England and Wales and in Northern Ireland by the Lord Chancellor; and
   (b) in Scotland by the Secretary of State.

(2) Any application made under the Convention by or on behalf of a person outside the United Kingdom may be addressed to the Lord Chancellor as the Central Authority in the United Kingdom.

(3) Where any such application relates to a function to be discharged under subsection (1) above by the Secretary of State it shall be transmitted by the Lord Chancellor to the Secretary of State and where such an application is addressed to the Secretary of State but relates to a function to be discharged under subsection (1) above by the Lord Chancellor the Secretary of State shall transmit it to the Lord Chancellor.

Judicial authorities

4. The courts having jurisdiction to entertain applications under the Convention shall be—

   (a) in England and Wales or in Northern Ireland the High Court; and
   (b) in Scotland the Court of Session.

Interim powers

5. Where an application has been made to a court in the United Kingdom under the Convention, the court may, at any time before the application is determined, give such interim directions as it thinks fit for the purpose of securing the welfare of the child concerned or of preventing changes in the circumstances relevant to the determination of the application.

Reports

6. Where the Lord Chancellor or the Secretary of State is requested to provide information relating to a child under Article 7(d) of the Convention he may—

   (a) request a local authority or a probation officer to make a report to him in writing with respect to any matter which appears to him to be relevant;
   (b) request the Department of Health and Social Services for Northern Ireland to arrange for a suitably qualified person to make such a report to him;
   (c) request any court to which a written report relating to the child has been made to send him a copy of the report;

and such a request shall be duly complied with.

Proof of documents and evidence
7. (1) For the purposes of Article 14 of the Convention a decision or determination of a judicial or administrative authority outside the United Kingdom may be proved by a duly authenticated copy of the decision or determination; and any document purporting to be such a copy shall be deemed to be a true copy unless the contrary is shown.

(2) For the purposes of subsection (1) above a copy is duly authenticated if it bears the seal, or is signed by a judge or officer, of the authority in question.

(3) For the purposes of Articles 14 and 30 of the Convention any such document as is mentioned in Article 8 of the Convention, or a certified copy of any such document, shall be sufficient evidence of anything stated in it.

Declarations by United Kingdom courts
8. The High Court or Court of Session may, on an application made for the purposes of Article 15 of the Convention by any person appearing to the court to have an interest in the matter, make a declaration or declarator that the removal of any child from, or his retention outside, the United Kingdom was wrongful within the meaning of Article 3 of the Convention.

Suspension of court's powers in cases of wrongful removal
9. The reference in Article 16 of the Convention to deciding on the merits of rights of custody shall be construed as a reference to—
    (a) making, varying or revoking a custody order, or any other order under section 1(2) of the Children and Young Persons Act 1969 or section 95(1), 97(2), 143(6) or 144 of the Children and Young Persons Act (Northern Ireland) 1968 (not being a custody order);
    (b) registering or enforcing a decision under Part II of this Act;
    (c) determining a complaint under section 3(5) or 5(4) of the Child Care Act 1980 or an appeal under section 6 or 67(2) or (3) of that Act;
    (d) determining a summary application under section 16(8), 16A(3) or 18(3) of the Social Work (Scotland) Act 1968;
    (e) making a parental rights order under section 104 of the Children and Young Persons Act (Northern Ireland) 1968 or discharging such an order, or giving directions in lieu of the discharge of such an order, under section 106(2) of that Act.

Rules of court
10. (1) An authority having power to make rules of court may make such provision for giving effect to this Part of this Act as appears to that authority to be necessary or expedient.

(2) Without prejudice to the generality of subsection (1) above, rules of court may make provision—
    (a) with respect to the procedure on applications for the return of a child and with respect to the documents and information to be furnished and the notices to be given in connection with any such application;
    (b) for the transfer of any such application between the appropriate courts in the different parts of the United Kingdom;
    (c) for the giving of notices by or to a court for the purposes of the provisions of Article 16 of the Convention and section 9 above and generally as respects proceedings to which those provisions apply;
    (d) for enabling a person who wishes to make an application under the Convention in a Contracting State other than the United Kingdom to obtain from any court in the United Kingdom an authenticated copy

of any decision of that court relating to the child to whom the application is to relate.

Cost of applications
11. The United Kingdom having made such a reservation as is mentioned in the third paragraph of Article 26 of the Convention, the costs mentioned in that paragraph shall not be borne by any Minister or other authority in the United Kingdom except as far as they fall to be so borne by virtue of the grant of legal aid or legal advice and assistance under Part 1 of the Legal Aid Act 1974, the Legal Aid (Scotland) Act 1967, Part I of the Legal Advice and Assistance Act 1972 or the Legal Aid Advice and Assistance (Northern Ireland) Order 1981.

Part II—Recognition and enforcement of custody decisions

The European Convention
12. (1) In this Part of this Act 'the Convention' means the European Convention on Recognition and Enforcement of Decisions concerning Custody of Children and on the Restoration of Custody of Children which was signed in Luxemburg on 20 May 1980.

(2) Subject to the provisions of this Part of this Act, the provisions of that Convention set out in Schedule 2 to this Act (which include Articles 9 and 10 as they have effect in consequences of a reservation made by the United Kingdom under Article 17) shall have the force of law in the United Kingdom.

Contracting States
13. (1) For the purposes of the Convention as it has effect under this Part of this Act the Contracting States other than the United Kingdom shall be those for the time being specified by an Order in Council under this section.

(2) An Order in Council under this section shall specify the date of the coming into force of the Convention as between the United Kingdom and any State specified in the Order.

(3) Where the Convention applies, or applies only, to a particular territory or particular territories specified by a Contracting State under Article 24 or 25 of the Convention references to that State in subsections (1) and (2) above shall be construed as references to that territory or those territories.

Central Authorities
14. (1) Subject to subsection (2) below, the functions under the Convention of a Central Authority shall be discharged—
  (a) in England and Wales and in Northern Ireland by the Lord Chancellor; and
  (b) in Scotland by the Secretary of State.

(2) Any application made under the Convention by or on behalf of a person outside the United Kingdom may be addressed to the Lord Chancellor as the Central Authority in the United Kingdom.

(3) Where any such application relates to a function to be discharged under subsection (1) above by the Secretary of State it shall be transmitted by the Lord Chancellor to the Secretary of State and where such an

application is addressed to the Secretary of State but relates to a function to be discharged under subsection (1) above by the Lord Chancellor the Secretary of State shall transmit it to the Lord Chancellor.

Recognition of decisions
15. (1) Articles 7 and 12 of the Convention shall have effect in accordance with this section.

(2) A decision to which either of those Articles applies which was made in a Contracting State other than the United Kingdom shall be recognised in each part of the United Kingdom as if made by a court having jurisdiction to make it in that part but—

>   (a) the appropriate court in any part of the United Kingdom may, on the application of any person appearing to it to have an interest in the matter, declare on any of the grounds specified in Article 9 or 10 of the Convention that the decision is not to be recognised in any part of the United Kingdom; and
>
>   (b) the decision shall not be enforceable in any part of the United Kingdom unless registered in the appropriate court under section 16 below.

(3) The references in Article 9(1)(c) of the Convention to the removal of the child are to his improper removal within the meaning of the Convention.

Registration of decisions
16. (1) A person on whom any rights are conferred by a decision relating to custody made by an authority in a Contracting State other than the United Kingdom may make an application for the registration of the decision in an appropriate court in the United Kingdom.

(2) The Central Authority in the United Kingdom shall assist such a person in making such an application if a request for such assistance is made by him or on his behalf by the Central Authority of the Contracting State in question.

(3) An application under subsection (1) above or a request under subsection (2) above shall be treated as a request for enforcement for the purposes of Articles 10 and 13 of the Convention.

(4) The High Court or Court of Session shall refuse to register a decision if—

>   (a) the court is of the opinion that on any of the grounds specified in Article 9 or 10 of the Convention the decision should not be recognised in any part of the United Kingdom;
>
>   (b) the court is of the opinion that the decision is not enforceable in the Contracting State where it was made and is not a decision to which Article 12 of the Convention applies; or
>
>   (c) an application in respect of the child under Part I of this Act is pending.

(5) Where the Lord Chancellor is requested to assist in making an application under this section to the Court of Session he shall transmit the request to the Secretary of State and the Secretary of State shall transmit to the Lord Chancellor any such request to assist in making an application to the High Court.

(6) In this section 'decision relating to custody' has the same meaning as in the Convention.

Variation and revocation of registered decisions

17. (1) Where a decision which has been registered under section 16 above is varied or revoked by an authority in the Contracting State in which it was made, the person on whose behalf the application for registration of the decision was made shall notify the court in which the decision is registered of the variation or revocation.

(2) Where a court is notified under subsection (1) above of the revocation of a decision, it shall—

(a) cancel the registration, and

(b) notify such persons as may be prescribed by rules of court of the cancellation.

(3) Where a court is notified under subsection (1) above of the variation of a decision, it shall—

(a) notify such persons as may be prescribed by rules of court of the variation; and

(b) subject to any conditions which may be so prescribed, vary the registration.

(4) The court in which a decision is registered under section 16 above may also, on the application of any person appearing to the court to have an interest in the matter, cancel or vary the registration if it is satisfied that the decision has been revoked or, as the case may be, varied by an authority in the Contracting State in which it was made.

Enforcement of decisions

18. Where a decision relating to custody has been registered under section 16 above, the court in which it is registered shall have the same powers for the purpose of enforcing the decision as if it had been made by that court; and proceedings for or with respect to enforcement may be taken accordingly.

Interim powers

19. Where an application has been made to a court for the registration of a decision under section 16 above or for the enforcement of such a decision, the court may, at any time before the application is determined, give such interim directions as it thinks fit for the purpose of securing the welfare of the child concerned or of preventing changes in the circumstances relevant to the determination of the application or, in the case of an application for registration, to the determination of any subsequent application for the enforcement of the decision.

Suspension of court's powers

20. (1) Where it appears to any court in which such proceedings as are mentioned in subsection (2) below are pending in respect of a child that

(a) an application has been made for the registration of a decision in respect of the child under section 16 above (other than a decision mentioned in subsection (3) below) or that such a decision is registered; and

(b) the decision was made in proceedings commenced before the proceedings which are pending.

the powers of the court with respect to the child in those proceedings shall be restricted as mentioned in subsection (2) below unless, in the case of an application for registration, the application is refused.

(2) Where subsection (1) above applies the court shall not—

    (a) in the case of custody proceedings, make, vary or revoke any custody order, or any other order under section 1(2) of the Children and Young Persons Act 1969 or section 95(1), 97(2), 143(6) or 144 of the Children and Young Persons Act (Northern Ireland) 1968 (not being a custody order);

    (b) in the case of proceedings on a complaint under section 3(5) or 5(4) of the Child Care Act 1980 determine, that complaint;

    (c) in the case of proceedings on an appeal under section 6 or 67(2) or (3) of that Act, determine that appeal;

    (d) in the case of proceedings in respect of a summary application under section 16(8), 16A(3) or 18(3) of the Social Work (Scotland) Act 1968, determine that application; or

    (e) in the case of proceedings on a complaint under section 104(1) of the Children and Young Persons Act (Northern Ireland) 1968 or on an application under section 106(2) of that Act, make a parental rights order under section 104 or, as the case may be, discharge or give directions in lieu of the discharge of such an order under section 106(2) of that Act.

  (3) The decision referred to in subsection (1) above is a decision which is only a decision relating to custody within the meaning of section 16 of this Act by virtue of being a decision relating to rights of access.

  (4) Paragraph (b) of Article 10(2) of the Convention shall be construed as referring to custody proceedings within the meaning of this Act.

  (5) This section shall apply to a children's hearing within the meaning of Part III of the Social Work (Scotland) Act 1968 as it does to a court.

Reports
21. Where the Lord Chancellor or the Secretary of State is requested to make enquiries about a child under Article 15(1)(b) of the Convention he may—

    (a) request a local authority or a probation officer to make a report to him in writing with respect to any matter relating to the child concerned which appears to him to be relevant;

    (b) request the Department of Health and Social Services for Northern Ireland to arrange for a suitably qualified person to make such a report to him;

    (c) request any court to which a written report relating to the child has been made to send him a copy of the report;

and any such request shall be duly complied with.

Proof of documents and evidence
22. (1) In any proceedings under this Part of this Act a decision of an authority outside the United Kingdom may be proved by a duly authenticated copy of the decision; and any document purporting to be such a copy shall be deemed to be a true copy unless the contrary is shown.

  (2) For the purposes of subsection (1) above a copy is duly authenticated if it bears the seal, or is signed by a judge or officer, of the authority in question.

  (3) In any proceedings under this Part of this Act any such document as is mentioned in Article 13 of the Convention, or a certified copy of any such document, shall be sufficient evidence of anything stated in it.

Decisions of United Kingdom courts

23. (1) Where a person on whom any rights are conferred by a decision relating to custody made by a court in the United Kingdom makes an application to the Lord Chancellor or the Secretary of State under Article 4 of the Convention with a view to securing its recognition or enforcement in another Contracting State, the Lord Chancellor or the Secretary of State may require the court which made the decision to furnish him with all or any of the documents referred to in Article 13(1)(b), (c) and (d) of the Convention.

(2) Where in any custody proceedings a court in the United Kingdom makes a decision relating to a child who has been removed from the United Kingdom, the court may also, on an application made by any person for the purposes of Article 12 of the Convention, declare the removal to have been unlawful if it is satisfied that the applicant has an interest in the matter and that the child has been taken from or sent or kept out of the United Kingdom without the consent of the person (or, if more than one, all the persons) having the right to determine the child's place of residence under the law of the part of the United Kingdom in which the child was habitually resident.

(3) In this section 'decision relating to custody' has the same meaning as in the Convention.

Rules of court

24. (1) An authority having power to make rules of court may make such provision for giving effect to this Part of this Act as appears to that authority to be necessary or expedient.

(2) Without prejudice to the generality of subsection (1) above, rules of court may make provision—

    (a) with respect to the procedure on applications to a court under any provision of this Part of this Act and with respect to the documents and information to be furnished and the notices to be given in connection with any such application;

    (b) for the transfer of any such application between the appropriate courts in the different parts of the United Kingdom;

    (c) for the giving of directions requiring the disclosure of information about any child who is the subject of proceedings under this Part of this Act and for safe-guarding its welfare.

Part III—Supplementary

Termination of existing custody orders, etc

25. (1) Where—

    (a) an order is made for the return of a child under Part I of this Act; or

    (b) a decision with respect to a child (other than a decision mentioned in subsection (2) below) is registered under section 16 of this Act,

any custody order relating to him shall cease to have effect.

(2) The decision referred to in subsection (1)(b) above is a decision which is only a decision relating to custody within the meaning of section 16 of this Act by virtue of being a decision relating to rights of access.

(3) . . .

(4) . . .

(5) . . .

(6) . . .

(7) . . .

Interpretation
27. (1) In this Act 'custody order' means any such order or authorisation as is mentioned in Schedule 3 to this Act and 'custody proceedings' means proceedings in which an order within paragraphs 1, 2, 5, 6, 8 or 9 of that Schedule may be made or in which any custody order may be varied or revoked.

(2) For the purposes of this Act 'part of the United Kingdom' means England and Wales, Scotland or Northern Ireland and 'the appropriate court', in relation to England and Wales or Northern Ireland means the High Court and, in relation to Scotland, the Court of Session.

(3) In this Act 'local authority' means—

   (a) in relation to England and Wales, the council of a non-metropolitan county, a metropolitan district, a London borough or the Common Council of the City of London; and
   (b) in relation to Scotland, a regional or islands council.

Schedule 1 – Convention on the Civil Aspects of International Child Abduction

CHAPTER 1. SCOPE OF THE CONVENTION

Article 3
The removal or the retention of a child is to be considered wrongful where—

   (a) it is in breach of rights of custody attributed to a person, an institution or any other body, either jointly or alone, under the law of the State in which the child was habitually resident immediately before the removal or retention; and
   (b) at the time of removal or retention those rights were actually exercised, either jointly or alone, or would have been so exercised but for the removal or retention.

   The rights of custody mentioned in sub-paragraph (a) above may arise in particular by operation of law or by reason of a judicial or administrative decision, or by reason of an agreement having legal effect under the law of that State.

Article 4
The Convention shall apply to any child who was habitually resident in a Contracting State immediately before any breach of custody or access rights. The Convention shall cease to apply when the child attains the age of sixteen years.

Article 5
For the purposes of this Convention—

   (a) 'rights of custody' shall include rights relating to the care of the person of the child and, in particular, the right to determine the child's place of residence;
   (b) 'rights of access' shall include the right to take a child for a limited period of time to a place other than the child's habitual residence.

CHAPTER 11. CENTRAL AUTHORITIES

Article 7

Central Authorities shall co-operate with each other and promote co-operation amongst the competent authorities in their respective States to secure the prompt return of children and to achieve the other objects of this Convention.

In particular, either directly or through any intermediary, they shall take all appropriate measures—

    (a) to discover the whereabouts of a child who has been wrongfully removed or retained;

    (b) to prevent further harm to the child or prejudice to interested parties by taking or causing to be taken provisional measures;

    (c) to secure the voluntary return of the child or to bring about an amicable resolution of the issues;

    (d) to exchange, where desirable, information relating to the social background of the child;

    (e) to provide information of a general character as to the law of their State in connection with the application of the Convention;

    (f) to initiate or facilitate the institution of judicial or administrative proceedings with a view to obtaining the return of the child and, in a proper case, to make arrangements for organising or securing the effective exercise of rights of access;

    (g) where the circumstances so require, to provide or facilitate the provision of legal aid and advice, including the participation of legal counsel and advisers;

    (h) to provide such administrative arrangements as may be necessary and appropriate to secure the safe return of the child;

    (i) to keep each other informed with respect to the operation of this Convention and, as far as possible, to eliminate any obstacles to its application.

CHAPTER III. RETURN OF CHILDREN

Article 8

Any person, institution or other body claiming that a child has been removed or retained in breach of custody rights may apply either to the Central Authority of the child's habitual residence or to the Central Authority of any other Contracting State for assistance in securing the return of the child.

The application shall contain—

    (a) information concerning the identity of the applicant, of the child and of the person alleged to have removed or retained the child;

    (b) where available, the date of birth of the child;

    (c) the grounds on which the applicants claim for return of the child is based;

    s of the child and the identity of the person with whom the child is presumed to be.

The application may be accompanied or supplemented by—

    (e) an authenticated copy of any relevant decision or agreement;

    (f) a certificate or an affidavit emanating from a Central Authority, or other competent authority of the State of the child's habitual residence, or from a qualified person, concerning the relevant law of that State;

(g) any other relevant document.

Article 9
If the Central Authority which receives an application referred to in Article 8 has reason to believe that the child is in another Contracting State, it shall directly and without delay transmit the application to the Central Authority of that Contracting State and inform the requesting Central Authority, or the applicant, as the case may be.

Article 10
The Central Authority of the state where the child is shall take or cause to be taken all appropriate measures in order to obtain the voluntary return of the child.

Article 11
The judicial or administrative authorities of Contracting States shall act expeditiously in proceedings for the return of children.

If the judicial or administrative authority concerned has not reached a decision within six weeks from the date of commencement of the pro-ceedings, the applicant or the Central Authority of the requested State, on its own initiative or if asked by the Central Authority of the requesting State, shall have the right to request a statement of the reasons for the delay. If a reply is received by the Central Authority of the requested State, that Authority shall transmit the reply to the Central Authority of the requesting State, or to the applicant, as the case may be.

Article 12
Where a child has been wrongfully removed or retained in terms of Article 3 and, at the date of the commencement of the proceedings before the judicial or administrative authority of the Contracting State where the child is, a period of less than one year has elapsed from the date of the wrongful removal or retention, the authority concerned shall order the return of the child forthwith.

The judicial or administrative authority, even where the proceedings have been commenced after the expiration of the period of one year referred to in the preceding paragraph, shall also order the return of the child, unless it is demonstrated that the child is now settled in its new environment.

Where the judicial or administrative authority in the requested state has reason to believe that the child has been taken to another State, it may stay the proceedings or dismiss the application for the return of the child.

Article 13
Notwithstanding the provisions of the preceding Article, the judicial or administrative authority of the requested State is not bound to order the return of the child if the person, institution or other body which opposes its return establishes that—
  (a) the person, institution or other body having the care of the person of the child was not actually exercising the custody rights at the time of removal or retention, or had consented to or subsequently acquiesced in the removal or retention; or
  (b) there is a grave risk that his or her return would expose the child to physical or psychological harm or otherwise place the child in an intolerable situation.

The judicial or administrative authority may also refuse to order the return of the child if it finds that the child objects to being returned and has attained an age and degree of maturity at which it is appropriate to take account of its views.

In considering the circumstances referred to in this Article, the judicial and administrative authorities shall take into account the information relating to the social background of the child provided by the Central Authority or other competent authority of the child's habitual residence.

Article 14
In ascertaining whether there has been a wrongful removal or retention within the meaning of Article 3, the judicial or administrative authorities of the requested State may take notice directly of the law of, and of judicial or administrative decisions, formally recognised or not in the State of the habitual residence of the child, without recourse to the specific procedures for the proof of that law or for the recognition of foreign decisions which would otherwise be applicable.

Article 15
The judicial or administrative authorities of a Contracting State may, prior to the making of an order for the return of the child, request that the applicant obtain from the authorities of the State of the habitual residence of the child a decision or other determination that the removal or retention was wrongful within the meaning of Article 3 of the Convention, where such a decision or determination may be obtained in that State. The Central Authorities of the Contracting State shall so far as practicable assist applicants to obtain such a decision or determination.

Article 16
After receiving notice of a wrongful removal or retention of a child in the sense of Article 3, the judicial or administrative authorities of the Contracting State to which the child has been removed or in which it has been retained shall not decide on the merits of rights of custody until it has been determined that the child is not to be returned under this Convention or unless an application under this Convention is not lodged within a reasonable time following receipt of the notice.

Article 17
The sole fact that a decision relating to custody has been given in or is entitled to recognition in the requested State shall not be a ground for refusing to return a child under this Convention, but the judicial or administrative authorities of the requested State may take account of the reasons for that decision in applying this Convention.

Article 18
The provisions of this Chapter do not limit the power of a judicial or administrative authority to order the return of the child at any time.

Article 19
A decision under this Convention concerning the return of the child shall not be taken to be a determination on the merits of any custody issue.

CHAPTER IV. RIGHTS OF ACCESS

Article 21
An application to make arrangements for organising or securing the effective exercise of rights of access may be presented to the Central Authorities of the Contracting States in the same way as an application for the return of a child.

The Central Authorities are bound by the obligations of co-operation which are set forth in Article 7 to promote the peaceful enjoyment of access rights and the fulfilment of any conditions to which the exercise of those rights may be subject. The Central Authorities shall take steps to remove, as far as possible, all obstacles to the exercise of such rights. The Central Authorities, either directly or through intermediaries, may initiate or assist in the institution of proceedings with a view to organising or protecting these rights and securing respect for the conditions to which the exercise of these rights may be subject.

CHAPTER V. GENERAL PROVISIONS

Article 22
No security, bond or deposit, however described, shall be required to guarantee the payment of costs and expenses in the judicial or administrative proceedings falling within the scope of this Convention.

Article 24
Any application, communication or other document sent to the Central Authority of the requested State shall be in the original language, and shall be accompanied by a translation into the official language or one of the official languages of the requested State or, where that is not feasible, a translation into French or English.

Article 26
Each Central Authority shall bear its own costs in applying this Convention.

Central Authorities and other public services of Contracting States shall not impose any charges in relation to applications submitted under this Convention. In particular, they may not require any payment from the applicant towards the costs and expenses of the proceedings or, where applicable, those arising from the participation of legal counsel or advisers. However, they may require the payment of the expenses incurred or to be incurred in implementing the return of the child.

However, a Contracting State may, by making a reservation in accordance with Article 42, declare that it shall not be bound to assume any costs referred to in the preceding paragraph resulting from the participation of legal counsel or advisers or from court proceedings, except insofar as those costs may be covered by its system of legal aid and advice.

Upon ordering the return of a child or issuing an order concerning rights of access under this Convention, the judicial or administrative authorities may, where appropriate, direct the person who removed or retained the child, or who prevented the exercise of rights of access, to pay necessary expenses incurred by or on behalf of the applicant, including travel expenses, any costs incurred or payments made for locating the child, the costs of legal representation of the applicant, and those of returning the child.

Article 27

When it is manifest that the requirements of this Convention are not fulfilled or that the application is otherwise not well founded, a Central Authority is not bound to accept the application. In that case, the Central Authority shall forthwith inform the applicant or the Central Authority through which the application was submitted, as the case may be, of its reasons.

Article 28

A Central Authority may require that the application be accompanied by a written authorisation empowering it to act on behalf of the applicant, or to designate a representative so to act.

Article 29

This Convention shall not preclude any person, institution or body who claims that there has been a breach of custody or access rights within the meaning of Article 3 or 21 from applying directly to the judicial or administrative authorities of a Contracting State, whether or not under the provisions of this Convention.

Article 30

Any application submitted to the Central Authorities or directly to the judicial or administrative authorities of a Contracting State in accordance with the terms of this Convention, together with documents and any other information appended thereto or provided by a Central Authority, shall be admissible in the courts or administrative authorities of the Contracting States.

Article 31

In relation to a State which in matters of custody of children has two or more systems of law applicable in different territorial units—
   (a) any reference to habitual residence in that State shall be construed as referring to habitual residence in a territorial unit of that State;
   (b) any reference to the law of the State of habitual residence shall be construed as referring to the law of the territorial unit in that State where the child habitually resides.

Article 32

In relation to a State which in matters of custody of children has two or more systems of law applicable to different categories of persons, any reference to the law of that State shall be construed as referring to the legal system specified by the law of that State.

Schedule 2 – European Convention on Recognition and Enforcement of Decisions Concerning Custody of Children

Article 1

For the purposes of this Convention:
   (a) 'child' means a person of any nationality, so long as he is under 16 years of age and has not the right to decide on his own place of residence under the law of his habitual residence, the law of his nationality or the international law of the State addressed;

(b) 'authority' means a judicial or administrative authority;

(c) 'decision relating to custody' means a decision of an authority in so far as it relates to the care of the person of the child, including the right to decide on the place of his residence, or to the right of access to him.

(d) 'improper removal' means the removal of a child across an international frontier in breach of a decision relating to his custody which has been given in a Contracting State and which is enforceable in such a State; 'improper removal' also includes:

   (i) the failure to return a child across an international frontier at the end of a period of the exercise of the right of access to this child or at the end of any other temporary stay in a territory other than that where the custody is exercised;

   (ii) a removal which is subsequently declared unlawful within the meaning of Article 12.

Article 4

(1) Any person who has obtained in a Contracting State a decision relating to the custody of a child and who wishes to have that decision recognised or enforced in another Contracting State may submit an applicaton for this purpose to the central authority in any Contracting State.

(2) The application shall be accompanied by the documents mentioned in Article 13.

(3) The central authority receiving the application, if it is not the central authority in the State addressed, shall send the documents directly and without delay to that central authority.

(4) The central authority receiving the application may refuse to intervene where it is manifestly clear that the conditions laid down by this Convention are not satisfied.

(5) The central authority receiving the application shall keep the applicant informed without delay of the progress of his application.

Article 5

(1) The central authority in the State addressed shall take or cause to be taken without delay all steps which it considers to be appropriate, if necessary by instituting proceedings before its competent authorities, in order:

   (a) to discover the whereabouts of the child;

   (b) to avoid, in particular by any necessary provisional measures, prejudice to the interests of the child or of the applicant;

   (c) to secure the recognition or enforcement of the decision;

   (d) to secure the delivery of the child to the applicant where enforcement is granted;

   (e) to inform the requesting authority of the measures taken and their results.

(2) Where the central authority in the State addressed has reason to believe that the child is in the territory of another Contracting State it shall send the documents directly and without delay to the central authority of that State.

(3) With the exception of the cost of repatriation, each Contracting State undertakes not to claim any payment from an applicant in respect of any measures taken under paragraph (1) of this Article by the central

authority of that State on the applicant's behalf, including the costs of proceedings and, where applicable, the costs incurred by the assistance of a lawyer.

(4) If recognition or enforcement is refused, and if the central authority of the State addressed considers that it should comply with a request by the applicant to bring in that State proceedings concerning the substance of the case, that authority shall use its best endeavours to secure the representation of the applicant in the proceedings under conditions no less favourable than those available to a person who is resident in and a national of that State and for this purpose it may, in particular, institute proceedings before its competent authorities.

Article 7
A decision relating to custody given in a Contracting State shall be recognised and, where it is enforceable in the State of origin, made enforceable in every other Contracting State.

Article 9
(1) *[Recognition and enforcement may be refused]* if:
  (a) in the case of a decision given in the absence of the defendant or his legal representative, the defendant was not duly served with the document which instituted the proceedings or an equivalent document in sufficient time to enable him to arrange his defence; but such a failure to effect service cannot constitute a ground for refusing recognition or enforcement where service was not effected because the defendant had concealed his whereabouts from the person who instituted the proceedings in the State of origin;
  (b) in the case of a decision given in the absence of the defendant or his legal representative, the competence of the authority giving the decision was not founded:
    (i) on the habitual residence of the defendant; or
    (ii) on the last common habitual residence of the child's parents, at least one parent being still habitually resident there, or
    (iii) on the habitual residence of the child;
  (c) the decision is incompatible with a decision relating to custody which became enforceable in the State addressed before the removal of the child, unless the child has had his habitual residence in the territory of the requesting State for one year before his removal.

(3) In no circumstances may the foreign decision be reviewed as to its substance.

Article 10
(1) *[Recognition and enforcement may also be refused]* on any of the following grounds:
  (a) if it is found that the effects of the decision are manifestly incompatible with the fundamental principles of the law relating to the family and children in the State addressed;
  (b) if it is found that by reason of a change in the circumstances including the passage of time but not including a mere change in the residence of the child after an improper removal, the effects of the original decision are manifestly no longer in accordance with the welfare of the child;

(c) if at the time when the proceedings were instituted in the State of origin:

    (i) the child was a national of the State addressed or was habitually resident there and no such connection existed with the State of origin;

    (ii) the child was a national both of the State of origin and of the State addressed and was habitually resident in the State addressed;

(d) if the decision is incompatible with a decision given in the State addressed or enforceable in that State after being given in a third State, pursuant to proceedings begun before the submission of the request for recognition or enforcement, and if the refusal is in accordance with the welfare of the child.

(2) Proceedings for recognition or enforcement may be adjourned on any of the following grounds:

(a) if an ordinary form of review of the original decision has been commenced;

(b) if proceedings relating to the custody of the child, commenced before the proceedings in the State of origin were instituted, are pending in the State addressed;

(c) if another decision concerning the custody of the child is the subject of proceedings for enforcement or of any other proceedings concerning the recognition of the decision.

Article 11

(1) Decisions on rights of access and provisions of decisions relating to custody which deal with the rights of access shall be recognised and enforced subject to the same conditions as other decisions relating to custody.

(2) However, the competent authority of the State addressed may fix the conditions for the implementation and exercise of the right of access taking into account, in particular, undertakings given by the parties on this matter.

(3) Where no decision on the right of access has been taken or where recognition or enforcement of the decision relating to custody is refused, the central authority of the State addressed may apply to its competent authorities for a decision on the right of access if the person claiming a right of access so requests.

Article 12

Where, at the time of the removal of a child across an international frontier, there is no enforceable decision given in a Contracting State relating to his custody, the provisions of this Convention shall apply to any subsequent decision, relating to the custody of that child and declaring the removal to be unlawful, given in a Contracting State at the request of any interested person.

Article 13

(1) A request for recognition or enforcement in another Contracting State of a decision relating to custody shall be accompanied by:

(a) a document authorising the central authority of the State addressed to act on behalf of the applicant or to designate another representative for that purpose;

(b) a copy of the decision which satisfies the necessary conditions of authenticity;

(c) in the case of a decision given in the absence of the defendant or his legal representative, a document which establishes that the defendant was duly served with the document which instituted the proceedings or an equivalent document;

(d) if applicable, any document which establishes that, in accordance with the law of the State of origin, the decision is enforceable;

(e) if possible, a statement indicating the whereabouts or likely whereabouts of the child in the State addressed;

(f) proposals as to how the custody of the child should be restored.

Article 15

(1) Before reaching a decision under paragraph (1)(b) of Article 10, the authority concerned in the State addressed:

(a) shall ascertain the child's views unless this is impracticable having regard in particular to his age and understanding; and

(b) may request that any appropriate enquiries be carried out.

(2) The cost of enquiries in any Contracting State shall be met by the authorities of the State where they are carried out.

Requests for enquiries and the results of enquiries may be sent to the authority concerned through the central authorities.

Article 26

(1) In relation to a State which has in matters of custody two or more systems of law of territorial application:

(a) reference to the law of a person's habitual residence or to the law of a person's nationality shall be construed as referring to the system of law determined by the rules in force in that State or, if there are no such rules, to the system of law with which the person concerned is most closely connected;

(b) reference to the State of origin or to the State addressed shall be construed as referring, as the case may be, to the territorial unit where the decision was given or to the territorial unit where recognition or enforcement of the decision or restoration of custody is requested.

(2) Paragraph (1)(a) of this Article also applies *mutatis mutandis* to States which have in matters of custody two or more systems of law of personal application.

Schedule 3 – Custody orders

PART I. ENGLAND AND WALES

1. (1) An order made by a court in England and Wales under any of the following enactments—

(a) section 7(2) of the Family Law Reform Act 1969;

(b) subsection (2) of section 1 of the Children and Young Persons Act 1969 (being an order made in pursuance of subsection (3)(c) of that section otherwise than in a case where the condition mentioned in subsection (2)(f) is satisfied with respect to the child);

(c) section 15(1) of the Children and Young Persons Act 1969 (being a care order made on the discharge of a supervision order other than a supervision order made in a case where the condition mentioned in section 1(2)(f) of that Act was satisfied with respect to the child);

(d) section 9(1), 10(1)(a) or 11(a) of the Guardianship of Minors Act 1971;

(e) section 42(1) or (2) or 43(1) of the Matrimonial Causes Act 1973;

(f) section 2(2)(b), 4(b) or (5) of the Guardianship Act 1973;

(g) section 17(1)(b), 33(1), 36(2) or 36(3)(a) of the Children Act 1975 or section 2(2)(b) or (4)(b) of the Guardianship Act 1973 as applied by section 34(5) of the Children Act 1975;

(h) section 8(2)(a), 10(1) or 19(1)(ii) of the Domestic Proceedings and Magistrates' Courts Act 1978;

(i) section 26(1)(b) of the Adoption Act 1976.

(2) After the commencement of section 26(1)(b) of the Adoption Act 1976 paragraph (g) of sub-paragraph (1) above shall have effect with the omission of the reference to section 17(1)(b) of the Children Act 1975.

(3) After the commencement of section 26(1)(b) of the Adoption Act 1976 paragraph (g) of sub-paragraph (1) above shall have effect with the omission of the reference to section 17(1)(b) of the Children Act 1975.

2. An order made by the High Court in the exercise of its jurisdiction relating to wardship so far as it gives the care and control of a child to any person.

3. An order made by the Secretary of State under section 25(1) of the Children and Young Persons Act 1969 (except where the order superseded was made under section 74(1)(a) or (b) or 78(1) of the Children and Young Persons Act (Northern Ireland) 1968 or was made under section 97(2)(a) of that Act on a complaint by a person under whose supervision the child had been placed by an order under section 74(1)(c) of that Act).

4. An authorisation given by the Secretary of State under section 26(2) of the Children and Young Persons Act 1969 (except where the relevant order, within the meaning of that section, was made by virtue of the court which made it being satisfied that the child was guilty of an offence).

Family Law Act 1986[1]

Part I – Child Custody

CHAPTER I. PRELIMINARY

Orders to which Part I applies
1. (1) Subject to the following provisions of this section, in this Part 'custody order' means—

(a) an order made by a court in England and Wales under any of the following enactments—

1 The Family Law Act 1986, Part I, comes into force on a day or days to be appointed (s 69(3)).

(i) section 9(1), 10(1)(a), 11(a) or 14A(2) of the Guardianship of Minors Act 1971 or section 2(4)(b) or 2(5) of the Guardianship Act 1973;

(ii) section 42(1) of the Matrimonial Causes Act 1973;

(iii) section 42(2) of the Matrimonial Causes Act 1973;

(iv) section 33(1) of the Children Act 1975 or section 2(4)(b) of the Guardianship Act 1973 as applied by section 34(5) of the Children Act 1975;

(v) section 8(2) or 19(1)(ii) of the Domestic Proceedings and Magistrates' Courts Act 1978;

(b) an order made by a court of civil jurisdiction in Scotland under any enactment or rule of law with respect to the custody, care or control of a child, access to a child or the education or upbringing of a child, excluding—

(i) an order committing the care of a child to a local authority or placing a child under the supervision of a local authority;

(ii) an adoption order as defined in section 12(1) of the Adoption (Scotland) Act 1978;

(iii) an order freeing a child for adoption made under section 18 of the said Act of 1978;

(iv) an order for the custody of a child made in the course of proceedings for the adoption of the child (other than an order made following the making of a direction under section 53(1) of the Children Act 1975);

(v) an order made under the Education (Scotland) Act 1980;

(vi) an order made under Part II or III of the Social Work (Scotland) Act 1968;

(vii) an order made under the Child Abduction and Custody Act 1985;

(viii) an order for the delivery of a child or other order for the enforcement of a custody order;

(ix) an order relating to the tutory or curatory of a child;

(c) an order made by a court in Northern Ireland under any of the following enactments—

(i) section 5 of the Guardianship of Infants Act 1886 (except so far as it relates to costs);

(ii) Article 45(1) of the Matrimonial Causes (Northern Ireland) Order 1978;

(iii) Article 45(2) of the Matrimonial Causes (Northern Ireland) Order 1978;

(iv) Article 10(2) or 20(1)(ii) of the Domestic Proceedings (Northern Ireland) Order 1980;

(d) an order made by the High Court in the exercise of its jurisdiction relating to wardship so far as it gives the care and control of a child to any person or provides for the education of, or for access to, a child, excluding an order relating to a child of whom care or care and control is (immediately after the making of the order) vested in a local authority or in the Northern Ireland Department of Health and Social Services.

(2) In this Part 'custody order' does not include—

(a) an order within subsection (1)(a) or (c) above which varies or revokes a previous order made under the same enactment;

Not yet in force.

(b) an order under section 14A(2) of the Guardianship of Minors Act 1971 which varies a previous custody order; or

(c) an order within paragraph (d) of subsection (1) above which varies or revokes a previous order within that paragraph.

(3) Subject to sections 32 and 40 of this Act, in this Part 'custody order' does not include any order which—

(a) was made before the date of the commencement of this Part;

(b) in the case of an order within subsection (1)(b) or (d) above or an order under any of the enactments mentioned in subsection (4) below, is made on or after that date on an application made before that date; or

(c) in any other case, is made on or after that date in proceedings commenced before that date.

(4) The said enactments are—

(a) sections 9(1) and 14A(2) of the Guardianship of Minors Act 1971 and section 33(1) of the Children Act 1975; and

(b) section 5 of the Guardianship of Infants Act 1886.

(5) For the purposes of subsection (3) above an order made on two or more applications which are determined together shall be regarded as made on the first of those applications.

(6) Provision may be made by act of sederunt prescribing, in relation to orders within subsection (1)(b) above, what constitutes an application for the purposes of this Part.

CHAPTER II. JURISDICTION OF COURTS IN ENGLAND AND WALES

Jurisdiction in cases other than divorce, etc
2. (1) A court in England and Wales shall not have jurisdiction to make a custody order within section 1(1)(a) of this Act, other than one under section 42(1) of the Matrimonial Causes Act 1973, unless the condition in section 3 of this Act is satisfied.

(2) The High Court in England and Wales shall have jurisdiction to make a custody order within section 1(1)(d) of this Act if, and only if,

(a) the condition in section 3 of this Act is satisfied, or

(b) the ward is present in England and Wales on the relevant date (within the meaning of section 3(6) of this Act) and the court considers that the immediate exercise of its powers is necessary for his protection.

Habitual residence or presence of child
3. (1) The condition referred to in section 2 of this Act is that on the relevant date the child concerned—

(a) is habitually resident in England and Wales, or

(b) is present in England and Wales and is not habitually resident in any part of the United Kingdom,

and, in either case, the jurisdiction of the court is not excluded by subsection (2) below.

(2) For the purposes of subsection (1) above, the jurisdiction of the court is excluded if, on the relevant date, proceedings for divorce, nullity or judicial separation are continuing in a court in Scotland or Northern Ireland in respect of the marriage of the parents of the child concerned.

(3) Subsection (2) above shall not apply if the court in which the other proceedings there referred to are continuing has made—

Not yet in force.

(a) an order under section 13(6) or 21(5) of this Act (not being an order made by virtue of section 13(6)(a)(i)), or

(b) an order under section 14(2) or 22(2) of this Act which is recorded as made for the purpose of enabling proceedings with respect to the custody of the child concerned to be taken in England and Wales,

and that order is in force.

(4) Subject to subsections (5) and (6) below, in this section 'the relevant date' means the date of the commencement of the proceedings in which the custody order falls to be made.

(5) In a case where an application is made for a custody order under section 9(1) or 14A(2) of the Guardianship of Minors Act 1971 or section 33(1) of the Children Act 1975, 'the relevant date' means the date of the application (or first application, if two or more are determined together).

(6) In the case of a custody order within section 1(1)(d) of this Act 'the relevant date' means—

(a) where an application is made for an order, the date of the application (or first application, if two or more are determined together), and

(b) where no such application is made, the date of the order.

Jurisdiction in divorce proceedings, etc
4. (1) The enactments relating to the jurisdiction of courts in England and Wales to make orders under section 42(1) of the Matrimonial Causes Act 1973 shall have effect subject to the modifications provided for by this section.

(2) In section 42(1)(b) of that Act (which enables orders as to custody and education to be made immediately, or within a reasonable period, after the dismissal of proceedings for divorce, etc) for the words 'within a reasonable period' there shall be substituted the words '(if an application for the order is made on or before the dismissal)'.

(3) A court shall not have jurisdiction to make a custody order under section 42(1)(a) of that Act after the grant of a decree of judicial separation if, on the relevant date, proceedings for divorce or nullity in respect of the marriage concerned are continuing in Scotland or Northern Ireland.

(4) Subsection (3) above shall not apply if the court in which the other proceedings there referred to are continuing has made—

(a) an order under section 13(6) or 21(5) of this Act (not being an order made by virtue of section 13(6)(a)(i)), or

(b) an order under section 14(2) or 22(2) of this Act which is recorded as made for the purpose of enabling proceedings with respect to the custody of the child concerned to be taken in England and Wales,

and that order is in force.

(5) Where a court—

(a) has jurisdiction to make a custody order under section 42(1) of the Matrimonial Causes Act 1973 in or in connection with proceedings for divorce, nullity of marriage or judicial separation, but

(b) considers that it would be more appropriate for matters relating to the custody of the child to be determined outside England and Wales,

Not yet in force.

the court may by order direct that, while the order under this subsection is in force, no custody order under section 42(1) with respect to the child shall be made by any court in or in connection with those proceedings.

(6) In this section 'the relevant date' means—

(a) where an application is made for a custody order under section 42(1)(a), the date of the application (or first application, if two or more are determined together), and

(b) where no such application is made, the date of the order.

Power of court to refuse application or stay proceedings

5. (1) A court in England and Wales which has jurisdiction to make a custody order may refuse an application for the order in any case where the matter in question has already been determined in proceedings outside England and Wales.

(2) Where, at any stage of the proceedings on an application made to a court in England and Wales for a custody order, or for the variation of a custody order, it appears to the court—

(a) that proceedings with respect to the matters to which the application relates are continuing outside England and Wales, or

(b) that it would be more appropriate for those matters to be determined in proceedings to be taken outside England and Wales,

the court may stay the proceedings on the application.

(3) The court may remove a stay granted in accordance with subsection (2) above if it appears to the court that there has been unreasonable delay in the taking or prosecution of the other proceedings referred to in that subsection, or that those proceedings are stayed, sisted or concluded.

(4) Nothing in this section shall affect any power exercisable apart from this section to refuse an application or to grant or remove a stay.

Duration and variation of custody orders

6. (1) If a custody order made by a court in Scotland or Northern Ireland (or a variation of such an order) comes into force with respect to a child at a time when a custody order made by a court in England and Wales has effect with respect to him, the latter order shall cease to have effect so far as it makes provision for any matter for which the same or different provision is made by (or by the variation of) the order made by the court in Scotland or Northern Ireland.

(2) Where by virtue of subsection (1) above a custody order has ceased to have effect so far as it makes provision for any matter, a court in England or Wales shall not have jurisdiction to vary that order so as to make provision for that matter.

(3) A court in England and Wales shall not have jurisdiction—

(a) to vary a custody order, other than one made under section 42(1)(a) of the Matrimonial Causes Act 1973, or

(b) after the grant of a decree of judicial separation, to vary a custody order made under section 42(1)(a) of that Act,

if, on the relevant date, proceedings for divorce, nullity or judicial separation are continuing in Scotland or Northern Ireland in respect of the marriage of the parents of the child concerned.

(4) Subsection (3) above shall not apply if the court in which the proceedings there referred to are continuing has made—

Not yet in force.

(a) an order under section 13(6) or 21(5) of this Act (not being an order made by virtue of section 13(6)(a)(i)), or

(b) an order under section 14(2) or 22(2) of this Act which is recorded as made for the purpose of enabling proceedings with respect to the custody of the child concerned to be taken in England and Wales,

and that order is in force.

(5) Subsection (3) above shall not apply in the case of a variation of a custody order within section 1(1)(d) of this Act if the ward is present in England and Wales on the relevant date and the court considers that the immediate exercise of its powers is necessary for his protection.

(6) Where any person who is entitled to the actual possession of a child under a custody order made by a court in England and Wales ceases to be so entitled by virtue of subsection (1) above, then, if there is in force an order for the supervision of that child made under—

(a) section 7(4) of the Family Law Reform Act 1969,

(b) section 44 of the Matrimonial Causes Act 1973,

(c) section 2(2)(a) of the Guardianship Act 1973

(d) section 34(5) or 36(3)(b) of the Children Act 1975, or

(e) section 9 of the Domestic Proceedings and Magistrates' Courts Act 1978,

that order shall cease to have effect.

(7) In this section 'the relevant date' means—

(a) where an application is made for a variation, the date of the application (or first application, if two or more are determined together), and

(b) where no such application is made, the date of the variation.

Interpretation of Chapter II
7. In this Chapter 'child' means a person who has not attained the age of eighteen.

CHAPTER V. RECOGNITION AND ENFORCEMENT

Recognition of custody orders: general
25. (1) Where a custody order made by a court in any part of the United Kingdom is in force with respect to a child who has not attained the age of sixteen, then, subject to subsection (2) below, the order shall be recognised in any other part of the United Kingdom as having the same effect in that other part as if it had been made by the appropriate court in that other part and as if that court had had jurisdiction to make it.

(2) Where a custody order includes provision as to the means by which rights conferred by the order are to be enforced, subsection (1) above shall not apply to that provision.

(3) A court in a part of the United Kingdom in which a custody order is recognised in accordance with subsection (1) above shall not enforce the order unless it has been registered in that part of the United Kingdom under section 27 of this Act and proceedings for enforcement are taken in accordance with section 29 of this Act.

Not yet in force.

Registration
27. (1) Any person on whom any rights are conferred by a custody order may apply to the court which made it for the order to be registered in another part of the United Kingdom under this section.

(2) An application under this section shall be made in the prescribed manner and shall contain the prescribed information and be accompanied by such documents as may be prescribed.

(3) On receiving an application under this section the court which made the custody order shall, unless it appears to the court that the order is no longer in force, cause the following documents to be sent to the appropriate court in the part of the United Kingdom specified in the application, namely—

  (a) a certified copy of the order, and
  (b) where the order has been varied, prescribed particulars of any variation which is in force, and
  (c) a copy of the application and of any accompanying documents.

(4) Where the prescribed officer of the appropriate court receives a certified copy of a custody order under subsection (3) above, he shall forthwith cause the order, together with particulars of any variation, to be registered in that court in the prescribed manner.

(5) An order shall not be registered under this section in respect of a child who has attained the age of sixteen, and the registration of an order in respect of a child who has not attained the age of sixteen shall cease to have effect on the attainment by the child of that age.

Cancellation and variation of registration
28. (1) A court which revokes, recalls or varies an order registered under section 27 of this Act shall cause notice of the revocation, recall or variation to be given in the prescribed manner to the prescribed officer of the court in which it is registered and, on receiving the notice, the prescribed officer—

  (a) in the case of the revocation or recall of the order, shall cancel the registration, and
  (b) in the case of the variation of the order, shall cause particulars of the variation to be registered in the prescribed manner.

(2) Where—

  (a) an order registered under section 27 of this Act ceases (in whole or in part) to have effect in the part of the United Kingdom in which it was made, otherwise than because of its revocation, recall or variation, or
  (b) an order registered under section 27 of this Act in Scotland ceases (in whole or in part) to have effect there as a result of the making of an order in proceedings outside the United Kingdom,

the court in which the order is registered may, of its own motion or on the application of any person who appears to the court to have an interest in the matter, cancel the registration (or, if the order has ceased to have effect in part, cancel the registration so far as it relates to the provisions which have ceased to have effect).

Not yet in force.

Enforcement

29.(1) Where a custody order has been registered under section 27 of this Act, the court in which it is registered shall have the same powers for the purposes of enforcing the order as it would have if it had itself made the order and had jurisdiction to make it; and proceedings for or with respect to enforcement may be taken accordingly.

(2) Where an application has been made to any court for the enforcement of an order registered in that court under section 27 of this Act, the court may, at any time before the application is determined, give such interim directions as it thinks fit for the purposes of securing the welfare of the child concerned or of preventing changes in the circumstances relevant to the determination of the application.

(3) The references in subsection (1) above to a custody order do not include references to any provision of the order as to the means by which rights conferred by the order are to be enforced.

Staying or sisting of enforcement proceedings

30. (1) Where in accordance with section 29 of this Act proceedings are taken in any court for the enforcement of an order registered in that court, any person who appears to the court to have an interest in the matter may apply for the proceedings to be stayed or sisted on the ground that he has taken or intends to take other proceedings (in the United Kingdom or elsewhere) as a result of which the order may cease to have effect, or may have a different effect, in the part of the United Kingdom in which it is registered.

(2) If after considering an application under subsection (1) above the court considers that the proceedings for enforcement should be stayed or sisted in order that other proceedings may be taken or concluded, it shall stay or sist the proceedings for enforcement accordingly.

(3) The court may remove a stay or recall a sist granted in accordance with subsection (2) above if it appears to the court—

(a) that there has been unreasonable delay in the taking or prosecution of the other proceedings referred to in that subsection, or

(b) that those other proceedings are concluded and that the registered order, or a relevant part of it, is still in force.

(4) Nothing in this section shall affect any power exercisable apart from this section to grant, remove or recall a stay or sist.

Dismissal of enforcement proceedings

31. (1) Where in accordance with section 29 of this Act proceedings are taken in any court for the enforcement of an order registered in that court, any person who appears to the court to have an interest in the matter may apply for those proceedings to be dismissed on the ground that the order has (in whole or in part) ceased to have effect in the part of the United Kingdom in which it was made.

(2) Where in accordance with section 29 of this Act proceedings are taken in the Court of Session for the enforcement of an order registered in that court, any person who appears to the court to have an interest in the matter may apply for those proceedings to be dismissed on the ground that the order has (in whole or in part) ceased to have effect in Scotland as a result of the making of an order in proceedings outside the United Kingdom.

Not yet in force.

(3) If, after considering an application under subsection (1) or (2) above, the court is satisfied that the registered order has ceased to have effect, it shall dismiss the proceedings for enforcement (or, if it is satisfied that the order has ceased to have effect in part, it shall dismiss the proceedings so far as they relate to the enforcement of provisions which have ceased to have effect).

Interpretation of Chapter V
32. (1) In this Chapter—
'the appropriate court', in relation to England and Wales or Northern Ireland, means the High Court and, in relation to Scotland, means the Court of Session;
'custody order' includes (except where the context otherwise requires) any order within section 1(3) of this Act which, on the assumptions mentioned in subsection (3) below—
(a) could have been made notwithstanding the provisions of this Part;
(b) would have been a custody order for the purposes of this Part; and
(c) would not have ceased to have effect by virtue of section 6, 15 or 23 of this Act.
(2) In the application of this Chapter to Scotland, 'custody order' also includes (except where the context otherwise requires) any order within section 1(3) of this Act which, on the assumptions mentioned in subsection (3) below—
(a) would have been a custody order for the purposes of this Part; and
(b) would not have ceased to have effect by virtue of section 6 or 23 of this Act,
and which, but for the provisions of this Part, would be recognised in Scotland under any rule of law.
(3) The said assumptions are—
(a) that this Part had been in force at all material times; and
(b) that any reference in section 1 of this Act to any enactment included a reference to any corresponding enactment previously in force.

CHAPTER VI. MISCELLANEOUS AND SUPPLEMENTAL

Power to order disclosure of child's whereabouts
33. (1) Where in proceedings for or relating to a custody order in respect of a child there is not available to the court adequate information as to where the child is, the court may order any person who it has reason to believe may have relevant information to disclose it to the court.
(2) A person shall not be excused from complying with an order under subsection (1) above by reason that to do so may incriminate him or his spouse of an offence; but a statement or admission made in compliance with such an order shall not be admissible in evidence against either of them in proceedings for any offence other than perjury.
(3) A court in Scotland before which proceedings are pending for the enforcement of an order for the custody of a child made outside the United Kingdom which is recognised in Scotland shall have the same powers as it would have under subsection (1) above if the order were its own.

Not yet in force.

Power to order recovery of child
34. (1) Where—
    (a) a person is required· by a custody order, or an order for the enforcement of a custody order, to give up a child to another person ('the person concerned'), and
    (b) the court which made the order imposing the requirement is satisfied that the child has not been given up in accordance with the order,
the court may make an order authorizing an officer of the court or a constable to take charge of the child and deliver him to the person concerned.
    (2) The authority conferred by subsection (1) above includes authority—
    (a) to enter and search any premises where the person acting in pursuance of the order has reason to believe the child may be found, and
    (b) to use such force as may be necessary to give effect to the purpose of the order.
    (3) Where by virtue of—
    (a) section 13(1) of the Guardianship of Minors Act 1971, section 43(1) of the Children Act 1975 or section 33 of the Domestic Proceedings and Magistrates' Courts Act 1978, or
    (b) Article 37 of the Domestic Proceedings (Northern Ireland) Order 1980,
a custody order (or a provision of a custody order) may be enforced as if it were an order requiring a person to give up a child to another person, subsection (1) above shall apply as if the custody order had included such a requirement.
    (4) This section is without prejudice to any power conferred on a court by or under any other enactment or rule of law.

Powers to restrict removal of child from jurisdiction
35. (1) In each of the following enactments (which enable courts to restrict the removal of a child from England and Wales)—
    (a) section 13A(1) of the Guardianship of Minors Act 1971,
    (b) section 43A(1) of the Children Act 1975, and
    (c) section 34(1) of the Domestic Proceedings and Magistrates' Courts Act 1978,
for the words 'England and Wales' there shall be substituted the words 'the United Kingdom, or out of any part of the United Kingdom specified in the order,'.
    (2) . . .
    (3) . . .
    (4) . . .
    (5) . . .

Effect of orders restricting removal
36. (1) This section applies to any order made by a court in the United Kingdom prohibiting the removal of a child from the United Kingdom or from any specified part of it.
    (2) An order to which this section applies shall have effect in each part of the United Kingdom other than the part in which it was made—

Not yet in force.

    (a) as if it had been made by the appropriate court in that other part, and

    (b) in the case of an order which has the effect of prohibiting the child's removal to that other part, as if it had included a prohibition on his further removal to any place except one to which he could be removed consistently with the order.

(3) The references in subsections (1) and (2) above to prohibitions on a child's removal include references to prohibitions subject to exceptions; and in a case where removal is prohibited except with the consent of the court, nothing in subsection (2) above shall be construed as affecting the identity of the court whose consent is required.

(4) In this section 'child' means a person who has not attained the age of sixteen; and this section shall cease to apply to an order relating to a child when he attains the age of sixteen.

Surrender of passports

37. (1) Where there is in force an order prohibiting or otherwise restricting the removal of a child from the United Kingdom or from any specified part of it, the court by which the order was in fact made, or by which it is treated under section 36 of this Act as having been made, may require any person to surrender any United Kingdom passport which has been issued to, or contains particulars of, the child.

(2) In this section 'United Kingdom passport' means a current passport issued by the Government of the United Kingdom.

Automatic restriction on removal of wards of court

38. (1) The rule of law which (without any order of the court) restricts the removal of a ward of court from the jurisdiction of the court shall, in a case to which this section applies, have effect subject to the modifications in subsection (3) below.

    (2) This section applies in relation to a ward of court if—

    (a) proceedings for divorce, nullity or judicial separation in respect of the marriage of his parents are continuing in a court in another part of the United Kingdom (that is to say, in a part of the United Kingdom outside the jurisdiction of the court of which he is a ward), or

    (b) he is habitually resident in another part of the United Kingdom,

except where that other part is Scotland and he has attained the age of sixteen.

(3) Where this section applies, the rule referred to in subsection (1) above shall not prevent—

    (a) the removal of the ward of court, without the consent of any court, to the other part of the United Kingdom mentioned in subsection (2) above, or

    (b) his removal to any other place with the consent of either the appropriate court in that other part of the United Kingdom or the court mentioned in subsection (2)(a) above.

Duty to furnish particulars of other proceedings

39. Parties to proceedings for or relating to a custody order shall, to such extent and in such manner as may be prescribed, give particulars of other proceedings known to them which relate to the child concerned (including proceedings instituted abroad and proceedings which are no longer continuing).

Not yet in force.

Interpretation of Chapter VI
40. (1) In this chapter—
'the appropriate court' has the same meaning as in Chapter V;
'custody order' includes (except where the context otherwise requires) any such order as is mentioned in section 32(1) of this Act.

(2) In the application of this Chapter to Scotland, 'custody order' also includes (except where the context otherwise requires) any such order as is mentioned in section 32(2) of this Act.

Habitual residence after removal without consent, etc
41. (1) Where a child who—
  (a) has not attained the age of sixteen, and
  (b) is habitually resident in a part of the United Kingdom,
becomes habitually resident outside that part of the United Kingdom in consequence of circumstances of the kind specified in subsection (2) below, he shall be treated for the purposes of this Part as continuing to be habitually resident in that part of the United Kingdom for the period of one year beginning with the date on which those circumstances arise.

(2) The circumstances referred to in subsection (1) above exist where the child is removed from or retained outside, or himself leaves or remains outside, the part of the United Kingdom in which he was habitually resident before his change of residence—
  (a) without the agreement of the person or all the persons having, under the law of that part of the United Kingdom, the right to determine where he is to reside, or
  (b) in contravention of an order made by a court in any part of the United Kingdom.

(3) A child shall cease to be treated by virtue of subsection (1) above as habitually resident in a part of the United Kingdom if, during the period there mentioned—
  (a) he attains the age of sixteen, or
  (b) he becomes habitually resident outside that part of the United Kingdom with the agreement of the person or persons mentioned in subsection (2)(a) above and not in contravention of an order made by a court in any part of the United Kingdom.

General interpretation of Part I
42. (1) In this Part—
'certified copy', in relation to an order of any court, means a copy certified by the prescribed officer of the court to be a true copy of the order or of the official record of the order;
'part of the United Kingdom' means England and Wales, Scotland or Northern Ireland;
'prescribed' means prescribed by rules of court or act of sederunt.

(2) For the purposes of this Part proceedings in England and Wales or in Northern Ireland for divorce, nullity or judicial separation in respect of the marriage of the parents of a child shall, unless they have been dismissed, be treated as continuing until the child concerned attains the age of eighteen (whether or not a decree has been granted and whether or not, in the case of a decree of divorce or nullity of marriage, that decree has been made absolute).

Not yet in force.

(3) For the purposes of this Part, matrimonial proceedings in a court in Scotland which has jurisdiction in those proceedings to make a custody order with respect to a child shall, unless they have been dismissed or decree of absolvitor has been granted therein, be treated as continuing until the child concerned attains the age of sixteen.

(4) Any reference in this Part to proceedings in respect of the marriage of the parents of a child shall, in relation to a child who, although not a child of both parties to the marriage, is a child of the family of those parties, be construed as a reference to proceedings in respect of that marriage; and for this purpose 'child of the family'—

    (a) if the proceedings are in England and Wales, means any child who has been treated by both parties as a child of their family, except a child who has been boarded out with those parties by a local authority or a voluntary organisation;

    (b) if the proceedings are in Scotland, means any child of one of the parties who has been accepted as one of the family by the other party;

    (c) if the proceedings are in Northern Ireland, means any child who has been treated by both parties as a child of their family, except a child who has been boarded out with those parties by or on behalf of the Department of Health and Social Services or a voluntary organisation.

(5) References in this Part to custody orders include (except where the context otherwise requires) references to custody orders as varied.

(6) For the purposes of this Part each of the following orders shall be treated as varying the custody order to which it relates—

    (a) an order which provides for a person to be given access to a child who is the subject of a custody order, or which makes provision for the education of such a child,

    (b) an order under section 42(6) of the Matrimonial Causes Act 1973 or Article 45(6) of the Matrimonial Causes (Northern Ireland) Order 1978.

    (c) an order under section 42(7) of that Act or Article 45(7) of that Order, and

    (d) an order under section 19(6) of the Domestic Proceedings and Magistrates' Courts Act 1978 or Article 20(6) of the Domestic Proceedings (Northern Ireland) Order 1980;

and for the purposes of Chapter V of this Part and this Chapter, this subsection shall have effect as if any reference to any enactment included a reference to any corresponding enactment previously in force.

(7) References in this Part to proceedings in respect of the custody of a child include, in relation to proceedings outside the United Kingdom, references to proceedings before a tribunal or other authority having power under the law having effect there to determine questions relating to the custody of children.

Not yet in force.

Appendix 2
Practice Directions, etc

Contents
A Practice Directions and Notes

A   PRACTICE DIRECTIONS AND NOTES

Practice Direction
[1972] 2 All ER 1360, [1972] 1 WLR 1047
Divorce Registry: Injunction

Order 13, Rule 6, of the County Court Rules 1981 (which applies to matrimonial causes proceeding in the Divorce Registry as in a divorce County Court) provides that applications for injunctions may be made ex parte (and in particular before the filing of a petition) only in cases of urgency. Normally two clear days' notice of the application is required (CCR Order 13, Rule 1(2), as modified by the Matrimonial Causes Rules [1977, Rule 122(2)]), although in proper cases the Court (which includes a Registrar) has power to abridge this time.

It is considered that only a small proportion of applications for injunctions are so urgent that no notice at all should be given.

To assist practitioners, arrangements have been made whereby in an application for injunctions for hearing at the Royal Courts of Justice in which a two day notice is to be given the solicitor need not attend to obtain the date for hearing. He may select any date on which the Court is sitting, at noon, and the date and time at which he, or Counsel, proposes to apply to the County Court Judge, and serve the requisite notice thereon on the Respondent to the application. He must at the same time send a copy of the notice to the Clerk of the Rules, Royal Courts of Justice, giving the title and number of the proceedings (or if none, so stating).

If, in a case of urgency, the Judge is prepared to order an interim injunction on an ex parte application, the form of injunction [(Form 16 County Court Forms Rules 1982)] provides for the grant of the injunction 'until the   day of   19   , upon which day this Court will consider whether this order shall be further continued'.

If the Judge makes an order in this form the time of the further hearing shall be obtained by the associate from the Clerk of the Rules and inserted in the order. Service of this order at least two clear days before the date fixed for the further hearing will constitute sufficient notice to the Respondent, provided that the Applicant seeks only a continuation of the injunction in the terms of the order made. If any further or other relief is sought notice of application for this must be filed and served by the Applicant.

This direction applies only to cases proceeding as in a divorce County Court. In High Court cases the recommended procedure is a specially fixed summons formally issued. The Clerk of the Rules of Divorce Registry will, however, on request, always fix the hearing for the earliest date consistent with the notice of two clear days or such shorter period as may be approved by the Registrar.

Compton Miller
Senior Registrar

10 July 1972

Practice Direction
[1973] 2 All ER 400, [1973] 1 WLR 657
Child: Removal from jurisdiction

1. Under r94(1) of the Matrimonial Causes Rules [1977] . . . in any matrimonial cause begun by petition either spouse may at any time apply ex parte for an order prohibiting the removal of any minor child of the family out of England and Wales without the leave of the court except on such terms as may be specified in the order.

Such an application may be made to a registrar (see [r 122(1)(a)] of the [1977] Rules). At the Divorce Registry any such application should be made to the registrar for the day.

2. Under r94(3) of the [1977] Rules . . . subject to r97(2) which deals with transfer of an application from a divorce county court to the High Court, an application for leave to remove a child out of England and Wales must be made to a judge except: (a) where the application is unopposed; or (b) where the application is for the temporary removal of the child [unless it is opposed on the ground that the child may not be duly returned and the registrar may make such order on the application as he thinks fit or may refer the application or any question arising thereon to a judge for his decision.]

In causes proceeding at the Divorce Registry practitioners who are in doubt whether an application should be made to a registrar or to a judge should consult the registrar for the day.

D Newton
Senior Registrar

8 May 1973

Practice Note
[1973] 2 All ER 512, [1973] 1 WLR 690
Wardship: Visit abroad

The following practice note has been issued by the President of the Family Division.

Where in wardship proceedings in the Family Division the court is satisfied that the ward should be able to leave England and Wales for temporary visits abroad without the necessity for special leave, an order may be made giving general leave for such visits, subject to compliance with the condition that the party obtaining the order (who will normally be the party having care and control of the ward) must lodge at the registry at which the matter is proceeding at least seven days before each proposed departure: (a) a written consent in unqualified terms by the other party or parties to the ward's leaving England and Wales for the period proposed; (b) a statement in writing giving the date on which it is proposed that the ward shall leave England and Wales, the period of absence and the whereabouts of the minor during such absence; and, unless otherwise directed, a written undertaking by the applicant to return the ward to England and Wales at the end of the proposed period of absence.

On compliance with these requirements a certificate, for production to the immigration authorities, stating that the conditions of the order have been complied with, may be obtained from the registry.

11 May 1973

D Newton
Senior Registrar

Practice Direction
[1974] 2 All ER 400, [1974] 1 WLR 576
Injunction: Undertaking as to damages

A form of interim injunction in a county court case [Form 16] includes a reference to an undertaking by the applicant, by his counsel or solicitor, in respect of damages sustained by the respondent. While such undertakings may be required when an interlocutory injunction is granted in an action under the general jurisdiction of the county court, they are unnecessary and inappropriate in High Court and county court matrimonial and children's matters concerning personal conduct. An undertaking as to damages will not be incorporated in an order for an injunction unless it is specifically required by the court and has been expressly given. This is likely to occur only when the injunction concerns property matters, and then only when the claim is to protect rights (as in application under section 17 of the Married Women's Property Act 1882) rather than to invoke discretionary powers (such as applications for the transfer of property).

Issued by the President of the Family Division with the concurrence of the Lord Chancellor.

26 April 1974

Registrar

Practice Direction
[1974] 2 All ER 1119, [1974] 1 WLR 936
Matrimonial Causes: Injunction

Following the general practice of the Chancery Division, although not that of the Queen's Bench Division, applications for injunctions in matrimonial cases in the Family Division and divorce county courts have hitherto been heard in open court. Experience of the present divorce law has led to the conclusion that in the interests of the parties and the better administration of justice this practice should be changed. Accordingly, as from 1 October 1974, a summons or notice of application to a judge in a matrimonial cause in the High Court or a divorce county court should be issued for hearing in chambers. Where the case is one of such urgency that even two days' notice in accordance with the President's direction of 10 July 1972 is impractical and the application has to be made ex parte it should likewise be made to a judge in chambers.

The judge's discretion to hear any particular application in open court is not affected by this direction.

The registrar's direction of 5 March 1957 (application for injunction prohibiting removal of child from jurisdiction to be made in open court) is hereby cancelled.

Issued by the President of the Family Division with the concurrence of the Lord Chancellor.

D Newton
24 June 1974   Senior Registrar

Practice Direction
[1977] 2 All ER 543, [1977] 1 WLR 609
Divisional Court: Appeal

1. This practice direction is issued with the approval of the President of the Family Division. It supplements RSC Ord 90, r 29 which governs the normal procedure for appeals to the Divisional Court of the Family Division (see also RSC Ord 90, r 9 and RSC Ord 105, r 11).

2. A notice of motion on appeal to the Divisional Court should be in the form set out in the appendix to this direction, with such modifications as may be necessary in any particular case.[1]

3. In addition to the certificate as to service and, where appropriate, the certificate as to delay (which can be in the form 'I certify that the reasons for delay are as set out in the Notice of Motion') required by virtue of RSC Ord 90, r 29(4),(d) and (e), the appellant's solicitor should certify whether or not there are any other matrimonial proceedings pending between the same parties. Wherever possible, all relevant certificates should be contained in the same document which should be lodged with the court on filing the notice of motion.

4. In addition to the other copies required to be lodged by RSC Ord 90, r 29, the appellant's solicitor (or the appellant if acting in person) must lodge in the Principal Registry three typescript copies of any manuscript document and two copies of any typescript document put in as an exhibit in the magistrates' court. Original exhibits are usually obtained by the Principal Registry from the magistrates' clerk shortly after entry of the appeal and, when necessary, the copies can be bespoken in the registry. Original exhibits cannot be handed out to solicitors for copying.

5. All documents lodged by or on behalf of the appellant must be clearly legible and preferably in double-spaced typing. Copies produced by photographic methods must be clear. Documents which do not come up to the required standard will be rejected.

This direction will also apply with necessary modifications to the practice in relation to adoption appeals to the Divisional Court (see Practice Direction dated 7th November 1962), but will not apply to an appeal from the magistrates' order in relation to contempt of court made under s 13 of the Administration of Justice Act 1960 (as to which see RSC Ord 109, r 2).

The President's Directions dated 20th November 1958 and 2nd October 1964, and the Practice Note dated 2nd July 1962 are hereby cancelled.

11 May 1977   Senior Registrar

1 The notion of motion is reproduced in Appendix 4, below.

Practice Direction
[1977] 3 All ER 451, [1977] 1 WLR 1065
Minor: Change of surname

1(a) Where a parent has by any order of the High Court or county court been given custody or care and control of a child and applies to the Central Office, Filing Department, for the enrolment of a deed poll to change the surname of such child who is under the age of 18 years (unless in the case of a female, she is married below that age), the application must be supported by the production of the consent in writing of the other parent.

(b) In the absence of such consent, the application will be adjourned generally unless and until leave is given to change the surname of such child in the proceedings in which the said order was made, and such leave is produced to the Central Office.

2(a) Where an application is made to the Central Office, Filing Department, by a parent who has not been given the custody or care and control of the child by any order of the High Court or county court for the enrolment of a deed poll to change the surname of such child who is under the age of 18 years (unless in the case of a female, she is married below that age), leave of the court to enrol such deed will be granted if the consent in writing of the other parent is produced or if the other parent is dead or beyond the seas or despite the exercise of reasonable diligence it has not been possible to find him or her or for other good reason.

(b) In case of any doubt the senior master or in his absence the practice master, will refer the matter to the Master of the Rolls.

(c) In the absence of any of the conditions specified above, the senior master or the Master of the Rolls, as the case may be, may refer the matter to the Official Solicitor for investigation and report.

(3) These directions are issued with the approval of the Master of the Rolls.

I H Jacob QC
Senior Master of the Supreme Court

24 May 1976

Practice Note
[1978] 2 All ER 919, [1978] 1 WLR 925
Matrimonial Cause: Injunction

The President is greatly concerned by the increasing number of applications being made ex parte in the Royal Courts of Justice for injunctions, which could and should have been made (if at all) on two clear days' notice to the other side, as required by the Rules. [CCR Ord 13 r 1(2); Matrimonial Causes Rules 1977, r 122(1)].

An ex parte application should not be made, or granted, unless there is real immediate danger of serious injury or irreparable damage. The recent examination of ex parte applications shows that nearly 50 per cent were unmeritorious, being made days, or even weeks, after the last incident of which complaint was made. This wastes time, causes needless expense, usually to the Legal Aid Fund, and is unjust to respondents.

Where notice of an application for an injunction is to be given and an early hearing date is sought, practitioners are reminded of the special arrangements which exist at the Royal Courts of Justice whereby the applicant's solicitors is able to select for the hearing any day on which the court is sitting. These arrangements are continued in the President's Practice Direction dated the 10th July 1972.[2]

26 June 1978   Senior Registrar

Practice Note
[1978] 2 All ER 1056, [1978] 1 WLR 1123
Injunction: Domestic Violence

To secure uniformity of practice, the President has issued the following note with the concurrence of the Lord Chancellor.

(1) Section 1(1)(c) of the Domestic Violence and Matrimonial Proceedings Act 1976 empowers a county court to include in an injunction provisions excluding a party from the matrimonial home or a part of the matrimonial home or from a specified area in which the matrimonial home is included. Where a power of arrest under section 2 of the 1976 Act is attached or an injunction containing such provisions, the respondent is liable to be arrested if he enters the matrimonial home or part thereof or specified area at any time while the injunction remains in force.

(2) It is within the discretion of the court to decide whether injunctions should be granted and, if so, for how long it should operate. But whenever an injunction is granted excluding one of the parties from the matrimonial home (or part thereof or specified area), consideration should be given to imposing a time limit on the operation of the injunction. In most cases a period of up to three months is likely to suffice, at least in the first instance. It will be open to the respondent in any event to apply for the discharge of the injunction before expiry of the period fixed, for instance on the ground of reconciliation or to the applicant to apply for an extension.

21 July 1978   Senior Registrar

Practice Direction
[1980] 1 All ER 288, [1980] 1 WLR 73
Child: Airport arrival

Where a person seeks an order for the return to him of children about to arrive in England by air and desires to have information to enable him to meet the aeroplane, the judge should be asked to include in his order a direction that the airline operating the flight, and, if he has the information, the immigration officer at the appropriate airport, should supply such information to that person.

To obtain such information in such circumstances in a case where a

2 [1972] 2 All ER 1360, [1972] 1 WLR 1047; see ante.

person already has an order for the return to him of children, that person should apply to a judge ex parte for such a direction.

Issued with the concurrence of the Lord Chancellor.

18 January 1980   Sir John Arnold P

Practice Direction
Unreported
Power of arrest: Procedure

Section 2 of the Domestic Violence and Matrimonial Proceedings Act 1976 provides that a person arrested under a power of arrest must be brought before a judge within 24 hours (not counting Christmas Day, Good Friday or Sundays) and the constable making an arrest must forthwith seek the directions of the court as to the time and place at which the person is to be brought before the judge.

The arrest may take place at a time when the period of 24 hours will expire before a court room is normally available. There is no power to remand the arrested person in custody or, if the proceedings are in a county court, to grant him bail. He must either be dealt with for contempt, if the evidence warrants it, or released.

Experience has now shown that the following procedure is appropriate and should be followed:

(1) Where on an ex parte application for an injunction which has been heard in private a judge decides to grant an injunction and to attach to it a power of arrest the terms of the injunction and the name of the person to whom it is addressed will be announced in open court in those cases where the judge is proceeding to hear other cases in open court. Where there is no further business in open court that day, the announcement will be made in open court at the next listed sitting of the court.

(2) Where a person arrested under section 2 cannot conveniently be brought before a judge sitting in a place normally used as a court room within 24 hours after the arrest, he may be brought before a judge at any convenient place but, as the liberty of the subject is involved, no impediment save such as may be required by local security should be put in the way of the press or any member of the public who wishes to be present.

(3) Any order of committal made by a judge otherwise than in public or a court room will be announced at the commencement of the next listed sitting of the court stating:

(a) the name of the person committed,

(b) in general terms the nature of the contempt of the court in respect of which the order of committal has been made, and

(c) if he has been committed for a fixed period, the length of that period.

Issued with the concurrence of the Lord Chancellor.

                                                              J L Arnold
23 January 1980   President

Practice Direction
[1980] 1 All ER 1008, [1980] 1 WLR 322
Family Division: Liberty to apply

Judges and registrars of the Family Division have found that there is mis-understanding among practitioners as to the meaning of the above words. In one sense there is always liberty to apply since the court can always be applied to by using the proper procedure, but it is emphasised that, except in a few special cases, the words 'Liberty to apply' do not give the right to apply to the court without using the procedures comprised in rule 122 of the Matrimonial Causes Rules 1977 and in the Non-Contentious Probate Rules, passim.

Under a summons for directions there is always liberty to apply for further directions without taking out a further summons. The court may give liberty to apply as to terms of compromise or as to the minor terms where property is settled. These examples are not exhaustive, but, in general applications should not be made under liberty to apply without using the procedures laid down by the Rules referred to.

4 March 1980   R L Bayne-Powell
                                                            Senior Registrar

Practice Note
[1980] 2 All ER 806
Child: Abduction: Press publicity

In cases where a child has been abducted, a judge may consider that press publicity may assist in tracing that child.

The President is of the opinion that in such cases the judge should adjourn for a period of about ten minutes to enable representatives of the press to attend, so that the widest publicity may be given.

22 June 1980   R L Bayne-Powell
                                                            Senior Registrar

Practice Note
[1981] 1 All ER 224, [1981] 1 WLR 27
Domestic Violence: Power of arrest

The police are holding some thousands of orders containing a power of arrest made under section 1(1)(c) of the Domestic Violence and Matrimonial Pro-ceedings Act 1976. Experience has shown that the police are rarely called on to take action on an injunction which is more than three months old, and the requirement that they should retain indefinitely the orders containing a power of arrest imposes an unnecessary burden on them.

The Practice Note dated the 21st July 1978 ([1987] 2 All ER 1056, [1978] 1 WLR 1123) recommended that consideration be given to imposing a time limit of three months on injunctions excluding a party from the matrimonial home or a specified area.

To assist in easing the burdens of the police and enabling them to concentrate on cases where action may be required, Judges should consider, at the time the power of arrest is attached to an injunction, for what period of time this sanction is likely to be required. Unless a judge is satisfied that a longer period is necessary in a particular case, the period should not exceed three months. In those few cases where danger to the applicant is still reasonably apprehended towards the expiry of the three months, application may be made to the court to then extend the duration of the injunction.

Issued by the President with the concurrence of the Lord Chancellor.

22 December 1980   Senior Registrar

Practice Note
[1982] 3 All ER 376, [1982] 1 WLR 1312
Court of Appeal: New procedure

October 4. Sir John Donaldson MR at his first sitting as Master of the Rolls in the Court of Appeal handed down the following written explanation and informal commentary on the more important changes in the practice and procedure of the Court of Appeal following the amendments to RSC Ord 59 made by the Rules of the Supreme Court (Amendment No 2) 1981 (SI 1981 No 1734 (L 21)).

References
Unless otherwise stated, references are to RSC Ord 59, as amended.

Leave to appeal
Applications for leave to appeal to the Court of Appeal will be heard by a single judge of the court sitting in chambers. No appeal will lie from his decision: Supreme Court Act 1981, section 54(6).

Notice of appeal
Heretofore the time for serving notice of appeal has varied according to the nature of the appeal. In future there will be a single time limit of four weeks from the date on which the judgment or order of the court below was signed, entered or otherwise perfected, unless this limit is abridged or extended by order of the court below, the registrar, the single judge of the Court of Appeal or the Court of Appeal: rule 4(1). The only exception will be social security appeals with a six-week limit. Applications for leave to serve notice of appeal out of time will be heard by the registrar. In view of the importance of parties knowing whether a judgment is final or is still subject to possible appeal, it will only be in exceptional cases that such leave will be granted.

The content of the notice of appeal is much more important than is generally realised. A notice of appeal which complies fully with RSC Ord 59, r 3 will both define and confine the area of controversy upon the hearing of the appeal, thus saving both time and expense to the parties. It is intended that wherever possible the members of the court will have read the notice of appeal and any respondent's notice and the reasons for the judgment under appeal before the appeal is called on and a properly drawn notice of appeal will enable counsel to come at once to the central issues without any or any prolonged opening. Failure to give the court this essential assistance by means of a carefully drawn notice of appeal may well lead to special orders being made in relation to time wasted and additional costs incurred.

The list of appeals
RSC Ord 59, r3(4) requires the notice of appeal to specify the list of appeals in which the appellant proposes that the appeal shall be set down. There are final and interlocutory lists of the following descriptions which are self-explanatory:

> Chancery Division, Chancery Divison (in Bankruptcy), Revenue Paper, Family Division, Queen's Bench Division, Queen's Bench Division (Admiralty), Queen's Bench Division (Commercial Court), Queen's Bench Division (Divisional Court), County Courts, County Courts (Divorce), County Courts (Admiralty), Appeal Tribunals (Land), Appeal Tribunals (Patent), Appeal Tribunal (Employment), Appeal Tribunal (Social Security Commission), Restrictive Practices Court.

In the light of experience the number of lists may require alteration from time to time, but full notice will be given of any change. Meanwhile it is only necessary to mention that apeals from the Commercial Court and from the Queen's Bench Divisional Court, both of which were formerly submerged in the general Queen's Bench Division lists, now have their own final and interlocutory lists.

Setting down the appeal
RSC Ord 59, r5 requires the appellant to 'set down' the appeal within seven days after the service of the notice of appeal on the parties. The time limit is important and will be strictly enforced. Any application for an extension of time must be made to the registrar. 'Setting down' means filing the notice of appeal with the court, accompanied by the documents specified in rule 5(1). The registrar and his staff will have to be satisfied that the required documentation is complete and will not hesitate to reject any notice where this is not the case. When they are so satisfied, the appeal will be given a serial number identifying the list in which it will be included and its position in that list. This list is not to be confused with the 'List of Forthcoming Appeals' in which appeals are included at a slightly later stage.

Respondent's notice
RSC Ord 59, r6 makes provision for the service of a respondent's notice within 21 days after the service of the notice of appeal. The content of any such notice is as important as that of the notice of appeal and for the same reason—it defines and confines the scope of the argument upon the appeal, enables the members of the court to inform themselves in advance of the hearing of what the appeal is about and so saves both time and expense. Again the time limit is important and will be strictly enforced, any application for an extension of time being made to the registrar unless the appeal is before the court itself at the time when the application is made.

Amendment of notice of appeal and respondent's notice
It is most desirable that both notices of appeal and respondents' notices should be full and accurate when first served. This should not be too difficult, since the judgment under appeal and the proceedings which led to it will be fresh in everyone's mind. Nevertheless it can happen that, on

reflection, it is thought desirable to amend such notices. Rule 7 allows this to be done without leave at any time before the appeal first appears in the 'List of Forthcoming Appeals'. Thereafter leave will be required and application should be made to the registrar on notice to all other parties, unless the appeal is already before the court for some other purpose. The registrar will require good reasons to be shown why the amendment was not made before the appeal appeared in the 'List of Forthcoming Appeals' and to be satisfied that the application has been made at the earliest possible moment.

Appearance of appeal in the List of Forthcoming Appeals
This is the second of the key stages in an appeal, the first being the service of the notice of appeal and the third the appearance of the appeal in the Warned List. Ultimately it will follow as soon as the appeal is set down as is reasonable, bearing in mind the steps which the appellant is then required to take. However, until the backlog of appeals has been reduced, there will be some cases in which there is a rather greater interval. The registrar is considering whether, and how, it will be possible to give solicitors advance notice that an appeal is to appear in the List of Forthcoming Appeals. However, it is the responsibility of the parties and their advisers to watch the Daily Cause List in which the List of Forthcoming Appeals will periodically be published.

Once an appeal appears in the List of Forthcoming Appeals, the appellant has seven days in which to lodge the various documents specified in rule 9.

Although the rules do not at present so require, it would greatly assist the efficient running of the court if at the same time as they are lodging documents pursuant to rule 9, appellants would provide an estimate of how much in-court time is likely to be needed for the hearing. In putting forward this estimate they should consult the respondents or their representatives and all concerned will no doubt wish to seek the views of counsel who will be appearing. It would also assist the court if appellants would indicate which counsel are being instructed by them and, where known, by the respondents. This will make it easier for the registrar when listing to take such account as is possible of counsel's other commitments, although it will be appreciated that this is only one factor amongst many which have to be considered if the current delays are to be eliminated and eliminated quickly.

It may be thought that seven days from the date when an appeal appears in the list of Forthcoming Appeals is rather a short time in which to do a lot of work, since the documentation required is substantially all that which will be needed for the hearing of the appeal. It is indeed a short time, but it must be remembered that parties and their advisers are free to file these documents as early as they like and the earlier that they in fact do so the better. As a matter of good practice they should start assembling the documents as soon as the appeal has been set down.

In the past much time has been wasted because appellants have failed to file all the appropriate documents, have filed an inadequate number of copies or have failed to ensure that bundles are properly paginated and are legible throughout. In the light of the contribution which this has made to the delay in hearing appeals, a serious view will be taken of any failure by appellants to comply with their obligations in this respect.

Directions by the registrar

RSC Ord 59, r 9 has been amended so as to include a new sub-rule (3) in the following terms:

> After the documents have been lodged the registrar shall give such directions in relation to the documents to be produced at the appeal, and the manner in which they are to be presented, and as to other matters incidental to the conduct of the appeal, as appear adapted to secure the just, expeditious and economical disposal of the appeal.

This is perhaps the most important single change in the rules. The conduct of appeals by way of oral hearing lies at the heart of the English tradition and practice and neither the Scarman Committee [set up in February 1978 under the chairmanship of Lord Scarman to examine ways and means of relieving the pressure in hearing civil appeals] nor anyone else has suggested that it should be abandoned in favour of a system of written appeals supplemented by oral hearings which are subject to strict time limits, as is the practice in some other jurisdictions. Nevertheless, an oral hearing involving the presence of the members of the court, shorthandwriters, court staff, counsel, solicitors and, sometimes, the parties is extremely expensive in terms of time and therefore of money. Furthermore, time, and particularly judicial time, is a scarce commodity of which the best possible use should be made, if the current level of delay is to be reduced. The problem is how to achieve a proper balance between what can be done by way of pre-reading by the members of the court in their rooms, which involves only judicial time, and what must be left to oral presentation and argument in court which involves the time of many others.

There can never be any single universal answer. Every appeal is different, although patterns do emerge. The sub-rule therefore contemplates that once the documentation is complete the registrar, either at the request of the parties or of his own motion, shall consider whether any special directions can be given which will expedite the hearing and render it less costly. We have as yet little experience of how this will work, although in exceptional cases it has in the past been attempted with some success by the court itself. The Scarman Committee suggested the use of 'perfected grounds of appeal' on the lines of those used in the Criminal Division of the Court of Appeal. These grounds of appeal often refer to the key authorities which will be relied upon and to the portions of the summing up and evidence which are relevant to each ground of appeal. They permit members of the court to pre-read the relevant material, much of which is non-controversial, and, thus informed, to consider and adjudicate upon the basis of a much abbreviated oral argument and to do so in a fraction of the time which would be necessary if they took their places in court knowing nothing of the appeal. In the context of civil appeals, it may be possible to use 'perfected grounds of appeal' but another possibility, which may be better, is for the parties to provide the court in advance with a skeleton outline of their respective arguments annotated by reference to the documents and authorities. The probability is that different approaches will be found appropriate to different types of appeal, but only time and experience will show which is the best method or methods.

What needs to be said now, and said with all possible emphasis, is that the better use of time is in the interests of everyone—the parties to the appeal, their advisers, parties to other appeals which will be delayed if time is not used to the best advantage and to the public at large which has an interest in the efficient administration of justice. Accordingly, the members of the court can look forward with some confidence to all concerned giving serious thought to, and, where appropriate, discussing with the registrar, how each individual appeal can best be presented. The registrar will be ready and willing to assist at any stage, but the appropriate moment will probably be at or about the time when an appeal appears in the List of Forthcoming Appeals. The Bar Council and The Law Society will not be concerned with individual appeals, but there will be the fullest and most frequent consultation with them as to what experiments are worth trying and as to the success of those experiments. As experience is built up, and in the light of that experience, we have no doubt the rate of disposal of appeals can be increased without detriment to, and even with an improvement in, the quality of the justice which is administered.

The single judge of the Court of Appeal
In the past a court consisting of at least two judges has had to consider incidental applications, such as those for leave to appeal, for the imposition or removal of orders staying execution or for the grant, variation or discharge of injunctions pending appeal. This represented an extravagant use of judicial time and rule 10 (9) will now enable all these matters to be considered and disposed of by a single judge sitting in chambers. All such applications will be made by motion: rule 14 (1).

Internal appeals and referrals
The amended RSC Ord 59 gives the registrar power to refer matters to a single judge and the single judge power to refer matters to the Court of Appeal: rule 14 (9) and (10). It also gives a right of appeal to the single judge from any determination of the registrar and from any determination of the single judge to the Court of Appeal. However, in respect of a determination by the registrar, there is no right of appeal to the Court of Appeal without the leave of that court if the registrar's determination has been reviewed by the single judge: rule 14 (11) and (12). Nevertheless, the advantages of the new system would be substantially eroded if appeals became a matter of course and parties and their advisers should give serious consideration to where their best interests lie before launching such appeals.

Listing of appeals for hearing—'the Warned List'*
The science, or more accurately the art, of a successful listing officer consists of an ability to quantify the unquantifiable and to predict the unpredictable. Factors of which he has to take account are the availability of judges, the availability of counsel, the speed with which the judges concerned will wish the argument to be presented, the inherent complexity of the appeal, the loquacity of counsel and the relative urgency of the appeal both objectively and in the eyes of the parties. If, against this background, a listing officer is instructed to give fixed dates for the hearing of all appeals and to specify far in advance by which court the appeal will be heard, the result is inevitable. Either he will over-estimate the hearing time needed for appeals and there will be gaps in the list which are too short to be filled by taking in other appeals or he will under-estimate and the fixed dates will not be met. Both have been happening, thereby causing delay and inconvenience to all concerned. Some new approach must be adopted, at least on an experimental basis.
　　The most obviously necessary change, and one recommended by the

---

* *Stop press*: see Practice Direction (List of Forthcoming Appeals) (1987) Times 3 October.

Scarman Committee, is to list for the Civil Division of the Court of Appeal as a whole and not for particular courts. This gives greater flexibility and will enable appeals originally destined for Court A, whose cases are over-running, to be switched to Court B where an appeal has been withdrawn or for some other reason judges have become available. This recommendation is being implemented and the registrar will be the listing officer for the whole of the civil division.

The next aspect which needs to be looked at is the concept of all or the vast majority of appeals being given fixed dates and given them far in advance of the hearing of the appeal. Clearly parties to appeals, and more particularly those appearing for them, have to be able to plan their work and need to know with a greater or lesser degree of precision, according to circumstances, when an appeal will be heard. But giving fixed dates which, because they are fixed must be very far ahead and well spaced out if they are to be guaranteed, is no real service to the parties. On the other hand, failing to space the appeals out and instead giving fixed dates to a con-secutive series of appeals will almost inevitably lead to a failure to meet some or all of these dates and that is worse than useless. Nevertheless, despite the difficulties inherent in a fixed date system, where appeals have already been given fixed dates, this commitment will be honoured if at all possible.

The reality is surely that only the most urgent appeals need to be heard with very short notice of the time of hearing and only a minority of appeals need to be allotted a fixed and guaranteed date far in advance. An obvious example of the latter category is the exceptionally heavy appeal upon which counsel, and to a lesser extent the court, will have to work for an extended period before the oral hearing begins. Listing is not unlike weather forecasting. The further away you are from the date for hearing, the more difficult it is to identify it precisely. But as you approach that day, it becomes more and more possible to do so and, in effect, to give a fixed date. Between the extremes of the very urgent appeal which must be heard almost at once, thus precluding substantial notice, and the exceptionally heavy case which requires long notice of a more or less fixed date, it may well be possible to meet the legitimate needs of the parties and of their advisers and also the public interest in reducing the number of appeals awaiting hearing by a system of long-range forecasting coupled slightly later with a more or less precise indication of the date for the hearing.

The maximum possible direct and continuing contact will be maintained between the court and the parties to appeals which are ready for hearing in order that they shall be heard as quickly as possible and with the minimum conflict with other commitments. However, it is only fair to the registrar and his staff to point out that the task of establishing an entirely new office, creating a new administrative infra-structure for the court and also a new centralised system of listing will involve great problems for them in the initial stages and there are bound to be teething troubles. In future com-munications should be easier than heretofore, because telex is being in-stalled in the Royal Courts of Justice. This will be the subject of a separate announcement.

Notwithstanding such communication, some form of published 'Warned List' containing appeals to be heard in the immediate future will still be needed. The existing 'Warned List' was designed to operate in connection with the unamended rules and is now inappropriate. Furthermore, cases appeared in it so long before they were likely to be heard that parties and their advisers, not unreasonably, did not regard themselves as being warned of anything. A new 'Warned List' will be published containing the appeals which are both ready for hearing and have already been given fixed dates, together with some other appeals of an urgent character. Meanwhile consideration will be given to what are the appropriate criteria for including appeals in a new style 'Warned List.'

In taking a fresh look at listing in the context of a new centralised system, the registrar and the court will be looking to both sides of the profession for constructive suggestions, advice and assistance, and experience shows that we shall not look in vain. This is supremely an area where it is necessary to try and to err before an effective system can be evolved.

Constitution of courts
Section 54 (4) of the Supreme Court Act 1981 and the Court of Appeal (Civil Division) Order 1982 (SI 1982 No 543) have authorised the constitution of courts consisting of two judges instead of three in certain specified circumstances, mainly appeals from interlocutory decisions, which includes most family and divorce matters, and appeals from the county courts. If the very serious backlog of appeals is to be reduced, it is essential that the fullest use be made of this power. The main theoretical objection to an appellate court of two judges is that they might disagree. Should this be likely to occur, it would be possible to relist the appeal for argument before a differently constituted court of three, but experience in the Divisional Court of the Queen's Bench Division suggests that this is most unlikely to occur in other than an insignificant number of cases. Nevertheless it will sometimes happen that whilst an appeal is of such a nature that there is jurisdiction for a two-judge court to hear it, it is well recognised that despite the need to make the best possible use of the available judge power, there are some appeals falling within the jurisdiction of a two-judge court which raise issues of such complexity or general importance that a three-judge court is desirable. Should this appear to the registrar to be the case, he will list the appeal for hearing by a three-judge court. Should it appear to the parties that this is the case, they will be free to apply to the registrar for a special listing before a three-judge court, but it is hoped that they will only adopt this course if there are really good reasons for so doing.

Oral hearings
It is hoped and expected that early consideration by the parties of the extent to which judges can profitably read papers before the hearing and the assistance of the registrar at the stage at which an appeal appears in the Forthcoming List of Appeals will enable the length of the oral hearing to be considerably reduced and that all concerned will know in advance what is expected of them. However, the way in which the hearing is conducted will, as always, be a matter to be determined by the members of the court hearing the appeal and if it appears to them that the directions which have been given were mistaken or need to be supplemented, the court will take the appropriate action.

Written judgments
Where the court has prepared written judgements, consideration will be given by the judges concerned to the advantage of giving copies to counsel, the law reporters and the representatives of the press present in court

instead of reading the judgments aloud. However where this is done, it must be understood that the purpose for which the copies are handed down is strictly limited, namely to save the parties the expense involved in prolonging the hearing, to allow the time saved to be devoted to deciding other appeals, to enable the representatives of the parties to make any necessary application following the announcement in the same way as they would have done if the judgments had been read out in court. Copies so handed down must not be reproduced without the leave of the court and the only recognised record of the written judgments will be that contained in the official transcript which will be obtainable from the court shorthandwriters and will record not only the written judgments, but also the exchanges between the court and counsel which follow the judgments being handed down.

4 October 1982

Practice Note
[1982] 3 A11 ER 924, [1982] 1 WLR 1420
Court of Appeal: Anton Piller Orders

November 5. Sir John Donaldson MR made the following statement. We have been discussing how this court should deal with *Anton Piller* orders. The applications are made ex parte in the court below. They are by their nature applications whose purpose could in some circumstances be frustrated if an appeal was heard in open court, although experience has shown that it is often possible to consider the matter in open court, relying upon the great responsibility and discretion which is always shown by those who report the cases on a regular basis (the members of the High Court Journalists' Association). Accordingly something out of the ordinary has to be shown before it would be right for the court to go into camera.

We would like it to be known that where counsel forms the view that it is necessary in the interests of justice that a preliminary application for an appeal against an ex parte refusal of an *Anton Piller* or similar order should be heard in camera, he should approach the registrar, indicating his view. The reasons should be put into writing, signed by counsel and handed to the registrar. In so doing it should be understood that counsel is expressing his personal view and is not making a submission on behalf of his client. This will enable the court to make a preliminary decision on whether the application should initially be made in camera or in open court. This procedure will avoid the problem which arises when the very reasons which justify a hearing in camera must themselves be put forward in camera if they are to be put forward at all.

5 November 1982

Practice Direction
[1983] 1 All ER 448, [1983] 1 WLR 85
Court of Appeal: Dismissal of Appeal

Consequent upon the creation of the office of Registrar of Civil Appeals, the existing practice direction reported in [1938] WN 89 and in *The Supreme Court Practice* 1982, p 933, note 59/5/3 is being amended to enable the registrar and any judge of the court to initial requests for the dismissal of civil appeals. In its amended form it reads:

> Where an appellant is sui juris and does not desire to prosecute an appeal, he may present a request signed by his solicitor stating that he is sui juris and asking to have the appeal dismissed, in which case (subject to the request being initialled by a judge of the court or by the Registrar of Civil Appeals) the appeal will be dismissed and struck out of the list, and an order will, if necessary, be drawn up directing payment of the costs by the appellant, such costs to be taxed in case the parties differ.
>
> Where the parties are sui juris and a settlement has been reached disposing of the appeal, they may present a request signed by the solicitors for all parties to the appeal, stating that they are sui juris, including the terms of settlement and asking that the appeal be dismissed by consent, in which case (subject to the request being initialled by a judge of the court or by the registrar of Civil Appeals) the appeal will be dismissed and struck out of the list and an order will, if necessary, be drawn up.
>
> If the appellant desires to have the appeal dismissed without costs, his request must be accompanied by a consent signed by the respondents' solicitors stating that the respondents are sui juris and consent to the dismissal of the appeal without costs, in which case (subject to the request being initialled by a judge of the court or by the Registrar of Civil Appeals) the appeal will be dismissed and struck out of the list.
>
> Where any party has no solicitor on the record, any such request or consent must be signed by him personally.
>
> All other applications as to the dismissal of an appeal and all applications for an order by consent reversing or varying the order under appeal will be placed in the list and dealt with in court.

11 January 1983   Sir John Donaldson MR

Practice Note
[1983] 2 All ER 34, [1983] 1 WLR 1055
Court of Appeal: Skeleton Arguments

Sir John Donaldson MR, sitting with Dunn and Purchas LJJ, handed down the following practice note.

As is well known, the judges of the Court of Appeal have been seeking new ways in which appeals can be presented and decided more quickly and at less expense to the parties. One innovation which has proved very successful in more complex appeals is the submission by counsel of what have been called 'skeleton arguments.'

It would be quite inappropriate to issue a practice direction in this context since whether skeleton arguments should be submitted, what form they should take and how they should be used will depend upon the peculiarities of the appeal concerned. However it may assist both branches of the profession if I mention the result of such experience as we have had of their use.

Skeleton arguments are, as their name implies, a very abbreviated note of the argument and in no way usurp any part of the function of oral argument in court. They are an aide-mémoire for convenience of reference before and during the hearing and no-one is inhibited from departing from their terms. Nevertheless experience shows that they serve a very real purpose.

Before the appeal is called on, the judges will normally have read the notice of appeal, any respondent's notice and the judgement appealed from. The purpose of this pre-reading is not to form any view of the merits of the appeal, but to familiarise themselves with the issues and scope of the dispute and thereby avoid the necessity for a lengthy, or often any, opening of the appeal. This process is assisted by the provision of skeleton arguments which are much more informative than a notice of appeal or a respondent's notice, being fuller and more recently prepared.

During the hearing of the appeal itself, skeleton arguments enable much time to be saved because they reduce or obviate the need for the judges to take a longhand note, sometimes at dictation speed, of the submissions and authorities and other documents referred to. Furthermore in some circumstances a skeleton argument can do double duty not only as a note for the judges but also as a note from which counsel can argue the appeal.

The usual procedure is for the skeleton argument to be prepared shortly before the hearing of the appeal at the same time as counsel is getting it up. It should contain a numbered list of the points which counsel proposes to argue, stated in no more than one or two sentences, the object being to *identify* each point, not to argue it or to elaborate upon it. Each listed point should be followed by full references to the material to which counsel will refer in support of it, ie, the relevant pages or passages in authorities, bundles of documents, affidavits, transcripts and the judgment under appeal. It should also contain anything which counsel would expect to be taken down by the court during the hearing, such as propositions of law, chronologies of events, lists of dramatis personae, and, where necessary, glossaries of terms. If more convenient, these can of course be annexed to the skeleton argument rather than being included in it. Both the court and opposing counsel can then work on the material without writing it down, thus saving considerable time and labour.

The document should be sent to the court as soon as convenient before the hearing, or—if for some reason this is not possible—handed in when counsel rises to address the court. It is however more valuable if provided to the court in advance. A copy should of course at the same time be sent or handed to counsel on the other side.

It cannot be over-emphasised that skeleton arguments are not formal documents to the terms of which anyone will be held. They are simply a tool to be used in the interests of greater efficiency. Experience shows that they can be a valuable tool. The judges of the court all hope that it will be possible to refine and extend their use.

Finally, even in simple appeals where skeleton arguments may be unnecessary, counsel should provide notes (preferably typed) of any material such as I have mentioned which would otherwise have to be taken down by the court more or less at dictation speed, thereby saving considerable time and labour.

12 April 1983

Practice Direction
[1983] 2 A11 ER 253, [1983] 1 WLR 558
Minor: Passport

In matrimonial, wardship and guardianship cases the court may grant an injunction restraining the removal of a child from the court's jurisdiction. In cases in which the apparent threat comes from the holder of a foreign passport this may be the only safe course. In cases in which the child holds, or the threat comes from the holder of, a British passport the court sometimes orders the surrender of any passport issued to, or which contains particulars of, that child.

Unless the Passport Office is aware that the court has ordered a British passport to be surrendered, there may be nothing to prevent a replacement passport from being issued. Accordingly in such cases, the court will in future notify the Passport Office in every case in which the surrender of a passport has been ordered.

Issued with the concurrence of the Lord Chancellor.

29 April 1983   Sir John Arnold P

Practice Note
[1983] 2 All ER 199, [1983] 1 WLR 598
Court of Appeal: New Procedure (No 2)

May 5. Sir John Donaldson MR, sitting with Dunn and Purchas LJJ, handed down the following practice statement.

In October of last year I made a statement, *Practice Note (Court of Appeal: New Procedure)* [1982] 1 WLR 1312, concerning changes being made in the procedure of the court. In the course of the 'informal commentary' which I issued at the same time, I drew attention to the fact that a single judge of the Court of Appeal would in future be able to consider incidental applications, such as those for leave to appeal [see section 54 (6) of the Supreme Court Act 1981], thus saving the time of the full court. I added that he would sit in chambers.

It has recently been suggested to us that on the true construction of the Supreme Court Act 1981 and RSC Ord 59, the sole exception to the general rule that the single judge will normally sit in chambers is the case where he is considering an application for leave to appeal and that he should then sit in open court. The practice has been altered accordingly and applications for leave to appeal are now being heard in open court.

Although it is now considered that the previous practice of hearing such applications otherwise than in open court was a procedural irregularity, the only result of such irregularity is that orders previously made in chambers could, in theory, be set aside if application were made for that purpose. As the merits will have been fully considered before the order was made, the applicant, on any such application, would be unlikely to succeed unless he satisfied the court that he had been prejudiced by the hearing having taken place in chambers rather than in open court.

5 May 1983

Practice Direction
[1983] 2 A11 ER 672, [1983] 1 WLR 790
Wardship: Parties to proceedings

In cases in which the ward has formed or is seeking to form an association, considered to be undesirable, with another person, that other person should not be made a party to the originating summons. He or she should be made a defendant in a summons within the wardship proceedings for injunction or committal. Such a person should not be added to the title of the proceedings nor allowed to see any documents other than those relating to the summons.

The judges of the Family Division consider that any such person should be allowed time within which to obtain representation and any order for injunction should in the first instance extend over a few days only.

This direction supersedes that dated December 15, 1961: see *Practice Direction (Parties to Wardship Proceedings)* [1962] 1 WLR 61.

Issued with the concurrence of the Lord Chancellor.

16 June 1983

B P Tickle
Senior Registrar

Practice Direction
[1983] 3 A11 ER 33, [1983] 1 WLR 922
Evidence: Documents

This practice direction applies to the Court of Appeal and to all divisions of the High Court. Any affidavit, exhibit or bundle of documents which does not comply with RSC, Ord 41 and this direction may be rejected by the court or made the subject for an order for costs.

Affidavits

1. *Marking*
At the top right hand corner of the first page of every affidavit, and also on the backsheet, there must be written in clear permanent dark blue or black marking: (i) the party on whose behalf it is filed; (ii) the initials and surname of the deponent; (iii) the number of the affidavit in relation to the deponent; and (iv) the date when sworn.

For example: '2nd Dft: E. W. Jones: 3rd: 24.7.82.'

2. *Binding*
Affidavits must not be bound with thick plastic strips or anything else which would hamper filing.

Exhibits
3. *Markings generally*
Where space allows, the directions under paragraph 1 above apply to the first page of every exhibit.

4. *Documents other than letters*
(i) Clearly legible photographic copies of original documents may be exhibited instead of the originals provided the originals are made available for inspection by the other parties before the hearing and by the judge at the hearing.

(ii) Any document which the court is being asked to construe or enforce, or the trusts of which it is being asked to vary, should be separately exhibited, and should not be included in a bundle with other documents. Any such document should bear the exhibit mark directly, and not on a flysheet attached to it.

(iii) Court documents, such as probates, letters of administration, orders, affidavits or pleadings, should never be exhibited. Office copies of such documents prove themselves.

(iv) Where a number of documents are contained in one exhibit, a front page must be attached, setting out a list of the documents, with dates, which the exhibit contains, and the bundle must be securely fastened. The traditional method of securing is by tape, with the knot sealed (under the modern practice) by means of wafers; but any means of securing the bundle (except by staples) is acceptable, provided that it does not interfere with the perusal of the documents and it cannot readily be undone.

(v) This direction does not affect the current practice in relation to scripts in probate matters, or to an affidavit of due execution of a will.

5. *Letters*
(i) Copies of individual letters should not be made separate exhibits, but they should be collected together and exhibited in a bundle or bundles. The letters must be arranged in correct sequence with the earliest at the top, and properly paged in accordance with paragraph 6 below. They must be firmly secured together in the manner indicated in paragraph 4 above.

(ii) When original letters, or original letters and copies of replies, are exhibited as one bundle, the exhibit must have a front page attached, stating that the bundle consists of so many original letters and so many copies. As before, the letters and copies must be arranged in correct sequence and properly paged.

6. *Paging of documentary exhibits*
Any exhibit containing several pages must be paged consecutively at centre bottom.

7. *Copies of documents generally*
It is the responsibility of the solicitor by whom any affidavit is filed to ensure that every page of every exhibit is fully and easily legible. In many cases photocopies of documents, particularly of telex messages, are not. In all cases of difficulty, typed copies of the illegible document (pages with 'a' numbers) should be included.

8. *Exhibits bound up with affidavit*
Exhibits must not be bound up with, or otherwise attached to, the affidavit itself.

9. *Exhibits other than documents*
The principles are as follows. (i) The exhibit must be clearly marked with the exhibit mark in such a manner that there is no likelihood of the contents being separated; and (ii) where the exhibit itself consists of more than one item (eg, a cassette in a plastic box), each and every separate part of the exhibit must similarly be separately marked with at least enough of the usual exhibit mark to ensure precise identification.

This is particularly important in cases where there are a number of similar exhibits which fall to be compared. Accordingly:

(a) The formal exhibit marking should, so far as practicable, be written on the article itself in an appropriate manner (eg, many fabrics can be directly marked with an indelible pen), or, if this is not possible, on a separate slip which is securely attached to the article in such a manner that it is not easily removable. (NB. Items attached by Sellotape or similar means are readily removable). If the article is then enclosed in a container, the number of the exhibit should appear on the outside of the container unless it is transparent and the number is readily visible. Alternatively, the formal exhibit marking may be written on the container, or, if this is not possible, on a separate slip securely attached to the container. If this is done, then either—(i) the number of the exhibit and, if there is room, the short name and number of the case, the name of the deponent and the date of the affidavit must be written on the exhibit itself and on each separate part thereof; or (ii) all these particulars must appear on a slip securely attached to the article itself and to each separate part thereof.

(b) If the article, or part of the article, is too small to be marked in accordance with the foregoing provisions, it must be enclosed in a sealed transparent container of such a nature that it could not be reconstituted once opened, and the relevant slip containing the exhibit mark must be inserted in such container so as to be plainly visible. An enlarged photograph or photographs showing the relevant characteristics of each such exhibit will usually be required to be separately exhibited.

10. *Numbering*
Where a deponent deposes to more than one affidavit to which there are exhibits in any one matter, the numbering of such exhibits should run consecutively throughout, and not begin again with each affidavit.

11. *Reference to documents already forming part of an exhibit*
Where a deponent wishes to refer to a document already exhibited to some other deponent's affidavit, he should not also exhibit it to his own affidavit.

12. *Multiplicity of documents*
Where, by the time of the hearing, exhibits or affidavits have become numerous, they should be put in a consolidated bundle, or file or files, and be paged consecutively throughout in the top right hand corner, affidavits and exhibits being in separate bundles or files.

Bundles of documents generally
13. The directions under 5, 6 and 7 above apply to all bundles of documents. Accordingly they must be (i) firmly secured together, (ii) arranged in chronological order, beginning with the earliest, (ii) paged consecutively at centre bottom, and (iv) fully and easily legible.

14. Transcripts of judgments and evidence must not be bound up with any other documents, but must be kept separate.

15. In cases for trial where the parties will seek to place before the trial judge bundles of documents (apart from pleadings) comprising more than 100 pages, it is the responsibility of the solicitors for all parties to prepare and agree one single additional bundle containing the principal documents to which the parties will refer (including in particular the documents referred to in the pleadings) and to lodge such bundle with the court at least two working days before the date fixed for the hearing.

21 July 1983   Lord Lane CJ

Practice Direction
[1983] 2 A11 ER 1066, [1983] 1 WLR 998
Family Division: Contempt of Court

The President has directed that on applications for the release of a contemnor from prison the contemnor should be present in court to hear the outcome of the application.

The only exception to this practice is in those cases in which the provisions of the Mental Health Act 1983 apply and it is considered by the solicitor conducting the application that in the particular circumstances it would not be desirable for the contemnor to attend.

Issued with the concurrence of the Lord Chancellor.

B P Tickle
25 July 1983   Senior Registrar

Practice Direction
[1983] 2 A11 ER 1088, [1983] 1 WLR 999]
Matrimonial Causes: Injunctions

Where relief is sought under the Matrimonial Homes Act 1983 the application must be made by originating summons. The procedure in the High Court is set out in Matrimonial Causes Rules 1977, rule 107³, which applies rule 104, with the necessary modifications. The summons should be headed 'In the matter of an application under section1 (or 9) of the Matrimonial Homes Act 1983.' The affidavit in support of the application should contain evidence of the applicant's rights of occupation of the matrimonial home and the circumstances in which the application is made. The form of order applied for should be an order (1) declaring the applicant's right of occupation of the matrimonial home, and (2) if ouster is sought, prohibiting the respondent from exercising any right to occupy such home from a specified date and time until further order.

The registrar's direction dated 21 December 1973, in so far as it relates to an initial hearing for directions will not apply to applications under section 1 (or 9) of the Matrimonial Homes Act 1983 for ouster injunctions.

The Principal Registry has no jurisdiction in relation to ouster injunctions under the Matrimonial Homes Act 1983 except in the High Court. Where there are pending divorce proceedings in the Principal Registry which are treated as pending in a divorce county court under the provisions of section 4 of the Matrimonial Causes Act 1967, and a party to those proceedings applies in the Principal Registry for ouster relief under section 1 (or 9) of the Matrimonial Homes Act 1983, a registrar or the judge hearing the section 1 (or 9) application, should be asked that the cause be transferred to the High Court.

RSC Ord 90, r 30
Applications in the Principal Registry for relief analogous to that available

---

3 Matrimonial Causes Rules 1977 rule 107 has been substituted by a new rule, S1 1984 1511.
  For the terms of rule 107 as substituted see Appendix 3, part c, post.

under section 1 of the Domestic Violence and Matrimonial Proceedings Act 1976 must also be made by originating summons in the High Court. The procedure to be followed is set out in RSC Ord 90, r 30. The originating summons should be headed 'In the matter of an application within the meaning of section 1 of the Domestic Violence and Matrimonial Proceedings Act 1976.'

B P Tickle,
Senior Registrar

Practice Direction
[1984] 1 A11 ER 684, [1984] 1 WLR 306
Family Division: Filing Affidavits (No 2)

1. Where in any cause or matter proceeding in the Principal Registry, a party wishes to file an affidavit or other document in connection with an application for which a hearing date has been fixed, the affidavit or other document must be lodged in the Principal Registry *not less than 14 clear days* before the appointed hearing date.
2. Where insufficient time remains before the hearing date to lodge the affidavit or other document as required by 1 above, it should, in case of an application before the judge, be lodged in Room 775 (Summons Clerk, Clerk of the Rules Department) at the Royal Courts of Justice as soon as possible *before* the hearing: where the application is before the registrar, it should be handed to the clerk to that registrar immediately before the hearing. Service should be effected upon the opposing party in the normal way.
3. The registrar's direction of 12 January 1981, *Practice Direction (Family Divison: Filing Affidavits)* [1981] 1 WLR 106, except paragraph 3, is cancelled.

7 February 1984

B P Tickle
Senior Registrar

Practice Direction
[1984] 1 A11 ER 783, [1984] 1 WLR 475
Family Division: Hearing Duration

1. Recent experience has shown that in some cases the estimated length of hearing of Family Division summonses and applications for hearing before a judge at the Royal Courts of Justice has been inaccurate, with a resultant waste of time for all concerned with litigation and a needless increase in costs. In order to remedy this situation the following procedure will apply with effect from the date of this registrar's direction.
2. On the issue of a summons or application (including restoring an adjourned summons or application or one referred to a judge) which is expected to last in excess of one day, the form of notice of estimate set out in the appendix to this registrar's direction, duly completed, must be

lodged with the Clerk of the Rules. The form should be signed by counsel, if already instructed, or by the solicitor acting for the party.

3. A copy of the completed notice must be served at once on every other party. Upon receipt by the solicitor he, or counsel if instructed, must consider the estimate and if he disagrees with it adopt the procedure in paragraph 6 as soon as possible.

4. A copy of the completed notice or any revised notice must be included in every set of instructions or brief sent to counsel.

5. It is the continuing responsibility of all solicitors and counsel when dealing with the case to consider whether or not the latest estimate recorded on the notice is accurate.

6. If any solicitor or counsel considers that the estimate needs revising either way a copy of the notice of estimate should be made, completed at box 5 with proposed revised estimate and served on the other parties and the Clerk of the Rules. The revised estimate should, whenever possible, be agreed with all other parties and signed jointly before being sent to the Clerk of the Rules. In the event of disagreement reference should be made to the Clerk of the Rules.

7. If an additional summons or a cross-summons is issued returnable on the same date, a separate notice of estimate should only be filed if the latest estimate is affected.

8. If within seven days of the date fixed for hearing it becomes apparent that the estimate requires revision, the Clerk of the Rules should be notified at once by telephone.

9. This registrar's direction does not apply to a party acting in person, but if the respondent(s) is represented by counsel or solicitor and he estimates that the matter will last in excess of one day he must immediately complete a notice of estimate and send it to the Clerk of the Rules.

10. The procedure relating to registrar's hearings, at the Divorce Registry, Somerset House, is not affected by this direction.

11. Copies of the form of notice of estimate, D208, are available from the Clerk of the Rules Department at the Royal Courts of Justice and Room G39 of the Divorce Registry in Somerset House.

B P Tickle
1 March 1984   Senior Registrar

Practice Direction
[1984] 2 All ER 407, [1984] 1 WLR 855
Ward: Removal from the jurisdiction

The judges of the Family Division are of the opinion, and it is accordingly hereby directed, that an application for leave to remove a child out of England and Wales in wardship and guardianship cases shall be made to a judge except in the following cases when it shall be made to the registrar, namely, (a) where the application is unopposed, or (b) where the application is for the temporary removal of the child unless it is opposed on the ground that the child may not be duly returned.

The registrar may make such order on the application as he thinks fit or may refer it or any question arising thereon to a judge.

Issued with the approval of the President.

B P Tickle
14 May 1984   Senior Registrar

Practice Direction
[1985] 1 A11 ER 1088, [1985] 1 WLR 739
Court of Appeal: Single Judge

18 March. Sir John Donaldson MR, at the sitting of the court, handed down the following practice direction.

At present, single judge applications are heard on Fridays by two nominated Lords Justice. This system suffers from certain drawbacks, in particular, the uneconomic use of judge-power, and it is therefore proposed that, as from the beginning of the Easter Term, a new system will be introduced on an experimental basis. This will involve the following changes to current procedures:

1. Upon setting down an application for hearing by a single Lord Justice, the following documents are to be lodged *in triplicate*: (a) the summons or, where the application is ex parte, the notice setting out the nature of the application; (b) the order under appeal; (c) in the case of an application for leave to appeal, the order of the court below refusing such leave; (d) the affidavit in support of the application, containing, in the case of an application for leave to appeal, the grounds of the proposed appeal.

2. A hearing date will no longer be given at the time of setting down. In the case of an inter partes application, notice of application should be served on the respondent(s) endorsed 'date and time to be notified by the Civil Appeals Office'.

3. Any further documents in support of the application must be lodged with the Civil Appeals General Office (Room 246) within 10 days of the date on which the application is set down, after which, unless the court directs that any further documents are to be filed, a hearing date will be fixed.

4. The Civil Appeals Office will notify the applicant and, in the case of inter partes applications, the respondent(s) of the time and date on which the application is to be heard.

18 March 1985

Practice Direction
[1986] 1 A11 ER 983, [1986] 1 WLR 475
Minor: Preventing removal abroad

The Child Abduction Act 1984 came into force in October 1984. Section 1 of the Act which relates to England and Wales provides that in relation to a child under 16 (and subject to certain exceptions) an offence is committed by (a) a parent or guardian of the child, or (b) a person to whom custody has been awarded by a court in England and Wales, or (c) if the child is illegitimate, a person in respect of whom there are reasonable grounds for believing that he is the father, if that person takes or sends the child out of the United Kingdom (i) without the consent of each person who is a parent or guardian or to whom sole or joint custody has been awarded by a court in England and Wales, or (ii) if the child is the subject of a custody order, without the leave of the court which made the order, or (iii) without leave of the court having been obtained under the Guardianship of Minors Acts 1971 and 1973. For the purposes of the Act of 1984, the term 'custody' includes 'care and control.'

Under section 2 of the Act, an offence is also committed in relation to a child under the age of 16 by any person who is not a parent or guardian or a person to whom custody has been granted if without lawful authority or reasonable excuse he takes or detains the child (a) so as to remove him from the lawful control of any person having such lawful control or (b) so as to keep him out of the lawful control of any person entitled thereto.

With effect from 2 May 1986 ports will be informed directly by the police (instead of the Home Office) when there is a real threat that a child is about to be removed unlawfully from the country. The police will provide a 24 hour service and will liaise with immigration officers at the ports in an attempt to identify children at risk of removal. It is not necessary first to obtain a court order in respect of a child under 16 before police assistance is sought. If an order has been obtained, however, it should be produced to them. Where the child is between the ages of 16 and 18, it will be an essential prerequisite that an order is obtained which restricts or restrains removal, or confers custody.

No ward, however, may be removed from the jurisdiction without the leave of the court. Evidence will need to be produced to the police that the child is a ward. This may either be an order confirming wardship, an injunction, or if no such order has been made, in cases of urgency, a sealed copy of the originating summons.

Any application for assistance to prevent a child's removal from the jurisdiction must be made by the applicant or his legal representative to a police station. This should normally be the applicant's local police station. However, in urgent cases, or where the wardship originating summons has just issued or where the court has just made the order relied on, contact may be made with any police station. If it is considered appropriate by the police, they will institute the 'port-alert' system to try to prevent removal from the jurisdiction.

Where the police are asked to institute a 'port-alert', they will need first to be satisfied that the danger of removal is *real* and *imminent*. 'Imminent' means within 24 to 48 hours and 'real' means that the port-alert is not being sought by or on behalf of the applicant merely by way of insurance.

The request for assistance should be accompanied by as much of the following information as possible.

The child: names, sex, date of birth, description, nationality, passport number (if known).

The person likely to remove: names, age, description, nationality, passport number (if known), relationship to child and whether child likely to assist him or her.

Person applying for a port-alert: names, relationship to child, nationality, telephone number (and solicitor's name and number if appropriate).

Likely destination

Likely time of travel and port of embarkation

Grounds for port-alert (as appropriate): 1. Suspected offence under section 1 of Child Abduction Act 1984; 2. Child subject to court order.

Details of person to whom the child should be returned if intercepted

If the police decide that the case is one in which the port-alert system should be used, the child's name will remain on the stop list for four weeks. After that time, it will be removed automatically unless a further application for a port stop is made.

Another measure which an interested party may take is to give notice in writing to the Passport Department, Home Office, that passport facilities should not be provided in respect of the minor either without leave of the court, or in cases other than wardship, the consent of the other parent, guardian, or person to whom custody or care and control has been granted, or the consent of the mother in the case of an illegitimate child.

The practice directions of 15 July 1963, *Practice Direction (Taking Child Out of Jurisdiction)* [1963] 1 WLR 947, of 18 July 1973, *Practice Direction (Child: Preventing Removal Abroad)* [1973] 1 WLR 1014, and of 20 July 1977, *Practice Direction (Ward: Removal from Jurisdiction)* [1977] 1 WLR 1018, are hereby cancelled.

Issued with the approval of the President and the concurrence of the Lord Chancellor.

B P Tickle
14 April 1986   Senior Registrar

Practice Direction
[1986] 1 FLR 630, [1986] Fam Law 258
Family Division: Long Vacation business

Business which will be taken at the Royal Courts of Justice during the Long Vacation will be:

(1) Injunctions.

(2) Committals to, and release from, prison.

(3) Custody, access or any other application relating to a child's welfare when the estimated length of hearing does not exceed one day.

(4) Any other matter which has been certified by a registrar as being fit for vacation business.

In any case falling within category (3), the estimate must be signed by the solicitor making the application or by counsel if instructed; it will only be in rare circumstances that a case, accepted for vacation hearing on the basis of an estimate of not more than one day but which takes longer, will be continued to be heard during the vacation after the first day.

In any case falling within category (4) a certificate signed by the solicitor making the application, or by counsel if instructed, must be supplied to the registrar that in his opinion (giving reasons) the matter is such that it must be dealt with during the vacation.

Whether the Clerk of the Rules lists an application within category

(3), or a registrar accepts as vacation business an application within category (4), will be entirely a matter for his discretion.

Issued with the approval of the President.

B P Tickle
16 May 1986   Senior Registrar

Practice Direction
[1986] 3 A11 ER 630, [1986] 1 WLR 1318
Appeals: Documentation

The purpose of this statement is to consolidate and expand the practice directions issued on 18 May 1983 (*Practice Note (Appeal: Documents)* [1983] 2 A11 ER 416) and 4 March 1985 (*Practice Note appeal: Documents)* [1985] 1 A11 ER 841) and at the same time to remind all concerned that it is the duty of those acting for appellants to ensure that the bundles of documents lodged for the use of the court comply with the relevant rules and directions. It is also their duty to lodge the bundles within the time limit prescribed by RSC Ord 59, r 9(1) (as amended). Neglect of these duties may lead to the appeal being struck out. Scrutiny of the bundles submitted has shown that there are certain errors and omissions which still occur very frequently. For that reason, attention is drawn, in particular, to the following requirements.

Transcripts
All transcripts lodged (whether of evidence or of the judgment) must be originals. Photocopies are not permitted: see *The Supreme Court Practice 1985*, paragraph 59/9/2.

Notes of judgment
In cases where there is no official transcript of the judge's judgment (eg county court cases and certain High Court hearings in chambers), either the judge's own note of his judgment must be submitted, or, where there is no such note, the counsel or solicitors who appeared in the court below must prepare an agreed note of the judge's judgment and submit it to him for his approval. A copy of the approved note of judgment must be included in each bundle. It should be noted, in the case of county court appeals, that concluding lines in the judge's notebook reading 'Judgment for the defendant with costs on scale 2' or the like are not 'the judge's own note of his judgment.' What is required is a note of the reasons for the decision.

In the majority of cases the county court judge gives an ex tempore judgment and, pending the introduction and supply of personal dictating machines, has no full written text of it. The same applies to those cases heard in the High Court for which no official transcript of judgment is available.

In all such cases a typed version of the appellant's counsel's note of the judgment (or the solicitor's note, if he appeared for the appellant in the court below) must be prepared, agreed with the other side, and submitted to the judge for his approval. Much delay has been caused in numerous cases by failure to put this in train promptly and expeditiously. To obviate such delays in future the following procedure must be adopted.

(i) Except where the county court judge handed down his judgment in writing, or it is known for certain that he has a full text of his reasoned decision, the appellant's solicitor should make arrangements for counsel's note of judgment (or, if the solicitor appeared in the court below, his own note) to be prepared, agreed with the other side, and then submitted to the judge, as soon as the notice of appeal has been served; he should not wait until the appeal has entered the List of Forthcoming Appeals. If that system is adopted, the approved note of judgment should be ready for inclusion in the bundles within the 14-day time limit for lodging documents, and no extension should be needed.

(ii) Where both sides were represented by counsel in the court below, it saves time if counsel for the appellant submits his note of judgment directly to counsel for the respondent.

(iii) Where the note of judgment has not been received back from the judge by the time the bundles are ready to be lodged, copies of the unapproved note of judgment should be lodged with the bundles; the approved note of judgment should then be substituted as soon as it is to hand.

(iv) In those cases where the appellant is appealing in person, counsel or solicitors for the other side must make available their notes of judgment, whether or not the appellant has himself made any note of the reasoned judgment.

County court notes of evidence

In county court cases a copy of the judge's notes of evidence must be bespoken from the county court concerned and a copy of these notes must be included in each bundle. Directives (Court Business 3/85, B1351, and 4/85, B1358, para. (3)) have been sent to county courts asking them to arrange for the notes of evidence to be transcribed as soon as the notice of appeal has been served on the county court registrar. The notes should then be ready for despatch to the appellant or his solicitors as soon as they formally request them and make provision for the copying charges. A directive (Court Business 4/85, B1358, para. (4)) has also been sent to county courts to the effect that the old practice which obtained in some county courts of refusing to make the notes of evidence available until counsel's agreed note of judgment has been submitted is to be discontinued.

Core bundles

In cases where the appellant seeks to place before the court bundles of documents comprising more than 100 pages, three copies of a core bundle containing the principal documents to which reference will be made must be lodged with the court. In such circumstances, it will not usually be necessary to lodge multiple copies of the main bundle. It will be sufficient if a single set of the full trial documents is lodged so that the court may refer to it if necessary.

Pagination and indexing

Bundles may be paginated clearly and there must be an index at the front of the bundle listing all the documents and giving the page references for each one. At present, many bundles are numbered merely by document. This is incorrect. Each page should be numbered individually and consecutively.

Binding of bundles

All the documents (with the exception of the transcripts) must be bound together in some form (eg. ring binder, plastic binder, or laced through holes in the top left-hand corner). Loose documents will not be accepted.

Legibility

All documents must be legible. In particular, care must be taken to ensure that the edges of pages are not cut off by the photocopying machine. If it proves impossible to produce adequate copies of individual documents, or if manuscript documents are illegible, typewritten copies of the relevant pages should also be interleaved at the appropriate place in the bundle.

Time limits

Time limits must be complied with and will be strictly enforced except where there are good grounds for granting an extension. The appellant's solicitor (or the appellant, if in person) should therefore set about preparing the bundles as soon as the notice of appeal has been lodged with the Civil Appeals Office (without waiting for the appeal to enter the List of Forthcoming Appeals); in that way, in most cases, the bundles should be ready to be lodged within the 14-day time limit prescribed by RSC Ord 59, r 9. An extension of time is unlikely to be obtained where the failure to lodge the bundles, transcripts, notes of judgment or notes of evidence within the prescribed time limit is due to failure on the part of the appellant's solicitors (or the appellant, if in person) to start soon enough on the preparation of the bundles or the obtaining of the other documents.

Responsibility of the solicitor on the record

It seems likely that the work of documentation is often delegated to very junior members of the solicitor's staff, often without referring them to the relevant rule and practice direction. Delegation is not, as such, objectionable, but (a) the member of staff must be instructed fully on what is required and be capable of ensuring that these requirements are met, and (b) the solicitor in charge of the case must personally satisfy himself that the documentation is in order before it is delivered to the court. London agents too have a responsibility. They are not just postmen. They should be prepared to answer any questions which may arise as to the sufficiency of the documentation.

22 October 1986   Sir John Donaldson MR

Practice Direction
[1987] 1 A11 ER 546
Family Division: Filing Affidavits (No 3)

Difficulties are being experienced because of the late filing of affidavits in cases proceeding in the Principal Registry.

The President and judges of the Family Division require the attention of practitioners to be drawn to the practice set out in the Registrar's Direction[4] of 7 February 1984 ([1984] 1 A11 ER 684, [1984] 1 WLR 306). Failure to comply with this practice may result in costs being disallowed or being ordered to be paid by the solicitor personally. Affidavits which are lodged

4 See above.

in the Principal Registry within 14 days before the hearing date instead of being lodged in the Clerk of the Rules' Department or with the clerk to the registrar may not be considered at all by the judge or the registrar as the case may be.

20 February 1987

B P Tickle
Senior Registrar

Practice Direction
[1987] 1 A11 ER 1087, [1987] 1 WLR 316
Family Division: Business: Transfer

1. These directions are given under section 37 of the Matrimonial and Family Proceedings Act 1984 by the President of the Family Division, with the concurrence of the Lord Chancellor, and apply to all family proceedings which are transferrable between the High Court and county courts under sections 38 and 39 of that Act. They supersede the directions given on 28 April 1986, Practice Direction (Family Division: Transfer of Business.[5] They do not apply to proceedings under the following provisions (which may be heard and determined in the High Court alone):

(a) sections 45(1) of the Matrimonial Causes Act 1973 (declaration of legitimacy or validity of a marriage);
(b) the Guardianship of Minors Acts 1971 and 1973 in the circumstances provided by section 15(3) of the Guardianship of Minors Act 1971;
(c) section 14 of the Children Act 1975 where the child is not in Great Britain (freeing for adoption);
(d) section 24 of the Children Act 1975 or section 6 of the Adoption Act 1968 (Convention adoptions);
(e) Part III of the Matrimonial and Family Proceedings Act 1984;

to an application for an adoption order where the child is not in Great Britain, or to an application that a minor be made, or cease to be, a ward of court.

2.(1) Family proceedings to which these directions apply (including interlocutory proceedings) shall be dealt with in the High Court where it appears to the court seised of the case that by reason of the complexity, difficulty or gravity of the issues they ought to be tried in the High Court.
(2) Without prejudice to the generality of sub-paragraph (1), the following proceedings shall be dealt with in the High Court unless the nature of the issues of fact or law raised in the case makes them more suitable for trial in a county court than in the High Court:

(a) petitions under section 1(2)(*e*) of the Matrimonial Causes Act 1973 which are opposed pursuant to section 5 of that Act;
(b) petitions in respect of jactitation of marriage;
(c) petitions for presumption of death and dissolution of marriage under section 19 of the Matrimonial Causes Act 1973;
(d) proceedings involving a contested issue of domicile;

5 [1986] 2 A11 ER 703, [1986] 1 WLR 1139.

(e) applications under section 5(6) of the Domicile and Matrimonial Proceedings Act 1973;

(f) applications to restrain a resident from taking or continuing with foreign proceedings;

(g) proceedings for recognition of a foreign decree;

(h) suits in which the Queen's Proctor intervenes or shows cause and elects trial in the High Court;

(i) proceedings in relation to a ward of court:—(i) in which the Official Solicitor is or becomes the guardian ad litem of the ward or of a party to the proceedings; (ii) in which a local authority is or becomes a party; (iii) in which an application for blood tests is made; (iv) where any of the matters specified in (j) below are in issue;

(j) proceedings concerning children in divorce and under the Guardianship Acts where: (i) an application is opposed on the grounds of want of jurisdiction; (ii) there is a substantial foreign element; (iii) there is an opposed application for leave to take a child permanently out of the jurisdiction or where there is an application for temporary removal of a child from the jurisdiction and it is opposed on the ground that the child may not be duly returned;

(k) applications for adoption or for freeing for adoption (i) which are opposed on the grounds of want of jurisdiction; (ii) which would result in the acquisition by a child of British citizenship;

(l) interlocutory applications involving—(i) Anton Piller orders; (ii) Mareva injunctions; (iii) directions as to dealing with assets outside the jurisdiction.

3. In proceedings where periodical payments, a lump sum or property are in issue the court shall have regard in particular to the following factors when considering in accordance with paragraph 2(1) above whether the complexity, difficulty or gravity of the issues are such that they ought to be tried in the High Court—(a) the capital values of the assets involved and the extent to which they are available for, or susceptible to, distribution or adjustment; (b) any substantial allegations of fraud or deception or non-disclosure; (c) any substantial contested allegations of conduct. An appeal in such proceedings from a registrar in a county court shall be transferred to the High Court where it appears to the registrar, whether on application by a party or otherwise, that the appeal raises a difficult or important question whether of law or otherwise.

4. Subject to the foregoing, family proceedings may be dealt with in a county court.

5. Proceedings in the High Court which under the foregoing criteria fall to be dealt with in a county court or a divorce county court, as the case may be, and proceedings in a county court which likewise fall to be dealt with in the High Court shall be transferred accordingly, in accordance with rules of court, unless to do so would cause undue delay or hardship to any party or other person involved.

23 February 1987   Sir John Arnold P

B EXTRACTS FROM THE CAUSE LISTS

1 Term time 'matrimonial causes and matters'

Urgent applications

Applications for hearing in County Court matrimonial causes made on notice must be served on the other side at least two clear days before the return date. Urgent applications for injunctions may be fixed for 12 o'clock noon on any day on which the Court is sitting which allows for such notice. A copy of the notice of application must immediately be sent to the Clerk of the Rules quoting the title and number of the proceedings (or, if none, so stating).

Applications which are so urgent that notice cannot be given may be made ex parte in the above Court at 10.30 am or 2 o'clock pm or, in extreme urgency, by leave of the Judge at any other time. It is the duty of solicitors to bespeak the Court file, if any, from the Registry to the Court in time for such applications.

Except where required by rule or so directed by the Judges, all applications will be heard in Chambers.

Where a copy order is required for immediate personal service, application should be made to the office of the Clerk of the Rules immediately after the hearing of the matter. Unless such a request is made all orders will be sent to the Registry for copying and service in the normal way.

Other applications

Applications for hearing in Chambers in County Court matrimonial causes estimated not to exceed one half hour and not reserved to a particular Judge should be issued in the Principal Registry of the Family Division and will be returnable on every Monday or Tuesday.

Chambers' applications estimated to exceed one half hour or reserved to a particular Judge should be issued in the office of the Clerk of the Rules.

Any settlement or alteration in the estimated duration of the hearing of an application should be notified to the Clerk of the Rules immediately.

2 Vacation hearings

Family Division matters proceeding in the High Court

Leave for urgent summons to be listed for hearing by the vacation Judge must first be obtained from a Registrar of the Principal Registry of the Family Division. The return date should then be obtained from the Judge's Clerk, after which the summons should be taken to the Clerk of the Rules Department (Room 772) the Royal Courts of Justice for formal issue.

Matrimonial causes pending the divorce courts

A Circuit Judge will be available during the period   to deal with urgent applications the matrimonial causes proceeding in the Divorce Registry and treated as pending in a Divorce County Court and in the London Periphery Divorce County Courts. Enquiries should be made in the first instance to the Clerk of the Rules Department, Room 772, Royal Courts of Justice (telephone No (01) 405 7641, extension 3007 or 3188).

Leave to issue an urgent application by notice should be obtained from a Registrar of a Principal Registry of the Family Division, after which the application should be taken to the Clerk of the Rules Department for a date to be fixed and for a formal issue of the application.

A Circuit Judge will pronounce decrees under the special procedure (rule 48) throughout the vacation and will commence regular sittings at the Royal Courts of Justice to hear matrimonial causes pending in divorce County Courts on

Appendix 3
Rules of Court

Contents

A Rules of the Supreme Court 1965, SI 1965/1776 (as amended)

Order 2

1. (1) Where, in beginning or purporting to begin any proceedings or at any stage in the course of or in connection with any proceedings, there has, by reason of any thing done or left undone, been a failure to comply with the requirements of these rules, whether in respect of time, place, manner, form or content or in any other respect, the failure shall be treated as an irregularity and shall not nullify the proceedings, any step taken in the proceedings, or any document, judgment or order therein.

(2) Subject to paragraph (3) the Court may, on the ground that there has been such a failure as is mentioned in paragraph (1) and on such terms as to costs or otherwise as it thinks just, set aside either wholly or in part the proceedings in which the failure occurred, any step taken in those proceedings or any document, judgment or order therein or exercise its powers under these rules to allow such amendments (if any) to be made and to make such order (if any) dealing with the proceedings generally as it thinks fit.

(3) . . .

2. (1) An application to set aside for irregularity any proceedings, any step taken in any proceedings or any document, judgment or order therein shall not be allowed unless it is made within a reasonable time and before the party applying has taken any fresh step after becoming aware of the irregularity.

(2) An application under this rule may be made by summons or motion and the grounds of objection must be stated in the summons or notice of motion.

Order 3

1. Without prejudice to section 5 of the Interpretation Act 1978, in its application to these rules, the word 'month,' where it occurs in any judgment, order, direction or other document forming part of any proceedings in the Supreme Court, means a calendar month unless the context otherwise requires.

2. (1) Any period of time fixed by these rules or by any judgment, order or direction for doing any act shall be reckoned in accordance with the following provisions of this rule.

(2) Where the act is required to be done within a specified period after or from a specified date, the period begins immediately after that date.

(3) Where the act is required to be done within or not less than a specified period before a specified date, the period ends immediately before that date.

(4) Where the act is required to be done a specified number of clear days before or after a specified date, at least that number of days must intervene between the day on which the act is done and that date.

(5) Where, apart from this paragraph, the period in question, being a

period of 7 days or less, would include a Saturday, Sunday or bank holiday, Christmas Day or Good Friday, that day shall be excluded.

In this paragraph 'bank holiday', means a day which is, or is to be observed as, a bank holiday or a holiday, under the Banking and Financial Dealings Act 1971, in England and Wales.

3. Unless the court otherwise directs, the month of August shall be excluded in reckoning any period prescribed by these rules or by any order or direction for serving, filing or amending any pleading.

4. Where the time prescribed by these rules, or by any judgment, order or direction, or doing any act at an office of the Supreme Court expires on a Sunday or other day on which that office is closed, and by reason thereof that act cannot be done on that day, the act shall be in time if done on the next day on which that office is open.

5. (1) The court may, on such terms as it thinks just, by order extend or abridge the period within which a person is required or authorised by these rules, or by any judgment, order or direction, to do any act in any proceedings.

(2) The court may extend any such period as is referred to in paragraph (1) although the application for extension is not made until after the expiration of that period.

(3) The period within which a person is required by these rules, or by any order or direction, to serve, file or amend any pleading or other document may be extended by consent (given in writing) without an order of the court being made for that purpose.

(4) In this rule references to the court shall be construed as including references to the Court of Appeal, a single judge of that court and the registrar of civil appeals.

Order 4
9. Where two or more causes or matters are pending in the same Division, then, if it appears to the court—
    (a) that some common question of law or fact arises in both or all of them, or
    (b) that the rights to relief claimed therein are in respect of or arise out of the same transaction or series of transactions, or
    (c) that for some other reason it is desirable to make an order under this rule
the court may order those causes or matters to be consolidated on such terms as it thinks just or may order them to be tried at the same time or one immediately after another or may order any of them to be stayed until after the determination of any other of them.

Order 7
1. The provisions of this Order apply to all originating summonses subject, in the case of originating summonses of any particular class, to any special

provisions relating to originating summonses of that class made by these Rules or by or under any Act.

2.(1) Every originating summons (other than an ex parte summons) shall be in Form No 8 or, if so authorised or required, in Form No 10 in Appendix A, and every ex parte originating summons shall be in Form No 11 in Appendix A.

(2) The party taking out an originating summons (other than an ex parte summons) shall be described as a plaintiff, and the other parties shall be described as defendants.

3. (1) Every originating summons must include a statement of the questions on which the plaintiff seeks the determination or direction of the High Court or, as the case may be, a concise statement of the relief or remedy claimed in the proceedings begun by the originating summons with sufficient particulars to identify the cause or causes of action in respect of which the plaintiff claims that relief or remedy.

(2) . . .

Order 10

1. (1) A writ must be served personally on each defendant by the plaintiff or his agent.

(2) A writ for service on a defendant within the jurisdiction may, instead of being served personally on him, be served—

(a) by sending a copy of the writ by ordinary first-class post to the defendant at his usual or last known address, or

(b) if there is a letter box for that address, by inserting through the letter box a copy of the writ enclosed in a sealed envelope addressed to the defendant.

In sub-paragraph (a) 'first-class post' means first-class post which has been pre-paid or in respect of which prepayment is not required.

(3) Where a writ is served in accordance with paragraph (2)—

(a) the date of service shall, unless the contrary is shown, be deemed to be the seventh day (ignoring Order 3, rule 2(5)) after the date on which the copy was sent to or, as the case may be, inserted through the letter box for the address in question;

(b) any affidavit proving due service of the writ must contain a statement to the effect that—

(i) in the opinion of the deponent (or, if the deponent is the plaintiff's solicitor or an employee of that solicitor, in the opinion of the plaintiff) the copy of the writ, if sent to, or, as the case may be inserted through the letter box for, the address in question, will have come to the knowledge of the defendent within 7 days thereafter; and

(ii) in the case of service by post, the copy of the writ has not been returned to the plaintiff through the post undelivered to the addressee.

(4) Where a defendant's solicitor indorses on the writ a statement that he accepts service of the writ on behalf of that defendant, the writ shall be

deemed to have been duly served on that defendant and to have been so served on the date on which the indorsement was made.

(5) Subject to Order 12, rule 7, where a writ is not duly served on a defendant but he acknowledges service of it, the writ shall be deemed, unless the contrary is shown, to have been duly served on him and to have been so served on the date on which he acknowledges service.

(6) Every copy of a writ for service on a defendant shall be sealed with the seal of the office of the Supreme Court out of which the writ was issued and shall be accompanied by a form of acknowledgment of service in Form No 14 in Appendix A in which the title of the action and its number have been entered.

(7) This rule shall have effect subject to the provision of any Act and these rules and in particular to any enactment which provides for the manner in which documents may be served on bodies corporate.

5. (1) The foregoing rules of this Order shall apply, with any necessary modifications, in relation to an originating summons (other than ex parte originating summons or an originating summons under Order 113) as they apply in relation to a writ, except that an acknowledgment of service of an originating summons shall be in Form No 15 in Appendix A.

(2) Rule 1 (1) (2) (3) and (4) shall apply, with any necessary modifications, in relation to a notice of an originating motion and a petition as they apply in relation to a writ.

Order 28
1. The provisions of this Order apply to all originating summonses subject, in the case of originating summonses of any particular class, to any special provisions relating to originating summonses of that class made by these rules or by or under any Act; and, subject as aforesaid, Order 32, rule 5, shall apply in relation to originating summonses as it applies in relation to other summonses.

1A. (1) In any cause or matter begun by originating summons (not being an ex parte summons) the plaintiff must, before the expiration of 14 days after the defendant has acknowledged service, or, if there are two or more defendants, at least one of them has acknowledged service, file with the office of the court out of which the summons was issued the affidavit evidence on which he intends to rely.

(2) In the case of an ex parte summons the applicant must file his affidavit evidence not less than 4 clear days before the day fixed for the hearing.

(3) Copies of the affidavit evidence filed in court under paragraph (1) must be served by the plaintiff on the defendant, or, if there are two or more defendants, on each defendant, before the expiration of 14 days after service has been acknowledged by that defendant.

(4) Where a defendant who has acknowledged service wishes to adduce affidavit evidence he must within 28 days after service on him of copies of the plaintiff's affidavit evidence under paragraph (3) file his own affidavit evidence in the office of the court out of which the summons is issued and

serve copies thereof on the plaintiff and on any other defendant who is
affected thereby.

(5) A plaintiff on whom a copy of a defendant's affidavit evidence has
been served under paragraph (4) may within 14 days of such service file in
court further affidavit evidence in reply and shall in that event serve copies
thereof on that defendant.

(6) No other affidavit shall be received in evidence without the leave of
the court.

(7) Where an affidavit is required to be served by one party on another
party it shall be served without prior charge.

(8) The provisions of this rule apply subject to any direction by the court
to the contrary.

(9) In this rule references to affidavits and copies of affidavits include
references to exhibits to affidavits and copies of such exhibits.

2. (1) In the case of an originating summons which is in Form No 8 in
Appendix A the plaintiff must, within one month of the expiry of the time
within which copies of affidavit evidence may be served under rule 1A
obtain an appointment for the attendance of the parties before the court
for the hearing of the summons, and a day and time for their attendance
shall be fixed by a notice (in Form No 12 in Appendix A) sealed with the
seal of the district registry (if any) in which the cause or matter is proceeding and, where the cause or matter is not proceeding in such a registry,
sealed with the seal—

(a) of the central office, where the cause or matter is assigned to the
Queen's Bench Division;
(b) of Chancery Chambers, where the cause or matter is assigned to
the Chancery Division;
(c) of the principal registry of the Family Division, where the cause or
matter is assigned to the Family Division.

(2) A day and time for the attendance of the parties before the court
for the hearing of an originating summons which is in Form No 10 in
Appendix A, or for the hearing of an ex parte originating summons, may
be fixed on the application of the plaintiff or applicant, as the case may be
and, in the case of a summons which is required to be served, the time
limited for acknowledging service shall, where appropriate, be abridged so
as to expire on the next day but one before the day so fixed, and the time
limits for lodging affidavits under rule 1A(2) and (3) shall, where
appropriate, be abridged so as to expire, respectively, on the fifth day
before, and the next day but one before, the day so fixed.

(3) Where a plaintiff fails to apply for an appointment under paragraph
(1) any defendant may, with the leave of the court, obtain an appointment
in accordance with that paragraph provided that he has acknowledged
service of the originating summons.

3. (1) . . .
(2) Not less than 4 clear days before the day fixed under rule 2 for the
hearing of an originating summons which is in Form No 10 in Appendix A,
the plaintiff must serve the summons on every defendant or, if any defendant has already been served with the summons, must serve on that
defendant notice of the day fixed for hearing.

6. Where in a cause or matter begun by originating summons an application is made to the court for an order affecting a party who has failed to acknowledge service, the court hearing the application may require to be satisfied in such manner as it thinks fit that the party has so failed.

Order 29

1. (1) An application for the grant of an injunction may be made by any party to a cause or matter before or after the trial of the cause of matter, whether or not a claim for the injunction was included in that party's writ, originating summons, counterclaim or third party notice, as the case may be.

(2) Where the applicant is the plaintiff and the case is one of urgency such application may be made ex parte on affidavit but, except as aforesaid, such application must be made by motion or summons.

(3) The plaintiff may not make such an application before the issue of the writ or originating summons by which the cause or matter is to be begun except where the case is one of urgency, and in that case the injunction applied for may be granted on terms providing for the issue of the writ or summons and such other terms, if any, as the court thinks fit.

2. (1) On the application of any party to a cause or matter the court may make an order for the detention, custody or preservation of any property which is the subject-matter of the cause or matter, or as to which any question may arise therein, or for the inspection of any such property in the possession of a party to the cause or matter.

(2) For the purpose of enabling any order under paragraph (1) to be carried out the court may by the order authorise any person to enter upon any land or building in the possession of any party to the cause or matter.

(3) Where the right of any party to a specific fund is in dispute in a cause or matter, the court may, on the application of a party to the cause or matter, order the fund to be paid into court or otherwise secured.

(4) An order under this rule may be made on such terms, if any, as the court thinks just.

(5) An application for an order under this rule must be made by summons or by notice under Order 25, rule 7.

(6) Unless the court otherwise directs, an application by a defendant for such an order may not be made before he acknowledges service of the writ or originating summons by which the cause or matter was begun.

3. (1) Where it considers it necessary or expedient for the purpose of obtaining full information or evidence in any cause or matter, the court may, on the application of a party to the cause or matter, and on such terms, if any, as it thinks just, by order authorise or require any sample to be taken of any property which is the subject-matter of the cause or matter or as to which any question may arise therein, any observation to be made on such property or any experiment to be tried on or with such property.

(2) For the purpose of enabling any order under paragraph (1) to be carried out the court may by the order authorise any person to enter upon any land or building in the possession of any party to the cause or matter.

(3) Rule 2(5) and (6) shall apply in relation to an application for an order under this rule as they apply in relation to an application for an order under that rule.

Order 32

1. Except as provided by Order 25, rule 7, every application in chambers not made ex parte must be made by summons.

2. (1) Issue of a summons by which an application in chambers is to be made takes place on its being sealed by an officer of the appropriate office.

(2) A summons may not be amended after issue without the leave of the court.

(3) In this rule 'the appropriate office' means—

(a) in relation to a summons in a cause or matter proceeding in a district registry, that registry;

(b) in relation to a cause or matter in the Chancery Division which is not proceeding in a district registry, Chancery Chambers;

(c) in relation to a summons in a cause or matter proceeding in the principal registry of the Family Division, that registry;

(d) in relation to a summons in an Admiralty cause or matter which is not proceeding in a district registry, the Admiralty Registry;

(e) in relation to a summons in any other cause or matter, the Central Office.

For the purposes of this paragraph, a cause or matter in which any jurisdiction is to be exercised by virtue of Order 34, rule 5(4) by a master or by the registrar of a district registry shall be treated, in relation to that jurisdiction, as proceeding in the Central Office, Chancery Chambers or that district registry as the case may be.

3. A summons asking only for the extension or abridgment of any period of time may be served on the day before the day specified in the summons for the hearing thereof but, except as aforesaid and unless the court otherwise orders or any of these rules otherwise provides, a summons must be served on every other party not less than two clear days before the day so specified.

4. (1) The hearing of a summons may be adjourned from time to time, either generally or to a particular date, as may be appropriate.

(2) If the hearing is adjourned generally, the party by whom the summons was taken out may restore it to the list on two clear days' notice to all the other parties on whom the summons was served.

5. (1) Where any party to a summons fails to attend on the first or any resumed hearing thereof, the court may proceed in his absence if, having regard to the nature of the application, it thinks it expedient so to do.

(2) Before proceeding in the absence of any party the court may require to be satisfied that the summons or, as the case may be, notice of the time appointed for the resumed hearing was duly served on that party.

(3) Where the court hearing a summons proceeded in the absence of a party, then, provided that any order made on the hearing has not been perfected, the court, if satisfied that it is just to do so, may re-hear the summons.

(4) Where an application made by summons has been dismissed without a hearing by reason of the failure of the party who took out the summons to attend the hearing, the court, if satisfied that it is just to do so, may allow the summons to be restored to the list.

6. The court may set aside an order made ex parte.

11. (1) The masters of the Queen's Bench Division and the registrars of the Family Division shall have power to transact all such business and exercise all such authority and jurisdiction as under the Act or these rules may be transacted and exercised by a judge in chambers except in respect of the following matters and proceedings, that is to say—

(a) . . .

(b) . . .

(c) . . .

(d) subject to paragraph (2) Order 50, rule 9, and Order 51, rule 2, proceedings for the grant of an injunction or other order under section 37 of the Act;

(e) . . .

(f) . . .

(g) . . .

(h) . . .

(2) Any such master or registrar shall have power to grant an injunction in the terms agreed by the parties to the proceedings in which the injunction is sought.

Order 41

1. (1) Subject to paragraphs (2) and (3) every affidavit sworn in a cause or matter must be entitled in that cause or matter.

(2) Where a cause or matter is entitled in more than one matter, it shall be sufficient to state the first matter followed by words 'and other matters,' and where a cause or matter is entitled in a matter or matters and between parties, that part of the title which consists of the matter or matters may be omitted.

(3) Where there are more plaintiffs than one, it shall be sufficient to state the full name of the first followed by the words 'and others,' and similarly with respect to defendants.

(4) Every affidavit must be expressed in the first person and, unless the court otherwise directs, must state the place of residence of the deponent and his occupation or, if he has none, his description, and if he is, or is employed by, a party to the cause or matter in which the affidavit is sworn, the affidavit must state that fact.

In the case of a deponent who is giving evidence in a professional, business or other occupational capacity the affidavit may, instead of stating the deponent's place of residence, state the address at which he works, the position he holds and the name of his firm or employer, if any.

(5) Every affidavit must be bound in book form, and, whether or not both sides of the paper are used, the printed, written or typed sides of the paper must be numbered consecutively.

(6) Every affidavit must be divided into paragraphs numbered consecutively, each paragraph being as far as possible confined to a distinct portion of the subject.

(7) Dates, sums and other numbers must be expressed in an affidavit in figures and not in words.

(8) Every affidavit must be signed by the deponent and the jurat must be completed and signed by the person before whom it is sworn.

5. (1) Subject to Order 14, rules 2(2) and 4(2) to Order 86, rule 2(1) to paragraph (2) of this rule and to any order made under Order 38, rule 3, an affidavit may contain only such facts as the deponent is able of his own knowledge to prove.

(2) An affidavit sworn for the purpose of being used in interlocutory proceedings may contain statements of information or belief with the sources and grounds thereof.

11. (1) Any document to be used in conjunction with an affidavit must be exhibited, and not annexed, to the affidavit.

(2) Any exhibit to an affidavit must be identified by a certificate of the person before whom the affidavit is sworn.

The certificate must be entitled in the same manner as the affidavit and rule 1(1) (2) and (3) shall apply accordingly.

Order 45

5. (1) Where—
   (a) A person required by a judgment or order to do an act within a time specified in the judgment or order refuses or neglects to do it within that time or as the case may be within the time as extended or abridged under Order 3, rule 5 or
   (b) A person disobeys a judgment or order requiring him to abstain from doing an act,

then subject to the provision of these rules the judgment or order may be enforced by one or more of the following means, that is to say—

   . . .

   (iii) Subject to the provision of the Debtors Acts 1869 and 1878 an order or committal against that person or, where that person is a body corporate, against any such officer.

6. (1) Notwithstanding that a judgment or order requiring a person to do an act specifies a time within which the act is to be done, the court shall, without prejudice to Order 3, rule 5, have power to make an order requiring the act to be done within another time, being such time after service of that order, or such other time, as may be specified therein.

(2) Where, notwithstanding Order 42, rule 2(1) or by reason of Order 42, rule 2(2) a judgment or order requiring a person to do an act does not specify a time within which the act is to be done, the court shall have power subsequently to make an order requiring the act to be done within such time after service of that order, or such other time, as may be specified therein.

(3) An application for an order under this rule must be made by summons and the summons must, notwithstanding anything in Order 65, rule 9, be served on the person required to do the act in question.

7. (1) In this rule, references to an order shall be construed as including references to a judgment.

(2) Subject to Order 24, rule 16(3), Order 26, rule 6(3) and paragraph (6) and (7) of this rule, an order shall not be enforced under rule 5 unless—
   (a) A copy of the order has been served personally on the person required to do or abstain from doing the act in question and
   (b) In the case of an order requiring a person to do an act, the copy has been so served before the expiration of the time within which he was required to do the act.

(4) There must be indorsed on a copy of an order served under this rule a notice informing the person on whom the copy is served—
   (a) In the case of service under paragraph (2) that if he neglects to obey the order within the time specified therein, or, if the order is to abstain from doing any act, that if he disobeys the order, he is liable to process of execution to compel him to obey it.

(5) With the copy of an order required to be served under this rule,

being an order requiring a person to do an act, there must also be served a copy of any order made under Order 3, rule 5, extending or abridging the time for doing the act and, where the first mentioned order was made under rule 5(3) or 6 of this Order, a copy of the previous order requiring the act to be done.

(6) An order requiring a person to abstain from doing an act may be enforced under rule 5 notwithstanding that service of a copy of the order has not been affected in accordance with this rule if the court is satisfied that, pending such service, the person against whom or against whose property it is sought to enforce the order has had notice thereof either—

(a) By being present when the order was made, or
(b) By being notified of the service of the order, whether by telephone, telegram or otherwise.

(7) Without prejudice to its powers under Order 65, rule 4, the court may dispense with service of a copy of an order under this rule if it thinks it just to do so.

Order 52

1. (3) Where contempt of court is committed in connection with any proceedings in the High Court, then, subject to paragraph (2), an order of committal may be made by a single judge of the Queen's Bench Division except where the proceedings were assigned or subsequently transferred to some other Division, in which case the order may be made by a single judge of that other Division.

The reference in this paragraph to a single judge of the Queen's Bench Division shall, in relation to proceedings in any court the judge or judges of which are, when exercising the jurisdiction of that Court, deemed by virtue of any enactment to constitute a court of the High Court, be construed as a reference to a judge of that court.

4. (1) Where an application for an order of committal may be made to a court other than a Divisional Court, the application must be made by motion and be supported by an affidavit.

(2) Subject to paragraph (3), the notice of motion, stating the grounds of the application and accompanied by a copy of the affidavit in support of the application, must be served personally on the person sought to be committed.

(3) Without prejudice to its powers under Order 65, rule 4, the court may dispense with service of the notice of motion under this rule if it thinks it just to do so.

5. Nothing in the foregoing provisions of this Order shall be taken as affecting the power of the High Court or the Court of Appeal to make an order of committal of its own motion against a person guilty of contempt of court.

6. (1) Subject to paragraph (2), the court hearing an application for an order for committal may sit in private in the following cases, that is to say—

(a) Where the application arises out of proceedings relating to the wardship or adoption of an infant or wholly or mainly to the guardianship, custody, maintenance or upbringing of an infant, or right of access to an infant;
(b) Where the application arises out of proceedings relating to a person suffering or appearing to be suffering from mental disorder within the meaning of the Mental Health Act 1983;

(c) Where the application arises out of proceedings in which a secret process, discovery or invention was in issue;

(d) Where it appears to the court that in the interests of the administration of justice or for reasons of national security the application must be heard in private;

But, except as aforesaid, the application should be heard in open court.

(2) If the court hearing an application in private by virtue of paragraph (1) decides to make an order of committal against the person sought to be committed, it shall in open court state—

(a) The name of that person,

(b) In general terms the nature of the contempt of court in respect of which the order is being made, and

(c) The length of the period for which he is being committed.

(3) Except with the leave of the court hearing an application for an order of committal, no grounds shall be relied upon at the hearing except the grounds set out in the statement under rule 2 or, as the case may be, in the notice of motion under rule 4.

The foregoing provision is without prejudice to the powers of the court under Order 20, rule 8.

(4) If on the hearing of the application the person sought to be committed expresses a wish to give oral evidence on his own behalf, he shall be entitled to do so.

7. (1) The court by whom an order of committal is made may by order direct that the execution of the order of committal shall be suspended for such period or on such terms or conditions as it may specify.

(2) Where execution of an order of committal is suspended by an order under paragraph (1), the applicant for the order of commital must, unless the court otherwise directs, serve on the person against whom it was made a notice informing him of the making and the terms of the order under that paragraph.

8. (1) The court may, on the application of any person committed to prison for any contempt of court, discharge him.

(2) Where a person has been committed for failing to comply with a judgment or order requiring him to deliver any thing to some other person or to deposit it in court or elsewhere, and a writ of sequestration has also been issued to enforce that judgment or order, then if the thing is in the custody or power of the person committed, the commissioners appointed by the writ of sequestration may take possession of it as if it were the property of that person and, without prejudice to the generality of paragraph (1), the court may discharge the person committed and may give such directions as it thinks fit.

Order 59

1. This Order applies, subject to the provisions of these rules with respect to particular appeals, to every appeal to the Court of Appeal (including so far as it is applicable thereto, any appeal to that court from an official referee, master or other officer of the Supreme Court or from any tribunal from which an appeal lies to that court under or by virtue of any enactment) not being an appeal for which other provision is made by these rules and references to 'the court below' apply to any court, tribunal or person from which such an appeal lies.

2. This Order (except so much of rule 3(1) as provides that an appeal shall be by way of rehearing and except rule 11(1) applies to an application to the Court of Appeal for a new trial or to set aside a verdict, finding or judgment after trial with or without a jury, as it applies to an appeal to that court, and references in this Order to an appeal and to an appellant shall be construed accordingly.

2A. In this Order 'a single judge' means a single judge of the Court of Appeal and 'registrar' means the registrar of civil appeals.

3. (1) An appeal to the Court of Appeal shall be by way of rehearing and must be brought by motion, and the notice of the motion is referred to in this Order as 'notice of appeal.'

(2) Notice of appeal may be given either in respect of the whole or in respect of any specified part of the judgment or order of the court below; and every such notice must specify the grounds of the appeal and the precise form of the order which the appellant proposes to ask the Court of Appeal to make.

(3) Except with the leave of the Court of Appeal, a single judge or the registrar, the appellant shall not be entitled on the hearing of an appeal to rely on any grounds of appeal, or to apply for any relief, not specified in the notice of appeal.

(4) Every notice of appeal must specify the list of appeals in which the appellant proposes that the appeal shall be set down.

(5) A notice of appeal must be served on all parties to the proceedings in the court below who are directly affected by the appeal; and, subject to rule 8, it shall not be necessary to serve the notice on parties not so affected.

(6) No notice of appeal shall be given by a respondent in a case to which rule 6(1) relates.

4. (1) Except as otherwise provided by this Order, every notice of appeal must be served under r 3(5) within 4 weeks from the date on which the judgment or order of the court below was sealed or otherwise perfected.

(2) . . .

(3) Where leave to appeal is granted by the Court of Appeal upon an application made within the time limited for serving notice of appeal under paragraph (1), a notice of appeal may, instead of being served within that time, be served within 7 days after the date when leave is granted.

5. (1) Within 7 days after the later of (i) the date on which service of the notice of appeal was affected, or (ii) the date on which the judgment or order of the court below was sealed or otherwise perfected, the appellant must lodge with the registrar—

  (a) a copy of the said judgment or order, and
  (b) two copies of the notice of appeal, one of which shall be indorsed with the amount of the fee paid, and the other indorsed with a certificate of the date of service of the notice, and

(2) Upon the said documents being left, the registrar shall file one copy of the notice of appeal and cause the appeal to be set down in the proper list of appeals; and the appeal shall come on to be heard according to its order in that list unless the Court of Appeal or a single judge or the registrar otherwise orders.

(3) The proper list of appeals for the purpose of paragraph (2) shall be decided by the registrar, without prejudice, however, to any decision of the Court of Appeal on the question whether the judgment or order appealed

against is interlocutory or final.

(4) Within 4 days after an appeal has been set down, the appellant must give notice to that effect to all parties on whom the notice of appeal was served, specifying the list in which the appeal is set down.

6. (1) A respondent who, having been served with a notice of appeal, desires—

    (a) to contend on the appeal that the decision of the court below should be varied, either in any event or in the event of the appeal being allowed in whole or in part, or

    (b) to contend that the decision of the court below should be affirmed on grounds other than those relied upon by that court, or

    (c) to contend by way of cross-appeal that the decision of the court below was wrong in whole or in part,

must give notice to that effect, specifying the grounds of his contention and, in a case to which paragraph (a) or (c) relates, the precise form of the order which he proposes to ask the court to make.

(2) Except with the leave of the Court of Appeal or a single judge or the registrar a respondent shall not be entitled on the hearing of the appeal to apply for any relief not specified in a notice under paragraph (1) or to rely, in support of any contention, upon any ground which has not been specified in such a notice or relied upon by the court below.

(3) Any notice given by a respondent under this rule (in this Order referred to as a 'respondent's notice') must be served on the appellant, and on all parties to the proceedings in the court below who are directly affected by the contentions of the respondent, and must be served within 21 days after the service of the notice of appeal on the respondent.

(4) A party by whom a respondent's notice is given must, within two days after a service of the notice, furnish two copies of the notice to the registrar.

7. (1) A notice of appeal or respondent's notice may be amended—

    (a) by or with the leave of the Court of Appeal, a single judge or the registrar, at any time;

    (b) without such leave, by supplementary notice served, before the date on which the appeal first appears in the List of Forthcoming Appeals referred to in r 9(1) on each of the parties on whom the notice to be amended was served.

(2) A party by whom a supplementary notice is served under this rule must, within 2 days after service of the notice, furnish two copies of the notice to the registrar.

8. (1) The Court of Appeal or a single judge or the registrar may in any case direct that a notice of appeal or respondent's notice be served on any party to the proceedings in the court below on whom it has not been served; or on any person not party to those proceedings.

(2) Where a direction is given under paragraph (1) the hearing of the appeal may be postponed or adjourned for such period and on such terms as may be just and such judgment may be given and such order made on the appeal as might have been given or made if the persons served in pursuance of the direction had originally been parties.

9. (1) Not more than 14 days after the appeal first appears in a list to be called 'the List of Forthcoming Appeals' the appellant must cause to be lodged with the registrar the number of copies for which paragraph (2) provides of each of the following documents, namely—

(a) the notice of appeal;

(b) the respondent's notice;

(c) any supplementary notice served under rule 7;

(d) the judgment or order of the court below;

(e) the originating process by which the proceedings in the court below were begun, any interlocutory or other related process which is the subject of the appeal, the pleadings (including particulars) if any, and, in the case of an appeal in an Admiralty cause or matter, the preliminary acts, if any;

(f) the transcript of the official shorthand note or record, if any, of the judge's reasons for giving the judgment or making the order of the court below or, in the absence of such a note or record, the judge's note of his reasons or, if the judge's note is not available, counsel's note of the judge's reasons approved wherever possible by the judge;

(g) such parts of the transcript of the official shorthand note or record, if any, of the evidence given in the court below as are relevant to any question at issue on the appeal or, in the absence of such a note or record, such parts of the judge's note of the evidence as are relevant to any such question;

(h) any list of exhibits made under Order 35, rule 11, or the schedule of evidence, as the case may be;

(i) such affidavits, exhibits, or parts of exhibits, as were in evidence in the court below and as are relevant to any question at issue on the appeal.

(2) Unless otherwise directed, the number of copies to be lodged in accordance with paragraph (1) is three copies except—

(a) where the appeal is to be heard by two judges in which case it is two copies; or

(b) in the case of an appeal in an Admiralty cause or matter, in which case it is four copies or, if the Court of Appeal is to hear the appeal with assessors, six.

(2A) When the transcripts, if any, referred to in items (f) and (g) of paragraph (1) have been bespoken by the appellant and paid for, the number of such transcripts required in accordance with paragraph (2) shall be sent by the official shorthand writer or transcriber direct to the registrar.

(3) At any time after an appeal has been set down in accordance with rule 5 the registrar may give such directions in relation to the documents to be produced at the appeal, and the manner in which they are to be presented, and as to other matters incidental to the conduct of the appeal, as appear best adapted to secure the just, expeditious and economical disposal of the appeal.

(4) The directions referred to in paragraph (3) may be given without a hearing provided always that the registrar may at any time issue a summons requiring the parties to an appeal to attend before him and any party to an appeal may apply at any time for an appointment before the registrar.

10. (1) In relation to an appeal the Court of Appeal shall have all the powers and duties as to amendment and otherwise of the High Court including, without prejudice to the generality of the foregoing words, the powers of the court under Order 36 to refer any question or issue of fact for trial before, or inquiry and report by, an official referee.

In relation to a reference made to an official referee, any thing required or authorised under Order 36, rule 9, to be done by, to or before the court shall be done by, to or before the Court of Appeal.

(2) The Court of Appeal shall have power to receive further evidence on questions of fact, either by oral examination in court, by affidavit, or by deposition taken before an examiner, but, in the case of an appeal from a judgment after trial or hearing of any cause or matter on the merits, no such further evidence (other than evidence as to matters which have occurred after the date of the trial or hearing) shall be admitted except on special grounds.

(3) The Court of Appeal shall have power to draw inferences of fact and to give any judgment and make any order which ought to have been given or made, and to make such further or other order as the case may require.

(4) The powers of the Court of Appeal under the foregoing provisions of this rule may be exercised notwithstanding that no notice of appeal or respondent's notice has been given in respect of any particular part of the decision of the court below or by any particular party to the proceedings in that court, or that any ground for allowing the appeal or for affirming or varying the decision of that court is not specified in such a notice; and the Court of Appeal may make any order, on such terms as the court thinks just, to ensure the determination on the merits of the real question in controversy between the parties.

(5) The Court of Appeal may, in special circumstances, order that such security shall be given for the costs of an appeal as may be just.

(6) The powers of the Court of Appeal in respect of an appeal shall not be restricted by reason of any interlocutory order from which there has been no appeal.

(7) Documents impounded by order of the Court of Appeal shall not be delivered out of the custody of that court except in compliance with an order of that court:

Provided that where a Law Officer or the Director of Public Prosecutions makes a written request in that behalf, documents so impounded shall be delivered into his custody.

(8) Documents impounded by order of the Court of Appeal, while in the custody of that court, shall not be inspected except by a person authorised to do so by an order of that court.

(9) In any proceedings incidental to any cause or matter pending before the Court of Appeal, the powers conferred by this rule in the court may be exercised by a single judge or the registrar.

Provided that the said powers of the Court of Appeal shall be exercisable only by that court or a single judge in relation to

(a) the grant, variation, discharge or enforcement of an injunction, or an undertaking given in lieu of an injunction; and

(b) the grant or lifting of a stay of execution or proceedings.

11. (1) On the nearing of any appeal the Court of Appeal may, if it thinks fit, make any such order as could be made in pursuance of an application for a new trial or to set aside a verdict, finding or judgment of the court below.

(2) The Court of Appeal shall not be bound to order a new trial on the ground of misdirection, or of the improper admission or rejection of evidence, or because the verdict of the jury was not taken upon a question which the judge at the trial was not asked to leave to them, unless in the opinion of the Court of Appeal some substantial wrong or miscarriage has been thereby occasioned.

(3) A new trial may be ordered on any question without interfering with the finding or decision on any other question; and if it appears to the Court of Appeal that any such wrong or miscarriage as is mentioned in paragraph (2) affects part only of the matter in controversy, or one or some only of the parties, the court may order a new trial as to that party only, or as to that party or those parties only, and give final judgment as to the remainder.

(4) . . .

(5) . . .

12. Where any question of fact is involved in an appeal, the evidence taken in the court below bearing on the question shall, subject to any direction of the Court of Appeal, or a single judge or the registrar, be brought before that court as follows—

(a) in the case of evidence taken by affidavit, by the production of a true copy of such affidavit;

(b) in the case of evidence given orally, by a copy of so much of the transcript of the official shorthand note as is relevant or by a copy of the judge's note, where he has intimated that in the event of an appeal his note will be sufficient, or by such other means as the Court of Appeal, or a single judge or the registrar, may direct.

13. (1) Except so far as the court below or the court of Appeal or a single judge may otherwise direct—

(a) an appeal shall not operate as a stay of execution or of proceedings under the decision of the court below;

(b) no intermediate act or proceeding shall be invalidated by an appeal.

(2) In an appeal from the High Court, interest for such time as execution has been delayed by the appeal shall be allowed unless the court otherwise orders.

14. (1) Unless otherwise directed, every application to the Court of Appeal, a single judge or the registrar which is not made ex parte must be made by summons and such summons must be served on the party or parties affected at least 2 clear days before the day on which it is heard or, in the case of an application which is made after the expiration of the time for appealing, at least 7 days before the day on which the summons is heard.

(2) Unless otherwise directed, any application to the Court of Appeal for leave to appeal (other than an application made after the expiration of the time for appealing) must be made ex parte in the first instance; but unless the application is then dismissed or it appears to that court that undue hardship would be caused by an adjournment, the court shall adjourn the application and give directions for the service of notice thereof on the party or parties affected.

(3) Where an ex parte application has been refused by the court below, an application for a similar purpose may be made to the Court of Appeal ex parte within 7 days after the date of the refusal.

(4) Wherever under these rules an application may be made either to the court below or to the Court of Appeal, it shall not be made in the first instance to the Court of Appeal, except where there are special circumstances which make it impossible or impracticable to apply to the court below.

(5) . . .

(6) . . .

(7) An application, not being an application for leave to appeal, which may be heard by a single judge shall unless otherwise directed be heard in chambers.

(8) An application which may under the provisions of this Order be heard by the registrar shall be heard in chambers.

(9) The registrar may refer to a single judge any matter which he thinks should properly be decided by a single judge, and, following such reference, the judge may either dispose of the matter or refer it back to the registrar with such direction as the single judge thinks fit.

(10) A single judge may refer to the Court of Appeal any matter which he thinks should properly be decided by that court, and, following such reference, that court may either dispose of the matter or refer it back to a single judge or the registrar, with such directions as that court thinks fit.

(11) An appeal shall lie to a single judge from any determination made by the registrar and shall be brought by way of fresh application made within 10 days of the determination appealed against.

(12) An appeal shall lie to the Court of Appeal from any determination by a single judge, not being the determination of an application for leave to appeal, and shall be brought by way of fresh application made within 10 days of the determination appealed against.

Provided that an appeal shall not lie to the Court of Appeal without the leave of that court in respect of a determination of the registrar which has been reviewed by a single judge.

15. (1) Without prejudice to the power of the Court of Appeal, a single judge or the registrar under Order 3, rule 5, to extend or abridge the time prescribed by any provision of this Order, the period for serving notice of appeal under rule 4 or for making application ex parte under rule 14(3) may be extended or abridged by the court below on application made before the expiration of that period.

19. (1) The following provisions of this rule shall apply to any appeal to the Court of Appeal from a county court other than an appeal against a decree nisi of divorce or nullity of marriage.

(2) The appellant must, within the time specified in rule 4, serve the notice of appeal on the registrar of the county court as well as on the party or parties required to be served under rule 3.

(3) In relation to the appeal rule 4(1) and rule 5(1) shall have effect as if for the words 'the date on which the judgment or order of the court below was sealed or otherwise perfected' there were substituted the words 'the date of the judgment or order of the court below.'

(4) It shall be the duty of the appellant to apply to the judge of the county court for a signed copy of any note made by him of the proceedings and of his decision, and to furnish that copy for the use of the Court of Appeal; and in default of production of such a note, or, if such a note is incomplete, in addition to such note, the Court of Appeal may hear and determine the appeal on any other evidence or statement of what occurred before the judge of the county court which appears to the Court of Appeal to be sufficient.

Except where the Court of Appeal or a single judge or the registrar of civil appeals otherwise directs, an affidavit or note by a person present in the county court shall not be used in evidence under this paragraph unless it was previously submitted to the judge for his comments.

(4A) . . .

(5) Rule 13(1)(a) shall not apply, but the appeal shall not operate as a stay of execution or of proceedings in the county court unless the judge of that court or the Court of Appeal so orders or unless, within 10 days after the date of the judgment or order appealed against, the appellant deposits a sum fixed by the judge not exceeding the amount of the money or the value of the property affected by the judgment or order, or gives such security for the said sum as the judge may direct.

(6) . . .

(7) In relation to any proceedings in the principal registry of the Family Division which by virtue of the matrimonial causes rules are treated as pending in a county court, paragraphs (1) to (5) shall have effect with the necessary modification as if the principal registry were a county court.

20. (1) In the case of an appeal to the Court of Appeal under section 13 of the Administration of Justice Act, 1960, the notice of appeal must be served on the proper officer of the court from whose order or decision the appeal is brought as well as on the party or parties required to be served under rule 3.

This paragraph shall not apply in relation to an appeal to which rule 19 applies.

(2) Where, in the case of an appeal under the said section 13 to the Court of Appeal or to the House of Lords from the Court of Appeal, the appellant is in custody, the Court of Appeal may order his release on his giving security (whether by recognizance, with or without sureties, or otherwise and for such reasonable sum as that court may fix) for his appearance within 10 days after the judgment of the Court of Appeal or, as the case may be, of the House of Lords on the appeal shall have been given, before the court from whose order or decision the appeal is brought unless the order or decision is reversed by that judgment.

(3) An application for the release of a person under paragraph (2) pending an appeal to the Court of Appeal or House of Lords under the said section 13 must be made by motion, and the notice of the motion must, at least 24 hours before the day named therein for the hearing, be served on the proper officer of the court from whose order or decision the appeal is brought and on all parties to the proceedings in that court who are directly affected by the appeal.

(4) Order 79, rule 9(6) (6A) (6B) and (8) shall apply in relation to the grant of bail under this rule by the Court of Appeal in a case of criminal contempt of court as they apply in relation to the grant of bail in criminal proceedings by the High Court, but with the substitution for references to a judge in chambers of references to the Court of Appeal and for references to the defendant of references to the appellant.

(5) When granting bail under this rule in a case of civil contempt of court, the Court of Appeal may order that the recognizance or other security to be given by the appellant or the recognizance of any surety shall be given before any person authorised by virtue of section 119 of the Magistrates' Courts Act 1980 to take a recognizance where a magistrates' court having power to take it has, instead of taking it, fixed the amount in which the principal and his sureties, if any, are to be bound.

An order by the Court of Appeal granting bail as aforesaid must be in Form 98 in Appendix A with the necessary adaptions.

(6) Where in pursuance of an order of the Court of Appeal under paragraph (5) of this rule a recognizance is entered into or other security given before any person, it shall be the duty of that person to cause the recognizance of the appellant or any surety or, as the case may be, a statement of the other security given, to be transmitted forthwith to the clerk of the court which committed the appellant; and a copy of such recognizance or statement shall at the same time be sent to the governor or keeper of the prison or other place of detention in which the appellant is detained, unless the recognizance or security was given before such governor or keeper.

(7) The jurisdiction of the Court of Appeal under section 13 of the Administration of Justice Act 1960 to hear and determine any appeal from an order or decision of the Crown Court dealing with an offence under section 6 of the Bail Act 1976 as if it were a contempt of court shall be exercised by the criminal division of the Court of Appeal.

(8) Subject to paragraph 7 the powers conferred on the Court of Appeal by paragraphs (2), (4), (5) and (6) of this rule may be exercised by a single judge.

Order 65

1. (1) Any document which by virtue of these rules is required to be served on any person need not be served personally unless the document is one which by an express provision of these rules or by order of the court is required to be so served.

(2) Paragraph (1) shall not affect the power of the court under any provision of these rules to dispense with the requirement for personal service.

2. Personal service of a document is effected by leaving a copy of the document with the person to be served.

4. (1) If, in the case of any document which by virtue of any provision of these rules is required to be served personally or a document to which Order 10, rule 1, applies, it appears to the court that it is impracticable for any reason to serve that document in the manner prescribed on that person, the court may make an order for substituted service of that document.

(2) An application for an order for substituted service may be made by an affidavit stating the facts on which the application is founded.

(3) Substituted service of a document, in relation to which an order is made under this rule, is effected by taking such steps as the court may direct to bring the document to the notice of the person to be served.

5. (1) Service of any document, not being a document which by virtue of any provision of these rules is required to be served personally or a document to which Order 10, rule 1, applies, may be effected—

(a) by leaving the document at the proper address of the person to be served, or
(b) by post, or
(c) where the proper address for service includes a numbered box at a document exchange, by leaving the document at that document exchange or at a document exchange which transmits documents every business day to that document exchange, or
(d) in such other manner as the court may direct.

In there rules 'document exchange' means any document exchange for the time being approved by the Lord Chancellor.

(2) For the purposes of this rule, and of section 7 of the Interpretation Act 1978, in its application to this rule, the proper address of any person on whom a document is to be served in accordance with this rule shall be the address for service of that person, but if at the time when service is effected that person has no address for service his proper address for the purposes aforesaid shall be—

    (a) in any case, the business address of the solicitor (if any) who is acting for him in the proceedings in connection with which service of the document in question is to be effected, or

    (b) in the case of an individual, his usual or last known address, or

    (c) in the case of indivuduals who are suing or being sued in the name of a firm, the principal or last known place of business of the firm within the jurisdiction, or

    (d) in the case of a body corporate, the registered or principal office of the body.

(2A) Any such document which is left at a document exchange in accordance with paragraph (1)(c) shall, unless the contrary is proved, be deemed to have been served on the same business day following the day on which it is left.

(3) Nothing in this rule shall be taken as prohibiting the personal service of any document or as affecting any enactment which provides for the manner in which documents may be served on bodies corporate.

In this rule 'business day' means any day other than a Saturday, a Sunday, Christmas Day, Good Friday or a bank holiday under the Banking and Financial Dealings Act 1971.

7. Any document (other than a writ of summons or other originating process) service of which is effected under rule 2 or under rule 5(1)(a) between 12 noon on a Saturday and midnight on the following day or after 4 in the afternoon on any other weekday shall, for the purpose of computing any period of time after service of that document, be deemed to have been served on the Monday following that Saturday or on the day following that other weekday, as the case may be.

8. Except as provided in Order 10, rule 1(3)(b) and Order 81, rule 3(2)(b) an affidavit of service of any document must state by whom the document was served, the day of the week and date on which it was served, where it was served and how.

9. Where by virtue of these rules any document is required to be served on any person but is not required to be served personally or in accordance with Order 10, rule 1(2) and at the time when service is to be effected that person is in default as to acknowledgment of service or has no address for service, the document need not be served on that person unless the court otherwise directs or any of these rules otherwise provides.

10. (1) No process shall be served or executed within the jurisdiction on a Sunday except, in case of urgency, with the leave of the court.

    (2) For the purposes of this rule 'process' includes a writ, judgment, notice, order, petition, originating or other summons or warrant.

Order 90
1. In this Order, 'principal registry' means the principal registry of the Family Division, and 'registrar' means a registrar of that Division.

2. All proceedings to which this Order relates shall be assigned to the Family Division and, except as provided by rules 3, 5 and 17, shall be begun in the principal registry.

2A. Unless the court otherwise directs in relation to any particular cause or matter or any particular document filed in a cause or matter, Order 63, r 4 shall apply to documents filed in the principal registry, or in a district registry in proceedings to which this Order relates, as it applies to documents filed in the Central Office.

3. (1) An application to make a minor a ward of court must be made by originating summons issued out of the principal registry or out of a district registry as defined by the matrimonial causes rules.

(2) Where there is no person other than the minor who is a suitable defendant, an application may be made ex parte to a registrar for leave to issue either an ex parte originating summons or an originating summons with the minor as defendant thereto; and, except where such leave is granted, the minor shall not be made a defendant to an originating summons under this rule in the first instance.

(3) Particulars of any summons under this rule issued in a district registry shall be sent by the district registrar to the principal registry for recording in the register of wards.

(3A) The date of the minor's birth shall, unless otherwise directed, be stated in the summons and the plaintiff shall—

    (a) on issuing the summons or before or at the first hearing thereof lodge in the registry out of which the summons issued a certified copy of the entry in the Register of Births or, as the case may be, in the Adopted Children Register relating to the minor, or

    (b) at the first hearing of the summons apply for directions as to proof of birth of the minor in some other manner.

(3B) The name of each party to the proceedings shall be qualified by a brief description in the body of the summons, of his interest in, or relationship to, the minor.

(4) Unless the court otherwise directs, the summons shall state the whereabouts of the minor or, as the case may be, that the plaintiff is unaware of his whereabouts.

(5) Every defendant other than the minor shall, forthwith after being served with the summons—

    (a) lodge in the registry out of which the summons issued a notice stating the address of the defendant and the whereabouts of the minor or, as the case may be, that the defendant is unaware of his whereabouts, and

    (b) unless the court otherwise directs, serve a copy of the notice on the plaintiff.

(6) Where any party other than the minor changes his address or becomes aware of any change in the whereabouts of the minor after the issue or, as the case may be, service of the summons, he shall, unless the court otherwise directs, forthwith lodge notice of the change in the registry out of which the summons issued and serve a copy of the notice on every other party.

(7) The summons shall contain a notice to the defendant informing him of the requirements of paragraphs (5) and (6).

(8) In this rule any reference to the whereabouts of a minor is a reference to the address at which and the person with whom he is living and any other information relevant to the question where he may be found.

3A. The power of the High Court to secure, through an officer attending upon the court, compliance with any direction relating to a ward of court may be exercised by an order addressed to the tipstaff.

4. (1) A minor who, by virtue of section 41 of the Supreme Court Act 1981, becomes a ward of court on the issue of a summons under rule 3 shall cease to be a ward of court—
- (a) if an application for an appointment for the hearing of the summons is not made within the period of 21 days after the issue of the summons, at the expiration of that period;
- (b) if an application for such an appointment is made within that period, on the determination of the application made by the summons unless the court hearing it orders that the minor be made a ward of court.

(2) Nothing in paragraph (1) shall be taken as affecting the power of the Court under section 41 of the said Act to order that any minor who is for the time being a ward of court shall cease to be a ward of court.

30. (1) An application to the High Court by a party to a marriage within the meaning of Section 1(1) of the Domestic Violence and Matrimonial Proceedings Act 1976 for an injunction containing one or more of the provisions mentioned in that sub-section shall, if no other relief is sought in the proceedings, be made by originating summons issued out of the Principal Registry or out of a District Registry as defined by the Matrimonial Causes Rules.

Any such summons shall be in Form 10 in Appendix A.

(2) A copy of any injunction to which a power of arrest has been attached under section 2 of the said Act of 1976 shall be delivered by the tipstaff to the officer for the time being in charge of any police station for the applicant's address.

(3) Where an order is made varying or discharging an injunction to which a power of arrest has been attached under the said section 2, a copy of the order shall be delivered by the tipstaff to the officer for the time being in charge of the police station at which time a copy of the injunction was delivered pursuant to paragraph (2) and, if the applicant has since changed her address, any police station for the new address, and a copy of the order shall be delivered to any officer so informed.

(4) The judge before whom a person arrested is brought pursuant to section 2(4) of the said Act of 1976 may exercise his power to punish him for disobedience to the injunction, notwithstanding that no copy of the injunction has been served on him in accordance with Order 45, rule 7(2) and that no application for an order of committal has been made (or notice of such an application has been served on him) pursuant to Order 52, rule 4.

31. Where a direction is given, under section 28 of the Domestic Proceedings and Magistrates' Courts Act 1978, that a magistrates' court to which a power of arrest is attached shall cease to have effect, the registrar shall immediately inform the officer for the time being in charge of the police station to which a copy of the magistrates' court order was sent, and, if the applicant for that order has since changed her address, any police station for the new address; and a copy of the direction shall be delivered to any officer so informed.

32. In this Part of this Order, unless the context otherwise requires:

(a) 'the Act' means the Child Abduction and Custody Act 1985 and words or expressions bear the same meaning as in the Act;

(b) 'the Hague Convention' means the convention defined in section 1(1) of the Act and 'the European Convention' means the convention defined in section 12(1) of the Act;

(c) 'the proper officer' means the Senior Registrar of the Family Division or any officer of the principal registry acting on his behalf.

33. (1) Except as otherwise provided by this Part, every application under the Hague Convention and the European Convention shall be made by originating summons, which shall be in Form No 10 in Appendix A.

(2) An application in custody proceedings for a declaration under section 23(2) of the Act shall be made by summons in those proceedings.

34. The originating summonms under which any application is made under the Hague Convention or the European Convention shall state—

(a) the name and date of birth of the child in respect of whom the application is made;

(b) the names of the child's parents or guardians;

(c) the whereabouts or suspected whereabouts of the child;

(d) the interest of the plaintiff in the matter and the grounds of the application; and

(e) particulars of any proceedings (including proceedings out of the jurisdiction and concluded proceedings) relating to the child,

and shall be accompanied by all relevant documents including but not limited to the documents specified in Article 8 of the Hague Convention or, as the case may be, Article 13 of the European Convention.

35. (1) In applications under the Hague Cpnvention, in addition to the matters specified in rule 34—

(a) the originating summons under which an application is made for the purposes of Article 8 for the return of a child shall state the identity of the person alleged to have removed or retained the child and, if different, the identity of the person with whom the child is presumed to be;

(b) the originating summons under which an application is made for the purposes of Article 15 for a declaration shall identify the proceedings in which the request that such a declaration be obtained was made.

(2) In applications under the European Convention, in addition to the matters specified in rule 34 the originating summons shall identify the decision relating to custody or rights of access which is sought to be registered or enforced or in relation to which a declaration that it is not to be recognised is sought.

36. The defendants to an application under the Act shall be—

(a) the person alleged to have brought into the United Kingdom the child in respect of whom an application under the Hague Convention is made;

(b) the person with whom the child is alleged to be;

(c) any parent or guardian of the child who is within the United Kingdom and is not otherwise a party,

(d) the person in whose favour a decision relating to custody has been made if he is not otherwise a party, and

(e) any other person who appears to the court to have a sufficient interest in the welfare of the child.

37. Notwithstanding Order 12, rule 9, the time limited for acknowledging service of an originating summons by which an application is made under the Hague Convention or the European Convention shall be seven days after service of the originating summons (including the day of service) or, in the case of a defendant referred to in rule 36(*d*) or (*e*), such further time as the court may direct.

38. Notwithstanding Order 28, rule 1A—

    (a) the plaintiff, on issuing an originating summons under the Hague Convention or the European Convention, may lodge affidavit evidence in the principal registry in support of his application and serve a copy of the same on the defendant with the originating summons;

    (b) a defendant to an application under the Hague Convention may lodge affidavit evidence in the principal registry and serve a copy of the same on the plaintiff within seven days after service of the originating summons on him;

    (c) the plaintiff in an application under the Hague Convention or the European Convention may within seven days thereafter lodge in the principal registry a statement in reply and serve a copy thereof on the defendant.

39. Any application under the Act (other than an application (a) to join a defendant, (b) to dispense with service or extend the time for acknowledging service, or (c) for the transfer of proceedings) shall be heard and determined by a judge and shall be dealt with in chambers unless the court otherwise directs.

40. The court may dispense with service of any summons (whether originating or ordinary) in any proceedings under the Act.

41. Notwithstanding Order 28, rule 5, the hearing of the originating summons under which an application under the Hague Convention or the European Convention is made may be adjourned for a period not exceeding 21 days at any one time.

42. (1) A party to proceedings under the Hague Convention shall, where he knows that an application relating to the merits of rights of custody is pending in or before a relevant authority, file in the principal registry a concise statement of the nature of the application which is pending, including the authority before which it is pending.

    (2) A party—

        (a) to pending proceedings under section 16 of the Act, or

        (b) to proceedings as a result of which a decision relating to custody has been registered under section 16 of the Act,

shall, where he knows that such an application as is specified in section 20(2) of the Act is pending in or before a relevant authority, file a concise statement of the nature of the application which is pending.

    (3) The proper officer shall on receipt of such a statement as is mentioned in paragraph (1) or (2) notify the relevant authority in which or before whom the application is pending and shall subsequently notify it or him of the result of the proceedings.

    (4) On the court receiving notification equivalent to that mentioned in paragraph (3) from the Court of Session or the High Court in Northern Ireland—

  (a) where the application relates to the merits of rights of custody, all further proceedings in the action shall be stayed unless and until the proceedings under the Hague Convention in the Court of Session or, as the case may be, the High Court in Northern Ireland are dismissed, and the parties to the action shall be notified by the proper officer of the stay and of any such dismissal accordingly, and

  (b) where the application is such a one as is specified in section 20(2) of the Act, the proper officer shall notify the parties to the action.

(5) In this rule 'relevant authority' includes the High Court, a county court, a magistrates' court, the Court of Session, a Sheriff Court, a Children's Hearing within the meaning of Part III of the Social Work (Scotland) Act 1968, the High Court in Northern Ireland, a county court in Northern Ireland, a court of summary jurisdiction in Northern Ireland or the Secretary of State.

43. (1) At any stage in any proceedings under the Act the court may, of its own motion or on the application by summons of any party to the proceedings issued on two days' notice, order that the proceedings be transferred to the Court of Session or the High Court in Northern Ireland.

(2) Where an order is made under paragraph (1) the proper officer shall send a copy of the order, which shall state the grounds therefor, together with the originating summons, the documents accompanying it and any evidence, to the Court of Session or the High Court in Northern Ireland, as the case may be.

(3) Where proceedings are transferred to the Court of Session or the High Court in Northern Ireland the costs of the whole proceedings both before and after the transfer shall be at the discretion of the Court to which the proceedings are transferred.

(4) Where proceedings are transferred to the High Court from the Court of Session or the High Court in Northern Ireland the proper officer shall notify the parties of the transfer and the proceedings shall continue as if they had been begun by originating summons under rule 33.

44. An application for interim directions under section 5 or section 19 of the Act may where the case is one of urgency be made ex parte on affidavit but shall otherwise be made by summons.

45. Without prejudice to the generality of Order 63, rule 4(1), any person who intends to make an application under the Hague Convention in a Contracting State other than the United Kingdom shall on satisfying the court as to that intention be entitled to obtain an office copy sealed with the seal of the Supreme Court of any order made in the High Court relating to the child in respect of whom the application is to be made.

46. (1) This rule applies to decisions which have been registered under section 16 of the Act and are subsequently varied or revoked by an authority in the Contracting State in which they were made.

(2) The court shall, on cancelling the registration of a decision which has been revoked, notify—

  (a) the person appearing to the court to have actual custody of the child;
  (b) the person on whose behalf the application for registration of the decision was made; and
  (c) any other party to that application
of the cancellation.

(3) The court shall, on being notified of the variation of a decision, notify—

  (a) the person appearing to the court to have actual custody of the child; and

(b) any party to the application for registration of the decision
of the variation and any such person may apply by summons in the
proceedings for the registration of the decision, for the purpose of making
representations to the court before the registration is varied.

(4) Any person appearing to the court to have an interest in the matter
may apply by summons in the proceedings for the registration of a decision
for the cancellation or variation of the registration.

Orders for disclosure of information
47. At any stage in proceedings under the European Convention the court
may, if it has reason to believe that any person may have relevant information about the child who is the subject of those proceedings, order that
person to disclose such information and may for that purpose order that
the person attend before it or file affidavit evidence.

B County Court Rules 1981, SI 1981/1687 (as amended)

Order 1

CITATION, APPLICATION AND INTERPRETATION

Computation of time
9. (1) Any period of time fixed by these rules or by a judgment, order or
direction for doing any act shall be reckoned in accordance with the
following provisions of this rule.

(2) Where the act is required to be done not less than a specified period
before a specified date, the period starts immediately after the date on
which the act is done and ends immediately before the specified date.

(3) Where the act is required to be done within or not less than a
specified period before a specified date, the period ends immediately
before that date.

(4) Where the act is required to be done within a specified period after
or from a specified date, the period starts immediately after that date.

(5) Where, apart from this paragraph, the period in question being a
period of 3 days or less would include a day on which the court office is
closed, that day shall be excluded.

(6) Where the time so fixed for doing an act in the court office expires on
a day on which the office is closed, and for that reason the act cannot be
done on that day, the act shall be in time if done on the next day on which
the office is open.

Order 2

OFFICES

Filing of documents
4. In these rules any reference to filing a document is a reference to filing it
in the court office by delivering it to the proper officer for entry by him in
the records of the court.

Order 3

COMMENCEMENT OF PROCEEDINGS

Originating applications
4. (1) Any proceedings authorised to be brought in a county court and not required by any Act or rule to be connected otherwise shall be brought by originating application.

(2) An originating application shall be in writing and shall state—
  (a) the order applied for and sufficient particulars to show the grounds on which the applicant claims to be entitled to the order;
  (b) the names and addresses of the persons (if any) intended to be served (in this rule called 'respondents') or that no person is intended to be served, and
  (c) the applicant's address for service.

(3) The applicant shall file—
  (a) the originating application together with as many copies as there are respondents; and
  (b) a request for the issue of the originating application.

(4) On the filing of the documents mentioned in paragraph (1) the proper officer shall—
  (a) enter the originating application in the records of the court and fix the return day;
  (b) prepare a notice to each respondent of the return day and annex to each such notice a copy of the application, and
  (c) deliver a plaint note to the applicant.

(5) The return day shall be a day fixed for the hearing of the originating application or, if the court so directs, a day fixed for a pre-trial review.

(6) Rule 3(2)(d)(ii) of this Order and the provisions of Order 7 shall apply, with the necessary modifications, to the service of an originating application as if the notice of the return day were a fixed date summons.

Title of proceedings
7. (1) Every document filed, issued or served in an action or matter shall bear the title of the action or matter and the distinguishing number allotted to it by the court.

(2) The title of an action or matter shall contain a reference to any Act, other than the County Courts Act 1984, by which the court is given power to entertain the proceedings.

Order 4

VENUE FOR BRINGING PROCEEDINGS

Originating applications and petitions
8. Proceedings by originating application or petition may be commenced—
  (a) in the court for the district in which—
    (i) the respondent or one of the respondents resides or carries on business, or
    (ii) the subject-matter of the proceedings is situated, or
  (b) if no respondent is named in the application or petition, in the court for the district in which the applicant or petitioner or one of the applicants or petitioners resides or carries on business.

Order 7

SERVICE OF DOCUMENTS

Part I—Generally

General mode of service
1. (1) Where by virtue of these rules any document is required to be served on any person and no other mode of service is prescribed by any Act or rule, the document may be served—
   (a) if the person to be served is acting in person, by delivering it to him personally or by delivering it at, or sending it by first-class post to, his address for service or, if he has no address for service—
      (i) by delivering the document at his residence or by sending it by first-class post to his last known residence, or
      (ii) in the case of a proprietor of a business, by delivering the document at his place of business or sending it by first-class post to his last known place of business;
   (b) if the person to be served is acting by a solicitor, by delivering the document at, or sending it by first-class post to, the solicitor's address for service.
   (2) In this Order 'first-class post' means first-class post which has been pre-paid or in respect of which prepayment is not required.

Personal service
2. Where any document is required by an Act or rule to be served personally—
   (a) service shall be effected by leaving the document with the person to be served;
   (b) the document may be served by—
      (i) a bailiff of the court or, if the person to be served attends at the office of the court, any other officer of the court; or
      (ii) a party to the proceedings or some person acting as his agent; or
      (iii) the solicitor of a party or a solicitor acting as an agent for such solicitor or some person employed by either solicitor to serve the document;
but service shall not be effected by any person under the age of 16 years.

Days on which no service permitted
3. Without prejudice to Order 40, rule 5(5), no process shall be served or executed within England or Wales on a Sunday, Good Friday or Christmas Day except, in the case of urgency, with the leave of the court.

Proof of service or non-service
6. (1) The person affecting service of any document shall—
   (a) if he is an officer of the court, make, sign and file a certificate showing the date, place and mode of service and any conduct money paid or tendered to the person served; and
   (b) if he is not an officer of the court, file an affidavit of service.
   (2) A bailiff who has failed to affect service of any document to be served by bailiff shall make, sign and file a certificate of non-service showing the reason why service has not been effected, and the proper officer of the bailiff's court shall send notice of non-service to the person at whose instance the document was issued.

Substituted service

8. (1) If it appears to the court that it is impracticable for any reason to serve a document in any manner prescribed by these rules for the service of that document, the court may, upon an affidavit showing grounds, make an order (in this rule called 'an order for substituted service') giving leave for such steps to be taken as the court directs to bring the document to the notice of the person to be served.

(2) Where a document is to be served by bailiff, the proper officer of the bailiff's court shall, if so requested, take such steps as may be necessary to provide evidence on which an order for substituted service may be made.

Order 13

APPLICATIONS AND ORDERS IN THE COURSE OF PROCEEDINGS

General provisions

1.(1) Except as otherwise provided, the following paragraphs of this rule shall have effect in relation to any application authorised by or under any Act or rule to be made in the course of an action or matter before or after judgment.

(2) Unless allowed or authorised to be made ex parte, the application shall be made on notice, which shall be filed and served on the opposite party not less than two days before the hearing of the application.

(3) Where the application is made ex parte, notice of the application shall be filed a reasonable time before the application is heard, unless the court otherwise directs.

(4) Unless allowed or authorised to be made otherwise, every application shall be heard in chambers.

(5) Where any party to the application fails to attend on the hearing the court may proceed in his absence if, having regard to the nature of the application, the court thinks it expedient to do so.

(6) The jurisdiction of the court to hear and determine the application may be exercised by the registrar and the applicant shall, unless the judge otherwise directs, make the application to the registrar in the first instance.

(7) Where the application is made to the registrar, he may refer to the judge any matter which he thinks should properly be decided by the judge, and the judge may either dispose of the matter or refer it back to the registrar with such directions as he thinks fit.

(8) The court may, as a condition of granting any application, impose such terms and conditions as it thinks fit, including a term or condition requiring any party to—

    (a) give security,

    (b) give an undertaking,

    (c) pay money into court,

    (d) pay all or any part of the costs of the proceedings, or

    (e) give a power of re-entry.

(9) Unless the court otherwise directs, the costs of the application shall not be taxed until the general taxation of the costs of the action or matter and, where an earlier taxation is directed, Order 38 shall apply as if the word 'claimed' were substituted for the word 'recovered' wherever it appears.

(10) An appeal shall lie to the judge from any order made by the registrar on the application and the appeal shall be disposed of in chambers unless the judge otherwise directs.

(11) An appeal under paragraph (10) shall be made on notice, which shall be filed and served on the opposite party within 5 days after the order appealed from or such further time as the judge may allow.

Directions

2. (1) In any action or matter the court may at any time, on application or of its own motion, give such directions as it thinks proper with regard to any matter arising in the course of the proceedings.

(2) In the exercise of the power conferred by paragraph (1) the court may, in particular, order any party to deliver any pleading or give any particulars which the court thinks necessary for defining the issues in the proceedings and may at the same or any subsequent time direct that the action or matter be dismissed or, as the case may be, the defendant be debarred from defending altogether or that anything in any pleading of which particulars have been ordered be struck out unless the order is obeyed within such time as the court may allow.

(3) 'Where the same judge is the judge for two or more districts and proceedings which are to be heard and determined by him are pending in the court for one of those districts, the judge or registrar may, in the exercise of the power conferred by paragraph (1), direct that the hearing in those proceedings shall take place in the court for another of those districts, and notice of any such direction shall be given by the proper officer to all parties who were not present when the direction was given.

(4) Where an application under paragraph (1) is made at a time when no day has been fixed for a pre-trial review, the court may, if it thinks it appropriate to do so, treat the hearing of the application as a day fixed for that purpose and the provisions of Order 17 shall apply accordingly.

(5) The provisions of this rule are without prejudice to Order 6, rule 7, Order 9, rule 11, and Order 17, rules 3 and 10.

Adjournment

3. (1) The court may at any time and from time to time, upon application or of its own motion, by order adjourn or advance the date of the hearing of any proceedings.

(2) Notice of any such adjournment or advancement shall be given by the proper officer to all parties who were not present when the order was made.

(3) If the hearing of any action or matter is adjourned generally, any party may apply to have a day fixed for the hearing and the proper officer shall fix a day and give notice of it to all parties.

(4) If no application is made under paragraph (3) within 12 months of the day on which the order was made adjourning the action or matter generally, the proper officer may give notice to all parties under this paragraph and, unless any party applies within 14 days after receipt of the notice to have a day fixed for the hearing or to have the hearing again adjourned and the application is granted, the action or matter shall be struck out.

Extension or abridgment of time

4. (1) Except as otherwise provided, the period within which a person is required or authorised by these rules or by any judgment, order or direction to do any act in any proceedings may be extended or abridged by consent of all the parties or by the court on the application of any party.

(2) Any such period may be extended by the court although the application for extension is not made until after the expiration of the period.

Application for injunction
6. (1) An application for the grant of an injunction may be made by any party to an action or matter before or after the trial or hearing, whether or not a claim for the injunction was included in that party's particulars of claim, originating application, petition, counterclaim or third party notice, as the case may be.

(2) Rule 1(6) shall not apply and, unless the registrar has power under any other provision of these rules to grant the injunction, the application shall be made to the judge.

(3) Where the applicant is the plaintiff and the case is one of urgency, the application may be made ex parte on affidavit but, except as aforesaid, the application must be made on notice, and in any case the affidavit or notice must state the terms of the injunction applied for.

(4) The plaintiff may not make an application before the issue of the summons, originating application or petition by which the action or matter is to be commenced except where the case is one of urgency and in that case—

   (a) the affidavit on which the application is made shall show that the action or matter is one which the court to which the application is made has jurisdiction to hear and determine, and

   (b) the injunction applied for shall, if granted, be on terms providing for the issue of the summons, originating application or petition in the court granting the application and on such other terms, if any, as the court thinks fit.

(5) Unless otherwise directed, every application not made ex parte shall be heard in open court.

(6) Except where the case is one of urgency, a draft of the injunction shall be prepared beforehand by the party making an application to the judge under paragraph (1) and, if the application is granted, the draft shall be submitted to the judge by whom the application was heard and shall be settled by him.

(7) The injunction, when settled, shall be forwarded to the proper officer for filing.

Order 20

EVIDENCE

Part II—Evidence generally

Evidence in chambers
5. In any proceedings in chambers evidence may be given by affidavit unless by any provision of these rules it is otherwise provided or the court otherwise directs, but the court may, on the application of any party, order the attendance for cross-examination of the person making any such affidavit, and where, after such an order has been made, the person in question does not attend, his affidavit shall not be used in evidence without the leave of the court.

Form and contents of affidavit
10. (1) Subject to the following paragraphs of this rule, the provision of the RSC with respect to—

   (a) the form and contents of an affidavit;

   (b) the making of an affidavit by two or more deponents or by a blind or illiterate deponent;

(c) the use of any affidavit which contains an interlineation, erasure or other alteration or is otherwise defective;

(d) the striking out of any matter which is scandalous, irrelevant or otherwise oppressive;

(e) the insufficiency of an affidavit sworn before any agent, partner or clerk of a party's solicitor; and

(f) the making and marking of exhibits to an affidavit,

shall apply in relation to an affidavit for use in a county court as they apply in relation to an affidavit for use in the High Court.

(2) Before any affidavit is used in evidence it must be filed, but in an urgent case the court may make an order upon the undertaking of a party to file, within such time as the court may require, any affidavit used by him before it is filed.

(3) Every affidavit must be indorsed with a note showing on whose behalf it is filed and the court may refuse to accept an affidavit which is not so indorsed.

(4) Unless the court otherwise orders, an affidavit may be used notwithstanding that it contains statements of information or belief.

(5) Every affidavit shall state which of the facts deposed to are within the deponent's knowledge and which are based on information or belief and shall give, in the former case, his means of knowledge and, in the latter case, the sources and grounds of the information or belief.

Order 22

JUDGMENTS AND ORDERS

Drawing up and service of judgments and orders

1. (1) Subject to the provisions of these rules with respect to particular judgments and orders, every judgment or final order and every order for directions made under Order 13, rule 2, or Order 17, rule 1, shall, unless the court otherwise directs, be drawn up and served by the proper officer on the party against whom it was given or made.

(2) Service shall be effected in accordance with Order 7, rule 1, and it shall not be necessary for the party in whose favour the judgment or order was made to prove that it reached the party to be served.

(3) Where judgment is entered in a default action under Order 9, rule 6(1), for payment forthwith, it shall not be necessary to draw up and serve the judgment unless—

(a) the judgment is for payment to the plaintiff or his solicitor:

(b) the plaintiff has abandoned part of his claim otherwise than by amending his particulars of claim and serving a copy on the defendant;

(c) the judgment is an interlocutory judgment for damages to be assessed.

(4) Any judgment given for the plaintiff in an action for principal money or interest secured by a mortgage or charge, and any order made on an appeal to a county court, shall be served on every party to the proceedings.

(5) Where a party to be served with a judgment or order is acting by a solicitor, service may, if the court thinks fit, be effected on the party as if he were acting in person.

Time for complying with other judgments
3. Every judgment or order requiring any person to do an act other than the payment of money shall state the time within which the act is to be done.

Order of appellate court
13. Where the Court of Appeal or High Court has heard and determined an appeal from a county court, the party entitled to the benefit of the order of the Court of Appeal or High Court shall deposit the order or an office copy thereof in the office of the county court.

Order 25

ENFORCEMENT OF JUDGMENTS AND ORDERS: GENERAL

Judgment creditor and debtor
1. In this Order and Orders 26 to 29 'judgment creditor' means the person who has obtained or is entitled to enforce a judgment or order and 'debtor' means the person against who it was given or made.

Production of plaint note
5. On filing—
  (a) a request for a warrant of execution, delivery or possession,
  (b) a request for a judgment summons or warrant of committal,
  (c) an application for a garnishee order under Order 30, rule 1, or
  (d) an application for a charging order,
the judgment creditor shall, if the judgment or order sought to be enforced is a judgment or order of a county court, produce the plaint note or originating process unless otherwise directed.

Description of parties
6. Where the name or address of the judgment creditor or the debtor as given in the request for the issue of a warrant of execution or delivery, judgment summons or warrant of committal differs from his name or address in the judgment or order sought to be enforced and the judgment creditor satisfies the proper officer that the name or address as given in the request is applicable to the person concerned, the judgment creditor or the debtor, as the case may be, shall be described in the warrant or judgment summons as 'C.D. of [*name and address as given in the request*] suing [*or sued*] as A.D. of [*name and address in the judgment or order*]'.

Recording and giving information as to warrants and orders
7. (1) Every registrar by whom a warrant or order is issued or received for execution shall from time to time state in the records of his court what has been done in the execution of the warrant or order.

  (2) If the warrant or order has not been executed within one month from the date of its issue or receipt by him, the proper officer of the court responsible for its execution shall, at the end of that month and every subsequent month during which the warrant remains outstanding, send notice of the reason for non-execution to the judgment creditor and, if the warrant or order was received from another court, to the proper officer of that court.

  (3) The registrar responsible for executing a warrant or order shall give such information respecting it as may reasonably be required by the judgment creditor and, if the warrant or order was received by him from another court, by the registrar of that court.

(4) Where money is received in pursuance of a warrant of execution or committal sent by one court to another court, the proper officer of the foreign court shall, subject to paragraph (5) and to section 41 of the Bankruptcy Act 1914 and section 326 of the Companies Act 1948 send the money, to the judgment creditor in the manner prescribed by the County Court Funds Rules and make return to the proper officer of the home court.

(5) Where interpleader proceedings are pending, the proper officer shall not proceed in accordance with paragraph (4) until the interpleader proceedings are determined and the registrar shall then make a return showing how the money is to be disposed of and, if any money is payable to the judgment creditor, the proper officer shall proceed in accordance with paragraph (4).

(6) Where a warrant of committal has been received from another court, the proper officer of the foreign court shall, on the execution of the warrant, send notice thereof to the proper officer of the home court.

Order 29

COMMITTAL FOR BREACH OF ORDER OR UNDERTAKING

Enforcement of judgment to do or abstain from doing any act

1. (1) Where a person required by a judgment or order to do an act refuses or neglects to do it within the time fixed by the judgment or order or any subsequent order, or where a person disobeys a judgment or order requiring him to abstain from doing an act, then, subject to the Debtors Acts 1869 and 1878 and to the provisions of these rules, the judgment or order may be enforced, by order of the judge, by a committal order against that person or, if that person is a body corporate, against any director or other officer of the body.

(2) Subject to paragraphs (6) and (7), a judgment or order shall not be enforced under paragraph (1) unless—

    (a) a copy of the judgment or order has been served personally on the person required to do or abstain from doing the act in question and also, where that person is a body corporate, on the director or other officer of the body against whom a committal order is sought, and

    (b) in the case of a judgment or order requiring a person to do an act, the copy has been so served before the expiration of the time within which he was required to do the act and was accompanied by a copy of any order, made between the date of the judgment or order and the date of service, fixing that time.

(3) Where a judgment or order enforceable by committal order under paragraph (1) has been given or made, the proper officer shall, if the judgment or order is in the nature of an injunction, at the time when the judgment or order is drawn up, and in any other case on the request of the judgment creditor, issue a copy of the judgment or order, indorsed with or incorporating a notice as to the consequences of disobedience, for service in accordance with paragraph (2).

(4) If the person served with the judgment or order fails to obey it, the proper officer shall, at the request of the judgment creditor, issue a notice calling on that person to show cause why a committal order should not be made against him, and subject to paragraph (7) the notice shall be served on him personally.

(5) If a committal order is made, the order shall be for the issue of a warrant of committal and a copy of the order shall be served on the person to be committed either before or at the time of the execution of the warrant unless the judge otherwise orders.

(6) A judgment or order requiring a person to abstain from doing an act may be enforced under paragraph (1) notwithstanding that service of a copy of the judgment or order has not been effected in accordance with paragraph (2) if the judge is satisfied that, pending such service, the person against whom it is sought to enforce the judgment or order has had notice thereof either—

(a) by being present when the judgment or order was given or made, or

(b) by being notified of the terms of the judgment or order whether by telephone, telegram or otherwise.

(7) Without prejudice to its powers under Order 7, rule 8, the court may dispense with service of a copy of a judgment or order under paragraph (2) or a notice to show cause under paragraph (4), if the court thinks it just to do so.

Discharge of person in custody
3. (1) Where a person in custody under a warrant or order, other than a warrant of committal to which Order 27, rule 8, or Order 28, rule 4 or 14, relates desires to apply to the court for his discharge, he shall make his application in writing attested by the governor of the prison (or any other officer of the prison not below the rank of principal officer) showing that he has purged or is desirous of purging his contempt and shall, not less than one day before the application is made, serve notice of it on the party, if any, at whose instance the warrant or order was issued.

(2) If the committal order does not direct that any application for discharge shall be made to the judge, it may, with leave of the judge, be made to the registrar.

(3) Nothing in paragraph (1) shall apply to an application made by the Official Solicitor in his official capacity for the discharge of a person in custody.

Order 47

DOMESTIC AND MATRIMONIAL PROCEEDINGS

Matrimonial Homes Act 1983
4. (1) Every application under section 1 or 9 of the Matrimonial Homes Act 1983 shall be dealt with in chambers unless the court otherwise directs.

(2) An application for an order under the said section 1 or 9 (except, subject to paragraph (5), an order to oust the respondent from the dwelling-house to which the application relates) may be heard and determined by the registrar.

(3) Subject to paragraph (4), paragraphs (1) and (2) of rule 2 shall apply in relation to the application as they apply in relation to an application under section 17 of the Married Women's Property Act 1882.

(4) Where matrimonial proceedings are pending between the parties in a county court, an application under the said section 1 or 9 shall be made in those proceedings in accordance with Order 13, rule 1.

(5) Where the application is for an order terminating the respondent's rights of occupation and it appears to the registrar, on the ex parte

application of the applicant, that the respondent is not in occupation of the dwelling-house to which the application relates and his whereabouts cannot after reasonable inquiries be ascertained, the registrar may dispense with service of the application on the respondent and hear and determine the application.

(6) This rule shall apply to an application for an order vacating the registration of a land charge of Class F or a notice or caution registered under section 2(7) of the Matrimonial Homes Act 1967 or a notice registered under section 2(8) of the Matrimonial Homes Act 1983, whether or not it is joined with an application under the said section 1 or 9, as it applies to an application under those sections.

(7) In this rule 'matrimonial proceedings' means—

(a) any proceedings to which sections 1 to 4 of the Matrimonial Causes Act 1967 apply, or

(b) proceedings under section 17 of the Married Women's Property Act 1882 concerning the matrimonial home.

Guardianship of Minors Act 1971 and 1973
6. (1) Every person appearing to be interested in, or affected by, an application under the Guardianship of Minors Acts 1971 and 1973 (except the minor with respect to whom the application is made) shall be made a respondent to the application, including, where the application is made under section 5 of the said Act of 1971 with respect to a minor who has been received into the care of a local authority under section 2 of the Child Care Act 1980, that authority.

(2) Where on an application made under section 9 of the said Act of 1971 relating to the custody of a minor under the age of 16 the court proposes to make an order under section 2(2)(b) of the Guardianship Act 1973 committing the minor to the care of a local authority, the proper officer shall fix a date for hearing any representation from the authority and shall, not less than 14 days before the date so fixed, send notice thereof to the authority and to the parties together with, in the case of the authority, a copy of the originating application.

(3) All proceedings under the said Acts of 1971 and 1973 shall be dealt with in chambers unless the court otherwise directs.

Domestic Violence and Matrimonial Proceedings Act 1976
8. (1) In this rule a section referred to by number means the section so numbered in the Domestic Violence and Matrimonial Proceedings Act 1976.

(2) An application under section 1 shall be made by originating application to the court for the district in which either the applicant or the respondent resides or the matrimonial home is situated.

(3) Order 7, rule 10(5), as applied by Order 3, rule 4(6), shall have effect in relation to the originating application as if for the period of 21 days mentioned in the said rule 10(5) there were substituted a period of 4 days.

(4) The originating application shall be dealt with in chambers unless the court otherwise directs.

(5) A copy of any injunction to which a power of arrest has been attached under section 2 shall be delivered to the officer for the time being in charge of any police station for the applicant's address.

(6) Where an order is made varying or discharging an injunction to which a power of arrest has been attached under section 2, an officer of the

court shall immediately inform the officer for the time being in charge of the police station at which a copy of the injunction was delivered pursuant to paragraph (5) and, if the applicant's address has since changed, any police station for the new address, and a copy of the order shall be delivered to any officer so informed.

(7) The judge before whom a person arrested is brought pursuant to section 2(4) may exercise his power to punish that person for dis-obedience to the injunction, notwithstanding that a copy of the injunction has not been served on him in accordance with Order 29, rule 1(2), and that no notice to show cause has been issued or served on him pursuant to Order 29, rule 1(4).

(8) In relation to a person who is in custody under such an order and warrant Order 29, rule 3 shall have effect as if the order and warrant were issued at the instance of the person who made the application under section 2(1).

Domestic Proceedings and Magistrates' Courts Act 1978
9. Where a direction is given under section 28 of the Domestic Pro-ceedings and Magistrates' Courts Act 1978 that a magistrates' court order shall cease to have effect—

  (a) the proper officer of the court giving the direction shall send notice thereof to the clerk of the magistrates' court, and
  (b) if a power of arrest is attached to the order, an officer of the court giving the direction shall forthwith inform the officer for the time being in charge of any police station to which a copy of the order was sent and, if the applicant's address has since changed, any police station for the new address, and a copy of the direction shall be delivered to any officer so informed.

Child Abduction and Custody Act 1985
10. (1) In this rule a section referred to by number means the section so numbered in the Child Abduction and Custody Act 1985.

(2) Where in pending proceedings relating to the merits of rights of custody (as construed in section 9) the court receives notification from the High Court, the Court of Session or the High Court in Northern Ireland of proceedings under the Hague Convention (as defined in section 1(1)), those pending proceedings shall be stayed unless and until the court is notified that the proceedings under the Hague Convention have been dismissed, and the proper officer shall notify the parties to the pending proceedings of the stay and any such dismissal accordingly.

(3) Where in pending proceedings such as are mentioned in section 20(2) the court receives notification from the High Court, the Court of Session or the High Court in Northern Ireland of proceedings under section 16 or of the registration of a decision under section 16 the proper officer shall notify the parties to the pending proceedings accordingly.

(4) Notwithstanding Order 50, rule 10(2), any person who intends to make an application under the Hague Convention in a Contracting State (as defined in section 2) other than the United Kingdom shall on satisfying the court as to that intention be entitled to obtain a copy bearing the seal of the court of any order made in the court relating to the child in respect of whom the application is to be made.

(5) An application for a declaration under section 23(2) in custody proceedings (as defined in section 27) shall be made by notice in those proceedings.

Order 50

GENERAL PROVISIONS

Powers of registrar when exercising his jurisdiction
2. (1) Where the registrar is authorised by or under any Act or these rules to hear and determine any action or matter or to deal with any proceedings or to exercise any other jurisdiction, he shall, within the limits of that authority and subject to any right of appeal to or review by the judge, have all the powers of the judge.

(2) Nothing in this rule shall authorise the registrar to commit any person to prison.

Notices
4. Every notice required by these rules shall be in writing unless the court authorises it to be given orally.

Matrimonial Causes Rules 1977, SI 1977/344 (as amended)

Application of other rules
3. (1) Subject to the provision of these Rules and of any enactment, the County Court Rules 1936 and the Rules of the Supreme Court 1965 shall apply, with the necessary modifications, to the commencement of matrimonial proceedings in, and to the practice and procedure in matrimonial proceedings pending in, a Divorce County Court and the High Court respectively.

(2) For the purpose of Paragraph (1) any provision of these Rules authorising or requiring anything to be done in matrimonial proceedings shall be treated as if it were, in the case of proceedings pending in a Divorce County Court, a provision of the County Court Rules 1936 and in the case of proceedings pending in the High Court, a provision of the Rules of the Supreme Court 1965.

Service of order
59.[1] (1) Where an order made in matrimonial proceedings has been drawn up, the registrar of the court where the order is made shall, unless otherwise directed, send a copy of the order to every party affected by it.

(2) Where a party against whom the order is made is acting by a solicitor, a copy may, if the registrar thinks fit, be sent to that party as if he were acting in person, as well as to his solicitor.

(3) It shall not be necessary for the person in whose favour the order was made to prove that a copy of the order has reached any other party to whom it is required to be sent.

(4) This rule is without prejudice to RSC Order 45, rule 7 (which deals with the service of an order to do or abstain from doing an act), CCR Order 25, rule 68 (which deals with orders enforceable by attachment), and any other rule or enactment for the purposes of which an order is required to be served in a particular way.

---

1 This rule is as amended by Matrimonial Causes (Amendment) Rules 1984 (SI 1984/1511).

Application for order under section 37(2)(a) of Act of 1973
84.[2] (1) An application under section 37(2)(a) of the Act of 1973 for an order restraining any person from attempting to defeat a claim for financial provision or otherwise for protecting the claim may be made to the Registrar.

(2) Rules 79[3] and 82[4] shall apply, with the necessary modifications, to the application as if it were an application for ancillary relief.

Committal and injunction
90. (1) Notwithstanding anything in RSC Order 52, rule 4(1) (which requires an application for an order of committal to be made by motion), but subject to rule 6 of that Order (which, except in certain cases, requires such an application to be heard in open court) an application for an order of committal in matrimonial proceedings pending in the High Court shall be made by summons.

(2) Where no judge is conveniently available to hear the application, then, without prejudice to CCR Order 25, rule 70(3) (which, in certain circumstances gives jurisdiction to a county court registrar), an application for—

(a) The discharge of any person committed, or

(b) The discharge by consent of an injunction granted by a judge, may be made to the registrar who, if satisfied of the urgency of the matter and that it is expedient to do so, may make any order on the application which a Judge could have made.

(3) Where an order or warrant for the committal of any person to prison has been made or issued in matrimonial proceedings pending in the divorce registry which are treated as pending in a divorce county court, that person shall, wherever he may be, be treated for the purposes of section [122] of the County Courts Act [1984] as being out of the jurisdiction of the divorce registry; but if the committal is for failure to comply with the terms of an injunction, the order or warrant may, if the judge so directs, be executed by the tipstaff within any county court district.

(4) For the purposes of Section [118] of the County Courts Act [1984] in its application to the hearing of matrimonial proceedings at the Royal Courts of Justice, the tipstaff shall be deemed to be an officer of the court.

Custody, care and supervision of children
92. (1) . . .
(2) . . .
(3) . . .
(4) . . .
(5) . . .
(6) . . .
(7) . . .
(8) Unless otherwise directed, any order giving a parent custody or care and control of a child shall provide that no step (other than the institution of proceedings in any court) be taken by that parent which would result in the child being known by a new surname before he or she attains the age of

2 The rule is as amended by Matrimonial Causes (Amendment) Rules 1978 (SI 1978/527), r 6 which came into force on 2 May 1978.
3 R 79 empowers the registrar to refer the application to the judge.
4 R 82 deals with the arrangements for hearing of application etc by judge.

18 years or, being a female, marries below that age, except with the leave of a judge or the consent in writing of the other parent.

Removal of child out of England and Wales
94.[5] (1) In any cause begun by petition the petitioner or the respondent may apply at any time for an order prohibiting the removal of any child of the family under 18 out of England and Wales without the leave of the court except on such terms as may be specified in the order.

Unless otherwise directed, an application under this paragraph may be made ex parte.

(2) Unless otherwise directed, any order relating to the custody or care and control of a child shall provide for the child not to be removed out of England and Wales without the leave of the court except on such terms as may be specified in the order.

(3) Subject to rule 97(2), an application for leave to remove a child out of England and Wales shall be made to a judge except in the following cases when it may be made to the registrar, namely—

    (a) where the application is unopposed, or

    (b) where the application is for the temporary removal of the child unless it is opposed on the ground that the child may not be duly returned and the registrar may make such order on the application as he thinks fit or may refer the application or any question arising thereon to a judge for his decision.

Notice of other proceedings relating to children
96. If, while a cause is pending, proceedings relating to any child of the family are begun in the High Court, a county court or a magistrates' court, a concise statement of the nature of the proceedings shall forthwith be filed by the person beginning the proceedings or, if he is not a party to the cause, by the petitioner.

Transfer of proceedings relating to children
97.[6] Rule 80 shall apply to proceedings for the exercise of any power under Part III the Act of 1973 as it applies to an application for ancillary relief.

Proceedings in High Court under section 17 of Act of 1882
104.[7] (1) An application to the High Court under section 17 of the Act of 1882 shall be made by originating summons in Form 23, which may be issued out of the divorce registry or a district registry, and at the same time the applicant shall, unless otherwise directed, file an affidavit in support of the summons and shall lodge in the court office a copy of the summons and of the affidavit for service on the respondent and on any mortgagee mentioned therein pursuant to paragraph (3).

(2) . . .

(3) Where the application concerns the title to or possession of land, the originating summons shall—

    (a) state, whether the title to the land is registered or unregistered, and, if registered, the Land Registry title number; and

    (b) give particulars, so far as known to the applicant, of any mortgage of the land or any interest therein.

---

5 This rule is as amended by Matrimonial Causes (Amendment) Rules 1978 (SI 1978/527).
6 Substituted by Matrimonial Causes (Amendment) Rules 1986 (SI 1986/634).
7 This rule is as amended by Matrimonial Causes (Amendment) Rules 1984 (SI 1984/1511).

(4) The registrar shall annex to the copy of the originating summons for service on the respondent a copy of the affidavit in support and an acknowledgment of service in Form 6.

(5) Where particulars of a mortgage are given pursuant to paragraph (3) the registrar shall serve on the mortgagee a copy of the originating summons and any person so served may apply to the court in writing, within 14 days after service, for a copy of the affidavit in support, within 14 days of receiving such an affidavit may file an affidavit in answer, and shall be entitled to be heard on the application.

(6) No appearance need be entered to the originating summons.

(7) If the respondent intends to contest the application, he shall within 14 days after the time limited for giving notice to defend, file an affidavit in answer to the application setting out the grounds on which he relies and lodge in the court office a copy of the affidavit for service by the registrar on the applicant.

(8) If the respondent fails to file an affidavit under paragraph (7), the registrar may by order specify a time within which the respondent must, if he wishes to defend, file an affidavit, and may, on or after making such an order, direct that the respondent shall be debarred from defending the application unless an affidavit is filed within that time.

(9) The registrar may grant an injunction in proceedings under the said section 17 if, but only so far as, the injunction is ancillary or incidental to any relief sought in those proceedings.

(10) Without prejudice to paragraph (7) of this rule, RSC Order 28, rule 7 (which enables a counterclaim to be made in an action begun by originating summons), shall apply, with the necessary modifications, to a respondent to an originating summons under this rule as it applies to a defendant who has entered an appearance to an originating summons.

(11) Rules 77(4) to (7), 78, 79 and 82 shall apply, with the necessary modifications, to an application under section 17 of the Act of 1882 as they apply to an application for ancillary relief.

(12) Subject to the provisions of this rule, these Rules shall, so far as applicable, apply, with the necessary modifications, to an application under section 17 of the Act of 1882 as if the application were a cause, the originating summons a petition, and the applicant the petitioner.

Proceedings under sections 1 and 9 of and Schedule 1 to the Matrimonial Homes Act 1983
107.[8] (1) Subject to paragraph (2) below the jurisdiction of the High Court under sections 1 and 9 of the Matrimonial Homes Act 1983 may be exercised in chambers and the provisions of rule 104 (except paragraph (2)) shall apply, with the necessary modifications, to proceedings under those sections as they apply to an application under section 17 of the Act of 1882.

(2) Where a cause begun in accordance with rule 8(1) is pending in the High Court an application under the said section 1 or section 9 by one of the parties shall be made as an application in that cause in accordance with rule 122(1)(b).

(3) An application for an order under the said section 1 or section 9 (except, subject to paragraph (4) below, an order to oust the respondent from the dwelling house to which the application relates) may be heard and determined by a registrar.

8 This rule was substituted by Matrimonial Causes (Amendment) Rules 1984 (SI 1984/1511).

(4) Where the applicant asks for an order under the said section 1 or section 9 terminating the respondent's right of occupation and it appears to the registrar, on the ex parte application of the applicant, that the respondent is not in occupation of the dwelling house to which the application relates and his whereabouts cannot after reasonable inquiries be ascertained, the registrar may dispense with service of the summons on the respondent and hear and determine the application.

(5) The jurisdiction of the court under Schedule 1 to the said Act of 1983 may be exercised by a registrar.

(6) Where an application is made for an order under the said Schedule 1, notice of the application (or, in the High Court, the summons by which the application is made) shall be served on—

(a) the spouse entitled as mentioned in paragraph 1 of that Schedule to occupy the dwelling house to which the application relates, and

(b) the landlord of the dwelling house,

and any person so served shall be entitled to be heard on the application.

(7) Any court in which an application for an order under the said Schedule is pending may, if it is a divorce county court, order the transfer of the application to the High Court or another divorce county court or, if it is the High Court, order the transfer of the application to a divorce county court, where the transfer appears to the court to be desirable and, unless the court otherwise directs, a transfer of the cause in which the decree is sought or granted shall include a transfer of the application.

Application for leave under section 13 of the Act of 1984
111A.[9] (1) An application for leave to apply for an order for financial relief under Part III of the Act of 1984 shall be made ex parte by originating summons issued in Form 25 out of the divorce registry and shall be supported by an affidavit by the applicant stating the facts relied on in support of the application with particular reference to the matters set out in section 16(2) of that Act.

(2) The affidavit in support shall give particulars of the judicial or other proceedings by means of which the marriage to which the application relates was dissolved or annulled or by which the parties to the marriage were legally separated and shall state, so far as is known to the applicant—

(a) the names of the parties to the marriage and the date and place of the marriage;

(b) the occupation and residence of each of the parties to the marriage;

(c) whether there are any living children of the family and, if so, the number of such children and full names (including surname) of each and his date of birth or, if it be the case, that he is over 18;

(d) whether either party to the marriage has remarried;

(e) an estimate in summary form of the approximate amount or value of the capital resources and net income of each party and of any minor child of the family;

(f) the grounds on which it is alleged that the court has jurisdiction to entertain an application for an order for financial relief under Part III of the said Act of 1984.

(3) The registrar shall fix a date and time for the hearing of the application by a judge in chambers and give notice thereof to the applicant.

9 Inserted by Matrimonial Causes (Amendment No 2) Rules 1985 (SI 1985/1315).

Application for an order for financial relief or an avoidance of transaction order under Part III of the Act of 1984

111B.[10] (1) An application for an order for financial relief under Part III of the Act of 1984 shall be made by originating summons issued in Form 26 out of the divorce registry and at the same time the applicant, unless otherwise directed, shall file an affidavit in support of the summons giving full particulars of his property and income.

(2) The applicant shall serve a sealed copy of the originating summons on the respondent and shall annex thereto a copy of the affidavit in support, if one has been filed, and a notice of proceedings and acknowledgment of service in Form 28, and rule 15 shall apply to such an acknowledgment of service as if the references in paragraph (1) of that rule to Form 6 and in paragraph (2) of that rule to eight days were, respectively, references to Form 28 and 31 days.

(3) Rules 72, 74, 75, 76A, 77(4), (6) and (7), and 82(1) and (2) shall apply, with the necessary modifications, to an application for an order for financial relief under this rule as they apply to an application for ancillary relief made by notice in Form 11 and the court may order the attendance of any person for the purpose of being examined or cross-examined and the discovery and production of any document.

(4) An application for an interim order for maintenance under section 14 or an avoidance of transaction order under section 23 of the Act of 1984 may be made, unless the court otherwise directs, in the originating summons under paragraph (1) or by summons in accordance with rule 122(1) and an application for an order under section 23 shall be supported by an affidavit, which may be the affidavit filed under paragraph (1), stating the facts relied on.

(5) If the respondent intends to contest the application he shall, within 28 days after the time limited for giving notice to defend, file an affidavit in answer to the application setting out the grounds on which he relies and shall serve a copy on the applicant.

(6) In respect of any application for an avoidance of transaction order the court may give such a direction or make such appointment as it is empowered to give or make by paragraph (3) and rule 74 shall apply, with the necessary modifications, to an application for an avoidance of transaction order as it applies to an application for an avoidance of disposition order.

(7) Where the originating summons contains an application for an order under section 22 of the Act of 1984 the applicant shall serve a copy on the landlord of the dwelling house and he shall be entitled to be heard on the application.

(8) An application for an order for financial relief under Part III of the Act of 1984 or for an avoidance of transaction order shall be determined by a judge.

Application for an order under section 24 of the Act of 1984 preventing a transaction

111C.[11] (1) An application under section 24 of the Act of 1984 for an order preventing a transaction shall be made by originating summons

---

10 Inserted by Matrimonial Causes (Amendment No 2) Rules 1985 (SI 1985/1315).
11 Inserted by Matrimonial Causes (Amendment No 2) Rules 1985 (SI 1985/1315).

issued in Form 27 out of the divorce registry and shall be supported by an affidavit by the applicant stating the facts relied on in support of the application.

(2) The applicant shall serve a sealed copy of the originating summons on the respondent and shall annex thereto a copy of the affidavit in support and a notice of proceedings and acknowledgment of service in Form 28, and rule 15 shall apply to such an acknowledgment of service as if the references in paragraph (1) of that rule to Form 6 and in paragraph (2) of that rule to eight days were, respectively, references to Form 28 and 31 days.

(3) If the respondent intends to contest the application he shall, within 28 days after the time limited for giving notice to defend, file an affidavit in answer to the application setting out the grounds on which he relies and shall serve a copy on the applicant.

(4) The application shall be determined by a judge.

(5) Rule 82 (save paragraph (3)) shall apply, with the necessary modifications, to the application as if it were an application for ancillary relief.

Service on solicitors

118.[12] (1) Where a document is required by these rules to be sent to any person who is acting by a solicitor, service shall, subject to any other direction or order, be effected—

    (a) by sending the document by first class post to the solicitor's address for service; or

    (b) where that address includes a numbered box at a document exchange, by leaving the document at that document exchange or at a document exchange which transmits documents daily to that document exchange.

(2) Any document which is left at a document exchange in accordance with paragraph (1)(b) shall, unless the contrary is proved, be deemed to have been served on the second day after the day on which it is left.

(3) Where no other mode of service is prescribed, directed or ordered, service may additionally be effected by leaving the document at the solicitor's address.

Service on person acting in person

119.[13] (1) Subject to paragraph (3) and to any other direction or order, where a document is required by these rules to be sent to any person who is acting in person, service shall be effected by sending the document by first class post to the address for service given by him or, if he has not given an address for service, to his last known address.

(2) Subject to paragraph (3), where no other mode of service is prescribed, directed or ordered, service may additionally be effected by delivering the document to him or by leaving it at the address specified in paragraph (1).

(3) Where it appears to the registrar that it is impracticable to deliver the document to the person to be served and that, if the document were left at, or sent by post to, the address specified in paragraph (1), it would be unlikely to reach him, the registrar may dispense with service of the document.

12 Substituted by the Matrimonial Causes (Amendment) Rules 1986 (SI 1986/634).

Service by bailiff in proceedings in divorce registry
120. Where, in any proceedings pending in the divorce registry which are treated as pending in a divorce county court, a document is to be served by bailiff, it shall be sent for service to the registrar of the county court within the district of which the document is to be served.

Mode of making application
122. (1) Except where these Rules, or any rules applied by these Rules, otherwise provide, every application on matrimonial proceedings—
  (a) Shall be made to a registrar;
  (b) Shall, if the proceedings are pending in the High Court, be made by summons or, if the proceedings are pending in a Divorce County Court, be made in accordance with CCR Order 13, rule 1 (which deals with applications in the course of proceedings).
  [(2) For the purposes of paragraph (1), CCR Order 13, rule 1 shall have effect as if for the period of one clear day mentioned in paragraph (1)(b)(i) of that rule (which prescribes the length of notice to be given) there were substituted the period of 2 clear days.]

Place of hearing of application by judge
123. (1) Any application in a cause which is to be heard by a judge otherwise than at the trial may, except where these Rules otherwise provide or the court otherwise directs, be heard—
  (a) if the cause is pending in the High Court—
      (i) at the Royal Courts of Justice, or
      (ii) in the case of an application in a cause proceeding in a district registry, at the divorce town in which that registry is situated or, if it is not situated in a divorce town, then at the appropriate divorce town, or
      (iii) in the cause of an application in a cause which has been set down for trial at a divorce town, at that town;
  (b) if the cause is pending in a divorce county court—
      (i) at that court if it is a court of trial and otherwise at the appropriate court of trial, or
      (ii) in the case of an application in a cause which has been set down for trial at a court of trial, at that court.
  (2) In this rule 'application' includes an appeal from an order or decision made or given by the registrar and 'appropriate divorce town' and 'appropriate court of trial' mean such divorce town or court of trial as in the opinion of the registrar is the nearest or most convenient.

Filing of documents at place of hearing, etc
126. Where the file of any matrimonial proceedings has been sent from one divorce county court or registry to another for the purpose of a hearing or for some other purpose, any document needed for that purpose and required to be filed shall be filed in the other court or registry.

Mode of giving notice
127. Unless otherwise directed, any notice which is required by these Rules to be given to any person shall be in writing and, if it is to be given by the registrar, shall be given by post.

---

13 Substituted by the Matrimonial Causes (Amendment) Rules 1986 (SI 1986/634).

Inspection etc of documents retained in court

130. (1) A party to any matrimonial proceedings or his solicitor or the Queen's Proctor or a person appointed under rule 72 or 115 to be the guardian *ad litem* of a child in any matrimonial proceedings may have a search made for, and may inspect and bespeak a copy of, any document filed or lodged in the court office in those proceedings.

(1A) Any person, not entitled to a copy of a document under paragraph (1) above, who intends to make an application under the Hague Convenvtion (as defined in section 1(1) of the Child Abduction and Custody Act 1985(c)) in a Contracting State (as defined in section 2 of that Act) other than the United Kingdom shall, if he satisfies the registrar that he intends to make such an application, be entitled to obtain a copy bearing the seal of the court of any order relating to the custody of the child in respect of whom the application is to be made.

(2) Except as provided by rules 48(3) and 95(3) and paragraphs (1) and (1A) of this rule, no document filed or lodged in the court office other than a decree or order made in open court, shall be open to inspection by any person without the leave of the registrar, and no copy of any such document, or of an extract from any such document, shall be taken by, or issued to, any person without such leave.

D The Magistrates' Courts (Matrimonial Proceedings) Rules 1980, SI 1980/1582

Interpretation and application

2. (1) In these Rules 'the Act' means the Domestic Proceedings and Magistrates' Courts Act 1978.

(2) Expressions used in these Rules have the meaning which they bear in the Act.

(3) Any reference in these Rules to a form is a reference to a form in the Schedule to these Rules and includes a reference to a form to the like effect with such variations as the circumstances may require.

(4) . . .

Notice to respondent of court's powers with regard to family protection orders

10. Where a summons is issued on an application for an order under section 16 or 17(1) of the Act, a notice in Form 12 indicating the powers conferred on a court by sections 16 and 18(1) shall be served on the respondent with the summons.

Jurisdiction in proceedings for order under section 2, 6, 7 or 16

11. In the case of an application for an order under section 2, 6, 7 or 16 of the Act a magistrates' court shall, subject to section 11 of the Administration of Justice Act 1964 and any determination of the committee of magistrates thereunder, have jurisdiction to hear the application if the applicant and the respondent last ordinarily resided together as man and wife within the commission area for which the court is appointed, as well as any such court as has jurisdiction by virtue of section 30(1) of the Act.

Transfer of proceedings for order under section 2, 6, 7 or 16

12.(1) Where an application is made to a magistrates' court for an order under section 2, 6, 7 or 16 of the Act and a summons has been issued in consequence thereof, then, on an application in that behalf made by the respondent in accordance with paragraph (2) below, a justice of the peace acting for the same place as that court may, if it appears that the case could be more conveniently heard in another magistrates' court having jurisdiction to hear it by virtue of rule 11 above, determine that the proceedings shall be removed into that other court.

(2) An application under paragraph (1) above may be made orally or in writing by or on behalf of the respondent and, unless the respondent applies in person, there shall be lodged with the clerk of the court in which the proceedings were begun a statutory declaration by the respondent which shall state—

    (a) the grounds upon which the application is made;

    (b) the address of the respondent to which notices may be sent;

    (c) a summary of the evidence which the respondent proposes to adduce in the proceedings, including the names, addresses and the occupation, if known, of any witnesses to be called by the respondent;

    (d) the occupation of the respondent and, if known, of the applicant in the proceedings.

(3) The justice adjudicating on an application under paragraph (1) above shall, unless he determines that the application shall be refused forthwith, afford to the person who applied for the order an opportunity of making representations, either orally or in writing, thereon.

(4) Where a justice determines under paragraph (1) above that proceedings shall be removed into another magistrates' court, he shall cause the clerk of the court in which the proceedings were begun to send to the clerk of that other court the complaint, a copy of the summons and any other relevant documents; and, on receipt thereof in that other court, the complaint shall be deemed to have been made in, and the summons to have been issued by, that other court, and any justice acting for the same place as that other court may appoint a time and place for the hearing of the proceedings which, upon notice thereof being sent to the parties to the proceedings, shall be deemed to have been the time and place appointed in the summons.

Consideration of application for family protection orders
13. (1) Where an application has been made to a magistrates' court for an order under section 16 of the Act and the applicant makes a statement to the clerk of the court, either orally or in writing, to the effect that there is imminent danger of physical injury to the applicant or a child of the family, the clerk shall take such steps as may be necessary to ensure that the court considers as soon as practicable whether or not to exercise its power to make an expedited order under section 16(2) and (6) of that Act.

(2) On an application to a magistrates' court for an order under section 16(3) of the Act, the date fixed for the hearing of the application shall be as soon as practicable and in any event not later than 14 days after the date on which the summons is issued.

Form of court orders
14. (1) . . .

(2) An order under section 16 of the Act shall be in Form 14.

(3) A power of arrest attached under section 18(1) of the Act to an order under section 16 shall be in Form 15.

(4) A warrant of arrest under section 18(4) of the Act shall be in form 16.

Entries in court's registers
15. (1) Where a clerk of a magistrate's court receives notice of any direction made by the High Court or a county court under section 28 of the Act
by virtue of which an order made by the magistrates' court under Part I of
the Act ceases to have effect, particulars thereof shall be entered in the
court's register.

(2) . . .

Notification of certain family protection orders
19. (1) Where a magistrates' court makes an expedited order under
section 16(2) and (6) of the Act (hereinafter referred to as an 'expedited
order'), the clerk of the court shall serve notice of the making of the order
on the respondent by causing a copy of the order to be delivered to the
respondent personally:

Provided that if a justice of the peace is satisfied by evidence on oath that
prompt personal service on the respondent is impracticable he may allow
service to be effected—

(a) by leaving a copy of the order for him with some person at his last
known or usual place of abode; or

(b) by sending a copy of the order by post in a letter addressed to him
at his last known or usual place of abode.

(2) (a) Where a magistrates' court makes an order under section 16 of the
Act to which a power of arrest is attached, the clerk of the court
shall cause a copy of the order to be sent to the officer for the time
being in charge of any police station for the address at which the
person who applied for the order resides.

(b) Where a magistrates' court makes an order under section 17(1) of
the Act varying or revoking any order under the said section 16 to
which a power of arrest is attached, the clerk of the court shall
cause a copy of the order under section 17(1) to be sent to the
officer for the time being in charge of the police station to which a
copy of the order under section 16 was sent in pursuance of sub-
paragraph (a) above and, if the person who applied for the order
under section 16 has since changed address, any police station for
the new address.

(3) In the case of an expedited order a copy thereof shall not be sent to
the police in pursuance of paragraph (2)(a) above until notice of the
making of the order has been served on the respondent in accordance with
paragraph (1) above and the clerk of the court shall, before sending it to
the police, enter on it an endorsement in Form 18 indicating that it has
been so served and the date on which the order takes effect.

(4) Where a copy of an expidited order is sent to the police in pursuance
of paragraph (2)(a) above, a copy of the order and its endorsement shall
also be sent to the person who applied for the order.

(5) Where, by virtue of section 16(8)(b) of the Act, an expedited order
to which a power of arrest is attached expires on the date of the commencement of the hearing by a magistrates' court of an application for an
order under section 16 of that Act, the clerk of the court shall cause notice
of the expiry to be sent to the officer for the time being in charge of the
police station to which a copy of the order was sent in pursuance of
paragraph (2)(a) above.

Service of documents
20. (1) Subject to the provisions of rule 19(1) above, service on any person of a document under these Rules may be effected—

    (a) by delivering it to him; or

    (b) by leaving it for him with some person at his last known or usual place of abode; or

    (c) by sending it to him by post in a letter addressed to him at his last known or usual place of abode or at an address given by him for that purpose.

    (2) In the case of a notice sent by post for the purposes of rule 12(4) above the notice shall be sent in a registered letter or by recorded delivery service.

Appendix 4
Precedents and forms

Contents

Precedents and Forms

The following precedents and forms are those which will be used in connection with the types of applications described in the text. The scope of this Appendix has been widened in this edition but practical considerations have made it impossible for every permutation to be included. Practitioners should therefore adapt the precedents and forms as appropriate to their individual requirements. As the factual circumstances of each case will vary considerably the affidavits are merely examples; the content of affidavits is discussed in the text. Adverse comment was made in *Pearson v Pearson*[1] as to the brevity, almost 'pro forma' nature of the applicant's affidavit.[2] The suggested content of an affidavit is to be regarded as a minimum, not a maximum. The court should always have as much information as possible, particularly where onerous relief, such as an exclusion injunction is sought.

Practitioners are also referred to *Atkin's Encyclopedia of Court Forms in Civil Proceedings*; in particular:

Affidavits	Vol 3	(1978 Issue)
Appeals	Vol 5	(1984 Issue)
Divorce	Vol 16	(1984 Issue)
Evidence	Vol 18	(1985 Issue)
Execution	Vol 19	(1984 Issue)
Husband and Wife	Vol 21	(1985 Issue)
Infants	Vol 21	(1985 Issue)
Injunctions	Vol 22	(1980 Issue)
Originating Summonses	Vol 29	(1983 Issue)
Pleadings	Vol 32	(1985 Issue)
Service of Process	Vol 35	(1983 Issue)

1 (1982) 3 FLR 137, CA.
2 Ibid, per Ormrod LJ at page 139 C–E.

A Applications: non-molestation, exclusion

1 **Originating summons** under the Domestic Violence and Matrimonial Proceedings Act 1976: High Court[1]

In the High Court of Justice   No   of 19
Family Division
Principal Registry (*or*   District Registry)

In the matter of the Domestic Violence and Matrimonial Proceedings Act 1976

Between:

A.B.   Plaintiff

and

C.D.   Defendant

LET C.D. of   (*address*)
attend before the Judge in Chambers at the Royal Courts of Justice, Strand, London WC2A 2LL   (*or insert address for the District Registry*)
On   day the   day of   19   at   o'clock in the   noon on the hearing of an application by the Plaintiff A.B. of   (*address*) that:

(1) The Defendant whether by himself his servants or agents or otherwise howsoever be restrained from assaulting molesting or otherwise interfering with the Plaintiff;

(2) the Defendant whether by himself his servant or agent or otherwise howsoever be restrained from assaulting molesting or otherwise interfering with-
              (*name*) being a child living with the Plaintiff;

(3) the Defendant do forthwith permit the Plaintiff to enter the matrimonial home known as the situate at   (*address*) and thereafter to permit the Plaintiff to remain therein;

(4) the Defendant be excluded from (*a part of*) the matrimonial home known as and situate at   (*address*) (*namely   part of house it is desired to exclude Defendant from*) and thereafter be restrained from returning thereto (*or approaching within thereto*);

(5) a power of arrest be attached to orders in the terms of paragraphs 1, 2 and 3 hereof.

AND LET the Defendant within   days after service of this summons upon him, counting the day of service, return the accompanying acknowledgement of Service to [the Principal Registry of the Family Division] *or* [the District Registry of the High Court].

Dated the   day of   19

NOTE:
This summons may not be served later than 12 calendar months beginning with the above date unless renewed by order of the Court.

This summons was taken out by
of
solicitor for the said Plaintiff whose address is as stated above.
or This summons was taken out by
of
agent for   of
solicitors for the said Plaintiff whose address is stated above.

or This summons was taken out by the said Plaintiff who resides at (*and (if the Plaintiff does not reside within the jurisdiction*) whose address for service is)
If the Defendant does not attend personally or by his Counsel or Solicitor at the time and place where mentioned such order will be made as the Court may think just and expedient.

Important
Directions for acknowledgement of service are given with the accompanying form.

---

1 Adapted from RSC Form 10, Appendix A

---

2 Originating application under the Domestic Violence and Matrimonial Proceedings Act 1976: county court

In the   County Court   Case No

In the matter of the Domestic Violence and Matrimonial Proceedings Act 1976

Between:

A.B.	Applicant
and	
C.D.	Respondent

I, A.B. of   in the County of   apply to the Court for an order in the following terms:

(1) That the Respondent by himself his servants agents or otherwise howsoever be restrained from assaulting molesting or otherwise interfering with the Applicant;

(2) that the Respondent by himself his servants agents or otherwise howsoever be restrained from assaulting molesting or otherwise interfering with (*name*) being a child living with the Applicant;

(3) that the Respondent be required to permit the Applicant forthwith to enter the property known as and situate at   (*address*) and that he/she thereafter permits the applicant to remain therein;

(4) that the Respondent be excluded from (*a part of*) the property known as and situate at   (*address*)   (namely the   (*part of house it is desired to exclude Respondent from*)) and that he/she be thereafter restrained from returning thereto (*or approaching within   thereof*);

(5) that a power of arrest be attached to orders in the terms of paragraphs 1, 2 and 4 hereof;

(6) that the Respondent be condemned in the costs of and occasioned by this application.

The grounds on which the Applicant claims to be entitled to orders in the above terms are:
The Applicant will rely upon the contents of the affidavit sworn the   day of   19   and served herewith.

The name and address of the person upon whom it is intended to serve this application is C.D. of   in the County of

The Applicant's address for service is: (*solicitor's address or if Applicant is acting in person [his or her] own address*).

Dated this   day of   19

(*Signed*)
(Applicant *or* Solicitor for the Applicant)

3 Originating summons under the Matrimonial Homes Act 1983: High Court[1]

[*Royal Arms*]

In the High Court of Justice   No 3456 of 1987
Family Division
[Principal *or*   District] Registry

In the Matter of an application under section [1 *or* 9] of the Matrimonial Homes
Act 1983

Between: A.B.   Applicant

                                  and

                                  B.B.   Respondent

LET B.B. of [*address*] attend before the Judge[2] in Chambers sitting at the [Royal
Courts of Justice, Strand, London WC2A 2LL *or address of District Registry*] on
[Tuesday] the [21st] day of [July 1987] at [10.30] o'clock in the [fore]noon on the
hearing of an application by the Applicant for an order in the following terms:

(*Continue as in Form 4, paragraphs 1–5*)

(6) [*Add if required eg*: That the respondent be liable for all outgoings in respect
of the said dwelling house, including the mortgage repayments to the
[Oxbridge] Building Society under a mortgage deed dated the [29th day of
October 1975] and made between the Respondent and the said Building
Society]

(7) [That the Respondent be restrained from assaulting, molesting or otherwise
interfering with the Applicant][3]

(8) That provision may be made for the costs of these proceedings.

Dated this 30th day of June 1987.

TAKE NOTICE that:

(1) A copy of the affidavit to be used in support of the application is delivered
herewith.

(2) You must complete the accompanying acknowledgment of service and send
it so as to reach the court within eight days after you receive this summons.

(3) If you wish to dispute the claim made by the applicant you must file an
affidavit in answer within 14 days after the time allowed for sending the
acknowledgment of service.

(4) If you intend to instruct a solicitor to act for you you should at once give him
all the documents served on you, so that he may take the necessary steps on
your behalf.

---

1 Adapted from the Matrimonial Causes Rules 1977 (SI 1977/344) App I Form 23. See
Matrimonial Homes Act 1983, ss 1, 9 27 *Halsbury's Statutes* (4th edn) MATRIMONIAL LAW
585. See also *Practice Direction* (Matrimonial Causes: Injunctions) [1983] 2 All ER 1088,
[1983], 1WLR 999 Appendix 2 for the wording of the claim.

2 The application must be made to a judge because it is sought to oust the respondent. For
the jurisdiction of judges and resgistrars see Matrimonial Causes Rules 1977, r 107(3) as
substituted (by SI 1984/1511): see Appendix 3. In any event a registrar does not have
jurisdiction to grant a non-molestation injunction except by consent (RSC Ord, 32,
r 11(1)(d)): see Appendix 3.

3 Add if required in which case the originating summons should also be intituled 'in the
Matter of the Domestic Violence and Matrimonial Proceedings Act 1976'.

4 Originating application under the Matrimonial Homes Act 1983: County Court[1]

In the Birmingham County Court   No 87 1234

In the Matter of the Matrimonial Homes Act 1983
And in the Matter of 41 Manchester Road, Bearwood, Birmingham, West Midlands

Between: A.C.   Applicant

                                  and

                                  D.C.   Respondent

I, A.C. of 41, Manchester Road, Bearwood, Birmingham, West Midlands, hereby apply to the Court for an Order in the following terms:
  (1) [That it be declared that the Applicant has rights of occupation in 41 Manchester Road aforesaid.][2]
  (2) That the Applicant be granted leave to enter and occupy 41 Manchester Road aforesaid.[3]
  (3) That the Respondent be forthwith required to permit the Applicant to exercise [her] rights of occupation in 41 Manchester Road aforesaid.[4]
  (4) [That the Respondent's rights of occupation in 41 Manchester Road aforesaid be terminated.][5]
  (5) That [alternatively to (4) above] the Respondent be prohibited[6] from exercising [his] rights of occupation in 41 Manchester Road aforesaid, or that [his] rights of occupation in 41 Manchester Road aforesaid be suspended[7] or restricted.[8]
  (6) That the Respondent be condemned in the costs of this application.

The grounds on which the Applicant claims to be entitled to orders in the above terms are set out in the Applicant's affidavit herein sworn the 1st June 1987.

Dated the 1st day of June 1987.

The name and address of the person on whom it is intended to serve this application is D. C. of [*address*].

The Applicant's address for service is [c/o *solicitor's address*] or [*own address if acting in person*]

---

1 There is no prescribed form of originating application.
2 Matrimonial Homes Act 1983, (27 *Halsbury's Statutes* (4th edn) 585 MATRIMONIAL LAW) s 1(2)(a); it is not necessary to seek such a declaration in respect of an applicant who is a joint owner of the matrimonial home. Ibid, s 9.
3 Ibid, s 1(1)(b)
4 Ibid, s 1(2)(c)
5 Ibid, s 1(2)(a); it is not possible to terminate the rights of occupation of a joint owner, ibid, s 9. A joint owner's rights may be restricted or suspended, or he may be prohibited from exercising his rights, ibid.
6 Ibid, s 1(2)(b).
7 Ibid.
8 Ibid.

5 **Notice of application** for injunctions interlocutory relief: divorce county court

In the   County Court   No of matter
(*or* In the Divorce Registry)   (*or*) No   of

Between:

A.B.	Petitioner
and	
C.B.	Respondent

TAKE NOTICE that the Petitioner intends to apply to the Judge of this Court sitting at   (*address*) on   day the   day of   19 at   o'clock for orders in the following terms:

(1) That the Respondent by himself his servants agents or otherwise howsoever be restrained from assaulting molesting or otherwise interfering with the Petitioner;
(2) that the Respondent be restrained from assaulting molesting or otherwise interfering with   (*name*) being a child of the family living with the Petitioner;
(3) that a power of arrest be attached to orders in the terms of paragraphs 1 and 2 hereof;
(4) that the Respondent be condemned in the costs of and occasioned by this application.

Dated this   day of   19

Signed

(Solicitors for the Petitioner *or* the Petitioner)

To the Registrar of the   County Court
And to the Respondent

6 **Summons for injunctions**: interlocutory relief: High Court[1]

                         No   of 19

In the High Court of Justice
Family Division
Principal Registry
Between

A.B	Petitioner
and	
C.B	Respondent
and	
D.E.	Party Cited

LET all parties attend before the Judge in Chambers at the Royal Courts of Justice, Strand London at or after 10.30 am.§
on   the   day of   19   on the hearing of an application on the part of the Respondent for an order that:

(1) The Petitioner be restrained from assaulting, molesting or otherwise interfering with the Respondent and F.B. and G.B. the children of the family.
(2) The Petitioner do forthwith permit the Respondent and the said children of the family to re-enter the matrimonial home at (*address*) and thereafter allow them to occupy the same.
(3) The Petitioner and the Party Cited be excluded from the matrimonial home   (*address*) and thereafter be restrained from returning thereto or approaching within   thereof.
(4) A power of arrest be attached to orders in the terms of paragraphs 1 and 3 hereof.
(5) The Petitioner and/or the Party Cited be condemned in the costs of this application.

DATED the   day of   19
The estimated duration of this summons is
Counsel will/will not* be appearing on behalf of the applicant

This summons was taken out by
of
Solicitors for the
To

Divorce Registry, Somerset House, Strand, London, WC2R 1LP

NOTES
§ In the case of Judges' summonses the number of the court and a better estimate of the actual time of commencement of hearing may be ascertained from the Daily Cause List published on the morning of the day of hearing, a draft of which may be seen at the office of the Clerk to the Rules, Room 772, Royal Courts of Justice at 3 pm the previous working day.
* Delete as applicable.

---

1 Adapted from Form D262 used in the Principal Registry. See also Matrimonial Causes Rules 1977 r 122(1)(b).

---

7 **Summons** under the Matrimonial Homes Act 1983: interlocutory relief; High Court

In the High Court of Justice   No 6543 of 1987
Family Division
Oxbridge District Registry

In the Matter of the Matrimonial Homes Act 1983
And in the Matter of [21 North Parks Road, Oxbridge in the County of Rutland]

Between:

	E.F.	Petitioner
	and	
	G.F	Respondent

LET all parties attend before the Judge in Chambers at the Oxbridge District Registry of the High Court, The Law Courts, Oxbridge, in the County of Rutland on [Tuesday] the [12th] day of [May 1987] at [11] o'clock in the [fore]noon on the hearing of an application on the part of the Petitioner for an Order that:

(*continue as in Form 4*)

Dated this [29th] day of [April 1987]

To the Respondent

This Summons (*conclude as in Form 6*)

8 Notice of Application under the Matrimonial Homes Act 1983: interlocutory relief; county court.

[Heading as in Form 5 with the inclusion of:

In the Matter of the Matrimonial Homes Act 1983
And in the Matter of (*address*)]

TAKE NOTICE that the [Petitioner] intends to apply to a judge of this court sitting
at (*address*) on day the day of 1987 at o'clock
in the noon for orders that:

(*continue as in Form 4*)

(*conclude as in Form 5*)

9 Affidavit in support of an application for non-molestation and ouster injunctions[1]

(*Heading as in Form 1, 2, 3, 4, 5, 6, 7, or 8*)

I, [Mavis Moan], of [201 Upper Lewisham Road, Lewisham, London SE 13[2]]
(*occupation*) the above-named [Applicant *or* Petitioner *or as the case may be*] Make
Oath and say as follows:

(1) I make this affidavit in support of my [Originating Summons, Originating
Application, Summons, Notice of Application *or as the case may be*] herein,
dated the 4th June 1987.

(2) *Either* [The [Respondent] and I were married on the [27th May 1980]] *or*
[The [Respondent] and I are not married but since about [May 1980] we
have cohabited at [201 Upper Lewisham Road]][3]

(3) There are [two] child[ren][4] of the [family *or* relationship] [John Moan, who
was born on the 21st October 1981, now aged six; and Ann Moan, who was
born on the 12th February 1984, now aged three.]

(4) *If the application is made as interlocutory relief in a suit for divorce or
judicial separation based on the respondent's behaviour it may be
appropriate to add*: [I crave leave to refer to my Petition[5] herein, filed [the
4th June 1987] and in particular paragraphs [11–26] thereof, the contents of
which are true.]

(5) *[If appropriate[6] add*: I crave leave to refer to the proceedings in this court
under [No 85 012345] being an application made by me against the Respondent under the provisions of the Domestic Violence and Matrimonial
Proceedings Act 1976. My Affidavit therein, sworn the 10th April 1985, set
out the grounds of my application. On the 29th April 1985 His Honour
Judge Bold granted an injunction restraining the Respondent from
assaulting, molesting or otherwise interfering with me and further ordered
him to vacate [201 Upper Lewisham Road] forthwith until further order.
The Respondent left in accordance with the order but about three months
later we reconciled when the Respondent promised to behave. Initially the
Respondent kept his promise.]

(6) The Property[7] [201 Upper Lewisham Road] is [freehold, leasehold, rented
or as the case may be] in [my *or* the Respondent's sole name *or* our joint
names]. [I, he *or* we] [purchased the same] *or* [was *or* were allocated the
tenancy by the council] in about [December 1983]. [The main reason for the
council granting [me, him *or* us] the tenancy was that I was pregnant.] The
monthly [mortgage instalment *or* rent] is [£] which is paid by [me, him
or us *or as the case may be*].

(7) [201 Upper Lewisham Road] is a [flat *or* house[8] *etc*] which consists of [[three] bedrooms, sitting room, kitchen, bathroom and lavatory]. [The Respondent occupies the main bedroom, [John] the small bedroom and since [*date*] [I have been sharing the second bedroom with Ann] *or* [as a result of the incident on [*date*] hereinafter referred to I have been living with [my mother] at [*address*]; where the children and I share one very small bedroom *or as the case may be*].

(8) [Our [marriage *or* relationship[9]] was happy until about [*date*] when the Respondent was made redundant. He was most upset at losing his job and became depressed. He squandered his redundancy money on gambling and drink.]

(9) [I have tried to encourage the Respondent to find a job but this has resulted in arguments particularly about money and in the course of these arguments the Respondent has frequently become violent to me. *Set out the major incidents of violence.*[10]]

(10) [At about 1.30 am on Saturday the 30th May 1987 the Respondent returned to the [flat] very drunk. He came into our bedroom and demanded that I cook his supper. I told him that there was no food in the house because he had not given me any housekeeping. The Respondent then falsely accused me of spending the housekeeping on bingo. He then demanded to have intercourse with me, and when I told him that I was too tired and that he was too drunk he became enraged and dragged me out of bed by my feet. This caused my head to fall on the floor and it hurt and was bruised.[11]]

(11) [When I got up off the floor the Respondent told me I had a choice of being 'screwed' or 'thrown out of the flat'. I tried to calm the Respondent down but he got more and more worked up, grabbed my hair and pushed me down the stairs. He then told me to 'bugger off out of his life' and then went into our bedroom and bolted the door behind him.]

(12) [I was very frightened by the violence, which was worse than it had ever been before. I was dazed and shaking with terror. I spent that night in Ann's bedroom [and have slept there ever since.] *or* [The next morning I left the [flat] [with [out] the children] and went to stay with my [parents] and still stay there.[12]]]

(13) [Since I moved [into Ann's bedroom] *or* [to stay with my parents] the Respondent has threatened me continually that unless I [return to the [flat]] and [resume sleeping with him] he will kill me.[13] I am very frightened of him and take his threats seriously especially as on the 2nd June 1987 he produced a flick knife and held it to my throat. He said that life was not worth living without me; he told me that he would kill me, [then our children] and then himself. He said that if he could not have me nobody would.]

(14) [There is insufficient room in the [flat] for us both to live there, separately and apart. I have nowhere else to go [and I feel that is essential for the children's welfare that we are able [to return to the [flat] *or* to live in peace at the [flat]]].

(15) [I recognise that the Respondent must live somewhere. In the long term it should be possible for him to rent a flat [*or* it may be that the [matrimonial home] will be sold and that there will be sufficient to rehouse us both]. In the short term[14] he could stay with his [brother] at   (*address*), which is a [three] bedroom property in which his [brother] lives alone.]

(16) [If this Honourable Court sees fit to exclude the Respondent from the [flat] I realise that he will probably wish to have access to the children. I feel that it is important for the children to have a good relationship with their father but at the present time I am concerned that his violence, which they have seen, has frightened them and they are reluctant to see him. [My mother and father] are willing to assist with access and I propose that, for the time being, the Respondent should have access on [Saturday afternoons] at my parents' home.]

(17) In all the circumstances I respectfully ask this Honourable Court to make orders in the terms of my [Originating Summons, Originating Application, Summons, Notice of Application *or as the case may be.*]

Sworn *etc*

---

1 For the general requirements of affidavits see RSC Ord 41, CCR Ord 20, r 10, Appendix 3; and see *Practise Note* (Evidence: Documents) [1983] 3 All ER 33, [1983] 1 WLR 922, Appendix 2. For filing see *Practice Direction* (Family Division; Filing Affidavits) [1984] 1 All ER 684, [1984] 1 WLR 306, and *Practice Direction* (Family Division: Filing Affidavits) (No 3) [1987] 1 All ER 546 Appendix 2. See also *Court Forms* Vol 21 (1985 Issue) title HUSBAND AND WIFE, Form 27.

2 The address may be excluded from the affidavit with the leave of the court; RSC Ord 41, r 1(4), CCR Ord 20, r 10(1)(a). An application to exclude an address should be made ex parte to a registrar at the time of issue of an application to be heard on notice, or to a judge at the hearing of an application ex parte for injunctions.

3 These are the factual circumstances which give the court jurisdiction under the Domestic Violence and Matrimonial Proceedings Act 1976, s 1 (27 *Halsbury's Statutes* 788 MATRIMONIAL LAW). See also Matrimonial Homes Act 1983, s 1 and 9 (27 *Halsbury's Statutes* 585 MATRIMONIAL LAW.

4 Give details of relevant children, stating their names, dates of birth, whether they are children of either or both parties and where they are living.

5 The facts which constitute the allegations of unreasonable behaviour (but not the evidence) will be pleaded in the petition (Matrimonial Causes Rules 1977, r 9 and Appendix 2 para 1(m)). The affidavit should give the supporting evidence. It is not necessary to exhibit the petition to the affidavit as the same is already on the court file. See also *Practice Direction* (Evidence: Documents) [1983] 3 All ER 33, [1983] 1 WLR 922 para 4 (iii) Appendix 2. Where an application is made ex parte, before the issue of proceedings it is permissable to exhibit a *draft* petition.

6 Details should be given of any previous or continuing relevant proceedings such as under the Domestic Violence and Matrimonial Proceedings Act 1976, the Matrimonial Homes Act 1983 or under the Guardianship of Minors Acts 1971 to 1973.

7 Particulars should be given about the matrimonial home, stating whether it is owned solely by one of the parties or jointly by both; whether it is freehold, leasehold or rented; the approximate amount of the mortgage repayments or rent and who pays the same.

8 Particulars should be given about the accommodation; the number of bedrooms; the sleeping arrangements, whether or not the parties continue to sleep together. Where the property is large the court will wish to have sufficient information to be able to decide whether the accommodation is large enough for the same to be divided between the parties as an interim solution.

9 Give brief background details about the marriage or the relationship.

10 Give full particulars about the respondent's conduct or the other circumstances which give rise to the application. It is important to state the effect of such conduct or circumstances on any children.

11 If a medical report has been obtained the same should be exhibited.

12 Where the applicant and any children have left the home details of their present accommodation should be given, particularly stating how permanent it is.

13 Where the application is made ex parte it is important that details should be given of the urgency of the application. Furthermore *all* incidents up to the date of the swearing of the affidavit should be included. It must be remembered that an applicant for an ex parte order has a heavy responsibility to disclose all relevant facts; see chapter 2 above.

14 Where it is sought to exclude the respondent from the home details should be given of any alternative accommodation which might be available to him. It is however very necessary to be realistic about the extent to which his friends and/or relatives will put him up. If the respondent spends nights away from the home with, for example, a girlfriend, the affidavit should say so.

B Service

10 Affidavit of service[1]

[Heading as in the proceedings]

I, Ivor Mackintosh, of 3 Railway Cutting, Streatham, London SW16, Inquiry Agent, Make Oath and say as follows:

(1) I am an Inquiry Agent in the firm of Seedie Mackintosh & Co and have been so for the past 5 years.

(2) I am over the age of 16 years (2).

(3) Acting on the instructions of Pick Shovel & Co, Solicitors for the [Petitioner], I did on [Tuesday the 24th February 1987[3]] at [10.30am] personally serve the [Respondent] at 27 Garage Mews, Islington, London N1 with [a] true [copy *or* copies] of [a summons issued by this Honourable Court, returnable on the [2nd March 1987] and an affidavit of the [Petitioner] sworn the 23rd February 1987 *or* an injunction granted by this Honourable Court on the 23rd February 1987] by handing[4] the said true [copy or copies] to [him] which [he] accepted (*or as the case may be*).

(4) There is now produced and shown to me marked 'I.M.1.' [a] true [copy *or* copies] of the [summons and affidavit *or* injunction] so served.

(5) At the time of service the [Respondent] admitted [his] identity to me and I recognised [him] from [having previously served [him] with documents (*specify*) in this matter on the 11th February 1987 *or* from description given to me by the [Petitioner] *or* from a photograph, now produced and shown to me marked 'I.M.2.', supplied to me by the [Petitioner] (*or as the case may be*)].

(6) At the time of such service I pointed out to the [Respondent] [the return date on the summons *or* the penal notice, which I read to [him]].

Sworn *etc*

---

1 RSC Ord 65, r 8; CCR Ord 7, r 6(1)(b); see Appendix 3. For the general requirements of affidavits see RSC Ord 41, CCR Ord 20, r 10, Appendix 3; and see *Practice Direction* (Evidence: Documents) [1983] 3 All ER 33, [1983] 1 WLR 922 Appendix 2; for filing see *Practice Direction* (Family Division: Filing Affidavits) [1984] 1 All ER 684, [1984] 1 WLR 306 and *Practice Direction* (Family Division: Filing Affidavits) [1987] 1 All ER 546, Appendix 2.

2 See CCR Ord 7, r 2, Appendix 2.

3 As to the times at which service may or may not be effected see *Supreme Court Practice*, para 65/2/2 and CCR Ord 7, r 5, Appendix 2.

4 Personal Service may be effected by leaving a copy with the person to be served. RSC Ord 65, r 2, CCR Ord 7, r 2, Appendix 3.

11 **Notice to a respondent** when a matter will be heard[1]

[*Royal Arms*]

In the   County Court

No of Matter

[In the Matter of the Domestic Violence and Matrimonial Proceedings Act 1976]

Between   Applicant

and   Respondent   Seal

To the Respondent:

A sealed copy of an originating application to the court is attached.

This matter will be heard by this court

at   (*address*)

on   (*date*)

at   o'clock when you should attend.

Failure to attend may result in an order being made in your absence.

Dated this   day of   19

---

1 Adapted from Form 8 County Court (Forms) Rules 1982 (SI 1982/586).

---

12 **Notice of bailiff service**[1]

I certify that the notice of which this is a true copy, was served by me on   (*date*) on the   (*Petitioner/Respondent*) personally at the address stated in the notice *or* at   (*address*)   (*or, if the notice is served in accordance with an order for substituted service state the manner of service*)

Bailiff/Officer of the Court

Notice of non-service

I certify that this notice has not been served for the following reasons:

(*set out reasons*)

Bailiff/Officer of the Court

---

1 To be endorsed on the reverse of Form 78 County Court (Forms) Rules 1982 (SI 1982/586). See Form 39 below.

C Orders

13 **Interim Injunction**: county court

In the   County Court

No of Matter

Between   Petitioner (*or*) Applicant

and   Respondent (*or*) Defendant

The [Petitioner (or) Applicant] undertaking by his [counsel (or) solicitor] to abide by any order this Court may make for the payment of damages in this case this Court shall hereafter find that the [Respondent (or) Defendant] has sustained any loss or damage by reason of this Order[1]

IT IS ORDERED that the [Respondent *or* Defendant] [whether by himself his servants agents, or otherwise] [be restrained] [do]

(set out terms of order)

until the   day of   19 .[2]
(*or*)
Until further order[3]
(*or*)
until the   day of   19   upon which day this Court will consider whether this Order shall be further continued.[4]

TAKE NOTICE THAT UNLESS YOU OBEY THE DIRECTIONS CONTAINED IN THIS ORDER YOU WILL BE GUILTY OF CONTEMPT OF COURT, AND WILL BE LIABLE TO BE COMMITTED TO PRISON[5]

Dated this   day of   19 .

Judge

---

1 This undertaking as to damages is in general inappropriate. *Practice Direction* [1974] 2 All ER 400, [1974] 1 WLR 576. See Appendix 2, above.
2 This should be used where the injunction is made inter partes for a fixed period.
3 This should be used where the injunction is made inter partes for an indefinite period.
4 This should be used where the injunction is made ex parte.
5 Notice in Form 77 incorporated in the order. See CCR Ord 29, r 1(3).

---

14 Injunction ex parte in proposed divorce proceedings[1]

In the Divorce Registry   No file[2]

His Honour Judge Bold   In Chambers

In the Matter of a proposed suit for divorce

Between: P.R.   Proposed Petitioner

and

S.R.   Proposed Respondent

Upon hearing [Counsel] for the Proposed Petitioner
And Upon reading the affidavit of the Proposed Petitioner, sworn today[3]
And Upon the Proposed Petitioner undertaking by [Counsel] to file a petition for dissolution of marriage within [48] hours[4]

It is Ordered that:

(1) [The Proposed Petitioner do have leave[5] to file a petition for divorce without filing a certificate of marriage, provided the same is filed within [21] days.]
(2) The Proposed Respondent, by himself, his servants or agents, or otherwise howsoever, is strictly enjoined and an injunction is hereby granted restraining him from:
    (i) assaulting, molesting or otherwise interfering with the Proposed Petitioner, and

(ii) removing the child[ren] of the family from the interim care and control of the Proposed Petitioner

until the   day of   1987, upon which day this Court will consider whether this order shall be further continued.

Dated this   day of   1987

(Penal Notice as in form 17)

---

1 Application may be made for an injunction prior to the issue of proceedings in a case of urgency, CCR Ord 13, r 6(4). See chapter 2 above. See also *Practice Direction* (Matrimonial Cause: Injunction) [1978] 2 All ER 919, [1978] 1 WLR 925, Appendix 2.
2 As proceedings have not been issued there will not be a file number.
3 If it has not been possible to swear the affidavit before making the application the judge may read the unsworn affidavit and hear the proposed petitioner's evidence that the contents are true; an undertaking must be given to swear and file the affidavit forthwith. In this context 'forthwith' and 'as soon as reasonably practical' have the same meaning and effect. It is important that there should be no default in compliance with such an undertaking. See *Refson & Co Ltd v Saggers* [1984] 3 All ER 111, [1984] 1 WLR 1025.
4 It is essential that the judge is told of any matter that would delay the issue of proceedings so that a realistic time will be set by the court. A solicitor who fails to issue proceedings within the specified time limit is, himself, in contempt. *Refson & Co Ltd v Saggers* above.
5 See Matrimonial Causes Rules 1977, r 12(2) (SI 1977/344).

---

15 Order under the Matrimonial Homes Act 1983 in divorce proceedings

[In the High Court of Justice
Family Division
Cardiff District Registry
or
In the Cardiff County Court]   No 87 D 4567·

In the Matter of the Matrimonial Homes Act 1983
And in the Matter of 83 Lake Road, Canton, Cardiff.

Between: W.P.   Petitioner

and

H.P.   Respondent

Upon hearing [*etc*]
And upon reading [*etc*]
It is Ordered that:

(1) [It is declared that the Petitioner has rights of occupation in 83 Lake Road aforesaid[1]]
(2) The Petitioner do have leave to enter and thereafter occupy 83 Lake Road aforesaid after [noon on the 16th May 1987[2]]
(3) The Respondent to permit the Petitioner to enter 83 Lake Road aforesaid [after noon on the 16 May 1987] and thereafter do permit the Petitioner to occupy the said premises[3]
(4) [The Respondent's rights of occupation in 83 Lake Road aforesaid be terminated[4] as from noon on the 16 May 1987]
or
[The Respondent be prohibited[5] from exercising [his] rights of occupation in 83 Lake Road aforesaid as from noon on the 16th May 1987 until further order]
or

[The Respondent's rights of occupation in 83 Lake Road aforesaid be suspended[6] from [noon on the 16th May 1987] for a period of [three months]

or

[The Respondent's rights of occupation in 83 Lake Road aforesaid be restricted[7] in that [he] may not enter [the main bedroom *or as the case may be*] until further order.

(5) [Petitioner's costs in any event]

(6) And it is directed that the Petitioner's rights of occupation shall not be brought to an end on the pronouncement herein of a decree of divorce but shall continue until the hearing of [her] application for ancillary relief.[8]

Dated this 6th day of May 1987.

---

1 Matrimonial Homes Act 1983, 27 *Halsbury's Statutes* (4th edn) 585, MATRIMONIAL LAW, s 1(2)(a). It is not necessary to apply for a declaration in respect of a joint owner of the matrimonial home, ibid, s 9.
2 Ibid, s 1(1)(b).
3 Ibid, s 1(2)(c).
4 Ibid, s 1(2)(a). The rights of occupation of a joint owner can not be terminated: ibid, s 9(1).
5 Ibid, s 1(2)(b).
6 Ibid.
7 Ibid.
8 Rights of occupation are brought to an end on the death of one spouse, ibid s 2(4)(a), or the termination (otherwise than by death) of the marriage, ibid s 2(4)(b), unless in the event of a matrimonial dispute or estrangement the court sees fit to direct otherwise by an order under s 1 during the subsistence of the marriage. Ibid, s 2(4).

---

16 Penal Notice High Court[1]

A Mandatory Injunction

If you the within named [A.B.] neglect to obey this Order by the time therein limited, you will be liable to process of execution for the purpose of compelling you to obey the same.

B Prohibitory Injunction:

If you the within-named [A.B.] disobey this Order, you will be liable to process of execution for the purpose of compelling you to obey the same.

---

1 See *Supreme Court Practice* para 45/7/6.

---

17 Notice as to consequences of disobedience to order of court: county court[1]

To   (*name*)
of   (*address*)
TAKE NOTICE that unless you obey the directions contained in this order you will be guilty of contempt of Court and will be liable to be committed to prison.

Dated this   day of   19 .

Registrar

---

1 Adapted from Form 77 County Court (Forms) Rules 1982.

18 Notice to police station of power of arrest

Domestic Violence and Matrimonial Proceedings Act 1976
To: the officer in charge of the police station for the Applicant's address
[In The Divorce Registry]   No   of 19 .

v

TAKE NOTICE that:

the enclosed copy order granting/varying/discharging an injunction, with a power of arrest attached, is delivered to you in accordance with court rules made pursuant to the above Act.

The relevant particulars are:

Applicant's name, address and telephone number (*if any*)

Applicant's solicitor's name, address and telephone number (*including emergency number if any*)

Name and address of person against whom order made

NOTES:
If an arrest is made under the Act,
    (i)   during weekdays (Monday to Friday) between 9 a.m. and 5 p.m., contact the [Clerk of the Rules Department (telephone number: 01 936 6000 Ext 6007 *or* 6188)]
    (ii) at any other time, follow normal Police Force instructions.
Dated

B. P. Tickle
Senior Registrar

D Wardship and children

19 Originating Summons: Wardship

[Royal Arms]

In the High Court of Justice   No 87 WG 123
Family Division
Oxbridge District Registry

In the Matter of Jane Smith (a minor)
And in the Matter of the Supreme Court Act 1981
And in the Matter of the Guardianship of Minors Act 1971 and 1973

Between: Rutland County Council   Plaintiff

and

Mary Smith   Defendant

To Mary Smith of 513 Stalin House, Karl Marx Estate, Oxbridge in the County of Rutland

LET the Defendant, within 14 days after service of this Summons on her, counting the day of service, return the accompanying Acknowledgment of Service to the Oxbridge District Registry of the High Court, The Law Courts, Oxbridge in the County of Rutland.

By this Summons, which is issued on the application of the Plaintiff, Rutland County Council of County Hall, Oxbridge, in the County of Rutland, the Plaintiff claims against the Defendant:
(1) that the minor continue to be a ward of this Honourable Court during her minority or until further order,
(2) that the minor be committed to the care of the Plaintiff pursuant to Family Law Reform Act 1969, s 7(2)
(3) that the Defendant be restrained from removing the minor from the care of the Plaintiff
(4) that the Defendant be restrained from communicating with the minor save through the Plaintiff
(5) that provision may be made for the costs of this Summons

The present whereabouts of the minor are that she resides at the Oxbridge Children's Home, 201 Rutland Road, Oxbridge, Rutland.

The minor was born on the 1st April 1982.

The Plaintiff's interest in the minor is statutory.
The Defendant is the mother of the minor.

Important Notice: It is a contempt of Court, which may be punished by imprisonment, to take any child named in this Summons out of England and Wales, even to Scotland, Northern Ireland, the Republic of Ireland, the Channel Islands or the Isle of Man, without the leave of the Court.

If a Defendant does not acknowledge service, such judgment may be given or order made against or in relation to her as the Court may think just and expedient.

Dated this 8th day of February 1987.

Note: *This Summons may not be served later than 12 calendar months beginning with the above date unless renewed by order of the Court.*

This Summons was taken out by Albert Bagg, of County Hall, Oxbridge, in the County of Rutland, Solicitor for the said Plaintiff whose address is stated above.

Important Directions for Acknowledgment of Service are given with the accompanying form.

To the Defendant (other than the minor)
Take Notice that, pursuant to Order 90, rule 3(5) and (6) of the Rules of the Supreme Court:
(1) you must forthwith after being served with this Summons lodge in the above mentioned Registry a notice stating your address and the whereabouts of the minor (or if it be the case that you are unaware of the minor's whereabouts) and unless the Court otherwise directs, you must serve a copy of such notice on the Plaintiff; and
(2) if you subsequently change your address or become aware of any change in the minor's whereabouts you must, unless the Court otherwise directs, lodge in the above mentioned Registry notice of your new address or of the new whereabouts of the minor, as the case may be and serve a copy of such notice on the Plaintiff.

Any notice required to be lodged in the above mentioned Registry should be sent or delivered to the Oxbridge District Registry of the High Court, The Law Courts, Oxbridge in the County of Rutland.

20 **Summons**: wardship[1]

In the High Court of Justice   No WG 89 of 1987
Family Division
Principal Registry

In the Matter of Alice Jones (a minor)
And in the Matter of the Supreme Court Act 1981
And in the Matter of the Guardianship of Minors Act 1971 and 1973

Between: Gerald Jones
                                      and
                          Hannah Jones (his wife)   Plaintiffs

                                      and

                          Alice Jones (a minor)
                          (by her Guardian ad Litem
                              the Official Solicitor)   Defendant

LET the Defendant and Jonathan Browne[2] of 412 Bennet Street, Deptford, London SE8 attend before one of the Judges of the High Court, sitting at the Royal Courts of Justice, Strand, London WC2A 2LL, on Friday the 8th day of May 1987 at or after 10.30 o'clock to show cause why an order should not be made that:

(1) the said Jonathan Browne be restrained from removing the minor from the care and control of the Plaintiffs
(2) the said Jonathan Browne be restrained from communicating with the minor in any way
(3) the said Jonathan Browne be condemned in the costs of this summons

Dated this 6th day of April 1987

To the Defendant and to the said Jonathan Browne.

This summons was taken out by Pick Shovel & Co, 22 Old Square, Lincoln's Inn, London, WC2, Solicitors for the Plaintiffs.

---

1 Adapted from Form FD586 used in the Principal Registry.
2 See *Practice Direction* (Wardship) (Parties to Proceedings) [1983] 2 All ER 672, [1983] 1 WLR 790, Appendix 2, above.

---

21 **Seek and find** order[1]

In the High Court of Justice   No WG 789 of 1987
Family Division
Principal Registry

Before Mr Justice Boggle   in Chambers

In the Matter of Richard Andrew Colts (a minor)
And in the Matter of the Supreme Court Act 1981
And in the Matter of the Guardianship of Minors Acts 1971 and 1973

Between:
                          Ruth Susan Colts   Plaintiff

                                      and

                          David John Colts   Defendant

UPON hearing [Counsel for the Plaintiff and for the Defendant AND upon reading the Affidavit of the Plaintiff sworn the 12th February 1987]

It is ordered that the Defendant do hand over the minor[s] into the custody of TT Tipstaff of this High Court of Justice his deputy or assistant

And it is directed that you the said Tipstaff, your deputy or assistant do receive the said minor[s] into your custody and deliver [him] to the Plaintiff

And in the event of the said Defendant failing to comply with the above handing over order these are therefore to command you the said Tipstaff and others in Her Majesty's name forthwith to apprehend the said Defendant and bring [him] before one of the Justices of the Family Division of the High Court at the Royal Courts of Justice, Strand, London as soon as possible after [his] apprehension

Dated the 12th day of February 1987

To the Defendant, the said David John Colts, of [*address*] and to TT Tipstaff of this High Court of Justice, his deputy or assistant and all other Constables and Peace Officers it may concern

---

1 Adapted from Form FD 589 used in the Principal Registry, this order, being directed to the Tipstaff, is not usually given to the party who applied for the order; if an order is made for continuation of the wardship, or for care and control, it will be drawn up separately.

22 Injunction: wardship[1]

In the High Court of Justice   No WG 234 of 1987
Family Division
Principal Registry

Before Mr Justice Stone   in Chambers

In the Matter of Adrian Green (a minor)
And in the Matter of the Supreme Court Act 1981
And in the Matter of the Guardianship of Minors Acts 1971 and 1973

Between: Catherine Green   Plaintiff

                                      and

                                 Ronald Green   Defendant

Upon the application of the Plaintiff by Summons dated the 26th day of January 1987

And upon hearing the Solicitor for the Plaintiff and Counsel for the Defendant

And upon reading the affidavit of the Plaintiff sworn the 26th day of January 1987 and the affidavit of the Defendant sworn the 30th day of January 1987

It is ordered that:
  (1) the Defendant Ronald Green, the father of the above mentioned minor Adrian Green whether by himself his servants or agents be restrained until further Order from doing the following acts or any of them that is to say taking the said minor Adrian Green out of the jurisdiction of this Court or permitting the said minor to go out of the jurisdiction
  (2) there be no order as to costs save that the costs of the Plaintiff and the Defendant be taxed in accordance with the provisions of Schedule 2 to the Legal Aid Act 1974.

Dated the 3rd day of February 1987.

---

1 The injunction should be indorsed with a penal notice in the following terms:
   'If you, the within-named Ronald Green disobey this order you will be liable to process of execution for the purpose of compelling you to obey the same.'
   See *Supreme Court Practice* 45/7/6, and see Form 16, above.

23 **Custody Order** in divorce proceedings[1]

In the Divorce Registry   No 1234 of 1986

Matrimonial cause proceeding in the Divorce
Registry treated by virtue of Section 42 of
the Matrimonial and Family Proceedings Act
1984 as pending in a divorce county court

His Honour Judge Block QC   in Chambers

Between:

Betty Jane Potts   Petitioner

and

Stuart Raymond Potts   Respondent

Upon hearing [Counsel on behalf of the Petitioner and of the Respondent] and
upon reading [the Court Welfare Officer's Report, the affidavits of the Respondent
sworn the 28th April 1986 and the 21st September 1986, the affidavit of the
Petitioner sworn the 1st July 1986] and upon taking the oral evidence [of the
petitioner and the Respondent]

It is Ordered that the child Mary Elizabeth Potts do remain in the [joint custody of
the parties with care and control to the Petitioner] until further order of the Court

And it is Directed:
  (1) that the said child be not removed from England and Wales without leave of
      the Court until [she] shall attain the age of 18 years; provided that if either
      parent do give a general written undertaking to the Court to return the said
      child to England and Wales when called upon to do so, and, unless otherwise
      directed, with the written consent of the other parent, that parent may
      remove the said child from England and Wales for any period specified in
      such written consent;[2] and
  (2) that no step (other than the institution of proceedings in any court) be taken
      by the said [Petitioner] which would result in [any of] the said child being
      known by a new surname before [she] attains the age of 18 years or, being
      female, marries below that age, except with the leave of a judge or the
      consent in writing of the other parent.[3]

Dated the 8th day of January 1987.

NOTE
Either parent may request the Passport Office (Clive House, Petty France, London
SW1) not to issue a passport allowing a child to go abroad without his or her
knowledge.

---

1 Adapted from Form D324 used in the Divorce Registry.
2 Matrimonial Causes Rules 1977, r 94(2)(SI 1977/344); see Appendix 3, above.
3 Ibid, r 92(8); see Appendix 3, above.

E Trespass and assault

24 Particulars of claim

In the Oxbridge County Court   Case No

Between:

A.B.   Plaintiff

and

C.D.   Defendant

PARTICULARS OF CLAIM

(1) The Plaintiff is and was at all material times the [leasehold *or* freehold owner] [tenant] of 53 Park Road Oxbridge in the County of Rutland.

(2) On divers days since about   (*date*) the Defendant has wrongfully entered the said premises:

(3) On divers days since about   (*date*) the defendant has frequently assaulted the plaintiff and has beaten her:

PARTICULARS

    (a) [*Set out all relevant incidents of trespass*]
    (b)
    (c) *etc.*

(4) By reason of the matters aforesaid the Plaintiff has suffered pain and injury loss and damage:

    (i) Injuries: [*Set out details of Plaintiff's injuries*]
    (ii) Treatment: [*Set out details of the treatment the Plaintiff received for his injuries*]
    (iii) Special Damage: [*Set out details of any expenses incurred by the Plaintiff such as mending windows and changing locks*

(5) The Defendant threatens and intends unless restrained by this Honourable Court to repeat the acts complained of.

and the Plaintiff claims:

    (i) Damages for assault limited to [£500].
    (ii) Damages for trespass limited to [£500].
    (iii) An injunction to restrain the Defendant whether by himself his servants or agents or otherwise howsoever from entering or attempting to enter the said premises.
    (iv) An injunction to restrain the Defendant by himself his servants or agents or otherwise howsoever from assaulting molesting or otherwise interfering with the Plaintiff.
    (v) Costs

Dated this   day of   1987.

To the Registrar and to the Defendant.

25 Notice of application for injunctions

In the Oxbridge County Court   Case No

Between:

A.B.   Plaintiff

and

C.D.   Defendant

NOTICE OF APPLICATION

TAKE NOTICE that the Plaintiff intends to apply to the Judge in court at the Oxbridge County Court   (*address*)   on   day the   day of   1982 at   o'clock in the   noon for an Order:

    (1) That the Defendant be restrained, until the trial of the Action herein or until further order, by himself his servants or agents or otherwise howsoever from entering or attempting to enter the premises known as the situate at 53 Park Road Oxbridge in the county of Rutland.

    (2) That the Defendant be restrained, until the trial of the Action herein or until further Order, by himself his servants or agents or otherwise howsoever from assaulting molesting or otherwise interfering with the Plaintiff.

    (3) That the Defendant be condemned in the costs of the application.

Dated this   day of   1987.

To the Registrar and to the Defendant.

26 Affidavit

In the Oxbridge County Court   Case No

Between: A.B.   Plaintiff

and

C.D.   Defendant

I, A. B. of 53 Park Road, Oxbridge in the County of Rutland, the above named Plaintiff, (*occupation*), Make Oath and say as follows:

    (1) I make this affidavit in support of my application herein, dated the   day of   1987, for injunctions.

    (2) I crave leave to refer to the Particulars of Claim herein, the contents of which are true.

    (3) I am the [owner *or* tenant] of 53, Park Road, Oxbridge and have been so since [the 15th April 1986] when I [purchased the house *or* was granted the tenancy of the house].

    (4) Between January 1983 and November 1985 I cohabited with the Defendant at a flat at 17B West Common Road, Northminster, Rutland. [There are [no] children of our relationship.]

    (5) Our relationship came to an end in November 1985 when I left the Defendant as a result of his violence and went to live at the Northminster Women's Refuge.

    (6) On the 20th November 1985 the Defendant came to the Refuge, broke down the door, and assaulted twelve of the residents, while trying to find out where I was.

    (7) The Police were called and they arrested the Defendant. He was charged with various offences and on the 10th January 1986 he pleaded guilty at Northminster Crown Court to one count of criminal damage, two counts of threats to kill and seventeen counts of assault occasioning actual bodily

harm. The prosecution did not proceed with the count of attempted murder. There is now produced and shown to me marked 'A. B. l' a true copy of the certificate of conviction. The Defendant was sentenced to 2 years imprisonment.

(8)   In April 1986 I moved to my present address so that the Defendant would not be able to find me on his release from prison. However the Defendant was released on the 18th May 1987 and has somehow discovered my whereabouts. Since the 25th May 1987 he has frequently forced his way into my home and has assaulted me.

(9)   (*Give details of the incidents pleaded in paragraphs 2 and 3 of the Particulars of Claim; Form 24 above.*)

(10) As a result of the Defendant's behaviour I am absolutely terrified; I am nervous and depressed. My whole life seems to be taken up with making sure that the Defendant is not following me or watching me. I cannot enjoy life while I am in such fear of the Defendant. I have to be on my guard when I go to work in the mornings, in case he is lying in wait for me. I have to watch out for him when I am travelling to and from work. I have to take care in case he follows me home or, worse still, has forced his way into my home while I have been out and is waiting for me.

(11) I am sure that the only way I can have any peace is if I am given the protection of the Court and I humbly ask this Honourable Court to grant orders in the terms of my application.

Sworn *etc*

27 Injunction[1]

In the Oxbridge County Court   Case No

Between: A.B.   Plaintiff

and

C.D.   Defendant

The Plaintiff undertaking by [her] [Counsel] to abide by any order this Court may make for the payment of damages in case this Court shall hereafter find that the Defendant has sustained any loss or damage by reason of this order[2]

It is Ordered that the Defendant whether by himself his servants or agents or otherwise be restrained from:

(1)   Assaulting or threatening the Plaintiff[3]

(2)   Entering or attempting to enter 53 Park Road Oxbridge in the County of Rutland

until the day after the day upon which this action shall be heard[4]

(*or*)

until further order[5]

(*or*)

until the   day of   1987 upon which day this Court will consider whether this Order shall be further continued[6]

TAKE NOTICE THAT UNLESS YOU OBEY THE DIRECTIONS CONTAINED IN THIS ORDER YOU WILL BE GUILTY OF CONTEMPT OF COURT AND WILL BE LIABLE TO BE COMMITTED TO PRISON[7]

Dated this   day of   1987

Judge

---

1 Adapted from Form 16 County Court (Forms) Rules 1982 (SI 1982/586).
2 The Practice Direction (Injunction: Undertaking as to Damages) [1974] 2 All ER 400, [1974] 1 WLR 576 does not apply to actions under the general jurisdiction of county courts. However in orders, such as this one, concerning personal conduct the court has a discretion whether or not such an undertaking should be given. The practice varies widely between individual courts.
3 Courts frequently refuse to restrain molestation falling short of threats or violence although it is submitted that there is no good reason for this.
4 This form is appropriate where the injunction is made as interlocutory relief on notice.
5 This form is appropriate where the injunction is made on the trial of the action.
6 This form is appropriate where the injunction is made ex parte.
7 Notice in Form 77 County Court (Forms) Rules 1982 incorporated in the order; see CCR Ord 29, r 1(3), Appendix 3.

F Preservation of assets

28 Summons or notice of application for an order under Matrimonial Causes Act 1973, section 37

(*Heading as in the suit: see Form 23*)
[LET all parties (*continue as in Form 7*)[1]
or
Take Notice that (*continue as in Form 8*)[1]
. . . for an order that:
    (1) the [Respondent] be restrained from disposing, selling, charging or otherwise dealing with [*set out the particular assets in respect of which an order is sought*]
    (2) the [Respondent] be condemned in the costs of this [summons *or* application]
               (*conclude as in Form 5 or 6*)

---

1 The application may be made to a registrar. See Matrimonial Causes Rules 1977, r 84(1), Appendix 3 above.

---

29 Notice of application for an interlocutory injunction in proceedings under Married Women's Property Act 1882

In the Divorce Registry[1]   No 9876 of 1987
In the Matter of an application by [Michael Simpson] under section 17 of the Married Women's Property Act 1882[2] and section 37 of the Matrimonial Proceedings and Property Act 1970[3]

Between: Michael Simpson   Applicant

                      and

                Susan Simpson   Respondent

TAKE NOTICE that the [Applicant] intends to apply to [the judge in chambers sitting at the Royal Courts of Justice, Strand, London WC2A 2LL *or* one of the Registrars in chambers at the Divorce Registry, Somerset House, London WC2R 1LP] on [Monday] the [7th] day of [September 1987] at [10.30] o'clock in the [fore] noon for orders that:

(1) The [Respondent] do forthwith deliver up to the [Applicant] all items of property specified in the First Schedule to the Originating Application herein[4]

(2) The [Respondent] be restrained from disposing, selling, charging or otherwise dealing with property specified in the Second Schedule to the Originating Application herein.[5]

(3) The [Respondent] be restrained from removing the property specified in the Third Schedule to the Originating Application herein[6] from the possession of the [Applicant].

(4) The [Respondent] be condemned in the costs of this application.

(conclude as in Form 5)

---

1 For the circumstances in which the Divorce Registry has jurisdiction to entertain proceedings under the Married Women's Property Act 1882 see Matrimonial Causes Rules 1977 (SI 1977/ 344), r 106.
2 27 *Halsbury's Statutes* (4th edn) 566 MATRIMONIAL LAW.
3 27 *Halsbury's Statutes* (4th edn) 652 MATRIMONIAL LAW
4 Property held by the Respondent but claimed by the Applicant; see 21 *Atkin's Court Forms* (1985) Issue) HUSBAND AND WIFE, Form 22.
5 Property held by the Respondent but owned jointly; see 21 *Atkin's Court Forms*, Form 22.
6 Property held by the Applicant but claimed by the Respondent, see 21 *Atkin's Court Forms*, Form 22.

---

30 Affidavit[1] in support

(Heading as in form 28)

I, *(name, address and occupation of deponent)* Make Oath and say as follows:

(1) I have made application to this Honourable Court for financial relief[2] in my [Petition *or*, Answer[3]] *or* [notice[4] of such application having been filed on *(date)*].

(2) So far as I am aware the Respondent's assets comprise *(here set them out shortly)*. I claim *(here set out the extent of the claim)*.

(3) I am informed by *(source)* and verily believe that the Respondent is about to transfer *(the property)* to his current girlfriend and that he is selling his other assets and intends to pay the net proceeds of sale of the same into his account with the Bank of America in Hollywood, California. His actions will result in there being no assets left in his possession in this country to meet whatever order this Honourable Court may make on my said application for financial relief.

(4) In the premises I respectfully ask this Honourable Court to make an order restraining the Respondent from effecting the transfer of *(property)* and to direct that the proceeds of sale of *(assets)* be deposited into a bank account in the joint names of our solicitors until my said application has been adjudicated upon.

Sworn *etc*

---

1 For the general requirements of affidavits see RSC Ord 41, CCR Ord 20 r 10, Appendix 3. See also *Practice Note*, (Evidence: Documents) [1983] 3 A11 ER 33, [1983] 1 WLR 922, Appendix 2. For filing of affidavits see *Practice Direction* (Family Division: Filing Affidavits) [1984] 1 A11 ER 684, [1984] 1 WLR 306, and see *Practice Direction* (Family Division: Filing Affidavits) [1987] 1 A11 ER 546, Appendix 2.
2 'Financial relief' is defined by Matrimonial Causes Act 1973, s 37(1) (27 *Halsbury's Statutes* (4th edn) 700 MATRIMONIAL LAW). See Appendix 1.

3 An application for maintenance pending suit, financial provision or property adjustment must be made in the petition or answer, if one is filed claiming relief. See Matrimonial Causes Rules 1977 (SI 1977 344), r 68(1).
4 An application, which should have been made in the petition or answer, may be made subsequently, by notice, with leave, Matrimonial Causes Rules 1977, r 68(2)(a). Where a petition or answer has not been filed by the applicant or the application is not required to be made in the petition or answer (eg an application for a variation order) the application is made by notice; see Matrimonial Causes Rules 1977, r 68(3). The notice is in Form 11 App 1 Matrimonial Causes Rules 1977.

31 **Injunction** under Matrimonial Causes Act 1973, section 37

(Heading as in the suit: see Form 23)
Upon the [Petitioner] undertaking to proceed expeditiously with [her] application for ancillary relief
And Upon hearing [Counsel on behalf of the Petitioner and on behalf of the Respondent] and upon reading [the affidavit of the Petitioner, sworn the 15th July 1987, and the affidavit of the Respondent, sworn the 22nd July 1987]

It is Ordered that:
(1) The order herein dated the 15th July 1987 be discharged.[1]
(2) The [Respondent], by himself, his servants, agents or otherwise be restrained from disposing of [*set out the asset eg* the proceeds of sale of Rose Cottage, The High Street, Little Market in the County of Norfolk] otherwise than by paying the same into an account in the joint names of the parties' solicitors pending the determination of the [Petitioner's] application for [ancillary relief], an agreement as to the division of the said proceeds of sale or further order.[2]
(3) The [Respondent], by himself, his servants, agents or otherwise be restrained from disposing, selling, charging or otherwise dealing with the following assets:
[(i) 200 shares in East Norfolk Motor Co Ltd;
(ii) a plot of freehold land situate at West Street Little Market in the County of Norfolk, the title of which is registered under Title No NK 12345 at HM Land Registry;
(iii) a quantity of antiques specified in a valuation dated the 3rd March 1982 by Slapdash & Co;
[(iv) a policy of assurance No QZ 99/5432/X, dated the 1st April 1970 with the Norfolk Permanent Mutual Assurance and Provident Benefit Society; and,
(v) the funds in account No AJ 13579 held at the Swaffham Branch of the King's Lynn Building Society, *or as the case may be*] pending the determination of the [Petitioner's] application for [ancillary relief], agreement or further order.]
(4) The [Respondent] be restrained from damaging or destroying, fair wear and tear excepted, any of the contents of the matrimonial home, The Old Mill, Swanton Bittering, Norfolk.
(5) The costs of this application [including costs reserved[3]] be reserved to the hearing of the [Petitioner's] application for ancillary relief (*or as the case may be*).
Dated this 24th day of July 1987

1 This assumes that an ex parte order was made on the 15th July 1987.
2 This form of wording was suggested in *Roche v Roche* (1981) 11 Fam Law 243, CA.
3 Costs of an ex parte hearing are normally reserved.

32 **Mareva** injunction

In the High Court of Justice   No: 2468 of 1987
Family Division
Principal Registry

Between: A. B.   Petitioner

                                      and

                                      C. B.   Respondent

UPON hearing [Counsel for the] [Petitioner] and upon reading the affidavit of the
[Petitioner] herein sworn the [day of   1987]
AND the [Petitioner] undertaking [, by Counsel,] to abide by any order this Court
may make as to damages in case the Court shall hereafter be of the opinion that the
[Respondent] shall have sustained any by reason of this order which the [Petitioner]
ought to pay

IT IS ORDERED and directed that the [Respondent C. B.] by himself his servants or
agents or otherwise howsoever be restrained, and an injunction is hereby granted
restraining him from:
disposing, selling, mortgaging, charging, pledging, transferring, or dealing howsoever with any [capital] assets the [Respondent] may have within the jurisdiction
of this court including and in particular [*set out any specific asset to be frozen as in
Form 31*] or removing or taking any steps to remove the same out of the jurisdiction
until [after the hearing of a summons returnable on the   day of   1987 *or*
after the hearing of the [Petitioner's] applications under Matrimonial Causes Act
sections 23 and 24 *add in any case* or until further order.]
    Costs [reserved *or* in the enquiry *or as the case may be*].
    Dated this   day of   1987.

33 **Anton Piller** order

In the High Court of Justice   No: 7531 of 1987
Family Division
Principal Registry

Between: E. G.   Petitioner

                                      and

                                      F. G.   Respondent

UPON motion this day made into this court by counsel for the Petitioner and upon
reading the affidavit of   (*name*) filed this day and the exhibits therein
referred to, and the Petitioner by counsel undertaking:
   (1) to serve this order together with a copy of the affidavit of   (*name*)
       by a solicitor of the Supreme Court;
   (2) to abide by any order this court may make as to damages in case this court
       shall hereafter be of the opinion that the Respondent shall have suffered any
       by reason of this order which the Petitioner ought to pay;
   (3) to notify the Respondent or the person on whom this order is served by the
       Solicitor of the Supreme Court who serves this order upon them that they
       may seek legal advice and to explain fairly and in everyday language the
       meaning and effect thereof;
   (4) to issue a summons within [24] hours to set aside the order made by Mr
       Justice Blank on the   day of   1986 on the ground, inter alia, of the
       Respondent's fraud and non-disclosure and to make such order for ancillary
       relief as may be just;]

AND the Solicitors for the Petitioner undertaking by counsel for the Petitioner, being their counsel for this purpose, that all documents obtained as a result of this order will be retained in their safe custody until further order.

IT IS ORDERED THAT the Respondent or such person as shall appear to be in charge of the premises at   (*address*) do forthwith permit the person who shall serve this order upon him, together with such persons not exceeding two as may be duly authorised by the Petitioner, to enter the premises at   (*address*) at any hour between 8 o'clock in the forenoon and 8 o'clock in the evening for the purpose of:
  (a) looking for and inspecting any of the following:
      (1) all documents relating to the Respondent's earnings, income and capital from   (*date*) to the date hereof;
      (2) all documents relating to (*set out particulars of any specific transaction*);
      (3) all bank statements, building society pass books, cheque stubs, paid cheques and paying-in books;
  (b) taking into the custody of the Petitioner's Solicitors all and any of the above-mentioned documents and of making copies of the same.
AND IT IS ORDERED THAT the Respondent and/or the person or persons appearing for the time being to be in charge of the premises aforesaid do produce forthwith to the person serving this order all of the documents referred to in the last preceeding order.
Liberty to apply.
Costs reserved.

Dated this   day of   1987.

---

1 Adapted from the order in *Emanuel v Emanuel* [1982] 2 All ER 342, [1982] 1 WLR 669, Wood J.

---

34 Originating summons under the Matrimonial and Family Proceedings Act 1984, section 24[1]

In the High Court of Justice   No: 76543 of 1987
Family Division
[Principal Registry]

In the Matter of an application under section 24 of the Matrimonial and Family Proceedings Act 1984[2]

Between: Mavis Doreen Kczepanskovitch   Applicant

                                and

                     Boris Igor Kczepanskovitch   Respondent

LET [Boris Igor Kczepanskovitch] of [The Hermitage, Moscow Road, Watford in the County of Hertford] attend before a judge of the Family Division in chambers at the Royal Courts of Justice, Strand, London, WC2A 2LL on [[Tues]day the [25th] day of [August] 19[87] at [10.30] o'clock in the [fore]noon *or* on a day to be fixed[3]] on the hearing of an application by the [Applicant] that the court shall make an order restraining you from making any disposition or transferring out of the jurisdiction or otherwise dealing with any property with intent to defeat a claim for financial relief by the Applicant under Part III of the Matrimonial and Family Proceedings Act 1984.

Dated this [18th] day of [August] 19[87].

This Summons was taken out by [Quick and Sharpe of 5 Lincoln's Inn Place, London WC2Q 3XZ]
[Solicitors for] the above named Applicant whose address is [25 Willesden Church Street, London NW6]

---

1 Adapted from Form 27, App 1, Matrimonial Causes Rules 1977, (SI 1977/344).
2 27 *Halsbury's Statutes* (4th edn) 853 MATRIMONIAL LAW.
3 The prescribed form provides that the application will be heard on 'a day to be fixed'. However, where it is feared delay would result in dissipation of assets an immediate application, often ex parte, should be made. See ch 2 and ch 10, above.

---

35 Notice of proceedings and acknowledgment of service under the Matrimonial and Family Proceedings Act 1984[1]

In the High Court of Justice
Family Division

Between   Applicant

and   Respondent

Read carefully this Notice of Proceedings before answering the questions which follow.

NOTICE OF PROCEEDINGS

(1) Or as the case may be.

TAKE NOTICE THAT an application [for financial relief] *or* [to prevent a transaction[2]] (1) has been presented to this Court. A sealed copy of it and a copy of the applicant's affidavit in support are delivered with this notice.

1. You must complete and detach the acknowledgment of service and send it so as to reach the Court within 31 days after you receive this notice, inclusive of the day of receipt. Delay in returning the form may add to the costs.

2. If you wish to dispute the claim made by the applicant you must file in the court an affidavit in answer within 28 days after the time allowed for sending the acknowledgment of service.

3. If you intend to instruct a lawyer to act for you, you should at once give him all the documents which have been served on you, so that he may send the acknowledgment to the Court on your behalf. If you do not intend to instruct a lawyer, you should nevertheless give an address for service in the acknowledgment so that any documents affecting your interests which are sent.to you will in fact reach you. This should be your place of residence or, if you do not reside in England and Wales the address of a place in England or Wales to which documents may be sent to you. Change of address should be notified to the Court.

ACKNOWLEDGMENT OF SERVICE

In the High Court of Justice
Family Division

Between   Applicant

and   Respondent

1. Have you received an originating summons
   and a copy of the supporting affidavit in respect of the proceedings mentioned above?
2. On what date and at what address did you   Date ....
   receive them?   Address ....
                                                ....
                                                ....
                                                ....

3. Are you the person named as the respondent
   in the originating summons?
4. Do you intend to defend the case?
   If your answer to this question is yes you must
   follow the instructions in paragraph 2 of the
   Notice of Proceedings.
5. Even if you do not intend to defend the case
   do you object to paying the costs of the proceedings, if so on what grounds?

Dated this   day of   19

                                                Signed ....
                                                              Respondent

[I am *or* We are] acting for the Respondent in this matter

                                                Signed ....
                                                Address   for   service   of
                                                documents

Dated   19 .

---

1 Adapted from Form 28, App 1, Matrimonial Causes Rules 1977, (SI 1977/344).
2 See Form 34, above.

---

36 **Writ** of ne exeat regno

In the High Court of Justice   No: 2323 of 1987
Family Division

[Principal *or*   District] Registry

Between: Maria Lombardi   Petitioner
                                and
                           Luigi Lombardi   Respondent

ELIZABETH THE SECOND, by the Grace of God, of the United Kingdom of Great
Britain and Northern Ireland and of Our other realms and territories Queen, Head
of the Commonwealth, Defender of the Faith To [TT] the Tipstaff attending Our
Supreme Court of Judicature, his deputy and all constables and other peace officers
GREETING
WHEREAS it is represented to us, in Our High Court of Justice on the part of Maria
Lombardi, Petitioner against Luigi Lombardi, Respondent amongst other things

that he the said Respondent is greatly indebted to the Petitioner and designs quickly to go into parts beyond the seas; as by oath made in that behalf appears; which tends to the great prejudice and damage of the said Petitioner's and

THEREFORE, in order to prevent this injustice, WE do hereby COMMAND you, that in the event that the said Luigi Lombardi should seek or attempt to depart from the jurisdiction of Our said court before having paid to the Petitioner or to [her] order the sum of [£10,000] you do without delay cause the said Luigi Lombardi personally to come before you and give sufficient bail or security in the sum of [£10,000] that the said Luigi Lombardi will not go or attempt to go into parts beyond the seas without leave of the said court.

AND when you have such bail or security you are forthwith to make and return a certificate thereof to Our said High Court of Justice distinctly and plainly under seal together with this writ.

AND in case the said Luigi Lombardi shall refuse to give bail or security then you are to bring him the said Luigi Lombardi before a judge of Our said court forthwith or as soon as is reasonably practicable.

WITNESS   (*name*) Lord High Chancellor of Great Britain the 16th day of July 1987.
This writ was issued by [Barber & Co] of [147 Seville Street, London WC2G 4JU] Solicitors for the [Petitioner].

---

1 Adapted from the form of order in *Thaha v Thaha* [1987] 2 FLR 142, [1987] Fam Law 234, Wood J.

G Enforcement

37 Summons for committal[1]

(Heading as in Form 6 or 7)

LET the Respondent attend before one of the Judges of the Family Division of the High Court of Justice sitting at the Royal Courts of Justice, Strand, London WC2A 2LL on [Tues]day the [16th] day of [June 1987] at [10.30] o'clock[2] on the hearing of an application by the Petitioner that the Respondent be committed to prison for his contempt of this Court in   [failing to (*set out the act ordered to be done*) vacate the matrimonial home by [noon on Wednesday the 10th day of June 1987] pursuant to an order dated the [3rd day of June 1987] made in this suit]
(*or*)
[(*set out the act(s) done by the Respondent alleged to be in breach of the order*) returning to the matrimonial home on the [11th day of June 1987] and [assaulting the Petitioner by punching her in the face and kicking her shins]] notwithstanding an order dated the [3rd day of June 1987] made in this suit and in breach of the injunction therein contained.

Dated the [12th day of June 1987]

This summons was issued by [Q. R. & Co] of (*address*) Solicitors for the Petitioner

To the Respondent

---

1 The application is by summons. Matrimonial Causes Rules 1977, (SI 1977/344).
2 The summons will be indorsed with a notice as to the likely time of the commencement of the hearing; see Form 6 above.

38 Notice of motion for committal

In the High Court of Justice   No.   of 1987
Family Division
[Principal *or* District Registry]

In the matter of the Domestic Violence and Matrimonial Proceedings Act 1976

Between: A. B.   Applicant

                                       and

                                      C. D.   Respondent

TAKE NOTICE that the High Court of Justice, Family Division sitting at the Royal Courts of Justice, Strand, London WC2A 2LL (*or insert address of District Registry*) will be moved before the Honourable Mr Justice   on   day the   day of 1987 at the sitting of the Court at   o'clock in the   noon or so soon thereafter as Counsel can be heard by Counsel on behalf of the Petitioner for an order that the said Respondent C.D. be committed to prison for his contempt of Court in (*here insert the failure to comply which is alleged for examples of which see Form 37*)
AND for an order that the Respondent do pay the costs of and occasioned by this application.
AND FURTHER TAKE NOTICE that the Applicant in support of the said application will rely upon the [affidavit of   sworn the   day of   and upon her affidavit sworn the   day of   ] which affidavit[s] [are *or* is] served herewith to support the said application.

Dated this   day of   19 .

                                              (*Signature*)
                                                  of
                                       Solicitors for the Applicant
To the Respondent, C.D. of

39 Notice to show cause why order of committal should not be made[1]

In the   County Court.
                                                        No of Matter
Between   Petitioner/Applicant
and   Respondent
To (*name*)
of (*address*)
TAKE NOTICE that the Petitioner/Applicant [*or* Respondent] will apply to this Court at
         (*address*) on   (*date*) at   o'clock for an order for your committal to prison

[for having disobeyed the order of this Court made on the   day of   19 restraining you from (*here set out the terms of the injunction*) by (*here set out the particular breach or breaches of the order alleged*)]

Or [for having neglected to obey the order made on the   day of   19 , requiring you to (*here set out the mandatory part of the order*)]

AND FURTHER TAKE NOTICE that you are required to attend the Court on the first-mentioned day to show cause why an order for your committal should not be made.

Dated this   day of   19 .

---

1 Adapted from Form 78 County Court (Forms) Rules 1982 (SI 1982/586).

40 Order of committal: High Court[1]

[Heading as in Form: 1, 3, 6, 7, 19, 20, 21 or 22]

Upon [motion *or* summons] this day made unto this Court by [Counsel] for the [plaintiff] and upon reading [an affidavit of   filed the   day of   19   of service on the [defendant]] of a copy of the order of the court dated the   day of   19
and of this [motion *or* summons]:
And it appearing to the satisfaction of the Court that the [defendant *name*] has been guilty of contempt of court in [*state the contempt*]:
It is ordered that for his contempt the [defendant] do stand committed to [Brixton] Prison to be there imprisoned [*until further order*][2]
[*Add where the order is suspended*: It is further ordered that this order shall not be executed if the [defendant *name*] complies with the following terms, namely, *set out terms of suspension*].
Dated this   day of   19   .

---

1 Adapted from Form 85 Appendix A, RSC Ord 1 r 9.
2 The court may imprison only for a fixed term. Contempt of Court Act 1981, s 14(1) (11 *Halsbury's Statutes* (4th edn) 174 CONTEMPT OF COURT). See also chapter 12 above.

41 Order of committal: county court[1]

In the   County Court

                                                                        No of Matter
Between   Petitioner/Applicant
and   Respondent
By an order of this Court, dated the   day of   19   , (*state the order*)

NOW, UPON THE APPLICATION of the (*Petitioner/Applicant or Respondent*) and upon hearing the (*Respondent or Petitioner/Applicant*) [*or if the (Respondent or Petitioner/Applicant) does not appear*, reading the affidavit or   [*or where service has been by a bailiff*, the indorsement of   a bailiff of this Court (*or* of the   County Court)] showing that a copy of the said order indorsed with a notice in Form 77[2] and notice of this application having been served upon the (*Respondent or Petitioner/Applicant*)] and upon (*state such evidence as may have been given*)

and the Court being of the opinion, upon consideration of the facts disclosed by the evidence given that   (*name*) has been guilty of a contempt of this Court by a breach of [or by neglecting to obey] the said order, namely (*here set out the particular matter of contempt*)

IT IS ORDERED that   (*name*) be committed for his contempt to Her Majesty's Prison at   (*name of prison used by the Court*) for   or until he shall be sooner discharged by due course of law and that a warrant for the arrest and committal of the said   (*name*) be issued forthwith.

AND IT IS ORDERED that the said   (*name*) do pay the costs of the (*Petitioner/Applicant or Respondent*) of this application and of the said committal, such costs to be taxed by the registrar and paid by the (*Respondent or Petitioner/Applicant*) into the office of this Court within fourteen days after the date of taxation.

[*Add if so ordered* AND IT IS FURTHER ORDERED that any application for the release of   (*name*) from custody shall be made to the judge.]

Dated this   day of   19   .

---

1 Adapted from Form 79 County Court (Forms) Rules 1982 (SI 1982/582).
2 See Form 17 above.

42 **Warrant** of committal

In the   County Court

No of Matter

Between   Petitioner/Applicant
and   Respondent

To the Registrar and Bailiffs of the Court, and to every constable within his jurisdiction, and to the Governor of Her Majesty's Prison at

On   the   day of   19   it was ordered that   (*name*) of (*address*) should be committed to prison for contempt of this Court.

YOU ARE THEREFORE required forthwith to arrest   (*name*) and deliver him to   Prison and you the Governor to receive   (*name*) and safely keep him in prison for   from the arrest under this warrant or until he shall be sooner discharged by due course of law.

Dated this   day of   19 .

---

1 Adapted from Form 80 County Court (Forms) Rules 1982 (SI 1982/582).

43 **Order for discharge** from custody under warrant of committal[1]

In the   County Court

No of Matter

Between   Petitioner/Applicant
and   Respondent

UPON APPLICATION made this   day of   19 , by   (*name*) who was committed to prison for contempt, by an Order of this Court, dated the day of   19 , and upon reading the application of   (*name*) attested on the   day of   19 , showing that he desirous of purging his contempt, and upon hearing
on behalf of the

[*Or, if no one appears for him* and upon being satisfied that the notice of this application has been duly served on the   ]

IT IS ORDERED that   (*name*) be discharged out of the custody of the Governor of Her Majesty's Prison at (*insert name of prison*) as to the contempt.

[*Add, if so ordered* AND IT IS ORDERED that   (*name*) do pay the sum of £   , the costs of this application, such costs to be taxed, into the office of this court on or before the   (*date*) (or within 14 days after taxation).]

Dated this   day of   19 .

---

1 Adapted from Form 83 County Court (Forms) Rules 1982 (SI 1982/582).

44 **Power of arrest** attached to injunction under section 2 of the Domestic Violence and Matrimonial Proceedings Act 1976

In the   County Court

No of Matter

Between   Petitioner/Applicant
and   Respondent

[Here set out the injunction Form 13, 14 or 15 endorsed with penal notice Form 17]

POWER OF ARREST

AND the Judge being satisfied that the Respondent has caused actual bodily harm to the Applicant [or the child concerned] and being of the opinion that he is likely to do so again, a power of arrest is attached to this injunction whereby any constable whom he has reasonable cause for suspecting of being in breach of the injunction as mentioned in section 2(3) of the Domestic Violence and Matrimonial Proceedings Act 1976.

[This power of arrest expires on the   day of   19 . *Delete as necessary*]

---

1 Adapted from Form 110 County Court (Forms) Rules 1982 (SI 1982/582). The form should be adapted when a power of arrest is attached to a High Court injunction.

45 **Order and warrant** for committal: Domestic Violence and Matrimonial Proceedings Act 1976[1]

In the   County Court

No of Matter

[In the Matter of the Domestic Violence and Matrimonial Proceedings Act 1976]

Between   Petitioner/Applicant
and   Respondent

To the Registrar and bailiffs of the Court and every constable within his jurisdiction and to the Governor of Her Majesty's Prison at   (*name of prison used by the court*).

By an order of this Court dated the   day of 19   , (*state the terms of the injunction*)

AND AS   (*name*) the Respondent (*or Petitioner/Applicant*) being suspected of a breach of the order has been arrested by a constable and brought before a Judge of this Court under section 2 of the Domestic Violence and Matrimonial Proceedings Act 1976

NOW UPON HEARING
and upon (*state such evidence as may have been given*)

AND the Judge being of the opinion, upon consideration of the facts disclosed by the evidence given, that   (*name*) has been guilty of a contempt of this Court by a breach of the order, namely (*set out the particular matter of contempt*)

IT IS ORDERED that   (*name*) be committed for his contempt to prison for
or until he shall be sooner discharged by due course of law.

YOU ARE THEREFORE required to keep   (*name*) under arrest and deliver him to prison and you the Governor to receive   (*name*) and safely keep him in prison for   from the arrest under this Warrant or until he shall be sooner discharged by due course of law.

[*Add if so ordered* AND IT IS FURTHER ORDERED that any application for the release of   (*name*) from custody shall be made to the Judge]

Dated this   day of   19

---

1 Adapted from Form 111 County Court (Forms) Rules 1982 (SI 1982/582).

H Magistrates courts

46 Notice to respondent of court's powers with regard to family protection orders[1]

Applications for an order under section 16
Respondents to an application for an Order under section 16 of the Domestic Proceedings and Magistrates' Courts Acts 1978 are informed that on hearing the application the Court (if satisfied as to certain circumstances involving violence or threats of violence) has power to make any order under section 16 of the Act, whether or not the Applicant asks for a particular kind of order to be made and, if so, whether or not the particular kind of order asked for by the Applicant is made.
Any or all of the following orders may be made under section 16:
   (i)   *Under section 16 (2)*
         (*a*) An order that the Respondent shall not use, or threaten to use, violence against the person of the Applicant;
         (*b*) An order that the Respondent shall not use, or threaten to use, violence against the person of a child of the family.
   (ii) *Under section 16 (3)*
         (*a*) An order requiring the Respondent to leave the matrimonial home;
         (*b*) An order prohibiting the Respondent from entering the matrimonial home.
   (iii) *Under section 16 (4)*
         If an order under section 16 (3) is made, a further order requiring the Respondent to permit the Applicant to enter and remain in the matrimonial home.
   (iv) *Under section 16 (10)*
         If an order under section 16 (2) is made, it may include provision that the Respondent shall not incite or assist another person to use, or threaten to use, violence against the person of the Applicant or, as the case may be, the child of the family.

Powers of arrest under section 18
In certain circumstances the court may attach a power of arrest to an order made under section 16. If so, a constable may arrest the Respondent without warrant if

he has reasonable cause for suspecting the Respondent of being in breach of the order.

---

1 Adapted from the Magistrates' Courts (Matrimonial Proceedings) Rules 1980, (SI 1980/1582) Schedule, Form 12. See ibid, r 10, Appendix 3, above; see also Domestic Proceedings and Magistrates' Courts Act 1978, ss 16, 18(1) (27 *Halsbury's Statutes* (4th edn) 791 MATRIMONIAL LAW); Appendix 1, above.

---

47 Family protection order[1]

Buckram Magistrates' Court (*Code*)

Date   19
Respondent: B. B.
Address:

On the application of

Applicant: A. B.
Address:

that
Substance of complaint: (*give particulars*)

IT IS ADJUDGED that the Complaint is true and it is ordered that:
Order: [The Respondent shall not use or threaten to use[2], violence against the person of the Applicant [and that the Respondent shall not incite or assist any other person[3] to use or threaten to use, violence against the person of the Applicant] *or*
The Respondent shall not use, or threaten to use[4], violence against the person of (*name*) being a child of the family [and that the Respondent shall not incite or assist any other person[5] to use, or threaten to use, violence against the person of (*name*)] *or*
The Respondent shall leave (*address*) being the matrimonial home[6] [and that the Respondent shall permit[7] the Applicant to enter and remain therein] *or*
The Respondent shall not enter[8] (*address*) being the matrimonial home [and that the Respondent shall permit[9] the Applicant to enter and remain therein]].
Here state any exceptions, conditions or other provisions[10].
[(*Where the order is not an expedited order*) This Order shall take effect[11] on
19   and shall expire on   19 .
or
(*where the order is an expedited order*) This Order shall take effect[12] [on the date when *or*   days after] notice of the making of the Order is served on the Respondent and shall expire on   19 (being 28 days after the date on which this order is made) or on the date of the commencement of the hearing, in accordance with the provisions of Part II of the Magistrates' Courts Act 1980, of the application, whichever occurs first.
Costs: And it is ordered that the Respondent pay costs of £   to the Applicant [forthwith *or* by [weekly *or* monthly] instalments of £   *or* not later than   ]
[(*Signature*)
Justice of the Peace
or By order of the Court
(*Signature*)
Justices' Clerk]

NOTES

If you disobey this order you could be sent to prison for up to two months or ordered to pay up to £2,000.

(*Where the order is an expedited order*) This is a *temporary* order only, and has been made because the Applicant has satisfied the court that there is imminent danger of physical injury to the Applicant or a child of the family. Before an ordinary (non-expedited) order is made, you will be able to be present in court and to explain your side of the matter.

---

1 Adapted from the Magistrates' Courts (Matrimonial Proceedings) Rules 1980, (SI 1980/1582) Schedule, Form 14. See ibid, r 14(2), Appendix 3, above.
2 Domestic Proceedings and Magistrates' Courts Act 1978, s 16(2) (27 *Halsbury's Statutes* (4th edn) 791 MATRIMONIAL LAW), Appendix 1, above.
3 Ibid s 16(10).
4 Ibid s 16(2).
5 Ibid s 16(10).
6 Ibid s 16(3).
7 Ibid s 16(4).
8 Ibid s 16(3).
9 Ibid s 16(4).
10 Ibid s 16(9).
11 Ibid s 16(9).
12 Ibid s 16(8)(as amended).

48 Power of arrest attached to family protection order[1]

(*Formal parts and order as in Form 46*)

The Court, having made an Order under Section 16 of the Domestic Proceedings and Magistrates' Courts Act 1978 which provides that the Respondent:

[(a) shall not use violence against the person of the applicant *or*
 (b) shall not use violence against the person of (*name*), being a child of the family, *or*
 (c) shall not enter (*address*), being the matrimonial home,]

and being satisfied that the Respondent has physically injured [the Applicant and/ or a child of the family] and considering that he is likely to do so again, a power of arrest is attached to the provision(s) mentioned at [(a) *or* (b) *or* (c)] above.

A CONSTABLE MAY ARREST without warrant a person whom he has reasonable cause for suspecting of being in breach of any such provision as is mentioned at [(a) *or* (b) *or* (c)] above by reason of that person's use of violence or, as the case may be, his entry into the matrimonial home.

---

1 Adapted from the Magistrates' Courts (Matrimonial Proceedings) Rules 1980, (SI 1980/1582) Schedule, Form 15. See ibid, r 14(3), Appendix 3, above. See also Domestic Proceedings and Magistrates' Courts Act 1978, s 18(1), (2) (27 *Halsbury's Statutes* (4th edn) 791 MATRIMONIAL LAW), Appendix 1, above.

49 **Indorsement** of expedited family protection order[1]

(Order as in Form 46)

This Order was served on the Respondent in accordance with rule 19 (1) of the Magistrates' Courts (Matrimonial Proceedings) Rules 1980 on   19   and [took effect on that date *or* will take effect on   19].

(Signature)
Justices' Clerk

---

1 Adapted from the Magistrates' Courts (Matrimonial Proceedings) Rules 1980, (SI 1980/1582) Schedule, Form 18. See ibid, r 19(3), Appendix 3, above. See also Domestic Proceedings and Magistrates' Courts Act 1978, s 16(8) (27 *Halsbury's Statutes* (4th edn) 791 MATRIMONIAL LAW), Appendix 1, above.

---

50 **Warrant** of arrest for breach of family protection order[1]

Buckram Magistrates' Court (*Code*)

Date: 19
Respondent: B. B.
Address:
Family Protection
order made by   Magistrates' Court on   19
Alleged breach of order:

<table>
<tr><td></td><td>Application on [oath or affirmation] having this day been made to me by (name)
that the Respondent has disobeyed the above order</td></tr>
<tr><td>Direction:</td><td>You, the constables of the Rutland Police Force are hereby required to arrest the Respondent and to bring the Respondent before the magistrates' court immediately.</td></tr>
<tr><td>[Bail:</td><td>On arrest, the accused shall be released on bail on entering into a recognizance in the sum of £   . [and providing   [surety or sureties] in the sum of £   [each]] for his appearance before the   Magistrates Court on   19   at   o'clock].</td></tr>
</table>

(Signature)

Justice of the Peace

---

1 Adapted from the Magistrates' Courts (Matrimonial Proceedings) Rules 1980, (SI 1980/1582) Schedule, Form 16. See ibid, r 14(4), Appendix 3, above. See also Domestic Proceedings and Magistrates' Courts Act 1978, s 18(4), (27 *Halsbury's Statutes* (4th edn) 791 MATRIMONIAL LAW), Appendix 1, above.

I Appeals

51 Notice of appeal to the Court of Appeal[1]

In the Court of Appeal
On Appeal from [The High Court of Justice
Family Division *or* The Divorce Registry
or The [Oxbridge] County Court *etc*]

[No 9367 of 1987
or 87 D 4687 *etc*[2]]

Between:
A. B.

[Plaintiff, Applicant
or Petitioner *etc*[3]]

and

C. [B. *or* D.]

[Defendant *or*
Respondent *etc*[4]]

NOTICE OF APPEAL

TAKE NOTICE that [pursuant to the leave[5] granted by [[His *or* Her] Honour Judge
    or the Honourable [Mr *or* Mrs] Justice   *or* the Right Honourable Lord
Justice   ] the Court of Appeal will be moved so soon as Counsel can be
heard by Counsel for the above-named [Plaintiff, Applicant *or* Petitioner] on
appeal from [the whole *or* a part] of the order herein of [[His *or* Her] Honour Judge
        or the Honourable [Mr *or* Mrs] Justice   ] made on   the day of
        1987 whereby it was ordered (*set out the terms of the order appealed
against*) FOR AN ORDER THAT (*set out the terms of the order[6] which is sought from
the Court of Appeal*) AND for an order that the [Defendant *or* Respondent] pay to
the [Plaintiff, Applicant *or* Petitioner] the costs of this appeal [and below (*or as the
case may be*)] to be taxed AND FURTHER TAKE NOTICE that the grounds[7] of this
appeal are that:
  (1) The learned Judge was wrong in law in holding that (*set out the conclusion of
      law which it is contended was wrongly decided*).[8] [The learned Judge ought to
      have held that (*set out the conclusion of law which it is contended that the
      judge should have reached*).]
  (2) The learned Judge erred in the exercise of [his *or* her] discretion:[9]
      (a) in that (*specify the way in which it is contended that the judge's discretion
          was exercised in a way that was wrong in principal*).
      (*or*)
      (b) in reaching [his *or* her] decision the learned Judge relied [in part] on
          (*specify the matter which it is contended that the judge should not have
          taken into account*) which was not relevant.
      (*or*)
      (c) in reaching [his *or* her] decision the learned Judge placed excessive
          weight on (*specify the matter*) and failed to take any or any sufficient
          account of (*specify the matter(s) which it is contended should have led to a
          different conclusion*). [Having regard to [all the circumstances of the case
          or the following circumstances namely (*set out all the relevant circum-
          stances*) the learned Judge should have (*specify the decision which it is
          contended the judge should have reached*).]
  (3) The learned Judge's conclusion that (*specify the conclusion*) is inconsistent
      with [his *or* her] finding of fact that (*specify the finding*). Having found that
      (*specify the finding*) the learned Judge should have [concluded *or* held] that
      (*specify the relevant conclusion or finding contended*).
AND FURTHER TAKE NOTICE that the [Plaintiff, Applicant *or* Petitioner] proposes
to apply to set down this appeal in the [Family Division *or* County Court] [(Final
and New Trial) *or* (Interlocutory)] List.

Dated the   day of   1987.

> (*Signature*)
> of (*address*) [Agents for
> (*name*)   of   (*address*)]
> Solicitor for the [Plaintiff,
> Applicant *or* Petitioner]

To the [Defendant *or* Respondent]
and to (*name*) of (*address*) [Agents
for (*name*) of (*address*)] [his *or* her]
Solicitors

To the [Defendant *or* Respondent] and [his *or* her] Solicitors:

No notice as to the date on which this appeal will be in the list for hearing will be given: it is the duty of solicitors to keep themselves informed as to the state of the lists. A respondent intending to appear in person should inform the office of the Registrar of Civil Appeals, Room 246, Royal Courts of Justice, Strand, London WC2A 2LL, of that fact and give his address; if he does so he will be notified to the address given of the date when the appeal is expected to be heard.

---

1 RSC Ord 59, r 3(1), and see ch 14 above.
2 The number used is that of the court below.
3 The parties are described as in the proceedings in the court below.
4 Where leave is necessary the grant should be recited. Leave is not required where an injunction is granted or refused. Supreme Court Act 1981, s 18(1)(h)(iii)(27 *Halsbury's Statutes* (4th edn) 756 COURTS); see also County Court Appeals Order (SI 1981/1749), Arts 2, 3.
5 The appellant may not, without leave, seek an order unless it is specified in the notice of appeal. RSC Ord 59, r 3(2).
6 The appellant may not, without leave, rely on any ground of appeal unless it is specified in the notice of appeal. RSC Ord 59, r 3(2).
7 It may be convenient to use numbered sub-paragraphs where several separate reasons are given.
8 An injunction is a discretionary remedy. To appeal against the exercise of a discretion the appellant must show that the decision is plainly wrong, that the judge failed to consider (or gave too little weight to) a relevant factor, that the judge gave too much weight to a relevant factor or took into account an irrelevant factor. *Evans v Bartlam* [1937] AC 473, [1937] 2 All ER 646, HL; and see *G v G (Minor: Custody Appeal)* [1985] 2 All ER 225, [1985] 1 WLR 647, HL. It may also be said that the decision is so wrong that the judge must have gone wrong somewhere; see *McLean v Burke* (1982) 3 FLR 70, CA.
9 See RSC Ord 59, r 3(4).

---

52 Notice of motion on appeal to the Divisional Court[1]

In the High Court of Justice   No   of 1987
Family Division
(Divisional Court)

In the matter of an appeal under [the Domestic Proceedings and Magistrates' Courts Act 1978 (*or as the case may be*)]

Between:

          A. B.   Appellant

          and

          C. D.   Respondent

TAKE NOTICE that the High Court of Justice, Family Division, Royal Courts of Justice, Strand, London WC2A 2LL will, on a date to be fixed and notified to the parties, consider an appeal by A. B. (the husband (*or*) wife of the respondent (*or*) father (*or*) mother of the child (*or as the case may be*)) against the order of the Magistrates' Court dated the   day of   19 .

   (1) The said order [*here set out details of the magistrates' order*] and [*if appropriate* the full names, surnames and dates of birth of the children referred to in the order are   ]

   (2) The appellant appeals against the whole of the said order [*or here set out the part or parts of the order appealed against*].

   (3) The appellant seeks an order that [*here set out the order that is sought from the Divisional Court*].

   (4) [*If appropriate*] Leave to appeal out of time[2] is required because [*here set out briefly the reason giving any dates that are relevant*].

   (5) The grounds of the appeal are [*all the grounds should be set out; it is not sufficient to state merely that the finding was against the weight of the evidence*].

Dated the   day of   19 .

This notice was filed by
whose address for service is: (*Signed*)
                             [*Solicitor for*] the above named appellant

---

1 Adapted from *Practice Direction* (Divisional Court: Appeal) [1977] 2 A11 ER 543, [1977] 1 WLR 609, see Appendix 2, above. See also *Practice Direction* [1978] 2 A11 ER 432, [1978] 1 WLR 797.

2 Where the delay is no more than six weeks (ie the notice is being filed within 12 weeks of the hearing) and has been occasioned by the obtaining of documents or legal aid and the respondent has been notified of the likelihood of an appeal, it will normally suffice to say so without giving details.

Appendix 5
Housing (Homeless Persons) Act 1977
Code of Practice

Practitioners should be aware of the following extracts from the Housing (Homeless Persons) Act 1977 Code of Practice (England and Wales)[1] in the event of having to negotiate with local authorities on behalf of homeless clients.

Homelessness

2.10 The Act also defines as homeless someone who has accommodation but cannot use it for one of the following reasons.

   (a) . . . .
   (b) His (or, more probably, her) attempt to return to the accommodation would be likely to be met with violence or threats of violence likely to be carried out by someone else in it.[2] Authorities are asked to respond sympathetically to applications from women who are in fear of violence; the fact that violence has not yet occurred does not, on its own, suggest that it is not likely to occur.
   (c) . . . .

2.11 A person is defined as 'threatened with homelessness' if he is likely to become homeless within 28 days.[3] Authorities should, however, be ready to advise and assist people where the possibility of their becoming homeless is known to the authority more than 28 days in advance. The earlier action can be taken, the greater is the likelihood that measures to avert homelessness can be effective. Authorities will wish to avoid adding the stress of uncertainty to existing stresses. Authorities should inform applicants as soon as is practicable of the arrangements which will be made to assist them.

2.12 Section 2[4] identifies those who have priority need, and for whom authorities are required to secure that accommodation is available. There are 4 main categories.

   (a) A person has priority need if he has one or more dependent children living with him or who might reasonably be expected to live with him.[5] The Act contains no definition of dependent children. The Secretaries of State consider that authorities should treat as such all those under the age of 16, and others under the age of 19 who are either receiving full-time education or training or are otherwise unable to support themselves. Dependants need not necessarily be the children of the applicant, but they may be related to the applicant in some other way (eg his grandchildren) or they may be adopted or foster-children. Child custody orders

---

1 Second Edition 1983, issued under Housing (Homeless Persons) Act 1977, s 12; repealed and replaced by the Housing Act 1985 Part III, s 71 (21 *Halsbury's Statutes*) 4th edn) 29 HOUSING).
2 Ibid, s 58(3)(b). The fact that a woman is living in a battered wives' refuge does not justify a local authority to refuse to treat her as homeless under Housing Act 1985, s 58. *R v Ealing London Borough Council, ex p Sidhu* (1982) 80 LGR 534; no reasonable authority, knowing that this particular applicant was living in one room with two children in a refuge, could fail to be satisfied that she had a priority need or that her homelessness and that of the children was unintentional.
3 Housing Act 1985, s 58(4).
4 The Housing (Homeless Persons) Act 1977, s 2 has been repealed and replaced by Housing Act 1985, Part III, s 59.
5 Ibid, s 59(1)(b).

should not be required.[6] One-parent families, including battered women with their children, are included.[7] Children need not actually be living with the applicant at the time. They may, for example, be staying temporarily with other relatives. Where however children are in care (but see paragraph 4.2 below) . . . the Secretaries of State consider they should be included only where it is reasonable that they live with the applicant. The advice of social services authorities will be important in any cases of this kind.

(b) . . .

(c) A person has priority need if he is, or if his household includes one or more members who are, vulnerable for one of the following reasons.

    (i) . . .

    (ii) . . .

    (iii) . . . Any other special reason.[8] Authorities should have particular regard to those who are vulnerable but do not come within either of the above categories. In particular, the Secretaries of State consider that it would be appropriate under this heading for authorities to secure whenever possible that accommodation is available for battered women without children who are at risk of violent pursuit or, if they return home, at risk of further violence; and for homeless young people who are at risk of sexual or financial exploitation (the problems to which such people may be exposed were indicted in the report, published in July 1976, of the Working Group on Homeless Young People).

(d) . . .

Intentional homelessness

2.16 In the opinion of the Secretaries of State, a battered woman who has fled the marital home should never be regarded as having become homeless intentionally[9] because it would clearly not be reasonable for her to remain, nor would it be appropriate that a homeless pregnant woman be treated as intentionally homeless simply because she is pregnant. If people can no longer afford to remain in their accommodation (eg because of a drop in income) and no further financial help is available, it should not be regarded as unreasonable for them to leave. In general authorities should not treat as intentionally homeless those who have been driven to leave their

6 Where a person is residing with dependent children a local authority is not entitled to require that person to obtain a final custody order in respect of the children before treating him as a person in priority need of accommodation. *R v Ealing London Borough Coucil, ex p Sidhu*, above.

7 Ibid.

8 Housing Act 1985, s 59(1)(c) (21 *Halsbury's Statutes* (4th edn) 29 HOUSING).

9 *R v Ealing London Borough Council, ex p Sidhu* above. A decision by a local authority that a person is intentionally homeless, within the meaning of Housing Act 1985, s 60 should be challenged in the High Court by judicial review and not by a claim in the county court, *Lambert v Ealing London Borough Council* [1982] 2 All ER 394, [1982] 1 WLR 550, CA. However judicial review is not an appropriate means of monitoring the actions of a housing authority save in exceptional circumstances, *Puhlhofer v Hillingdon London Borough Council* [1986] AC 484, [1986] 1 All ER 467, HL. Where a homeless person unreasonably refuses an offer of accommodation by the local authority, there is then no further duty on the authority to make offers of other accommodation, *R v Westminster City Council, ex p Chambers* (1982) 4 FLR 487, 81 LGR 401.

accommodation because conditions had degenerated to a point when they could not in all the circumstances reasonably be expected to remain —perhaps because of overcrowding or lack of basic amenities or severe emotional stress. But in considering whether it would have been reasonable[10] for people to remain where they were, authorities may have regard to the general housing conditions of the area; eg whether there are many people in the area living in worse conditions than the applicants.

Accommodation
4.2 Accommodation is 'available' only if it is available for occupation by all those who might reasonably be expected to live together.[11] The practice of splitting families is not acceptable, even for short periods. The social cost, personal hardship and long term damage to children, as well as the expense involved in receiving children into care, rules this out as an acceptable course, other than in the exceptional case where professional social work advice is that there are compelling reasons, apart from homelessness, for separating a child from his family. The provision of shelter from which one partner is excluded is also unacceptable unless there are sound reasons, for example where a woman is seeking temporary refuge following violence from another member of the household and it is undesirable that she be under pressure to return.

Co-operation
7.2 Perhaps the main occasions when one housing authority will need to collaborate with another housing authority will be in circumstances where a householder has moved across local authority borders.[12] Paragraphs 2.21–2.22 above deal with the question of which housing authority is responsible for securing accommodation; but there will be other circumstances where a housing authority do not necessarily wish (or are unable) to make a notification under section 5,[13] but where they may seek the assistance of another authority in relation, for example, to their inquiries about the circumstances as described by an applicant. Or if there are special difficulties in securing accommodation for an applicant—for example, if it is advisable for a battered woman to be rehoused in another area because of the continuing risk of violence from her partner—another authority may be able to assist.[14] Where an authority have estates outside their own area they may find it helpful to agree policy on certain matters with the authorities in whose areas the estates are situated (see paragraph 7.4 below).

10 A woman living with a man who becomes intentionally homeless is not necessarily barred by his conduct or by the fact that he might benefit undeservingly if she were given accommodation from being entitled to the relief available under Housing Act 1985, Part III to a person who had not become homeless intentionally: *Lewis v North Devon District Council* [1981] 1 All ER 27, sub nom *R v North Devon District Council, ex p Lewis* [1981] 1 WLR 328. The policy of Housing Act 1985, Part III requires a housing authority to consider the family unit as a whole and may take into account the conduct of other members of the family; in the absence of evidence to the contrary an authority may assume that other members of the family acquiesce in the conduct of the head of the household, ibid.
11 Housing Act 1985, Part III, s 75 (21 *Halsbury's Statutes* (4th edn) HOUSING).
12 Housing Act 1985, s 67.
13 Housing (Homeless Persons) Act 1977, s 5 has been repealed and replaced by Housing Act 1985, Part III, s 67.
14 Where a housing authority has carefully considered the risk of domestic violence before referring the applicant to another authority the court will not interfere with its conclusion, *R v Bristol City Council, ex p Browne* [1979] 3 All ER 344, [1979] 1 WLR 1437.

Index